650.142 C932d
Criscito, Pat, 1953 –
Designing the perfect resume /

Grass Lake Branch
Jackson District Library   11/22/05

WITHDRAWN

W9-BIK-401

DESIGNING THE PERFECT
RÉSUMÉ

THIRD EDITION

by Pat Criscito, CPRW
President and Founder
ProType, Ltd.
Colorado Springs

Author of Barron's
*e-Résumés, Interview Answers in a Flash,
How to Write Better Résumés and Cover Letters,*
and *Guide to Distance Learning*

BARRON'S

The résumés in this book are real résumés used by real people to get real jobs.
The names and contact information have been changed to protect their privacy.
Thank you to all the clients for their inspiration and permission to use their résumés.
Thank you to members of the National Résumé Writers Association (NRWA) for submitting résumés for this book.

© Copyright 2006, 2000, 1995 by Pat Criscito
ProType, Ltd.
Colorado Springs, Colorado
Phone: (719) 592-1999
E-mail: pat@patcriscito.com
Web site: www.patcriscito.com

All rights reserved.
No part of this book may be reproduced
in any form, by photostat, microfilm, xerography,
or any other means, or incorporated into any
information retrieval system, electronic or
mechanical, without the written permission
of the copyright owner.

All inquiries should be addressed to:
Barron's Educational Series, Inc.
250 Wireless Boulevard
Hauppauge, New York 11788
http://www.barronseduc.com

Library of Congress Control Number: 2005053037
    ISBN-13: 978-0-7641-2895-0
    ISBN-10: 0-7641-2895-7

Library of Congress Cataloging-in-Publication Data

Criscito, Pat, 1953-
    Designing the perfect resume/by Pat Criscito.--3rd ed.
       p. cm.
    Includes index.
    ISBN-10: 0-7641-2895-7
    ISBN-13: 978-0-7641-2895-0
       1. Résumés(Employment) I. Title.

  HF5383.C74 2005
  650.14'2--dc22

                                        2005053037

PRINTED IN THE UNITED STATES OF AMERICA
9 8 7 6 5 4 3 2 1

Contents

650.142 C932d
Criscito, Pat, 1953 –
Designing the perfect resume /

Grass Lake Branch
Jackson District Library

11/22/05

Contributing Résumé Writers

Thank you to all of the writers who contributed to this edition. For complete contact information on any of these résumé writers, search by their last name at the Web site for the National Résumé Writers Association *(www.nrwa.com)*.

Marcia Baker	reachmsmab@cavtel.net	Pages 124–125
Rosie Bixel	aps@bhhgroup.com	Pages 74–75, 103, 123, 165, 218, 223, 294
Arnold G. Boldt	Arnoldsmth@aol.com	Pages 232–233, 296
Karen S. Carli	kscarli@comcast.net	Pages 76–77
Amy Charland	amy@charlandcareerconsulting.com	Pages 59, 64, 73
Sean P. Colfer	winwithcpm@peoplepc.com	Pages 62–63
Beth Colley	resume@chesres.com	Pages 163, 222, 295, 315
Pat Criscito	pat@protypeltd.com	Pages 38–46, 48–49, 57–58, 65–67, 78–79, 82–83, 88–89, 90–96, 99, 107, 115–117, 119–121, 126–127, 130–134, 136–137, 143, 146–148, 151–157, 161–162, 164, 167–168, 170, 176–177, 182–183, 186–187, 189–191, 199–200, 210, 212–215, 228, 238–239, 246–248, 256–276, 278–280, 283–285, 288, 302–305, 307–311, 314
Jean Cummings	jcummings1@verizon.net	Pages 100–101, 242–243
Norine Degliano	ndagliano@yahoo.com	Pages 54–56, 110, 202–203
Anne-Marie Ditta	Amditta@firstimpressioncareerservices.com	Pages 50–51, 108, 188, 196–197, 208-209
Louise Garver	careerpro@cox.net	Pages 102, 128–129, 159, 192
Jill Grindle	j.grindle@comcast.net	Pages 236–237
Lee Anne Grundish	GrafixServices@aol.com	Pages 166, 179
Alice Hanson	alicehanson@aimresumes.com	Pages 118, 144–145, 234–235
La-Dana R. Jenkins	info@lrjconsulting.net	Pages 109, 111, 184, 219
Maggie Jones	resumewriter@wcnet.org	Pages 80, 104–105
Billie P. Jordan	bjordan1@ec.rr.com	Pages 122, 160, 252–253
Barbara Kanney	bkanney64@sssnet.com	Pages 60, 70–71, 254–255, 293, 313-314
Myriam-Rose Kohn	myriam-rose@jedaenterprises.com	Pages 169, 204–205, 220–221, 226–227
Lorie Lebert	lorie@coachingroi.com	Pages 158, 180–181
Angie Maizlish	angie@firstimpressionscareer.com	Pages 240–241
Murray Mann	MurrayMann@aol.com	Pages 250–251, 300
Marjii Middleton	awaywords@comcast.net	Page 112
Cheryl Minnick	Cherbear199@aol.com	Pages 138–139
Gerald R. Moore	Jmoorecprw@wmconnect.com	Pages 193, 195
Melanie A. Noonan	PeriPro1@aol.com	Pages 53, 206–207, 216–217, 224–225, 282, 298
Edie Rische	erische@door.net	Pages 52, 61, 68, 84–85, 106, 140, 178, 194, 198, 281, 286, 297, 306, 312, 316
Barbara Safani	info@careersolvers.com	Pages 86–87
Rosie St. Julian	rosiecprw@prodigy.net	Pages 230–231
Janice Steffen	resumeoptions@aol.com	Pages 244–245
Chris Van Petten	chris@yourpro.com	Pages 81, 299
Rosa E. Vargas	creatingprints@earthlink.net	Pages 72, 287, 301

1 The Perfect Résumé?

The only *perfect* résumé is the one that fits the personality of its owner, tempered of course by the expectations of the industry. That means there are as many "perfect résumés" as there are kinds of people and kinds of jobs! Well, you won't find millions of résumés in *this* book, but you should find at least one that is a good match with your personality and industry. The ideas in this book can be used in your personal résumé or, if you are a professional résumé designer or career consultant, in your work with other people's résumés.

This third edition is different from the first two, which contained résumés designed by me exclusively. Nearly all of the résumés in this edition are new, and half of them were written and designed by members of the National Résumé Writers Association (NRWA). At the back of this book is a listing of NRWA résumé writers with their contributions. Feel free to contact any of the writers by navigating to www.nrwa.com and searching for them by name.

Remember, a résumé is just a way to get your foot in the door. It is a marketing tool—an advertisement. The *perfect* résumé will stand out in a two-inch stack of résumés on a busy executive's desk and help you get that all-important interview by making a strong first impression.

Even though content is important, many times well-qualified people aren't considered for positions because a poorly designed résumé didn't grab the reader's attention long enough to make sure the words were read. Just the opposite can be true as well. Even if your qualifications aren't the greatest, a well-designed résumé improves your chances of getting an interview because it stands out in a crowd of poorly designed ones.

Because I feel strongly that a résumé should reflect the personality of the person it represents, I respect my clients' wishes when it comes to the actual design of their résumés. This means that, even though my staff and I write and design nearly a thousand résumés every year for clients in 42 countries, no two are exactly alike. You won't like every résumé in this book, and you shouldn't. Each one is designed and written to reflect an individual's personal career goals, industry, and personality.

Even though Chapter 2 is devoted to writing the words in your résumé, the rest of the book is intended to help you express yourself visually in the design of your résumé. The choice of overall style, type font, graphics, and even paper color says something about your personality. If you consider yourself to be more conservative and if you are in a traditional job in senior management, banking, or accounting, you will probably be drawn to the conservative résumés in this book. Throughout the book, but especially in Chapters 12 and 17, you will find résumés for more creative types, like actors, graphic designers, artists, and advertising professionals.

The number one rule in the résumé business is "It depends!" The length of your résumé depends on your relevant experience and education. It also depends on your industry—a CV for a doctor, college professor, or other professional can be as long as it needs to be (see Chapter 16). Whether you choose to put your photograph on your résumé depends on whether your appearance is a bonafide occupational qualification in your industry (model, news anchor, actor; see Chapter 9). Whether you can place a graphic design on your résumé or use creative lines depends on how creative your industry is and the expectations of hiring managers in that industry (see Chapters 11, 12, and 17). Whether you choose to use a functional style instead of a pure reverse chronological style depends on your work history—do you have gaps in employment that you want to make less obvious, is every job repetitive, are you entering the job market for the first time and most of your experience is non-paid (see Chapter 14)? If you are sending your résumé overseas to an international company or you are a college student whose leadership is proven in your activities, then a list of personal interests might be an appropriate addition to your résumé (see Chapter 9).

Choose elements from various résumés that create a personalized look just for you, but keep in mind where you will be sending your résumé. Today, many large companies and recruiters who receive a lot of résumés scan résumés into electronic databases. Because of this trend, certain design elements are not appropriate for scanning. For those of you who know you will be sending résumés to Fortune 1000 and large high-tech companies, read Chapter 3 closely and let it guide you through your design choices.

This book is *not* devoted strictly to scannable résumés. Only about 24 percent of job openings today require a résumé that is scannable. The remaining 76 percent can be designed with your personality and industry in mind without a second thought to scannability. For those of you who will mix sending your résumé to companies that scan résumés and those who don't, it is possible to create a perfectly scannable ASCII text résumé (see page 46) that can be printed and sent along with a handsomely designed résumé that may not be scannable. Then your recipient has a choice of which résumé to scan.

Although this book focuses on design, it doesn't mean you should neglect the words on your résumé. Chapter 2 will guide you through an award-winning twelve-step résumé writing process that will help you get your experience and accomplishments down on paper. Remember, once your résumé design has grabbed your reader's attention, the words must then keep that attention.

About half of the book is devoted to the various design elements of a résumé with full-page samples: name, address, headings, dates, geographic locations, fonts, bullets, graphic lines, and other graphic design elements. Chapter 13 will show you the visual difference between laying out your résumé with bulleted short lines and paragraphs. Chapter 14 will provide you with samples of functional résumés and functional/chronological combinations. Curriculum vitae and executive/professional résumés have unique needs addressed in Chapters 15 and 16. Then we get to have some fun with creative résumés for artists, advertising professionals, actors, dancers, models, and other artistic people. In Chapter 18, you will find sample cover letters on various letterhead styles and a discussion of paper color, type, and size.

You have a wealth of designs and job descriptions in this book from which to choose—more than in any other résumé book on the market today. If you find wording that works for you, please feel free to use it as a foundation for the words on your own résumé. The index at the end of this book will help you find specific job titles that might help you to describe your experience. Every job title from every résumé in the book has been pulled out in alphabetical order to make it easier for you to locate specific job descriptions.

Now that you know what this book offers, let's get started writing your résumé!

2 How to Write the Perfect Résumé

Writing your résumé is often one of the most difficult things you will ever do! Think about it . . . you must turn your life history into a one- or two-page advertisement that highlights a lifetime of experience, accomplishments, and education. Since we have been taught all of our lives not to blow our own horn, most people find this ultimate advertisement difficult to write.

Before you can begin to design your résumé on paper, you need to have the words. Use the following twelve-step writing process to help clarify your experience, accomplishments, skills, education, and other background information, which will make the job of condensing your life onto a sheet of paper a little easier. I expanded this twelve-step process into an entire book for Barron's—*How to Write Better Résumés and Cover Letters*—which you can find at your local bookstore or online. If you want to download the questionnaires developed for that book, you can find them free at my Web site—*www.patcriscito.com*—by clicking on *bookstore*. You can also copy the forms from the Appendix in the back of this book.

❑ Step One: Focus

The first step in writing the perfect résumé is to know what kind of job you will be applying for. A résumé without a focus is never as effective as one that relates to a specific job description.

Now, decide what type of job you will be applying for and then write it at the top of a piece of paper. This can become your objective statement, should you decide to use one, or it can become the first line of the profile section of your résumé to give your reader a general idea of your area(s) of expertise.

An objective is not required on a résumé, and often the cover letter is the best place to personalize your objective for each job opening. There is nothing wrong with using an objective statement on a résumé, however, provided it does not limit your job choices. As an alternative, you can alter individual résumés with personalized objectives that reflect the actual job title for which you are applying. Just make sure that the rest of your information is still relevant to the new objective.

Never write an objective statement that is not precise. You want to name the position so specifically that, if a janitor came by and knocked over the stacks of sorted résumés on a hiring manager's desk, he could put yours back in its right stack without even thinking about it. That means saying, "A marketing management position with an aggressive international consumer goods manufacturer" instead of "A position that utilizes my education and experience to mutual benefit."

❏ Step Two: Education

The second step in writing your résumé is to think about your education. That means all of your training and not just formal education (college, university, or trade school).

The education section of your résumé will include degrees, continuing education, professional development, seminars, workshops, and sometimes even self-study.

Under your objective statement, list any education or training that might relate. If you are a recent college graduate and have little relevant experience, then your education section will be placed at the top of your résumé. As you gain more experience, your education almost always gravitates to the bottom.

There is an exception to every rule in the résumé business, however, so use your common sense. If you are changing careers and recently returned to college to obtain new credentials, your education section will appear at the top of the résumé even if you have years of experience. Think about your strongest qualifications and make certain they appear in the top half of page one of your résumé.

If you participated in college activities or received any honors or completed any notable projects that relate directly to your target job, this is the place to list them.

Computerized applicant tracking systems are programmed to show that you have college study but not a degree if they see from–to dates. For instance, writing 1999–2001 implies that you did not graduate. If you graduated with a degree, list only the year you graduated (2001).

When you attend a trade school, you receive either a diploma or certificate. This type of schooling can be listed under the "Education" heading or under a separate heading called "Training" or "Technical Training."

Listing high school education and activities on a résumé is only appropriate when you are under 20 and have no education or training beyond high school. Once you have completed either college courses or specialized technical training, drop your high school information altogether.

Continuing education shows that you care about lifelong learning and self-development, so think about any relevant training since your formal education was completed. *Relevant* is the key word here. Always look at your résumé from the perspective of a potential employer. Don't waste space by listing training that is not directly or indirectly related to your target job. This section can include in-services, workshops, seminars, corporate training programs, conferences, conventions, and other types of training.

❏ Step Three: Job Descriptions

Get your hands on a written description of the job you wish to obtain and for any jobs you have held in the past, as well as for your current job. If you are presently employed, your human resource department is the first place to look. If not, then go to your local library and ask for a copy of *The Dictionary of Occupational Titles* or the *Occupational Outlook Handbook* (which can also be found on the Internet—see below). These industry standard reference guides offer volumes of occupational titles and job descriptions for everything from Abalone Divers to Zoo Veterinarians (and thousands in between).

Another resource available at your local library or college career center is *Job Scribe,* a computer software program with more than 3,000 job descriptions.

Other places to look for job descriptions include:

- Your local government job service agencies
- Professional and technical organizations
- Recruiters
- Associates who work in the same field
- Newspaper advertisements for similar job
- Online job postings, which tend to have longer job descriptions than print ads.

Here are some other sources for job descriptions on the Internet:

- America's Career InfoNet: *www.acinet.org*
- Career Guide to Industries: *www.bls.gov/oco/cg/*
- Careers Online Virtual Careers Show: *http://www.careersonline.com.au/show/menu.html*
- Dictionary of Occupational Titles: *www.oalj.dol.gov/libdot.htm*
- JobProfiles.com: *www.jobprofiles.org*
- Occupational Outlook Handbook: *www.bls.gov/oco/home.htm*
- Occupational Outlook Quarterly: *www.bls.gov/opub/ooq/ooqhome.htm*

Performance evaluations, depending on how well they are written, generally list a description of your major responsibilities, a breakdown of individual tasks, and highlights of your accomplishments. You should *always* keep a folder at home of performance evaluations from every job you have ever held. If you haven't kept them up until now, please start.

Now, make copies of these performance evaluations so you can highlight them as you write your résumé. Use a different colored pen to highlight accomplishments—the things you did above and beyond the call of duty.

Also make copies of the job descriptions you discovered and mark the sentences that describe anything you have done in your past or present jobs. These job descriptions are important sources of keywords, so pay particular attention to nouns and phrases that you can incorporate into your own résumé.

❏ Step Four: Keywords

In today's world of computerized applicant tracking systems, make sure you know the buzzwords of your industry and incorporate them into the sentences you are about to write. Keywords are the nouns, adjectives, and sometimes verbs and short phrases that describe your experience and education that might be used to find your résumé in a keyword search of a résumé database. They are the essential knowledge, abilities, and skills required to do your job.

Keywords are generally concrete descriptions like: C++, UNIX, fiber optic cable, network, project management, among others. Even well-known company names (Intel, IBM, Hewlett-Packard) and universities (Harvard, Yale, Princeton, SMU, Stanford, Tulane, Columbia, etc.) are sometimes used as keywords, especially when it is necessary to narrow down an initial search that calls up hundreds of résumés from a résumé database.

Acronyms and abbreviations here can either hurt you or help you, depending on how you use them. One example given to me by an engineer at Yahoo! Resumix was the abbreviation "IN." Think about it. "IN" could stand for *intelligent networks, Indiana,* or the word *in.* It is better to spell out the abbreviation if there could be any possible confusion. However, if a series of initials is so well known that it would be recognized by nearly everyone in your industry and would not likely be confused with a real word, then the keyword search will probably use those initials (i.e., IBM, CPA, UNIX). When in doubt, always spell it out at least one time on your résumé. A computer only needs to see the combination one time for it to be considered a "hit" in a keyword search.

Soft skills are often not included in search criteria, especially for very technical positions, although I have interviewed some companies that use them extensively for the initial selection of résumés for management positions. For instance, "communicate effectively," "self-motivated," "team player," and so on, are great for describing your abilities and are fine to include in your profile, but concentrate more on your hard skills, especially if you are in a high-tech field.

In the end of this chapter, you will find a more in-depth description of keywords and some examples of keywords for specific industries, although there is no such thing as a comprehensive listing of keywords for any single job. The computerized candidate management programs used by most companies and online résumé databases allow the recruiter or hiring manager to personalize his or her list of keywords for each job opening, so it is an evolving process. You will never know whether you have listed absolutely every keyword possible, so focus instead on getting on paper as many related skills as possible, remembering to be absolutely honest and accurate.

The job descriptions and performance evaluations you found in Step Three are some of the most important sources for keywords. You can also be certain that nearly every noun and some adjectives in a job posting or advertisement will be keywords, so make sure you use those words somewhere in your résumé, using synonyms wherever you can. Just make sure you can justify every word on your résumé—don't exaggerate. If you don't have the experience or skill, don't use the keyword.

Make a list of the keywords you have determined are important for your particular job search and then list synonyms for those words. There is a form for this purpose in the appendix. As you incorporate these words into the sentences of your résumé, check them off.

One caution. Always tell the truth. The minute a hiring manager speaks with you on the telephone or begins an interview, any exaggeration of the truth will become immediately apparent. It is a bad idea to say, "I don't have experience with Excel computer software" just to get the words *Excel* or *computer software* on paper so your résumé will pop up in a keyword search. In a cover letter, it might be appropriate to say that you "don't have five years of experience in marketing but can add two years of university training in the subject to three years of in-depth experience as a marketing assistant with Hewlett-Packard." That is legitimate reasoning, but anything more manipulative can be hazardous to your job search.

❑ Step Five: Your Jobs

Now that you have the basic information for your résumé, you need to create a list of jobs and write basic sentences to describe your duties. Start by using a separate "Experience" form (you will find them in the appendix) for each job you have held for the past 10 to 15 years. You can generally stop there unless there is something in your previous work history that is particularly relevant to the new job you are seeking.

Starting with your present position, list the title of every job you have held, along with the name of the company, the city and state, and the years you worked there. You don't need to list full addresses and zip codes, although you will need to know that information when it comes time to fill out an application. You should use a separate page for each job title even if you worked for the same company in more than one capacity.

You can list years only (1996–present) or months and years (May 1996–present), depending on your personality. People who are more detail oriented are usually more comfortable with a full accounting of their time. Listing years alone covers some gaps if you have worked in a position for less than a full year while the time period spans more than one calendar year. For instance, if you worked from December 2000 through January 2001, saying 2000–2001 certainly looks better. If you are concerned about gaps in your work history, then listing years only is to your advantage.

From the perspective of recruiters and hiring managers, most don't care whether you list the months and years or list the years only. However, if you are writing a Resumix résumé for a U.S. government job, you will be required in almost every case to list the beginning and ending month and year for each job. Regardless of which method you choose, be consistent throughout your résumé, especially within each section. Don't use months sometimes and years alone other times within the same section. Consistency of style is important on a résumé, since it is that consistency that makes your résumé neat, clean, and easy to read.

❑ Step Six: Duties

Under each job on its separate page, make a list of your duties, incorporating phrases from the job description wherever they apply. You don't have to worry about making great sentences yet or narrowing down your list. Just get the information on paper.

This is the most time-consuming part of the résumé writing process. Depending on how quickly you write/type, it could take an entire day just for this step. Anything worth doing, however, is worth doing right, so you will want to take the time to do this step to the best of your ability.

Don't forget to list internships, practicums, and unpaid volunteer work in your experience section. Experience is experience, whether you are paid for it or not. If the position or the knowledge you gained is relevant to your current job search, then put it on your résumé. You can either include unpaid experience along with your paid experience, or you can create a separate section just for your volunteer history.

❑ Step Seven: Accomplishments

When you are finished with your work history, go back to each job and think about what you might have done above and beyond the call of duty. What did you contribute to each of your jobs? How did you measure your success? Did you:

- Exceed sales quotas by 150 percent each month?
- Save the company more than $100,000 by developing a new procedure?
- Generate new product publicity in trade press?
- Control expenses or cut overhead?
- Expand the business or attract/retain customers?
- Improve the company's image or build new relationships?
- Improve the quality of a product?
- Solve a problem?
- Do something that made the company more competitive?
- Make money?
- Save money or time?
- Improve quality or service?
- Increase productivity?
- Improve workplace safety?
- Increase efficiency or make work easier?

Go back to the experience forms in the last step and write down any accomplishments that show potential employers what you have done in the past, which translates into what you might be able to do for them in the future. This is not *bragging*, which is a prideful exaggeration. Instead, it is *advertising*, which is "to make known the positive features of a product (you)."

Quantify and diversify whenever possible. Numbers are always impressive. But don't duplicate wording throughout the résumé. If you use dollars in one case, use percentages in another. Overused words lose their effectiveness, like a song played on the radio again and again.

Remember, you are trying to motivate the potential employer to buy . . . you! Convince your reader that you will be able to generate a significant return on their investment in you. Try to focus on "before" and "after" examples. Identify a problem and explain how you corrected it.

❏ Step Eight: Delete

Now that you have the words on paper, make a copy of each sheet. It pays to be a packrat if you decide to change careers in the future. Store the original worksheets in the same file you created for your performance evaluations and job descriptions. Use the copies for this step.

Decide which jobs are relevant to today's job search. Set aside the jobs that are too old or irrelevant (like flipping hamburgers back in high school if you are now an electrical engineer with ten years of experience). Try to limit your list of final jobs to no more than six, although you can list more if they are truly relevant or contain valuable experience.

Remember, your résumé is just an enticer, a way to get your foot in the door. It isn't intended to be all-inclusive. You can choose to go back only as far as your jobs relate to your present objective.

Then focus on the sentences and do the same. Which ones are the most powerful? Which ones summarize your experience best? Which ones highlight your accomplishments best? Be careful not to delete sentences that contain the keywords you identified in Step Four.

Next, do the same for your education and training worksheets. Copy them, file away the originals, and cross out anything that doesn't relate to your current job goal.

This does not apply to your formal education, however. Even if you have a graduate degree in your career field and your undergraduate degree is unrelated, leave them both on your résumé. Your reader will need to see the progression of your formal education.

If you have a bachelor's degree and an associate degree, you don't need to list them both unless there is something about the major of your associate degree that is not included in your bachelor's degree and is relevant to your current search. Remember, it is okay to list almost anything on your résumé as long as it is relevant to your job search.

One last thing, if you have lied about (or exaggerated) anything on your résumé up to this point, delete it now! Did you know that it is against the law to lie on a résumé? You could be committing a felony. If you are caught and convicted, you could land in jail! And that's not all. If you claim to have a college degree you didn't earn and it leads to higher pay, you could be accused of criminal fraud by your employer, even if this is discovered years later.

According to a survey conducted by the Society for Human Resource Management, among the 87 percent of hiring managers who check all references, 90 percent say they've caught job applicants making false claims and, of those liars, 35 percent fabricated a previous employer. Reuters reports that ADP Screening and Selection Services found that more than 50 percent of the people on whom it conducted employment and education checks in 2003 had submitted false information, compared with about 40 percent a year earlier.

Anne Fisher of *Fortune* magazine says, "The vast majority of companies view lying on a résumé as grounds for firing or for putting a candidate right out of the running, so forget it." Companies are fighting back. They are conducting more thorough background checks of candidates and even long-time employees. This includes not only references but also criminal checks. If you are job hunting, you will likely have to prove you really did earn your degree. Expect to be asked for an official transcript of your college work.

❑ Step Nine: Sentences

It's time to do some serious writing now. You must make dynamic, attention-getting sentences of the duties and accomplishments you have listed under each job, combining related items to avoid short choppy phrases. Here are the secrets to great résumé sentences:

- Never use personal pronouns (I, my, me). Instead of saying: *"I planned, organized, and directed the timely and accurate production of code products with estimated annual revenues of $1 million"* you should say: *"Planned, organized, and directed . . ."* Writing in the first person makes your sentences more powerful and attention grabbing, but using personal pronouns throughout a résumé is awkward. Your reader will assume that you are referring to yourself, so the personal pronouns can be avoided.
- Make your sentences positive, brief, and accurate. Since your ultimate goal is to get a human being to read your résumé, remember to structure the sentences so they are interesting to read.
- Use verbs at the beginning of each sentence (designed, supervised, managed, developed, formulated, and so on) to make them more powerful (see the list at the end of this chapter).
- Incorporate keywords from the list you made in Step Four.
- Make certain each word means something and contributes to the quality of the sentence.

If you find it difficult to write clear, concise sentences, take the information you have just written to a professional writer who can help you turn it into a winning résumé. Choose someone who is a Nationally Certified Résumé Writer (NCRW), Master Résumé Writer (MRW), or Certified Professional Résumé Writer (CPRW). That way you can be assured that the person has passed the strictest tests of résumé writing and design in the country, including peer review, administered by the National Résumé Writers' Association (NRWA), Career Masters Institute (CMI), and Professional Association of Résumé Writers (PARW).

To find certified résumé writers, check these Web sites:

- National Résumé Writers' Association: *www.nrwa.com*
- Professional Association of Résumé Writers: *www.parw.com*
- Career Masters Institute: *www.cminstitute.com*
- Professional Résumé Writing and Research Association: *www.prwra.com*
- Certified Résumé Writers Guild: *www.certifiedresumewritersguild.com*
- Certified Résumé Writers: *www.certifiedresumewriters.net*

What are the benefits of partnering with a professional résumé writer? According to the NRWA, you will gain access to:

- Expert résumé writing, editing, and design skills.
- Needed objectivity and expertise to play up your strengths, downplay your weaknesses, and position yourself for interview success.
- The precise know-how to target your career and industry correctly.
- Winning résumé, job search, interviewing, and salary negotiation strategies from recognized experts.
- Experienced professionals who have passed rigorous résumé industry exams and demonstrated their commitment to the profession by obtaining ongoing training.

Résumé writers work in one of three ways: 1) they gather all of the information they need from you in a personal interview, 2) they require that you complete a long questionnaire before they begin working on your résumé, or 3) they use a combination of both methods. In any case, you have already done most of the data collection if you have followed the steps in this chapter. This preparation sometimes makes the résumé easier to write and many professional résumé writers will pass on that savings to you in the form of lower fees.

❏ Step Ten: Rearrange

You are almost done! Now, go back to the sentences you have written and think about their order of presentation. Put a number 1 by the most important description of what you did for each job. Then place a number 2 by the next most important duty or accomplishment, and so on until you have numbered each sentence.

Again, think logically and from the perspective of a potential employer. Keep related items together so the reader does not jump from one concept to another. Make the thoughts flow smoothly.

The first sentence in a job description is usually an overall statement of the position's major responsibilities. The rest of the sentences should begin with your most important duties and accomplishments and proceed to lesser ones.

Let me give you an example of a job description in rough draft format and one that has been rearranged, and I'm sure you will see what I mean.

JOHNSON UNIVERSITY HOSPITAL, New Brunswick, New Jersey (2000 – 2003)
Director, Pediatric Emergency Department
- Recently developed and implemented an expansion of the department into a new children's hospital.
- Hired and managed a staff of 40 employees, directed performance improvement initiatives, and implemented departmental standards of care.
- Analyzed trends for key indicators to improve subsequent code responses.
- Member of the Performance Improvement Committee.
- Analyzed 72-hour readmission trends to find problems with practice patterns.
- Selected for the Code Response Team: Developed a new performance improvement form.
- Redesigned resuscitation guidelines for residents and nursing staff.
- Directed clinical and administrative operations of a 12,000-visit-per-year pediatric emergency department.
- Developed and managed an operating budget of $1.3 million.

- Developed staffing standards and evaluated the qualifications/competence of department personnel to provide appropriate levels of patient care.
- Member of the Health Policy and Strategic Planning Committee responsible for preparing the hospital and staff for JCAHO accreditation reviews.
- Implemented a pain initiative.

After numbering and rearranging the sentences, the section reads much stronger and has a better flow.

JOHNSON UNIVERSITY HOSPITAL, New Brunswick, New Jersey (2000 – 2003)
Director, Pediatric Emergency Department
- Directed clinical and administrative operations of a 12,000-visit-per-year pediatric emergency department.
- Developed and managed an operating budget of $1.3 million.
- Hired and managed a staff of 40 employees, directed performance improvement initiatives, and implemented departmental standards of care.
- Developed staffing standards and evaluated the qualifications/competence of department personnel to provide appropriate levels of patient care.
- Member of the Health Policy and Strategic Planning Committee responsible for preparing the hospital and staff for JCAHO accreditation reviews.

Key Accomplishments:
- Recently developed and implemented an expansion of the department into a new children's hospital.
- Member of the Performance Improvement Committee: Analyzed 72-hour readmission trends to find problems with practice patterns. Implemented a pain initiative. Redesigned resuscitation guidelines for residents and nursing staff.
- Selected for the Code Response Team: Developed a new performance improvement form. Analyzed trends for key indicators to improve subsequent code responses.

Here is my reasoning for rearranging the sentences:

1. The first sentence was selected because it was a good overall statement of the job's major responsibility.
2. The second sentence added a further sense of scope by describing the size of the director's budget.
3. As did the third sentence by discussing the number of employees managed and other supervisory responsibilities.
4. The next two sentences are secondary job duties and special assignments.
5. In order to emphasize achievements, key accomplishments were pulled out into a separate section.
6. The first bullet was the most important accomplishment and the most recent.
7. All of the bullets that applied to the Performance Improvement Committee were listed together in a separate paragraph.
8. The last accomplishment was the least important.

❏ **Step Eleven: Related Qualifications**

At the bottom of your résumé (or sometimes toward the top), you can add anything else that might qualify you for your job objective. This includes licenses, certifications, special skills, languages, credentials, publications, speeches, presentations, exhibits, grants, special projects, research, affiliations, volunteer activities, civic contributions, honors, awards, distinctions, professional recognitions, computer skills, international experience, and sometimes even interests if they truly relate. For instance, if you want a job in sports marketing, stating on your résumé that you play tennis or are a triathlete would be an asset.

❑ Step Twelve: Profile

Last but not least, write four or five sentences that give an overview of your qualifications. This profile or qualifications summary should be placed at the beginning of your résumé. You can include some of your personal traits or special skills that might have been difficult to get across in your job descriptions.

Some HR professionals might disagree with me. They say that they skip over descriptions of unverifiable claims about personal strengths, but there are just as many HR managers who read every word. Besides, you want to make sure you cover your soft skills for e-résumés where keywords defined in job requisitions often request such strengths.

Here is a sample profile section for a computer systems technician looking for a job with a military contractor:

- Experienced systems/network technician with significant communications and technical control experience in the military sector.
- Focused and hard working; willing to go the extra mile for the customer.
- Skilled in troubleshooting complex problems by thinking outside the box.
- Possesses a high degree of professionalism and dedication to exceptional quality.
- Current Top Secret security clearance with access to Sensitive Compartmented Information.

It is also acceptable to use a keyword summary like the one below to give a "quick and dirty" look at your qualifications:

- **Certifications:** CompTIA A+ Certified, Certified Work Group Manager.
- **Networks:** Networking concepts and architecture, client/server and peer-to-peer local-area and wide-area networks (LAN/WAN), servers, routers, switches, hubs, cabling in Ethernet environments, command and control networks, secure SIPR nets, Windows NT, Windows 2000, Exchange, Proxy Server, Microsoft System Management Server (SMS), UNIX.
- **Equipment:** Network interface cards, sound cards, SCSI cards, tape drives, hard drives, printers, and peripherals.
- **Software:** MS Word, Excel, PowerPoint, Access, Outlook, Internet Explorer, Remedy, MS Exchange, SQL Server, Norton Antivirus, Ghost, MS Proxy, Sidewinder Firewall.

This type of laundry list isn't very interesting for a human being to read, but a few recruiters in high-tech industries like this list of terms because it gives them a quick overview of an applicant's skills. You can use whichever style you prefer.

Busy recruiters spend as little as ten seconds deciding whether to read a résumé from top to bottom. You will be lucky if the first third of your résumé gets read, whether it is an electronic résumé or a paper one, so make sure the information at the top entices the reader to read it all.

This profile section must be relevant to the type of job for which you are applying. It might be true that you are "compassionate," but will it help you get a job as a high-pressure salesperson? Write this profile from the perspective of a potential employer. What will convince this person to call you instead of someone else?

Another important reason for adding this profile section to your résumé is to ensure that the clerk who classifies your résumé into a category and summarizes your information into the applicant tracking software doesn't have to read your entire résumé and guess what words are important. Even large companies that don't scan résumés or receive them through e-mail or Web-based e-forms (which includes the majority of companies) still have computerized systems for tracking résumés or they outsource the scanning of paper résumés, so these words of advice apply to all résumés, not just the electronic kind.

❑ You're Done: Well, Almost

Now it's time to put all of this information together into the perfect résumé. You have a qualifications summary, your education, experience, and other relevant information. The only thing you lack is your contact information.

For the contact information, you can use your full name, first and last name only, or shortened names (Pat Criscito instead of Patricia K. Criscito).

Do not use work telephone numbers or a work e-mail address on your résumé. Potential employers tend to consider that an abuse of company resources, which implies you might do the same if you are working for them. Listing a cellular telephone number on your résumé gives a hiring manager a way to reach you during working hours.

Avoid the use of "cutesy" e-mail addresses on a résumé. If you use *babycakes@aol.com* for your personal e-mail, create a second e-mail address under your account that will be more professional. If your only access to the Internet is at work, then create a free-mail account at *hotmail.com, juno.com, usa.net, yahoo.com, mail.com, excite.com, e-mail.com,* or *altavista.com.* Check *www.refdesk.com/freemail.html* for a list of even more free e-mail services.

Now it's time to typeset your information in a style that reflects your personality for your paper résumé. There is a science behind laying out a paper résumé, just like there is a science behind designing advertisements, and you need to feel comfortable with your word processing software before you even start. If you are not, then you should call in a professional typesetter, designer, or résumé writer for this part. You have just finished the hardest part of a résumé—the writing of it—so you may be able to save some money by shopping around when getting it typeset. Make sure the designer knows you need a résumé that will scan perfectly and that you need a copy of the file on a computer disk so you can create your e-mailable version.

An experienced résumé writer and designer can take the work you have done and enhance it with a wealth of seasoned knowledge, turning it into a finely tuned marketing instrument that truly reflects who you are. The finished résumé will attract a reader to learn more about you in an interview, which is the whole purpose of your résumé anyway.

Whether you typeset your résumé yourself or hire someone else to do it for you, the ultimate responsibility for the accuracy of your résumé is *yours*. Make sure every word is spelled correctly and that your grammar is perfect. Double proofread your dates, address, phone number, and any other numbers that might appear in your résumé. Make sure punctuation is consistent and that you haven't used the ampersand (&) in place of the word *and* (except in the case of a company name when the company uses it that way). When you are absolutely certain it is perfect, then have someone else read it again just to make sure!

❏ **Power Verbs**

Just because a computer will screen your résumé in the beginning and look for keywords is no excuse for poor writing. Your ultimate goal is to entice a human being to read your résumé, so keep the sentences interesting by using positive power verbs. Try to use a variety of these words. It is easy to choose the same one to begin every sentence, but there are synonyms buried within this list that will make your writing better.

A

abated
abbreviated
abolished
abridged
absolved
absorbed
accelerated
accentuated
accommodated
accompanied
accomplished
accounted for
accrued
accumulated
achieved
acquired
acted
activated
actuated
adapted
added
addressed
adhered to
adjusted
administered
adopted
advanced

advertised
advised
advocated
affirmed
aided
alerted
aligned
allayed
alleviated
allocated
allotted
altered
amassed
amended
amplified
analyzed
answered
anticipated
appeased
applied
appointed
appraised
approached
appropriated
approved
arbitrated
aroused
arranged
articulated

ascertained
aspired
assembled
assessed
assigned
assimilated
assisted
assumed
assured
attained
attended
attracted
audited
augmented
authored
authorized
automated
averted
avoided
awarded

B

balanced
bargained
began
benchmarked
benefitted
bid

billed
blended
blocked
bolstered
boosted
bought
branded
bridged
broadened
brought
budgeted
built

C

calculated
calibrated
canvassed
capitalized
captured
cared for
carried
carried out
carved
catalogued
categorized
caught
cautioned
cemented

centralized
certified
chaired
challenged
championed
changed
channeled
charged
charted
checked
chose
chronicled
circulated
circumvented
cited
clarified
classified
cleaned
cleared
closed
coached
co-authored
coded
cold called
collaborated
collated
collected
combined
commanded
commenced
commended
commissioned
communicated
compared
competed
compiled
complemented
completed
complied
composed
compounded
computed
conceived
concentrated
conceptualized
concluded
condensed

conducted
conferred
configured
confirmed
confronted
connected
conserved
considered
consolidated
constructed
consulted
consummated
contacted
continued
contracted
contributed
controlled
converted
conveyed
convinced
cooperated
coordinated
copied
corrected
correlated
corresponded
counseled
counted
created
credited with
critiqued
cultivated
customized
cut

D

dealt
debated
debugged
decentralized
decided
decoded
decreased
dedicated
deferred
defined
delegated

deleted
delineated
delivered
demonstrated
deployed
depreciated
derived
described
designated
designed
detailed
detected
determined
developed
devised
devoted
diagnosed
diagramed
differentiated
diffused
directed
disbursed
disclosed
discounted
discovered
discussed
dispatched
dispensed
dispersed
displayed
disposed
disproved
dissected
disseminated
dissolved
distinguished
distributed
diversified
diverted
divested
divided
documented
doubled
drafted
dramatized
drew up
drove

E

earned
eased
economized
edited
educated
effected
elaborated
elected
elevated
elicited
eliminated
embraced
emphasized
employed
empowered
enabled
encountered
encouraged
ended
endorsed
enforced
engaged
engineered
enhanced
enlarged
enlisted
enriched
enrolled
ensured
entered
entertained
enticed
equipped
established
estimated
evaluated
examined
exceeded
exchanged
executed
exercised
exhibited
expanded
expedited
experienced
experimented

explained
explored
exposed
expressed
extended
extracted
extrapolated

F

fabricated
facilitated
factored
familiarized
fashioned
fielded
filed
filled
finalized
financed
fine-tuned
finished
fixed
focused
followed
forecasted
forged
formalized
formatted
formed
formulated
fortified
forwarded
fostered
fought
found
founded
framed
fulfilled
functioned as
funded
furnished
furthered

G

gained
garnered
gathered

gauged
gave
generated
governed
graded
graduated
granted
graphed
grasped
greeted
grew
grouped
guaranteed
guided

H

halted
halved
handled
headed
heightened
held
helped
hired
honed
hosted
hypnotized
hypothesized

I

identified
ignited
illuminated
illustrated
implemented
imported
improved
improvised
inaugurated
incited
included
incorporated
increased
incurred
indicated
individualized
indoctrinated

induced
influenced
informed
infused
initialized
initiated
innovated
inspected
inspired
installed
instigated
instilled
instituted
instructed
insured
integrated
intensified
interacted
interceded
interfaced
interpreted
intervened
interviewed
introduced
invented
inventoried
invested
investigated
invigorated
invited
involved
isolated
issued
itemized

J

joined
judged
justified

L

launched
learned
leased
lectured
led
lessened

leveraged
licensed
lifted
lightened
limited
linked
liquidated
listened
litigated
loaded
lobbied
localized
located
logged

M

made
maintained
managed
mandated
maneuvered
manipulated
manufactured
mapped
marked
marketed
mastered
maximized
measured
mediated
memorized
mentored
merchandised
merged
merited
met
minimized
mobilized
modeled
moderated
modernized
modified
molded
monitored
monopolized
motivated

mounted
moved
multiplied

N

named
narrated
navigated
negotiated
netted
networked
neutralized
nominated
normalized
noticed
notified
nurtured

O

observed
obtained
offered
officiated
offset
opened
operated
optimized
orchestrated
ordered
organized
oriented
originated
outdistanced
outlined
outperformed
overcame
overhauled
oversaw
owned

P

paced
packaged
packed
paid

pared
participated
partnered
passed
patterned
penalized
penetrated
perceived
perfected
performed
permitted
persuaded
phased out
photographed
piloted
pinpointed
pioneered
placed
planned
played
polled
posted
praised
predicted
prepared
prescribed
presented
preserved
presided
prevailed
prevented
priced
printed
prioritized
probed
processed
procured
produced
profiled
programmed
progressed
projected
promoted
prompted
proofread
proposed
protected

proved
provided
pruned
publicized
published
purchased
pursued

Q

quadrupled
qualified
quantified
queried
questioned
quoted

R

raised
rallied
ranked
rated
reached
reacted
read
realigned
realized
rearranged
reasoned
rebuilt
received
reclaimed
recognized
recommended
reconciled
reconstructed
recorded
recovered
recruited
rectified
redesigned
redirected
reduced
re-engineered
referred
refined

refocused
regained
registered
regulated
rehabilitated
reinforced
reinstated
reiterated
rejected
related
released
relied
relieved
remained
remediated
remodeled
rendered
renegotiated
renewed
reorganized
repaired
replaced
replicated
replied
reported
represented
reproduced
requested
required
requisitioned
researched
reserved
reshaped
resolved
responded
restored
restructured
retained
retooled
retrieved
returned
revamped
revealed
reversed
reviewed
revised
revitalized
revolutionized

rewarded
risked
rotated
routed

S

safeguarded
salvaged
saved
scanned
scheduled
screened
sculptured
searched
secured
segmented
seized
selected
sent
separated
sequenced
served as
serviced
settled
set up
shaped
shared
sharpened
shipped
shortened
showed
shrank
signed
simplified
simulated
sketched
skilled
slashed
smoothed
sold
solicited
solidified
solved
sorted

sourced
sparked
spearheaded
specialized
specified
speculated
spent
spoke
sponsored
spread
spurred
stabilized
staffed
staged
standardized
started
steered
stimulated
strategized
streamlined
strengthened
stressed
stretched
structured
studied
subcontracted
submitted
substantiated
substituted
succeeded
suggested
summarized
superceded
supervised
supplied
supported
surpassed
surveyed
swayed
swept
symbolized
synchronized
synthesized
systemized

T

tabulated
tackled
tailored
talked
tallied
targeted
tasted
taught
teamed
tempered
tended
terminated
tested
testified
tied
tightened
took
topped
totaled
traced
tracked
traded
trained
transacted
transcribed
transferred
transformed
transitioned
translated
transmitted
transported
traveled
treated
trimmed
tripled
troubleshot
turned
tutored
typed

U

uncovered
underlined

underscored
undertook
underwrote
unearthed
unified
united
updated
upgraded
upheld
urged
used
utilized

V

validated
valued
vaulted
verbalized
verified
viewed
visited
visualized
voiced
volunteered

W

weathered
weighed
welcomed
widened
withstood
witnessed
won
worked
wove
wrote

Y

yielded

❏ **Keywords**

As discussed in Step Four of the résumé writing process, using the right keywords for your particular experience and education is critical to the success of your résumé if it is ever scanned or e-mailed into an electronic résumé database. Without the right keywords, your résumé will float in cyberspace forever waiting for a hiring manager to find it. If your résumé contains all of the right keywords, then you will be among the first candidates whose résumés are reviewed. If you lack only one of the keywords, then your résumé will be next in line after résumés that have them all, and so on.

Remember, your keywords are the experience and skills that come from the specific terminology used in your job. For instance, *operating room* and *ICU* immediately classify the experience of a nurse, but *pediatric ICU* narrows it down even further.

Don't try to limit your résumé by using fewer words. If your information is longer than one page, a reader looking at a computer screen won't be able to tell, but the computer doing a keyword search will know if a word is not there. Recall, however, that you only need to use a word one time for it to be considered a "hit" in a keyword search. Try to use synonyms wherever possible to broaden your chances of being selected.

You should also understand the difference between a simple keyword search and a concept search. When a recruiter brings up an e-mailed résumé onto the screen and sends the computer on a search for a single word like *marketing*—which one can do in any word-processing program with a few clicks of a mouse or function key—he or she is performing a keyword search.

You are also performing a keyword search when you type a word or combination of words into the command line of a search engine like Yahoo! or Google. In that case, sometimes the computer searches entire documents for matches and other times it looks only at headers or extracts from the files.

A concept search, on the other hand, can bridge the gap between words by reading entire phrases and then using sophisticated artificial intelligence to interpret what is being said, translating the phrase into a single word, like *network*, or a combination of words, like *project management*.

For example, in a simple keyword search on "Manager of Product Sales," ordinary software would return a match on a candidate's résumé that reads "worked for a Manager of Product Sales." Using a concept search, Yahoo! Resumix can distinguish between this résumé and another candidate's résumé that indicated "served as a Manager of Product Sales."

The software that extracts data from scanned and e-mailed résumés and Web sources is incredibly sophisticated. Yahoo! Resumix, one such program used by recruiters in large companies and government agencies, reads the grammar of noun, verb, and adjective combinations and extracts the information for placement on the form that will become your entry in a résumé database. Its expert system extraction engine uses a complex knowledge base of more than 197,000 rules and over ten million résumé terms. It recognizes grammatical structure variations, including synonyms and context within natural language text.

It even knows the difference between *Harvard Graphics* (a computer software program) and *Harvard* (the university) by its placement on the page and its relationship to the header that precedes it *(Computer Skills* or *Education)*.

Because of this complicated logic, and because each company and each hiring manager has the ability to personalize the search criteria for each job opening, it is impossible to give you a concrete list of the thousands of possible keywords that could be used to search for any one job.

For instance, StorageTek, a high-tech company in Louisville, Colorado, graciously conducted a keyword search for me of their Resumix database and brought up the following criteria from two different hiring managers for the same job title. These are keywords extracted from real job requisitions written by hiring managers.

FINANCIAL ANALYST/SENIOR ACCOUNTANT:

REQUIRED:
- BS in finance or accounting with 4 years of experience or
- MBA in related field with 2 years of relevant experience
- certified public accountant
- forecasting

REQUIRED:
- BS in finance or accounting with 4 years of experience or
- MBA in related field with 2 years of relevant experience
- accounting
- financial reporting
- financial statement
- Excel

DESIRED:
- accounting
- financial
- trend analysis
- financial statement
- results analysis
- trends
- strategic planning
- develop trends
- financial modeling
- personal computer
- microcomputers
- DCF
- presentation skills
- team player

DESIRED:
- ability
- customer
- new business
- financial analysis
- financial
- forecasting
- process improvement
- policy development
- business policies
- PowerPoint
- Microsoft Word
- analytical ability

You can see why it is so difficult to give definitive lists of keywords and concepts. However, it is possible to give you samples of actual keyword searches used by the recruiters at StorageTek to give you some ideas.

Let me emphasize again that you should list only experience you actually have gained. Do not include the keywords on the following pages in your résumé just because they are listed here.

ACCOUNT EXECUTIVE

REQUIRED:
- BS degree
- 3 years technical selling experience
- Fortune 500 account management experience
- sales
- storage industry
- solution selling

DESIRED:
- Siebel
- quota levels
- VAD
- VAR

ACCOUNTING ANALYST

REQUIRED:
- BA or MBA
- 2–4 years of experience
- asset management
- SAP
- accounting

DESIRED:
- fixed assets
- capital assets
- corporate tax
- US GAAP

BASE SALES REPRESENTATIVE

REQUIRED:
- 2–4 years of sales or contract management experience
- 2+ years of telemarketing or telesales experience

DESIRED:
- Siebel
- storage industry

BUSINESS MANAGER, CENTRAL ARCHIVE MANAGEMENT

REQUIRED:
- BS in engineering or computer science

- 10 years of related engineering and/or manufacturing experience
- strategic planning
- network
- product management
- program management

DESIRED:
- business plan
- line management
- pricing
- team player
- CAM
- marketing
- product strategy
- vendor
- general management
- OEM
- profit and loss

BUSINESS OPERATIONS SPECIALIST

REQUIRED:
- bachelor's degree
- 4 years of directly related experience
- production schedule
- project planning

DESIRED:
- ability to implement
- CList
- data analysis
- off-shift
- team player
- automation
- ability to plan
- customer interaction
- VM
- CMS
- JCL
- REXX
- MVS
- UNIX
- analytical ability
- customer interface
- network
- skills analysis
- automatic tools

DEVELOPMENT ENGINEER, ADVISORY

REQUIRED:
- BS/BA, Masters desired

- 5–10 years mechanical engineering experience
- 10+ years experience in hardware design
- EMC/EMI debug
- mechanical design
- tape drive

DESIRED:
- DFSS (Design for Six Sigma)
- ANSYS or Metlab
- mechanisms design
- shock
- vibration
- NARTE
- tape library
- data storage

FINANCIAL ANALYST, STAFF

REQUIRED:
- BS in Finance or Accounting
- 1–2 years related experience
- customer-focused experience
- excellent written communication skills
- collection
- financial forecast
- financial modeling
- financial reporting
- financial consolidation
- reconciliation

DESIRED:
- international finance
- hyperion consolidation software
- channel experience

ORDER SPECIALIST

REQUIRED:
- BS degree
- 1–3 years experience
- order administration
- order fulfillment
- invoice processing
- Microsoft Word
- Excel

DESIRED:
- database

PROJECT MANAGER, HUMAN RESOURCES

REQUIRED:
- bachelor's degree in human resources, business, or related field
- 6 years broad experience

DESIRED:
- communications
- project management
- milestone development
- time management
- credibility
- recruiting
- long-range planning
- sourcing

SECRETARY III

REQUIRED:
- high school education or equivalent
- 5 years of experience
- typing skill of 55–60 wpm
- interpersonal skills
- oral communication

DESIRED:
- administrative assistance
- clerical
- data analysis
- file maintenance
- material repair
- PowerPoint
- project planning
- reports
- screen calls
- troubleshoot
- answer phones
- communication skills
- document distribution
- mail sorting
- Microsoft Word
- presentation
- publication
- schedule calendar
- secretarial
- appointments
- confidential
- edit
- material

- policies and procedures
- problem solving
- records management
- schedule conference
- telephone interview

SOFTWARE ENGINEER—EMBEDDED, ADVISORY LEVEL

REQUIRED:
- BS or MS degree in one of the computer sciences or engineering
- 12–14 years of experience minimum
- controller architecture design experience
- disk controller
- fiber channel
- SCSI design
- embedded systems

DESIRED:
- open systems
- product development

SOFTWARE ENGINEER—EMBEDDED, STAFF

REQUIRED:
- BS or MS degree in one of the computer sciences or engineering
- 3–5 years of experience minimum
- C++
- embedded systems
- realtime

DESIRED:
- pSOS
- iCLinux

SOFTWARE ENGINEER, SENIOR

REQUIRED:
- BS/MS in engineering, computer science or closely related field
- 8 to 9 years of experience

DESIRED:
- C+
- customer
- hiring/firing
- prototype
- structured design
- code development
- DASD
- methodology
- real time

- supervision
- communication skills
- experiment design
- problem solving
- software design
- testing

SYSTEMS ENGINEER, SENIOR

REQUIRED:
- BS degree in related field
- 8–10 years of experience
- pre-sales
- systems engineering
- MVS
- data storage

DESIRED:
- systems configuration
- capacity planning
- DFHSM
- HSC
- presentation skills

3 Designing the Perfect Scannable Résumé

What happens when you create a beautiful paper résumé and mail or fax it to a company that scans résumés into a computerized database instead of forwarding it to a hiring manager for review? It ends up in cyberspace instead of on someone's desk. This automated process requires some special design considerations in order to make your résumé scanner friendly, which is what this chapter addresses.

According to *U.S. News & World Report*, more than 10,000 unsolicited résumés arrive every week at most Fortune 500 companies, and before the days of computerized applicant tracking systems, 80 percent were thrown out after a quick review. In a recent conversation with a Chicago recruiter with access to Coca-Cola's résumé database, I learned that Coke receives as many as 100,000 résumés a month!

It was simply impossible to keep track of that much paper until now. Instead of opening and reading thousands of paper résumés, companies can scan them or receive them by e-mail or via their online application forms and sort them by keywords. The resulting applicant database becomes an HR department's most valuable asset that contains the credentials of hundreds of thousands of potential employees.

Recent sources indicate that nearly all large companies with 1,000 employees or more are using computerized applicant tracking systems that scan résumés. Even if they don't do it themselves, companies turn to service bureaus to manage their résumé scanning or to recruiters to find potential employees for them, who in turn scan résumés into their proprietary databases. Even though these numbers sound large, in actuality they represent only 24 percent of companies nationwide. According to a survey conducted by the Society of Human Resource Managers, 76 percent of companies do not scan résumés.

As more and more companies have established a presence on the Internet and opened up their computer databases to e-mailed résumés, the scannability of your résumé has become less of an issue. The majority of résumés are sent as attachments to e-mails or in the body of e-mail messages.

When you e-mail your résumé directly to a company, you have total control over whether or not your information is correct. You are not at the whim of a scanner's ability to read your font or formatting. However, Fortune 1000 companies that scan résumés will continue to use their investment in this technology as long as they receive enough paper résumés to make the process worthwhile.

The U.S. government has invested a great deal of money over the past five years creating their Resumix applicant tracking system, so making your paper résumé scanner friendly will continue to be important when sending your résumé to government agencies.

This chapter is devoted to helping you avoid the pitfalls that commonly cause a résumé to scan poorly. This includes choosing the right fonts, laying out the text of your résumé in such a way that it is scanner friendly, selecting the right paper color, etc. With these guidelines, your résumé will be ready for a hiring manager's computerized keyword search.

If you would rather not worry about whether your résumé is scannable, then simply send your formatted résumé (styled any way you like) along with an unformatted (ASCII text) résumé like the one on page 46. Your recipient will then have a choice whether to scan the "ugly" one or to send the formatted one to the hiring manager for review. You can never go wrong when you send both styles.

For complete instructions on how to format and use an ASCII text file, both on paper and on the Internet, you should obtain a copy of Barron's *e-Résumés*. In it you will learn everything you need to know to take full advantage of the Internet and the three types of electronic résumés—scannable, e-mailable, and Web-based.

❑ Understanding the Technology

When your paper résumé is received by a human resource department that uses a computerized applicant tracking system, your résumé must first be transferred from paper into binary information that a computer can read before it can be stored in the résumé database. This is accomplished with a scanner that is connected to a computer running a special kind of software that can examine the dots of ink on your printed page and determine by their shapes which letters they represent. This is called optical character recognition, or OCR for short.

This software matches patterns with sets of characters stored in its memory, which is one of the reasons why it is important to choose a type style (or font) for your résumé that conforms to normal letter shapes. If you use a highly decorative type style, the OCR software will have difficulty making matches and will misinterpret letters. This means your words won't be spelled correctly, which of course means that a keyword search for the word *bookkeeping* will never turn up your résumé if the OCR thought you typed *bmkkeepmg*.

For now, let's assume that you have designed a résumé that the scanner can read. First, depending on the company's procedures, your résumé will be received directly by the recruiter assigned to fill a certain position (if the job was advertised) or by the human resource department in general (if you have sent your résumé unsolicited).

When the recruiter has finished reviewing your information, your résumé is added to the stacks of résumés to be processed by the computer that day. A clerk will then put your résumé into the automatic feeder bin of a flatbed scanner, separating your résumé from the one above and below it with a blank piece of paper. Within seconds, the scanner has passed its light over your pieces of paper and the software interprets the black dots of ink as letters of the alphabet. The computer then begins extracting information to fill in its electronic form, which will become part of your electronic résumé file.

❏ Your Name

Let's start at the top of your résumé and work our way down. Since your résumé is basically an advertisement for you and your skills, you should think about the design of your résumé from a marketing standpoint. When you see a well-designed ad, what is the first thing you notice (besides a picture of the product)? The product name, of course. Since you *are* the product, your name should be the first thing a reader sees and remembers.

The size and boldness of the type of your name should be larger than the largest font used in your text, but for a scannable résumé it should be no larger than 20-point type. You may use all capital letters, a combination of upper and lower case, or capitals combined with small capitals (LIKE THIS). Following is an example of a Times Roman Bold font in a few good point sizes for the name on a scannable résumé:

- **14 POINT NAME**
- **16 POINT NAME**
- **18 POINT NAME**
- **20 POINT NAME**

Avoid using decorative fonts like these for either your name or your text if your résumé will be scanned:

- **Bodini Poster**
- **Broadway Engraved**
- Bard
- *Commercial Script*
- **COTTONWOOD**

- Crazed
- *Freestyle Script*
- **Lalique**
- *Kaufmann*
- Linotext

Using reverse boxes to print white type on a black (or gray shaded) background is another mistake in a scannable résumé. Scanners can't read them and your name will be missing from your résumé! Here is a sample of a reverse boxed name:

> **PAT CRISCITO**

Lastly, make certain your name is at the top of each page of your résumé. The clerks who scan résumés are often dealing with hundreds of pieces of paper every day. It is not a good idea to staple a scannable résumé, so it is very easy for the pages of your résumé to become separated from each other.

❏ Address

Next comes your contact information. It isn't always necessary to put your address at the top of your scannable résumé. Today's sophisticated applicant tracking systems know by more than position on the résumé whether the text is an address or phone number. It doesn't matter whether you put your contact information at the top or bottom of your résumé; this is your personal preference. However, always list your e-mail address in addition to your home and cellular telephone numbers and postal information.

❑ Fonts

Use popular fonts that are not overly decorative in order to ensure optimum scannability.

This sentence is typeset in a decorative font that is known to cause problems with résumé scannability (Sanvito).

So is this sentence (AGaramond Italic).

Following are some samples of good fonts for a scannable résumé:

Serif Fonts *(traditional fonts with little "feet" on the edges of the letters)*

Bookman .... The quick brown fox jumps over a lazy dog
THE QUICK BROWN FOX JUMPS OVER A LAZY DOG

Candida .... The quick brown fox jumps over a lazy dog
THE QUICK BROWN FOX JUMPS OVER A LAZY DOG

Century Schoolbook .... The quick brown fox jumps over a lazy dog
THE QUICK BROWN FOX JUMPS OVER A LAZY DOG

Charter .... The quick brown fox jumps over a lazy dog
THE QUICK BROWN FOX JUMPS OVER A LAZY DOG

Garamond .... The quick brown fox jumps over a lazy dog
THE QUICK BROWN FOX JUMPS OVER A LAZY DOG

Palatino .... The quick brown fox jumps over a lazy dog
THE QUICK BROWN FOX JUMPS OVER A LAZY DOG

Times Roman .... The quick brown fox jumps over a lazy dog
THE QUICK BROWN FOX JUMPS OVER A LAZY DOG

Utopia .... The quick brown fox jumps over a lazy dog
THE QUICK BROWN FOX JUMPS OVER A LAZY DOG

Sans Serif *(contemporary fonts with no decorative "feet")*

Antique Olive .... **The quick brown fox jumps over a lazy dog**
THE QUICK BROWN FOX JUMPS OVER A LAZY DOG

Arial (Helvetica) .... The quick brown fox jumps over a lazy dog
THE QUICK BROWN FOX JUMPS OVER A LAZY DOG

Arial (Helvetica) Narrow .... The quick brown fox jumps over a lazy dog
THE QUICK BROWN FOX JUMPS OVER A LAZY DOG

Avant Garde .... The quick brown fox jumps over a lazy dog
THE QUICK BROWN FOX JUMPS OVER A LAZY DOG

Myriad Roman .... The quick brown fox jumps over a lazy dog
THE QUICK BROWN FOX JUMPS OVER A LAZY DOG

News Gothic .... The quick brown fox jumps over a lazy dog
THE QUICK BROWN FOX JUMPS OVER A LAZY DOG

Optima (Humanist, CG Omega) .... The quick brown fox jumps over a lazy dog
THE QUICK BROWN FOX JUMPS OVER A LAZY DOG

It doesn't make any difference whether you choose a serif or a sans serif font, but the font size should be no smaller than 9 or 10 points and no larger than 12 points for the text. Having said that, you will notice that the fonts in the previous examples are all slightly different in size even though they are exactly the same point size. Every font has its own designer and its own personality, which means that no two typefaces are exactly the same. Look at the difference between the 9-point Avant Garde and the 9-point Times Roman fonts below:

- Times Roman—9 point
- Avant Garde—9 point

You will notice that the Times Roman appears considerably smaller and could potentially cause problems with a scanner, while the 9-point Avant Garde (and the other sans serif fonts above) scanned fine in all of our tests.

The key to choosing a font for a scannable résumé is that none of the letters touch one another at any time. This can be caused by poor font design, by adjusting the kerning (the spacing between letters) in your word processor, or by printing your résumé with a low-quality printer. Even some ink-jet printers can cause the ink to run together between letters with the wrong kind of paper.

Any time one letter touches another, a scanner will have a difficult time distinguishing the shapes of the letters and you can end up with misspellings on your résumé. A keyword search looks for words that are spelled correctly, so a misspelled word is as good as no word.

Don't use underlining on your résumé for the same reason. Underlines touch the descenders on letters like g, j, p, q, and y and make it difficult for an OCR program to interpret their shapes. Take a look at these words and see if you can tell where a scanner would have trouble:

- The quick brown fox jumps over a lazy dog
- *The quick brown fox jumps over a lazy dog*
- The quick brown fox jumps over a lazy dog
- The quick brown fox jumps over a lazy dog

Related to fonts are bullets—special characters used at the beginning of indented short sentences to call attention to individual items on a résumé. These characters should be round and solid (•) for a scannable résumé. Scanners interpret hollow bullets (0) as the letter "o." Don't use any unusually shaped bullets (□, ✣) that the scanner will try to interpret as letters.

While we are on the topic of special characters, the percent (%) and ampersand (&) signs used to cause problems for some OCR software, but that isn't a problem anymore. From the perspective of good writing, however, you should always spell out the word *and,* except in cases where the ampersand appears in the name of a company. Foreign accents and letters that are not part of the English alphabet can be misinterpreted by optical character recognition.

Even though you have probably heard that italics are a no-no on a scannable résumé, today's more sophisticated optical character recognition software can read italics without difficulty, provided one letter does not touch another. The engineers I spoke with who designed résumé scanning software all stated that their software has no problem reading italics, and my staff has confirmed that with tests. We have even scanned résumés typeset in all italics without a problem, although I don't recommend that simply from a readability standpoint. The key is to choose a font that is easy to read, is not overly decorative, and does not have one letter touching another. The italic typefaces of any of the samples in this chapter would be fine to use as accents on your résumé.

❑ Format

Rely on white space to define sections. Scanners like white space. They use it to determine when one section has ended and the next has begun. Horizontal lines can also be used to define sections since they are usually ignored by OCR software, provided they do not touch any of the letters on the page. However, avoid the use of short, vertical lines or small boxes since scanners try to interpret these as letters.

Don't use columns (like a newspaper) on your résumé. Scanners read from left to right and often have difficulty determining how to arrange text that was originally set in columns. Although the keywords will be intact, your résumé may end up looking like garbage in the ASCII text version created during the OCR process.

In today's job market, résumés (whether electronic or paper) don't have to be limited to one page. Craig MacDonald, in a special report for the *Seattle Post-Intelligencer*, says, "The cold, hard truth is, writing a résumé is just like advertising. Effective advertising means capturing the audience's attention quickly, concisely describing why someone should want to buy the product (you), and then closing the sale by suggesting a means of rapidly making the purchase. This has nothing to do with length, but a lot to do with format, language, tone, and style."

With e-résumés in particular, the more keywords and synonyms you are able to use, the better your chances of being selected in a keyword search. Therefore, it is better to have a two-page résumé with all your skills and qualifications listed than to have a one-page résumé with information missing because you tried to conserve space. Here is the general rule for a résumé today.

- New graduates—one page
- Most people—one or two pages
- Senior executives—two or three pages

One caution, however. The reader sees only one screen at a time and may decide to stop reading after the first screen if something doesn't entice him or her to read on. Therefore, you should make certain that the meat of your résumé is on the first half of the first page. This can be accomplished with a profile or keyword summary, followed by a list of your achievements.

Remember to keep your sentences powerful and interesting to read. Cyberspace doesn't negate the need for good writing. You still want a human being to read your résumé sooner or later!

❏ Paper

Print your résumé on a high-quality, light-colored paper (white, off-white, or *very* light gray). Never use papers with a background (pictures, marble shades, or speckles). The scanner tries to interpret the patterns and dots as letters. This is a good rule to follow even for paper résumés that will never be scanned. Often, companies will photocopy your résumé to hand to a hiring manager, and dark colors or patterns will simply turn into dark masses that make your résumé difficult to read. If a company has multiple locations, the original résumé may even get faxed from one site to another and the same thing would happen.

Avoid using photocopies of your résumé unless you have access to a high-quality copier. Original laser printed masters are best, although a high-quality ink-jet printer is acceptable.

Print on only one side of the page and use standard-size 8½" × 11" paper. The scanner cannot turn your page over, so the reverse side might be missed when the clerk puts your résumé into the automatic document feeder. That same process is the reason why you should not use 11" × 17" size paper. The pages would have to be cut into 8½" × 11" sheets and the printing on the reverse side would not get scanned.

Don't fold your résumé, since the creases make it harder to scan. It is much better to invest in flat 9" × 12" envelopes and an extra two bits of postage to make a good first impression. Laser print and copier toner tend to crack off the page when creased, making the letters on the fold line less than solid, which a scanner could easily misinterpret. Staple holes can cause the pages of a résumé to stick together, so never put a staple in a résumé you know will be scanned.

Now that you know all the secrets for designing a résumé that will pass the scannability test, let's look at some sample résumés that scanned well.

Molly Fitch

PROFILE	• Experienced advertising account executive with a diverse background. • Dedicated professional who works until the job is done. • Well-organized but flexible problem solver who enjoys being challenged. • Effective team player with strong interpersonal and communication skills.

EXPERIENCE

ACCOUNT EXECUTIVE (2000 – present)
RPM Advertising (formerly Graham Advertising), Colorado Springs, Colorado
• Plan, coordinate, and direct advertising campaigns for clients.
• Responsible for more than $2.5 million in total advertising budgets, focusing on the automotive industry.
• Confer with clients to determine advertising requirements and budget limitations, utilizing knowledge of products, media capabilities, and audience characteristics.
• Work with agency artists and other media production specialists to select media type and cost, and to determine media timing.
• Negotiate contracts with newspapers and billboard advertisers.
• Coordinate activities of workers engaged in market research, copywriting, artwork layout, media buys, development of special displays and promotional items, and other production activities as needed to carry out approved campaign.
• Design preliminary newspaper ad layouts and write scripts for television and radio advertising.

MANAGER IN TRAINING (1998 – 2000)
Abercrombie and Fitch, Denver, Colorado
• Responsible for opening and closing the store, regulating saleable and damaged merchandise, collecting money for sales, and researching/collecting returned checks.
• Input payroll for more than 50 sales associates and balanced the books.
• Provided customer service in a retail environment and ensured customer satisfaction.

ASSISTANT MANAGER (1994 – 1998)
Cook's Nook, Fort Worth, Texas
• Assisted customers with purchases and maintained inventory of merchandise.
• Opened and closed the store each day, and balanced cash register receipts.

MARKETING INTERNSHIP (1993 – 1994)
The Marketing Group, Dallas, Texas
• Organized, edited, and distributed mass mailings for promotional campaigns.

RECEPTIONIST (Summers 1991, 1992, 1993)
Vidmar Motor Company, Pueblo, Colorado
• Contacted newspaper and radio stations to schedule advertising, make recommendations, and monitor trafficking.
• Assisted in editing television commercial promotions.
• Regulated telephone calls for 60 associates and maintained mail correspondence.

SALES REPRESENTATIVE (1992 – 1993)
Texas Christian University Skiff, Fort Worth, Texas
• Marketed advertisements for TCU's newspaper, *The Skiff*.
• Assisted in the design and layout of advertisements.

EDUCATION

BACHELOR OF ARTS, ADVERTISING/PUBLIC RELATIONS (1994)
Texas Christian University, Fort Worth, Texas
• Emphasis in Business

ADDRESS

1234 Samuel Point, Colorado Springs, Colorado 80906, Cellular (719) 555-1234

38

EDWARD L. PETERSON

1234 Arequa Ridge Drive • Colorado Springs, Colorado 80919 • (719) 555-1234 • ELPeterson@protypeltd.com

QUALIFICATIONS
- Experienced project manager with a background in military logistics and the private sector.
- Profit-oriented, conscientious manager with strong organizational skills.
- Exceptional communication skills; able to motivate others to function as a successful team.

EXPERIENCE

JAMITCH ENTERPRISES, Peterson AFB, Colorado (2002 – present)
Project Manager, Standard Base Supply System Contract
- Responsible for the overall planning, directing, and resource management of a private-sector contract with the U.S. Air Force ($150 million of inventory and 110,000 transactions per month).
- Realized a profit through efficient utilization of resources, cost controls, safety and quality control, problem resolution, and budget programming.
- Selected and managed a work force of approximately 140 personnel at four locations, ensuring effective staffing and union negotiations.

TECOM, INC., Peterson AFB, Colorado (1993 – 2002)
Project Manager, Standard Base Supply System Contract (1997 – 2002)
Project Manager, Transient Alert Services (1996 – 1997)
Consultant (1993 – 1996)
- Responsible for the same duties as above for five years.
- Managed Transient Alert Services, including the provision of appropriate arrival and departure services for 500–600 transient aircraft per month.
- Supervised, trained, and scheduled a staff of 26.
- Served as a consultant for three years in the preparation of proposals for base supply and aircraft maintenance contracts, including staffing, organization, PWS responses, quality control plans, and safety procedures.

USAF ACADEMY AERO CLUB, Colorado (1993 – 1996)
Contract Flight Instructor
- Taught student pilots to commercial/instrument ratings, accumulating 650+ hours.

UNITED STATES AIR FORCE (1978 – 1993)
Assistant to the Deputy Chief of Staff for Logistics, USAF Academy, Colorado
Director of Supply, USAF Academy, Colorado
Deputy Base Commander, RAF Alconbury, England
Supply Squadron Commander, RAF Alconbury, England
Staff Supply Officer, Directorate of Civil Engineering, HQ USAF
- More than 24 years of logistics experience, including materiel management, inventory, supply, budgeting, transportation, fuels, and procurement.
- Assisted the Deputy Chief of Staff with supply, contracting, transportation, logistics plans, and program directorates, including squadron commander responsibilities for more than 325 personnel.
- As Deputy Base Commander, administered the support requirements for 6,000 personnel, including involvement with security police, legal services, personnel, recreation services, civil engineering, and equal opportunity/affirmative action policies.
- Formulated, analyzed, and evaluated policy methods and procedures and implemented directives necessary for facilities management support.
- As Supply Squadron Commander, managed the efforts of more than 250 personnel to provide supply support to three squadrons.
- Developed a new concept for contracting supply support that was employed by a majority of air force bases.

EDUCATION

BACHELOR OF SCIENCE, University of Missouri
U.S. AIR FORCE TRAINING: Industrial College of the Armed Forces, Squadron Officers School, Staff Supply Officer Course

Nick A. Dayton

1234 Harlan Court • Lake Forest, Illinois 60045 • (847) 555-1234 • E-mail: nadayton@protypeltd.com

PROFILE

- Dynamic leader with proven quality assurance and operations management experience, including:
  - Strategic Planning
  - Supervision and Training
  - Production Management
  - Quality Engineering
  - FDA Good Manufacturing Practices
  - Design Control Requirements
  - ISO 9000 Certification
  - Process Improvements
- Able to use a strong technical background to analyze complex processes and develop innovative solutions to challenges.
- Track record of gaining greater efficiencies from existing resources.
- Especially adept at increasing profitability without negatively impacting the organization.
- Strong communication and interpersonal skills; skilled in building effective teams to maximize results.

EXPERIENCE

ABBOTT LABORATORIES (1982 – present)
Director, Quality Assurance (1996 – present)
Hospital Products Division, Abbott Park, Illinois

- Managed quality engineering, label control, specifications and documentation, vendor/supplier quality assurance, compliance auditing, complaint handling, and clinical affairs quality assurance for this manufacturer of drugs, solutions, and medical devices with division sales of $2 billion.
- Developed and supervised the implementation of the division's quality assurance guidelines and policies to maintain ISO 9000 certification.
- Ensured that third-party vendors and customers met quality standards.
- Collaborated with plant quality assurance managers from 12 plants to develop corrective actions in response to FDA Good Manufacturing Practice (GMP) observations by internal auditors and external regulatory inspectors.
- Developed 21 CFR Part 11, compliance methodologies to improve the audit trail, system security, and system self-check.
- Successfully implemented an advanced electronic documentation management system to improve the accuracy of product databases and to permit a systems approach to complaint handling.
- Hired, supervised, and evaluated 5 department managers responsible for a staff of 85.
- Developed and administered a $10 million budget with no overruns.
- Served as the division trainer for the Situational Leadership II management development program.

Site Quality Assurance Manager, Hematology Business Unit (1993 – 1996)
Diagnostics Division, Santa Clara, California

- Selected to manage all quality and regulatory compliance functions for this Abbott acquisition, including quality assurance for manufacturing, vendors, software, and research and development.
- Managed GMP compliance, label control and specifications, and 501(k) submittals.
- Passed FDA audits with no citations in spite of a very complex operation and the introduction of 3 new products (advanced hematology analyzers).
- Achieved ISO 9000 certification for product design, software development, and manufacturing operations in only 12 months.
- Responsible for hiring and supervising 55 direct reports; grew the operation from 300 to 500 employees.
- Succeeded in increasing the number of products offered and substantially reducing the product development-to-market time.
- Increased revenues from $12 million to $300 million in less than 3 years.

Plant Quality Assurance Manager, Critical Care/Electronic Drug Delivery Systems (1989 – 1993)
Hospital Products Division, Mountain View, California

- Directed plant quality assurance program for this new Abbott acquisition with 600 employees and $100 million in annual sales.
- Achieved ISO 9000 certification for the manufacture of infusion pumps, cardiac output computers, and Opticaths.
- Increased throughput and investment in research and development while reducing costs.
- Created an ergonomics program with a multi-disciplinary team of specialists from quality assurance, industrial engineering, safety, and industrial hygiene departments that significantly reduced injuries.

EXPERIENCE **(continued)**	**Manufacturing Unit Manager** (1985 – 1989) **Hospital Products Division, Austin, Texas**

- Supervised all wet-side manufacturing operations on four shifts operating seven days per week.
- Recruited, hired, and supervised 30 production supervisors and 4 production managers.
- Managed preparation, filling, sterilization, inspection/overwrap, packaging, and shipping of intravenous solutions.
- Increased production volumes from 90 million to 300 million units per year while meeting an annual cost reduction of $3–9 million per year.

Production Manager (1982 – 1985)
Hospital Products Division, Austin, Texas

- Built the production operations from the ground up for this start-up operation, including staffing the plant with 980 production workers, training, developing/validating production processes and procedures, and scheduling.
- Selected, installed, and tested all production equipment and refined operating procedures.

TRACOR, INC., Aerospace Group, Austin, Texas (1978 – 1982)
Product Line Manager (1980 – 1982)
Manufacturing Manager (1978 – 1980)

- Managed the manufacturing operations and marketing of military countermeasures, teletypewriters, and digital systems.

TEACHING

ADJUNCT PROFESSOR (Fall Semester 1999)
DePaul University, Kellstadt Graduate School of Business, Chicago, Illinois

- Taught MBA courses in quality assurance and operations management

CERTIFICATIONS

- Situational Leadership II, Blanchard Training and Development
- Quality Assurance Systems, Zenger-Miller
- Frontline Leadership, Zenger-Miller

EDUCATION

DOCTOR OF BUSINESS ADMINISTRATION (1999)   GPA 3.94/4.0
The University of Sarasota, Florida
Emphasis in Health Care Administration
Dissertation: *Critical Success Factors in Total Quality Management Systems:*
A Practitioner-Based Study of U.S. Quality Systems

MASTER OF ARTS IN ORGANIZATIONAL MANAGEMENT (1994)   GPA 3.95/4.0
University of Phoenix, Northern California Campus, San Jose, California
Thesis: *ISO 9000 Program Development and Implementation*

BACHELOR OF ARTS IN INDUSTRIAL MANAGEMENT (1979)
St. Edward's University, Austin, Texas

AFFILIATIONS

Parenteral Drug Association (PDA): Core Team Member of the Task Group for Computer Validation and 21 CFR Part 11, Electronic Records/Signatures
American Society of Quality, Illinois
American Society of Quality, Biomedical Division, Santa Clara, California
American Electronics Association, Santa Clara, California

KENNETH L. DAVIS
12345 Quiet Circle East
Colorado Springs, CO 80917-2009

SSN: 123-45-6789

Home: (719) 555-1234
Work: (303) 555-1234, ext. 33
E-mail Address: kldavis@protypeltd.com

This is the scannable format preferred by many government agencies. Often, it can be used instead of a Form SF-171 or Form OF-612.

SKILLS

More than twenty years of logistical management experience, including procurement, budgeting, supply sources, reconciliation, account tracking, forecasting, manpower, research, receiving, delivery, inventory management, stock levels, records, reports of survey, forklift operation, and military supply rules. Detail-oriented with a talent for developing innovative solutions to problems. Team player who is willing to work long hours to get the job done. Computer literate with experience in Windows 95, Alpha Five Database, MS Word, Excel, WordPerfect, Quattro Pro, and MAPCON.

WORK EXPERIENCE
March 1997 to present
40 hours per week
Job Title: Property Administration Specialist
Pay: $31,000 per year
Employer: Antarctic Support Associates, 1234 Inverness Drive East, Englewood, CO 80112
Supervisor: Jane Doe, (303) 555-1234
Description: Responsible for purchasing, receiving, and warehousing of $80 million in inventory. Conducted annual inventories in the Antarctic, New Zealand, and at three U.S. sites. Accountable for 9,500 line items of capital equipment.

September 1993 to March 1997
56 hours per week
Job Title: Senior Materialsperson
Pay: $27,560 per year
Employer: McMurdo Power and Water Plants, Antarctica, Antarctic Support Associates, 1234 Inverness Drive East, Englewood, CO 80112
Supervisor: John Doe, (303) 555-1234
Description: Contracted to manage and account for supplies, parts, and equipment needed to maintain the operation of the power and water plants. Coordinated the requisitioning of parts and equipment through MAPCON Power "1000." Conducted aisle audits to ensure proper accounting and receipt of items issued from stock. Performed any other duties required by plant or logistics supervisor. Performed duties as Galley Pad Food Supervisor responsible for the unloading of McMurdo's year supply of food and proper storage of dry and frozen foods.

April 1993 to September 1993 (between contracts) and August 1991 to September 1992
40 hours per week
Job Title: Material Handler
Pay: WG-5
Employer: U.S. Army, Terminal Operations, DOL, Ft. Carson, CO 80913
Supervisor: James Doe, (719) 555-1234
Description: Received supplies and equipment and moved items by forklift, handcart, conveyor, etc.

September 1992 to April 1993
56 hours per week
Job Title: Materialsperson
Pay: $25,500 per year
Employer: Palmer Station on the Peninsula, Antarctica, Antarctic Support Associates, 1234 Inverness Drive East, Englewood, CO 80112
Supervisor: Jane Doe, (303) 555-1234
Description: Interfaced with laboratory supervisor to ensure timely requisition, receipt, and distribution of science cargo for various science groups. Automated Palmer Station's parts and supply inventory into MAPCON. Hazardous cargo packing/shipping for transport on commercial and DOD systems.

March 1991 to August 1992
30 hours per week
Job Title: Administrative Clerk, volunteer
Employer: University of Southern Colorado, Extended Studies, 229 East Pikes Peak Avenue, Colorado Springs, CO 80903
Supervisor: John Doe, (719) 555-1234
Counseled veterans regarding their education benefits part-time while attending the university.

August 1966 to September 1989
40 hours per week
Job Title: Supply/Accounting Sergeant
Pay: E-7
Employer: U.S. Army, 4th Division Support Command, Ft. Carson, CO 80913
Supervisor: Natalia Armstrong
Description: Twenty-four years of active duty military service, including fifteen years of logistical experience and nine years of aviation maintenance experience. Instrumental in managing three separate property book accounting teams for three different Army divisions made up of 27 combat units/companies each. Maintained document files and property records for equipment totaling $800 million to $2.5 billion. Supervised the Retail Supply operation for 52 units, including requisition, warehousing, and issue procedures for Army equipment and repair parts. Managed a multinational work force of 30 Korean nationals and 31 military personnel. Identified areas requiring change and specifically revised logistical practices and procedures, which streamlined property storage, distribution, and accountability. Conducted cyclic inventories and logistic operation inspections. Managed all capital and organizational equipment requisitioning. Coordinated retrograde procedures for unserviceable equipment. Assistant logistics manager for brigade-level supply operations, maintaining authorized levels of organizational equipment and repair parts. Successfully coordinated the deployment and fielding of two Patriot Missile Batteries to Germany, controlling and establishing accountable property records for $1.3 billion in equipment.

EDUCATION
Undergraduate studies toward a Bachelor of Science in Business Administration (March 1991 to August 1995), University of Southern Colorado, Extended Studies, 229 East Pikes Peak Avenue, Colorado Springs, CO 80903

Associate of General Studies (August 1988 to January 1991), Pikes Peak Community College, 5675 S. Academy Boulevard, Colorado Springs, CO 80906

"I certify that, to the best of my knowledge and belief, all of my statements are true, correct, complete, and made in good faith." February 2, 2005

KENNETH L. DAVIS

SSN: 123-45-6789

1234 Meridian Road • Englewood, Colorado 80831
Home: (719) 555-1234 • Cell: (719) 555-5678 • E-mail: clw0152@protype.com

VACANCY ANNOUNCEMENT: 02OC2210A13

INFORMATION TECHNOLOGY SPECIALIST

> Government jobs often require KSA statements that go beyond the information you provide in your résumé. The italics indicate the original questions.

KNOWLEDGE, SKILLS, AND ABILITIES

1. Extensive knowledge of computer systems and related computer concepts, principles, and practices related to the DoD IA/CND environment.

From 1998 to 2002, I worked directly with the US Space Command and AFSPC IA offices in direct support of classified NUIS network systems. From 2002 to 2004, I served as the Telecommunications Manager for the Air Force Space Command (AFSPC) Information Assurance/Computer Network Defense (IA/CND) organization responsible for the security of AFSPC classified and unclassified networks. I also served as Chief of the Networks Management Section, which provided technical oversight for world-class network upgrades to the local base network supporting more than 6,500 customers, including 26 general officers, 5 major commands, and geographical support units located worldwide. Analyzed, designed, and implemented enterprise computer networks and telecommunications systems, including system engineering, technical architecture development, software security integration, systems integration, configuration/data management, and network performance evaluation and testing, Deployed with the AFSPC IA/CND teams and assisted in network security assessments. Responsible for implementation of the AFSPC Network Operations and Security Center (NOSC) on Peterson AFB which included CND computer systems in support of AFSPC and Air Force wide computer systems. Oversaw the Honeypot system project implemented at Peterson AFB.

2. Ability to interpret and develop policy, regulations, procedures, and system processes.

Used an extensive knowledge of DoD policies, regulations, procedures, and system processes to develop statements of work, contract documentation, and budgets, to negotiate service-level agreements, to analyze business operations and perform strategic planning, for process re-engineering, and in procurement and outsourcing activities,

3. Broad knowledge of telecommunications systems policies, procedures, and practices.

I have more than 30 years of telecommunications/ADP systems operations and maintenance experience with the DoD, which includes writing and interpreting National Agency (NSA, DIA), U.S. Air Force, U.S. Army, and command-level telecommunications systems policies, procedures, and practices. For the past two years, I have gained commercial telecommunications systems experience with a major telecom corporation where I have written system-level procedures/policies based on detailed process engineering and analysis. I would bring the best practices of both worlds to this organization.

4. Ability to make sound decisions and develop program doctrine, policy, procedures to meet administrative requirements applicable to systems and agencies supported by USNORTHCOM.

With more than 18 years of management experience with the DoD, I have developed and implemented program doctrines, policies, and procedures at the national agency level.

5. Comprehensive knowledge of federal Automated Data Process (ADP) security laws, policies, and guidelines to plan future computer security requirements and to conduct complex studies and analyses.

As the Chief of the Networks Management Section at Peterson AFB, I conducted complex studies and analyses and was responsible for the security of a computer network supporting more than 6,500 customers in five major commands. I analyzed and designed enterprise computer networks and telecommunications systems and performed complex cost-benefit analyses. For the Intelligence and Security Command in Virginia, I analyzed business operations, performed process re-engineering, and prepared five-year strategic plans, feasibility studies, and resource/financial plans. I was also responsible for information and software security.

6. Broad knowledge of related computer disciplines such as systems, networks, communication lines, intrusion detection systems, firewall, routers, and current IA and CND reporting procedures.

From 2002 to 2004 I was responsible for the engineering of AFSPC classified and unclassified networks, which included the design and implementation of cryptographic equipment, Barrier Reef (Sidewinder firewalls/routers/switches) at all AFSPC bases and GSUs. I was also responsible for initial implementation of the IA/CND mission within the AFSPC NOSC. From 1997 to 2000 I was the technical telecommunications/ network expert in support of engineering the NUIS classified network, which included cryptographic equipment, ATM systems, routers, switches, hubs, network management systems, and other security devices. From 1993 to 1998 I was the Intelligence and Security Command (INSCOM) lead technical advisor for telecommunications, network, and ADP systems.

7. Maintains a broad knowledge of technical information necessary to evaluate alternative approaches for satisfying data storage system development and management, and computer systems interoperability requirements.

My current position allows me to stay on top of state-of-the-art network systems and engineering practices in the Worldwide MCI Data Center data storage systems and automated high-speed backup procedures between the diverse computer systems on the enterprise backbone.

8. Broad based technical knowledge of current DoD IA/CND, and JCS crisis procedures.

My DoD/JCS knowledge, which I gained in more than 13 years with the DoD, is only two years old. It would take a minimal amount of time to come up to speed on the changes since my departure from DoD in 2003.

9. Ability to communicate effectively, both orally and in writing.

All of my positions over the past 15 years have required extensive report writing and presentations to high-level internal and external customers. I have developed a reputation as an open, honest communicator with proven briefing skills.

10. Knowledge of Department of Defense Contract and procurement procedures.

I was the Contracting Officer Representative (COR) and Technical Quality Assurance Evaluator (TQAE) on numerous DoD contracts, where I ensured that contractors complied with all aspects of the contract and operated within DoD guidelines and Federal Acquisition Regulations (FARS). I also have been responsible for all procurement and outsourcing activities of large projects.

LESLIE A. MARTIN
123 North Cascade Avenue #29
Colorado Springs, Colorado 80903
Phone: (719) 555-1234
E-mail: martin@protypeltd.com

If you would rather not worry about whether your résumé is scannable, simply save the file as a DOS text file and reformat it like this. Send it along with your formatted résumé.

PROFILE
~~~~~~~~~~~~~~~~~~~~~~~~~~~~~~~~~~~
Goal-oriented sales and customer support professional with successful experience in account management, needs assessment, high-tech sales, promotion, training, and relationship building. Strong background in building new territories and using creative marketing approaches. Respected for problem solving skills; willing to go the extra mile to make the customer happy. Demonstrated ability to create client loyalty above and beyond the sales relationship. Self-motivated and flexible; comfortable working independently with little supervision. Computers: Solomon, MS Word, Excel, Access, Outlook, Lotus Notes, ACT!, Support Magic, Winzip, Windows, PC Anywhere, Passport, MS Explorer.

EXPERIENCE
~~~~~~~~~~~~~~~~~~~~~~~~~~~~~~~~~~~
DEALER SALES AND MARKETING REPRESENTATIVE (1999 to present)
ARI Network Services, Inc., Colorado Springs, Colorado
Successfully sold software to the outdoor power industry for parts lookup, e-commerce, and warranty tracking. Formulated, designed, and conducted sales presentations to small engine dealers, repair centers, and ATV/snowmobile dealers. Established and developed a commercial account base throughout the United States. Successfully turned around customers who were unhappy with the merger through effective marketing, professional sales presentations, and follow-up. Won President's 100 Percent Club Award for meeting 100 percent of quota for the fiscal year 1998 to 1999.

LEVEL I TECHNICAL SUPPORT (1997 to 1999)
Powercom 2000, Colorado Springs, Colorado
Hand picked by the transition manager to demonstrate the business component of the software (invoicing, inventory, point-of-sale) to a potential buyer, a transaction ultimately worth several million dollars. Consistently exceeded sales quotas through cold calling and referrals. Effectively taught technophobic customers and made them feel comfortable with the technology. Began the position as a temp-to-hire, survived two downsizings, and was hired by the purchasing company in 1999.

ACADEMIC COUNSELOR (1993 to 1997)
National University, San Diego, California
Generated student enrollments for this private university for adult learners. Made biweekly presentations and recruited local community college students for the undergraduate degree programs. Enrolled and counseled potential students and provided financial aid advice. Regularly exceeded quotas, enrolling up to 52 students per month. Selected as one of the top three sales representatives. Supervised, trained, and motivated eight academic advisors. Translated academic transcripts and ensured the accuracy of credit transfers. Served as an intermediary between students and faculty and reported recurring problems with faculty to senior management.

ASSISTANT MANAGER (1991 to 1993)
Adventure Car Rentals, San Diego, California
Financed college education by managing a rental car agency specializing in high-end sports cars. Hired and supervised staff and resolved problems with insurance companies.

EDUCATION
~~~~~~~~~~~~~~~~~~~~~~~~~~~~~~~~~~~
BACHELOR OF BEHAVIORAL SCIENCE (1996)
National University, San Diego, California
Graduated cum laude; maintained a 3.5 GPA while working full time.

4 Stand-out Names

Since your résumé is basically an advertisement for you and your skills, you should think about the design of your résumé from a marketing standpoint. When you see a well-designed ad, what is the first thing you notice (besides a picture of the product)? The product name, of course. Since *you* are the product, your name should be the first thing a reader sees and remembers. To accomplish that, there is really only one rule to remember: *Your name should be easy to read and it should stand out above the rest of the text.* That can be done by using:

A Larger Font in Upper/Lower Case

ALL CAPS

FIRST LETTER LARGER

A Creative Font

On the samples in this section, you will also notice the use of graphic elements and lines to help define the name and separate it from the rest of the text. Even scanned clip art letters or a signature can be used to enhance a résumé, but the latter only works when you have great handwriting. Your name, however, should not distract the reader from the message. Make it part of the overall design of your résumé but separate it from the body text with lines or white space.

The most important thing is to make sure the style of your name reflects your personality, tempered by the expectations of your industry. If you are flamboyant and are looking for a job in the arts, then you have a license to be creative. Go for it! If, on the other hand, you work in a conservative industry or you feel uncomfortable with your name printed large, then it is important to tone it down.

If you are trying to make your résumé scannable, designer fonts, names with graphic elements in the place of letters, reverse boxes, and script names will not scan.

Terri Shaner

1234 Weather Vane Drive
Colorado Springs
Colorado 80920
(719) 555-1234
ts@protypeltd.com

QUALIFICATIONS
- Highly motivated professional with a strong desire to use a recent chemistry degree in a biochemical, industrial, or research setting.
- Extensive research experience using differential scanning calorimetry.
- Additional research in plant molecular biology, molecular breeding, gene targeting, and antifreeze proteins.
- Dedicated, well-organized manager who is able to solve problems using innovative thinking.
- Effective team player with proven technical writing, communication, and interpersonal skills.
- Proficient in Windows, MS Word, Excel, PowerPoint, MathCAD, and Origin by MicroCal.

EDUCATION

BACHELOR'S DEGREE IN CHEMISTRY, EMPHASIS ON BIOCHEMISTRY (2001)
University of Colorado, Colorado Springs
- Received the Department of Chemistry's *Award for Outstanding Performance in Materials Science*, 2000 – 2001
- Scientific course work included: Problem Solving in Engineering, Chemistry Independent Study (Special Projects I/II), Physical Chemistry I/II and Lab, Analytical Chemistry and Lab, Materials Science, Chemistry Seminar I/II, Physics I/II and Lab, Biochemistry, Genetics, Molecular Genetics, Organic Chemistry I/II and Lab, Cellular Biology, Physics for Life Sciences I/II and Lab, General Chemistry I/II and Lab
- Mathematics course work included: Calculus I/II, Introduction to Calculus, Algebra
- Major course work GPA 3.2

LAB SKILLS

- MOPAC
- CNMR
- HNMR
- Oscilloscope
- Abbe3-l Refractometer
- Titrations
- Gas Chromatography
- Microscale Extractions
- Gel Electrophoresis
- Infrared Spectrophotometer
- Differential Scanning Calorimetry
- Digital Multimeter

PUBLICATIONS

Krescheck, G. C., and Shaner, T. (2003). "Observation of complex thermal transitions for mixed micelle solutions containing alkyldimethylphosphine oxides and phospholipids and the accompanying cloud points," *Chemistry and Physics of Lipids*, pp. 123-145.

PRESENTATIONS
- Shaner, T. (2001). *H-Atom transfer is a preferred antioxidant mechanism of curcumin.* Colorado Springs, CO: University of Colorado.
- Shaner, T. (2001). *The evolution of advanced gas-to-liquids technology.* Colorado Springs, CO: University of Colorado.

INDEPENDENT RESEARCH

RESEARCH ASSISTANT (2000 – 2001)
Dr. Gordon C. Kresheck, Colorado Springs, Colorado
- Researched the solution properties of protein molecules in the crystalline state in order to make an *a priori* prediction of the way a low-molecular-weight substance binds to a given protein.
- Helped to develop a model system to study the interaction of ligands with macromolecules in a systematic way, including the micelle formation of surfactants.
- Expanded the studies to a thermodynamic investigation of the interaction of the same surfactant molecules with synthetic polypeptides and proteins.
- Used solution calorimetry to determine the enthalpy change and stoichiometry for the binding processes.

Mary Mitchell Rex

PROFILE
- Experienced escrow processor with a proven background in:
  - Escrow processing
  - Customer service
  - Loan document processing
  - Billing and collections
  - Process efficiencies
  - Purchasing
  - Coordination
  - Real estate
  - Accounting
- Flexible professional who works hard and welcomes new challenges.
- Effective team player with a great sense of humor and consistent positive attitude.
- Proficient in Windows, MS Word, Outlook, Internet Explorer, Impact, and FastWeb.

EXPERIENCE

ESCROW PROCESSOR
Title America, Inc., Colorado Springs, Colorado (1997 – 2004)
Lawyers Title Company, Colorado Springs, Colorado (1996 – 1997)
First American Title Company, Colorado Springs, Colorado (1991 – 1993)
Processed escrow files and served as a liaison between real estate agents, sellers, buyers, and lenders. Prepared and recorded legal documents for closings, including trustee and estate documents, deeds of trust, warranty deeds, marriage certificates, and other documents. Ordered payoff statements and executed payoffs from such sources as mortgage lenders, banks, credit unions, attorneys, collection companies, private individuals, and IRS tax liens. Prepared releases for judgments and liens. Assisted lenders and builders with the generation of draws and payments on building projects. Drafted borrower collection letters and set up structured payments to ensure reimbursement of outstanding balances. Provided customer service and answered multi-line telephones. Maintained inventory of office supplies, opened and delivered mail, and performed filing and other general office duties.
- Ensured that closings were completed on time every day in order to avoid legal repercussions.
- Authorized check signer on the recording account for more than seven years.
- Calculated, balanced, and made daily deposits for the entire office, which were often in excess of $1 million.
- Minimized losses by expediting lender documents.
- Developed a tickler system for outstanding tasks on each account, which made processing more efficient and saved significant man hours.
- Created letters to customers that were sent automatically after each closing asking for referrals and suggestions for improvement.
- Received the Title America Stellar Performance Award for three consecutive years (2001, 2002, 2003).
- Survived industry downturns as the only original employee of the company after seven years.

RELOCATION ADVISOR
Prudential Patterson Group Realtors, Inc., Colorado Springs, Colorado (1993 – 1996)
Scheduled appointments for showing of homes by coordinating between Realtors, buyers, and sellers. Typed MLS listings and drafted sales contracts. Assisted corporate clients with the relocation of recruits by setting up apartments or houses, rental cars, and whole house furnishings, purchasing groceries, and providing area information. Coordinated appraisals, surveys, and home inspections. Answered multi-line telephones and performed other administrative tasks.
- Searched and selected rentals that met the client's relocation criteria.
- Compiled information regarding entertainment, schools, churches, shopping, etc., specific to each area of town.

EDUCATION

CERTIFICATE IN BUSINESS MANAGEMENT
Blair Business College, Colorado Springs, Colorado
- Completed a two-year program with a GPA of 3.5

MEDICAL TERMINOLOGY COURSE
Memorial Hospital, Colorado Springs, Colorado
- Completed a six-month course

CONTACT

123 Columbine Avenue • Colorado Springs, Colorado 80904
Home: (719) 555-1234 • Cellular: (719) 555-5678 • Email: maryrex@protypeltd.com

YOKO AKINOHARA

1234 Midland Avenue
Bronxville, NY 10708
Home / Fax: (914) 555-1234
Mobile: (917) 555-1234
E-mail: yoko@protypeltd.com

Marketing / Promotions Specialist / Public Relations / Business Development

Results-orientated marketing professional accomplished in creating and leading market campaigns to consistently meet business objectives in language and entertainment. Initiates groundbreaking programs that deliver sustainable revenue growth in global markets. Highly intuitive style with a demonstrated ability to drive business development, conduct market research and analysis, perform accurate sales forecasting, and build customer satisfaction.

SOFTWARE

Adobe Illustrator, Adobe Photoshop, Quark Express, PowerPoint, Satori Bulk Mailer, MS Entourage, MS Word, MS Excel, FTP

LANGUAGES

Fully fluent in Japanese and English–Navigational in Spanish

PROFESSIONAL EXEPERIENCE

ESPRIT LINE COMPANY, LTD, Greenwich, CT 1999–present
Assistant Marketing Manager
Leading international direct response advertiser known for successful sales and marketing of language instruction materials throughout the United States, Japan, Canada, Europe, and South America. Managed an eight-person staff with full responsibility for results driven sales and customer service leadership. Liaison to headquarters in Japan with control of $200,000 annual marketing budget. Implemented administrative processes attributed with establishing sales goals, performance, policies, and procedures. Orchestrated copywriting, design, and print production of marketing materials, advertising, catalogues, and Web site with ROI analysis.

- Led the development and execution of marketing strategies that produced rapid growth of up to 164 percent revenue gains.

- Initiated advertising campaigns that delivered record-breaking results and reduced costs by 20 percent with penetration into Japanese and Brazilian markets.

- Introduced direct mail marketing strategies and account databases attributed with tripled revenue growth and strengthening customer retention.

- Directed market research, competitive analysis, and trend modeling to identify new product lines and product expansion to sustain sales growth. Favorably led win-win negotiations of purchase terms, pricing, and quality control.

50

PROFESSIONAL EXPERIENCE continued

INTERNATIONAL PRODUCTION GROUP, INC. New York, NY 1996–1999
Talent Representative / A&R Coordinator
Boutique agency, facilitating a broad range of record engineering and video production services for popular Japanese recording artists in the United States. Managed overseas concert tour for internationally recognized recording group, Rockapella. Coordinated performances at locations such as the Bottom Line (Nagoya, Japan), The Blue Note (Fukuoka and Osaka, Japan), and Bay Hall (Yokohama, Japan). Arranged for chart topping Japanese musicians to cut music with studios such as Sony Music Studios. Played an instrumental role in selection and hiring of musicians. Ensured projects were completed on time and within budget. Hunted scenic locations and coordinated artists' photo shoots for use in print advertising and public relations materials.

- ☛ Created marketing strategy that delivered 100% sell through rate on music CDs and licensed products.
- ☛ Scouted new artist that was offered a contract with For Life, one of Japan's leading record labels.

EIDAI INDUSTRIES, INC. Ridgefield, NJ 1995–1996
Assistant Manager
Major import / export trading company conducting trading in Brazil, Puerto Rico, and Japan. Coordinated import / export trading between Brazil and Puerto Rico with full responsibility for purchase orders, A / R billing, and collections.

- ☛ Introduced strategies that reduced past due accounts from $1 million per month to $20,000.

PROFESSIONAL AFFILIATIONS

Active Member, DIRECT MARKETING ASSOCIATION

RELEVANT INTERESTS

Salsa Music and Dance: Studied with Duplessey-Monic Walker, Glenda Heffer, Becky Bliss, and Ernest Barthelemy

Travel: Turkey, Spain, Portugal, Italy, Australia, China

EDUCATION

MBA: Marketing SACRED HEART UNIVERSITY, Fairfield, CT (1995)

BA: Communication HOKUSEI GAKUEN UNIVERSITY, Sapporo, Japan (1992)

Angelina B. Cabanellie

PROFILE
- Excellent proofreading skills
- Type 95 wpm; Gregg Shorthand 75 wpm
- Transcription experience
- Superior telephone courtesy utilizing positive attitude
- Personable communicator with caring demeanor
- Technologically proficient

PROFESSIONAL EXPERIENCE

Owner, ANGIE'S TYPING SERVICE, Lubbock, Texas   2000 – present

Offer typing services to students and professionals in the community. Services include reports, research papers, theses, presentations, proposals, books, short stories, etc. Desktop publishing includes certificates, signs, flyers, invitations, greeting cards, business cards, and advertising. Other functions include marketing, mentoring, tutoring, and customer service.

Working knowledge of Microsoft Word, Excel, PowerPoint, Outlook, Adobe PhotoShop, WordPerfect, Lotus, and the Internet.
- **Grew business from zero to client base of 300 in five years.**
- **Gained a profit from first year on.**

Part-time Secretary, SARAH HIGGINS INSURANCE, Lubbock, Texas 1998 – 2000

Acted as personal secretary to independent life and health insurance agent. Assisted with outside work for her insurance association, to include a golf tournament and convention. Generated memos to clients and insurance companies. Maintained client database. Placed calls to insurance companies daily to follow up on claims. Maintained files and forms inventory.
- **Commended for thoroughness and accuracy.**
- **Praised for never missing a day of work.**

OTHER EXPERIENCE
- Constructed, edited, and distributed newsletters for several organizations
- Created presentation materials for Make-A-Wish Auto Show
- Conceived and produced logo for local car club
- Donate desktop publishing to local social club

HOBBIES AND INTERESTS
- Visiting the elderly in nursing homes
- Traveling
- Investing

EDUCATION

Secretarial Science Program, 1999, San Antonio, Junior College, San Antonio, Texas

Accounting and Business courses, El Paso Community College, El Paso, Texas

P. O. Box 1234
Tahoka, Texas 79373
acab@protypeltd.com
(806) 555-1234

Ben Bartlett

12345 Dixon Place
Minnetonka, MN 55343
(612) 555-1234

Technical Manager
Manufacturing Operations

PROFILE

A solutions-driven and customer-focused leader with excellent analytical, planning, team building, and time/resource management skills. More than 20 years of expertise in heavy mechanical, pneumatic, hydraulic, and conveyor systems. Strong, consistent track record of contributions to increased productivity, quality control, cost efficiency, and profitability.

PROFESSIONAL EXPERIENCE

1988 to present TRAUTWEIN COMPANY, RIVER FALLS, MN

Plant Manager, directing all manufacturing processes for production of gear drives and fluid mixers for various industries. Oversee 2 supervisors and 18 production workers. In charge of troubleshooting and repair of custom machinery. Coordinate purchasing, scheduling, and outside services. Demonstrated effectiveness and accomplishments in the following areas:

Plant Enhancements

- Designed three new machines used for specific purposes in the manufacturing process, replacing obsolete and labor intensive equipment. Collaborated closely with engineers at machinery company throughout all stages of building and debugging.
- Once new machinery was operational, achieved increases of 25 percent in productivity and 35 percent in profitability. Realized paybacks on each machine far ahead of projected ROI.
- Made possible a 47 percent reduction in unproductive labor (from 38 to 20 employees), saving approximately $400,000 in annual salary expenses.

Operational Improvements

- Took charge of company move to 50 percent smaller quarters, saving substantial rent and utility costs.
- Designed floor plan for most efficient space utilization. Handled all rigging and placement of machinery, accomplishing this move with only one day of downtime.
- Set work standards based on machine capabilities and model operator performance, which increased operational control and predictablity of scheduling.
- Managed a $.5 million purchasing budget for all materials and outside services. Negotiated vendor contracts for win-win outcomes.
- Saved approximately $30,000 a year in technician fees by performing most maintenance and repairs on production machinery in-house, with troubleshooting guidance by phone.
- Enforced safety regulations, acting on suggestions of workers' compensation insurance carrier. During entire tenure, maintained record of no major accidents, OSHA/EPA violations, or lawsuits.

Human Resources Management

- Developed a loyal and motivated workforce through a merit evaluation program that encouraged employees to meet productivity goals. Created advancement opportunities for superior employees.
- Cross-trained staff to take over during absences of regular employees, thereby minimizing backlogs in production scheduling and shipping.
- Instituted part-time work schedules for mothers, allowing them to put in their time during the hours their children were in school. As a result, maintained full production without payout of benefits.
- Provided small incentives for workers to exercise greater care and catch defects early in the process, which has cut overall waste of materials from 22 percent to less than 6 percent while eliminating customer rejects.

TRAINING

1981 to 1983   ALLTRADES LEARNING CENTER, MINNEAPOLIS, MN
Completed certificate course in Applied Electronic Technology.

Michael Hutchinson

→

123 Founders Circle, Hyattstown, MD 20871
301.555.1234 ▪ hutchinson@protypeltd.com

Profile

Microsoft trained and certified professional offering 19+ years of cross-functional experience:

Web Developer – develop Internet-based Web applications; specialize in database applications and Web forms; possess a keen foresight for Internet technology trends – ASP and .Net proficient.

Web Designer – design custom Web sites; maintain and update content; create user interfaces, and revitalize aging Web sites – Adobe Photoshop specialist.

Database Administrator – demonstrate proficient relational database experience; create, maintain, and backup database servers – MS SQL 2000 expert.

Entrepreneurial Thinker – provide top-notch customer service to forge and enhance long-term customer partnerships; known for turning around underperforming Web sites while keeping overall costs under targeted goals.

Professional Experience

Web Designer / Web Developer / Webmaster   2003 to present
The Job Connection, LLC (www.jobconnection.com)   Chevy Chase, MD

An Internet-based recruiting site connecting employers and job seekers through industry-specific Web sites (38 main and 11 group sites), job board posting, and an applicant resume bank/database. Recipient of the 2005 Hiring Aide, Inc., *Premier Recruiting Site* Award.

► Brought on-board three years after site was launched. Redesigned entire network through implementation of numerous technologies that transformed a text-based site to a top competitor in the recruitment industry. Weekly sales revenues nearly tripled within the first 12 months of site redesign; user numbers increased from 450k to over 800k.

Formula for success:
   – Redesigned and currently maintain 49 core Web sites using Microsoft Visual Studio.NET Enterprise Developer Edition.
   – Updated site code to more current Web standards—more than 25 percent of present employer's Web pages are ASP.NET; 75 percent are ASP.
   – Designed cascading style sheets, which created graphics continuity and streamlined editing procedures.
   – Developed all site images, marketing images, and logos using Adobe Photoshop.
   – Maintain complete administrator rights and responsibilities for entire network. Provide 24/7 on-call support to both hardware and software functionality.
   – Ensure Web servers are fully up to date on virus utilities and software patches.

► Built and implemented technology tools to support marketing and customer service center (Angola, Indiana). Improved service efficiency and customer relations while decreasing business costs.

Formula for success:
   – Installed a voice-over IP phone system (Artisoft/TeleVantage), with servers in Chevy Chase and Angola. Created a virtual office connection with the six customer service representatives and the home office.
   – Designed an interface with the contact management database using Visual Basic.
   – Review all marketing materials prior to dissemination through mass faxing and e-mailing campaigns (weekly distribution of over one-million).
   – Support Customer Service Center by responding to any user questions that reach beyond technical capabilities of the customer service reps.

Professional Experience (Continued)

Web Designer / Web Developer/ Webmaster　　　　　　　　　1999 to 2002
eWholesalers Office Supplies, Inc.　　　　　　　　　　　　　Annadale, VA

A small dot com start-up catering to office supply retailers and wholesalers nationwide.

► Recruited during initial business development phase to develop and maintain all of the company's corporate sites, intranet, and customer Web sites. Excelled in a deadline intensive environment while juggling multiple responsibilities.

► Built ten or more custom sites around existing databases, conferring with customers throughout all phases of Web development. Maintained solid customer relations as the single point of contact for all content updates.

Lotus Notes Web Developer　　　　　　　　　　　　　　　　1996 to 1999
Web Information Services　　　　　　　　　　　　　　　　　Columbia, MD

The technology company that purchased BND Technologies and provided Internet visibility and support to client companies.

► Managed entire Web site development lifecycle, executing Lotus Notes Domino to create a Web presence and designing relational databases. Worked extensively with Windows 95/98 and Windows NT operating systems.

► Employed prior hardware expertise in training an out-of-state team of computer technicians in the complexities of building network servers.

Network Engineer, Computer Technician　　　　　　　　　　1985 to 1996
BND Technologies, Inc　　　　　　　　　　　　　　　　　　Baltimore, MD

An independent corporation supplying high-end computer networks for government agencies and businesses.

► Installed, repaired, and/or modified nearly 1000 Windows network systems in government buildings throughout the DC-Baltimore business corridor. Installed and maintained Windows software, computer hardware, and printers. Built over 250 Windows NT network servers.

► Represented company mission of putting the customer first while professionally interfacing with technical and non-technical personnel to define and satisfy end-user needs.

Entrepreneurial Venture

Solopreneur　　　　　　　　　　　　　　　　　　　　　　2002 to present
eMagic.com (www.emagic.com)　　　　　　　　　　　　　　Hyattstown, MD

► Conceived and launched an independent business to help small companies establish a prominent Web presence. Build custom Web sites, orchestrating complete project lifecycle from defining site requirements with customers to designing, developing, and maintaining sites.

► Design site graphics using Adobe Photoshop. Create interactive on-line Web forms; incorporate existing databases and build user-friendly contact management systems.

Education and Technical Training

Microsoft Certified Solutions Developer (MCSD VB6) ► **Lotus Notes CLPP Application Developer** ► **Visual Basic.NET Certification** (in progress)

Associate of Science, Computer Science, Montgomery Community College, Rockville, MD
43 credits completed, including Java, C, Basic, Fortran, Pascal

Graduate, North Hyattstown High School, Hyattstown, MD

Michael Hutchinson

123 Founders Circle, Hyattstown, MD 20871
301.555.1234 ▪ hutchinson@protypeltd.com
Page 3

Internet Expert
Customer Relations Specialist

Technical Addendum

Demonstrated proficiency in the following areas:

Microsoft Technologies

Windows Services (VB.NET)	ASP	Visual SourceSafe
Visual Interdev/Studio.NET	ASP.NET	Visual Basic 6
Internet Information Server (IIS)	Win32 API	VBScript
Windows NT/2000/2003 Servers	SQL Server 2000	Office Suite/Access

Internet Technologies

CSS - Cascading Style sheets	HTTPS	FTP	XML/XSL
Image Optimization (gif, jpeg)	HTML	DHTML	JavaScript
Search Engine Optimization	ADO	PDF	Intranet / Extranet
Image Printing Requirements (dpi)	ODBC	TCP/IP	Web Site Redesign

Miscellaneous Technologies

Network Monitoring and Alerting Applications	Electronic Data Interchange (EDI)
E-mail Server Maintenance and Optimization	SPAM Maintenance
Web Server Optimization	ACT! API
Artisoft / TeleVantage Voice-over IP	Adobe Photoshop
Mass E-mail Marketing Software	Rational ClearQuest

Gloria R. Conner

PROFILE
- Experienced, hard working flight attendant with a great customer service attitude.
- Able to foster cooperative relationships and generate enthusiasm.
- Skilled in taking the initiative—self-confident and conscientious.
- Traveled extensively in the United States, Hawaii, Mexico, and Europe.

EXPERIENCE

FLIGHT ATTENDANT
Frontier Airlines, Denver, Colorado (2000 – present)
Western Pacific Airlines, Colorado Springs, Colorado (1999 – 2000)
- Provide top-of-the-line service to airline customers during flights.
- Assure the safety and comfort of passengers on domestic and international flights.
- Greet passengers, verify tickets, record destinations, and direct passengers to their assigned seats.
- Explain the use of safety equipment, serve meals and beverages, and perform other personal services.
- Evaluate passengers for those who might pose a possible security risk, and ensure the safety of the flight deck and pilots.
- Interview candidates for flight attendant positions and make hiring recommendations.
- Certified for CPR, first aid, automated external defibrillator, water ditching, and self-defense.

STAFF ASSISTANT, DRUG COMMISSION OFFICER
United States Anti-Doping Agency, Colorado Springs, Colorado (2000 – 2002)
United States Olympic Committee, Colorado Springs, Colorado (1997 – 2000)
- Assisted drug commission officers in the collection of samples to test for performance-enhancing substances in athletes who compete in Olympic, Paralympic, and Pan American games and/or train in the United States.
- Traveled throughout the U.S. to conduct doping controls both in competition and out of competition without notice.
- Monitored urine collection to ensure the integrity of samples, reduced the chances of sample contamination, and maintained the security of each sample up to shipment.
- Completed forms with personal data, drug use history, sport, and other information.

FOOD AND COCKTAIL SERVER
Maggie Mae's Restaurant, Colorado Springs, Colorado (1995 – 1997)
McKay's Restaurant, Colorado Springs, Colorado (1994 – 1995)
- Provided high-quality customer service in family-style restaurants.

EDUCATIONAL ASSISTANT
George C. Round Elementary, Manassas, Virginia (1993 – 1994)
Solomon Elementary, Schofield Barracks, Hawaii (1991 – 1993)
- Managed a classroom of twelve children; tutored and tested small groups of children.
- Assisted four kindergarten classroom teachers in instruction and non-instructional tasks.

PHYSICAL AND HEALTH TRAINER
Straub Clinic and Hospital, Inc., Wahiawa, Hawaii (1990 – 1991)
Darmstadt Military Community, Darmstadt, Germany (1987 – 1990)
- Taught aerobics and helped people to reach their health and fitness goals.

EDUCATION

FLIGHT ATTENDANT TRAINING, Frontier Airlines, Denver, Colorado (1998)
- Completed three and a half weeks of flight attendant training

FLIGHT ATTENDANT TRAINING, Western Pacific Airlines, Colorado Springs, Colorado (1997)
- Completed three and a half weeks of intensive training

GROUP EXERCISE LEADER BASIC TRAINING COURSE, St. Louis, Missouri (1987)

1234 East 12TH Avenue #105 • Thornville, Colorado 80233 • Email: gconner@protypeltd.com
Home: (303) 555-1234 • Cellular: (720) 555-5678

57

Sean R. Callaghan

12345 Jefferson Court ▼ Providence, RI 02904 ▼ (401) 555-1234 ▼

Seeking opportunity for progressive challenges in the areas of
Public Relations, Advertising, or Marketing

PROFILE

- ▲ Effective team collaborator with proven written and oral communication skills.
- ▲ Take responsibilities seriously and willing to go the extra mile to meet client needs.
- ▲ Good listener, open minded, and quick to learn.
- ▲ Enjoy creative brainstorming, analyzing ideas, and developing persuasive concepts.
- ▲ Computer literate with working knowledge of MS Word, Excel, and PowerPoint; experience using QuarkXPress, Photoshop, and Sound Edit programs.

EDUCATION

University of Rhode Island, Providence, RI
B.A. *cum laude* Marketing   August 2004
Relevant courses included: Publicity Methods, Public Relations, Writing for the Media

PROJECTS

- ▲ Received group grade of "A" as member of a 4-person team that put together a publicity campaign to increase attendance for shows at campus theater. Worked within a limited advertising budget to raise public awareness within the community. Researched low-cost or free methods to distribute information outside of campus, resulting in 20 percent greater than anticipated ticket sales for final show of the season.
- ▲ Utilized various publicity techniques in assembling a press kit for upcoming events at Coliseum Arena. Created press releases, fact sheets, and newsletters for inclusion in the press kit to generate interest in minor league hockey and football games, concerts, children's shows, and circus performances.

INTERNSHIP

Coliseum Arena, Marketing and Group Sales Department   Spring 2003

- ▲ Interacted with management and important clients, contributing own perspective in writing press releases, assembling information for newsletters, and designing flyers for shows.
- ▲ Attended press conferences, interviewed hockey players, and wrote articles for monthly newsletter.

EMPLOYMENT

URI Campus Alumni Association   School years 2000 to 2003

- ▲ Telemarketer for 9 hours per week. Contacted alumni to raise funds for construction of new stadium, receiving 60 percent pledge responses.

COMMUNITY SERVICE

- ▲ Habitat for Humanity: Devoted time and resources during spring 2000 semester to help in building housing for indigent families in Cranston, Rhode Island.
- ▲ PETA volunteer since 2001, active in raising public concern about animal cruelty and responsible pet ownership.
- ▲ Visit area nursing homes, bringing selected pets for the enjoyment of the elderly residents.

Jessica A. Dwyer

OBJECTIVE   Clinical Trials Support Specialist Lead

SUMMARY OF QUALIFICATIONS

▶ Associate of Science degree, with emphasis in Biology.
▶ Ability to work under pressure and handle multiple priorities while maintaining quality control.
▶ Familiar with Microsoft Word, Excel, and Access; able to learn new technologies quickly.
▶ Recognized for attention to detail and dependability; excellent driving record.
▶ Proven record of managing and improving workflow processes through effective team leadership.

PROFESSIONAL EXPERIENCE

Production Technician Specialist: Celestica, Rochester, MN, 1998 – 2005

▶ Managed multiple operations concurrently in a fast-paced circuit board production line.
▶ Motivated team to efficiently learn and implement new procedures while continuously meeting daily deadlines; praised for empowering employees to take pride in their work.
▶ Ensured uninterrupted production by immediately finding and fixing equipment malfunctions.
▶ Attended training sessions focusing on new technologies and quality improvement issues.
▶ Used conflict management skills to assist team members in resolving personal conflicts.
▶ Guaranteed quality control of product before it left the production area by checking each board under the microscope and entering data accurately into database.
▶ Followed OSHA guidelines, as a volunteer on the Emergency Response Team, ensuring safety of team and staff when cleaning chemical spills.
▶ Promoted from technician to technician specialist in 1998 due to high work ethic, willingness to be flexible, and positive attitude.

Electronic Technician: Benchmark, Winona, MN, 1997 – 1998

▶ Worked as a team to sustain product flow through test area.
▶ Solved problems arising on the floor; used computer program to pinpoint failure locations.

Production Operator: IBM, Rochester, MN, 1996 – 1997

▶ Worked on production line ensuring the final product was free of defects.

Electronics Internship: IBM, Rochester, MN, 1996

▶ Repaired and resolved problems related to motors and circuit boards.

EDUCATION

A.S. Degree (emphasis in **Biology**), May 2005
Rochester Community and Technical College, Rochester, MN

Electronic Technician Certificate, August 1994
Minnesota Riverland Technical College, Rochester, MN

12345 6th St SW ▲ Rochester, MN 55902 ▲ (507) 555-1234 ▲ dwyer@protypeltd.com

John H. Millerton

4321 10th Street NE
Massillon, OH 44646
330-555-1234

CAREER TARGET: FORCE PROTECTION OFFICER

Eager to support the United States in a position that will assist in fighting the war against terrorism.

PROFILE

Driven, self-motivated team player with a record of problem solving and paying strict attention to detail. Qualifications include:

- One year joint responsibility for camp security in a war zone.

- Assisted in supply operations for one year at A Team level, 5th Special Forces Group.
- High endurance qualities—work out, run, cycle, swim three times a week.
- Capable of strenuous labor—lift heavy appliances frequently.
- Mechanically adept—qualified in outdoor equipment and small appliance repair.
- Valid U.S. driver's license.
- U.S. Citizen.

MILITARY SERVICE

United States Army   1985–1988
  Operations and Intelligence Specialist (11F2S)
  Served one Vietnam tour at A Team level in the 5th Special Forces Group. Successfully completed combat medic training. Airborne qualified. Honorably discharged, 1988. Received various medals/awards as follows:

- Bronze Star-Oak Leaf Cluster	- CIB–Combat Infantry Badge
- VSM–Vietnamese Service Medal	- VCM–Vietnamese Commendation Medal
- Parachute Badge	- NDSM–National Defense Service Medal

EMPLOYMENT HISTORY

Diversified Home Services   1994–present
(Multi-faceted business specializing in the repair of major appliances, hot tubs, and outdoor power equipment providing service to 10,000+ customers)
  Owner/Operator
  - Proficiently diagnose, estimate, and repair consumer products.
  - Successfully maintained profitability for 20+ years through two economic recessions.
  - Utilize leadership, organizational, mechanical, and team building skills – manage successful service team of four technicians.
  - Handle weekly payroll, maintain monthly balance sheet, and accounts payable/receivable and manage inventory.

J.C. Penney Product Service   1988–1994
(Large international retail department store serving customers with high-quality merchandise at affordable prices)
  Service Technician
  - Diagnosed and repaired appliances and outdoor power equipment

EDUCATION

Degree Program: Business Administration, The University of Akron, 18 months

REBA WOODWARD

1234 Oracal Ave.
Sunny, Texas 79000
(798) 555-1234 (H)
(798) 555-5678 (C)
rwood@protypeltd.com

PROFILE

Energetic "multitasker" with 25 years of nursing experience in administrative, clinical, ER, OR, and direct patient care settings. Equivalent of BSN from four years training at two schools. Plan and teach in-services and continuing education seminars. Proficiently write and revise policies and procedures. Easily establish relationships with broad cross-section of people. Driven achiever with competitive nature. Remain open minded, adjust well to change, and honor differences. Expertise includes:

Assertive Communication	*Focused Listening*	*Community Relations*
Problem Solving / Critical Thinking	*Relationship Building*	*Fund Raising*
Time Management / Prioritization	*Teamwork*	*Accurate Record Keeping*
Professionalism	*Decisiveness*	*Teaching / Instructing / Mentoring*

PROFESSIONAL EXPERIENCE

2002 – present   *RN, Operating Room Circulator,* ANDERSON SURGICENTER, Sunny, Texas
Manage the operating room of a cataract surgery center, coordinating activities of five others. Assist patients with pre-op paperwork, screening for allergies and gathering medical history. Assess vital signs and start IVs. Monitor and maintain patient status during surgery. Teach patients post-op care.

1991 – 2002   *Director of Health Services / School Nurse,* PARKWOOD ISD, Parkwood, Texas
Provided all health services to students and staff of entire school district of nine schools. Administered daily activities of the clinic. Performed health screenings and dispensed medications. Counseled students and trained staff for emergencies. Consistently monitored district for compliance with public school and state regulations regarding: environment, safety, and immunization requirements.

Managed own office: entered computer data, filed, composed and mailed letters / notices, maintained records, and wrote / revised policies and procedures. Interacted with and mediated between parents, students, and school administration. Interfaced with other state agencies, i.e., Child Protective Services (CPS) and Texas Education Agency (TEA).

Key Contributions:
- **Planned and managed assemblies, workshops, health fairs, immunization clinics, and fund-raising events.**
- **Gained exposure in the community.**
- **Chaired committee that developed and promoted drug–free schools policy.**
- **Provided a safe environment where students were comfortable and able to learn.**
- **Established strong rapport with parents and students.**
- **Accommodated requests and inquiries 24 hours a day.**

1988 – 1991   *Charge Nurse*, DON KEY MEDICAL / SURGICAL CENTER, Fairweather, Texas
Supervised five nurses: assigned duties, delegated responsibility, and monitored progress. Assisted doctor with rounds and transcribed orders. Assisted staff with procedures and gave full daily assessment on every patient. Provided direct patient care, including medication and self-care instruction.

EDUCATION

1986 – 1988   **Registered Nurse (RN),** BAPTIST HOSPITAL SCHOOL OF NURSING, Sunny, Texas

COMPUTER SKILLS

PC literate with knowledge of Windows, Microsoft Word, Outlook Express, and Internet

ORGANIZATIONS

1991 – 2002   President (two years), Texas Association of School Nurses

CHRIS HOWELL

T: (636) 555-1234 ✦ C: (636) 555-5678 ✦ E: chowell@protypeltd.com

Results-focused Vice President of Operations

AN INTRODUCTION

Troubleshooting is my forte. I am able to quickly assess a situation, develop a plan, and then implement it. I have always believed that every problem contains its own solution if one makes the effort to understand the obstacle. I have a bachelor's degree in business administration and more than 20 years of experience delivering increases in sales, market and product ranges, production, and efficiency.

KEY POINTS

- ☑ BUDGET AND BUSINESS PLAN DEVELOPMENT
- ☑ FORECASTING MARKET TRENDS
- ☑ CROSS-MARKETING
- ☑ BUSINESS START-UP AND DEVELOPMENT
- ☑ NEW PRODUCT LINES
- ☑ INCENTIVE PROGRAMS
- ☑ TROUBLESHOOTING
- ☑ MARKETING CAMPAIGNS
- ☑ INVENTORY MANAGEMENT

KEY ACCOMPLISHMENTS

- ☑ DRAMATICALLY INCREASED SALES THROUGH DYNAMIC CROSS-MARKETING CAMPAIGNS.[1]
- ☑ REDUCED OVERHEAD 90 PERCENT.[2]
- ☑ INCREASED PRODUCTION 45 PERCENT THROUGH AUTOMATION.[3]
- ☑ BOOSTED SALES 39 PERCENT. [4]

RECORD OF EXPERIENCE

☑ **CHRIS HOWELL COMMODITY TRADER CONSULTING, INC., Chicago, IL**   **2001–present**
PRESIDENT/FOUNDER

COMPANY PROFILE:
This firm employs three people and helps commodities traders improve their bottom line. Clients are members of the Chicago Board of Trade, Chicago Mercantile Exchange, and New York Energy Exchange.

- Saved the Chicago Board of Trade $15 million by analyzing experimental trading programs.
- Discussed the commodities market, futures, market trends, trading tips, and choice picks in nationally distributed magazines and television programs.

☑ **GEM STAR PROMOTIONS, INC., Palatine, IL**   **1989–2001**
PRESIDENT/FOUNDER

COMPANY PROFILE:
This company employed four people and specialized in promotions for food-related corporations. Developed various cross-marketing programs for Frigidaire, Libby-Owens Foods, Admiral Appliances, Montgomery Ward, and others.

Continued …

- [1]Increased sales by 79,500 units for Montgomery Ward and Admiral Appliance by developing and implementing compelling cross-marketing sales incentives. Launched equally successful programs for Frigidaire and Libby-Owens.
- [2]Reduced overhead 90 percent by restructuring the business.
- Developed advertising campaigns so successful the *Chicago Tribune* showcased them in their advertising.

▣ CHOICE CUT BEEF MARKETS, INC., Imperial, IL   1983–1989
PRESIDENT/FOUNDER

COMPANY PROFILE:
Built this company from the ground up with a *federally inspected* processing plant and 13 retail outlets. We employed 50 people and specialized in packaging and selling premium-quality meats to both retail consumers and commercial customers such as Johnsonville Sausage, Swiss Colony Foods, and Neiman-Marcus.

- [3]Boosted productivity 45 percent by automating processing lines.
- [4]Boosted sales 39 percent by implementing revolutionary marketing concepts such as preferred buyers clubs and home delivery.
- Built the first 100 percent wood-free processing plant in the United States that served as a model for the USDA and industry representatives from around the world.

▣ HOWELL BROS. WHOLESALE MEAT COMPANY, INC., Decatur, IL   1980–1983
VICE PRESIDENT OF OPERATIONS

COMPANY PROFILE:
This company employed 30 people and specialized in packaging and selling premium-quality meats to commercial clientele. It consisted of a federally inspected meat packing facility and one retail outlet.

- Amassed $3.5 million in annual sales.

TECH SKILLS

▣ OPERATING SYSTEMS:
- MS Windows 95–XP including NT

▣ SOFTWARE:
- MS Office Professional Edition and MS Project
- Bloomberg Professional and Peachtree Premium

THANK YOU.   636.555.1234

Samantha J. Wiley, RT-M

12345 6th Street NW ∽ Rochester, MN 55901 ∽ 507-555-1234 ∽ sjwiley@protypeltd.com

Profile

- More than 12 years of radiology experience; certified by ARRT.
- Respected for producing high-quality images that meet and exceed departmental standards.
- Strong interpersonal skills used to comfort patients and work effectively with care staff.
- Self-starter with high work ethic. Able to work independently and as part of a team.
- Dedicated to continuing professional education; strong interest in patient pathology.
- Voted "most caring" by co-workers completing a survey regarding patient treatment.

Professional Experience

Radiological Technologist (Mammographer)
Olmsted Medical Center, Rochester, MN, 1997 – present

- Ensure optimum images for care team by developing partnerships with patients during exams.
- Conduct needle localization, mammography, and ductography examinations.
- Perform fluoroscopic, surgical, trauma, portable, and general radiology.
- Serve on student advisory board that oversees, coordinates, and evaluates internship program.
- Instrumental in creating system to ensure supplies are always well stocked for the Radiology Department, resulting in more efficient patient care.
- Carry out Dexa scans and train personnel how to effectively use equipment.
- Organize and distribute tuberculosis information to make sure all patients and staff are aware of screening procedures. Serve on tuberculosis screening task force.

Radiological Technologist (Mammographer)
Austin Community Hospital, Austin, MN, 1994 – 1997

- Positioned patients and set up equipment for stereotactic breast biopsy examinations.
- Performed general, fluoroscopic, and portable radiology.

Radiological Technologist (Mammographer)
St. Joseph Community Hospital, St. Joseph, MN, 1992 – 1994

- Provided breast health education to patients utilizing visual media; encouraged self-exam.
- Performed fluoroscopic, portable, geriatric, and trauma radiology.
- Ensured quality control during processing; used teleradiography equipment.

Radiological Technologist (Mammographer)
Allied Professional Temporary Services, Roseville, MN, 1991 – 1992

- Performed orthopedic and general radiology in a variety of clinic and hospital settings.

Certifications

Certified Mammographer, American Registry of Radiologic Technology (ARRT), 1993 – present
Certified Radiographer, American Registry of Radiologic Technology (ARRT), 1992 – present
Certified Basic Life Support, American Heart Association (AHA), 1991 – present

Education

Associate of Science, **Radiography**, 1991
Mayo School of Health Related Sciences, Rochester, MN

Bachelor of Science, Horticulture, University of Minnesota, St. Paul, MN, 1982

"Samantha's patient care is exceptional. Due to her experience and attention to detail, she is able to foresee the need to take extra images during an exam."
-Doctor

"Samantha takes great pride in her work and it shows."
-Supervisor

"Samantha literally saved my life! She detected an abnormality that is not usually picked up by the routine breast exam. She went the extra mile and the result was that we detected the breast cancer early."
-Patient

Rosalyn C. Marlin

1234 Fair Dawn Drive • Colorado Springs, Colorado 80920
Home: (719) 555-1234 • Email: rcmarlin@protypeltd.com

PROFILE
- Self-motivated student who achieves goals through discipline and hard work.
- Detail-oriented, extroverted team player who always goes beyond the expected.

EDUCATION

RAMPART HIGH SCHOOL, Colorado Springs, Colorado (May 2005)
- Current grade point average 3.78.
- Focus on the arts.
- Currently taking advanced placement and weighted classes.
- Selected for the Honor Roll every semester every year.

SPECIAL TRAINING
- Radio Theater, Bemis School, Colorado Springs, Colorado (2000)

THEATER

ROLE	PERFORMANCE	VENUE	DATE
Annabel	Robin Hood	Rampart High School	2004
Assistant Director	God's Favorite	Rampart High School	2004
Hot Box Dancer	Guys and Dolls	Rampart High School	2004
Time	Snow White	Rampart High School	2004
Assistant Director	All My Sons	Rampart High School	2003
Dorca's Little Sister	Seven Brides for Seven Brothers	Rampart High School	2003

MUSIC

RAMPART HIGH SCHOOL MARCHING BAND (Squad Leader)
- Pikes Peak March of Champions—Placed first in 2004 and 2001, exhibitioned in 2003.
- Douglas County Marching Invitational—Placed second in 2004, second in 2003, and fifth in 2002.
- Southern Colorado Regional Competitions—Placed second in 2004, first in 2003, first in 2002, and first in 2001.
- Pomona Marching Invitational Competitions—Placed third in 2004, grand champion in 2003, third in 2002, and seventh in 2001.
- Colorado Bandmasters Association State Competition—Placed third in 2004, second in 2003, third in 2002, and ninth in 2001.
- Dallas Invitational—Won the Best Marching Band Award in 2004.
- Colorado Springs Festival of Lights Parade—Won the Best Band Award in 2002, 2003, and 2004.
- Winter Guard—Placed second in 2003.

RAMPART HIGH SCHOOL CONCERT BAND
- Served as an instructor for other students in the section.
- Wind Ensemble (2002-2005), Symphonic Band (2001-2002).
- Dallas Invitational—Won the Best Concert Band Award in 2004.

RAMPART HIGH SCHOOL JAZZ BAND

RAMPART HIGH SCHOOL CHOIR
- Festival Choir (2003-2004), Chamber Singers (2004-2005), All-State Choir (2005).

VOLUNTEER
- Volunteer Missionette, Assemblies of God Church (1990-present)—Service projects, including helping the elderly, caroling, nursing homes, remodeling the church building, yard work, and babysitting.
- Elected as historian of the Band Council (2004-2005)
- Helped serve meals for the youth choir's fund-raising dinner at the Sunbird Restaurant.
- Volunteered at the Colorado Springs Balloon Classic Festival (2002, 2003).
- Served meals at the Heritage Christian Center Thanksgiving outreach.

BERNADETTE D'EVES

EXPERIENCE

XEROX CORPORATION, Denver, Colorado
Xerox Engineering Systems Division – Versatec Products

Engineering Systems/Wide Format Specialist (1993 – 1996, 1998 – present)
Market large format engineering printers, plotters, and document management systems in a four-state region. Provide focused expertise and marketing sales support in complex sales cycles that include demonstrations, surveys, and presentations to the highest levels of corporate management. Support 35 sales representatives when their customers need wide-format products. Delivered a plan of more than $3,000,000 in systems priced from $5,000 to $500,000. Responsible for maintaining dealer and rural agent channels, third-party software alliances, and close communication with service technicians to maintain market share and maximize customer satisfaction. Developed long-term relationships with major accounts in the aerospace, manufacturing, architectural, and engineering industries with national implications resulting in significant long-term revenue.

- Number 1 out of 150 worldwide and 90 nationally in 1998.
- Number 1 in Western region sales for three years.
- Achieved President's Club 90% of the time (top 10% of sales corporate-wide).
- Received the "Honorary Sales Support Quality Award" from Lucent Technologies in 1998.

High Volume Account Manager (1997)
Achieved the district's product and revenue objectives by providing system sales leadership, training, and support for seven sales representatives in a six-state region selling high-end engineering printers/plotters and electronic engineering document storage/retrieval systems. Conducted closing sales calls and plan/review sessions with the sales representatives to formulate and evaluate account management sales strategies and developmental action plans. Implemented quarterly seminars and technology symposiums for the team to improve market penetration. Utilized and leveraged key third-party alliance system solutions to meet customer requirements. Provided to top management accurate monthly, quarterly, and yearly business forecasts for the district's systems performance.

- Exceeded annual sales quota of $15.0 million.
- Number 4 out of 14 high volume account managers nationally.

High-Volume Engineering Systems Sales Executive (1990 – 1991)
Supervised a team of seven territory sales representatives in a five-state region, delivering a plan of more than $4.0 million in large-ticket products greater than $75,000. Responsibilities included resource management, account maintenance, sales training, prospect development, 90-day action plans, monthly plan and review sessions, major account calls, implementation of national marketing actions, and operation reviews to senior management.

- President's Club, 1990 (top 15% nationally).
- Number 2 of 6 in volume in Midwest region.

EDUCATION

MASTER OF BUSINESS ADMINISTRATION, University of Arizona, Tucson, Arizona

BACHELOR OF SCIENCE IN ACCOUNTING, University of Arizona, Tucson, Arizona

TRAINING

XEROX: Sales Training; Quality Improvement Process; Facilitator Training; Management Studies; Solution Sales

CONTACT

1234 Capella Drive, Monument, Colorado 80132, Cell: (719) 555-1234, Email: bdeves@protypeltd.com

DEREK N. OLMSTEAD

College: 1234 18th Street, Greeley, CO 80631
Home: 1234 Bear Cloud Drive, Colorado Springs, CO 80919
Cellular: (719) 555-1234 • Home: (719) 555-5678

SUMMARY OF QUALIFICATIONS

Email: dno4726@protypeltd.com

- Dynamic sales representative with the proven ability to establish common ground quickly and connect with prospects.
- Second-generation salesman who has learned how to maintain long-term, profitable relationships.
- Loyal team player with exceptional interpersonal, communication, and presentation skills.
- Energetic and self-motivated professional; able to handle multiple projects simultaneously and manage time efficiently.

EDUCATION

BACHELOR OF ARTS IN COMMUNICATIONS, University of Northern Colorado, Greeley, Colorado (December 2006)
- Minor in Public Relations and Media Studies
- Relevant courses completed: Inquiry in Speech Communications, Family Communications, Communications and Leadership, History of Mass Communications, Introduction to Rehabilitation Services, Introduction to Speech Communications, Intercultural Communications, Small Group Communications, Persuasion, Stress Management, Speaking Evaluation, Basics of Public Speaking
- Developed a community lacrosse team as a civics project for speech class. Interviewed athletic directors, recruited students, and presented the programs at local schools.

EXPERIENCE

SALES REPRESENTATIVE, The Buckle, Greeley, Colorado (2003 – 2004)
- Sold contemporary clothing to both male and female customers using an active sales approach.
- Completed quarterly formal sales training and learned to develop repeat business through relationship selling.
- Consistently earned a commission on top of an hourly base rate by aggressively selling high volumes every month.

PERSONAL FITNESS CONSULTANT, World Gym, Colorado Springs, Colorado (Summer 2004)
- Sold gym memberships both inside and outside the facility.
- Achieved top sales representative status for two of the four months on the job, consistently meeting or exceeding sales quotas every month.
- Developed and implemented promotional campaigns at local night clubs, Sam's Club stores, and special events throughout the community.
- Promoted the gym through special on-location radio contests offering free memberships for winners.
- Helped to create ideas for group deals offered to apartment complexes through newsletters.
- Worked on Territory Day programs, military events, television/video productions, posters, and other promotions.

COUNSELOR, High Trails, Colorado Springs, Colorado (Summer 2002)
- Served as a counselor for this week-long outdoor camp for junior high students sponsored by the school district.
- Selected based on the recommendation of two high school teachers.

HONORS & AWARDS

- Received the University of Northern Colorado Scholastic Achievement Award (2003).
- Honored with an award from the University of Northern Colorado Office of Multicultural Affairs for high GPA (2003).

ACTIVITIES

- Member, University of Northern Colorado Lacrosse Team (2002 – 2004), Treasurer (2003 – 2004).
- Member, League of United Latin Students (2004).
- Leader in the YoungLife program—completed multiple semesters of leadership training to impact the lives of youth and prepare them for the future; served as a leader for middle school students while in high school.
- Lettered in varsity and junior high school varsity wrestling—played in regional competitions.
- Lettered in varsity and junior varsity high school lacrosse—played in state tournaments; selected for the Vail All Star Team during senior year.
- Played varsity and junior varsity high school football.
- Avid weight lifter (trained with two former Mr. Colorados); enjoy rock climbing (participated in competitions).

MALINDA MARIE MCFADDEN

1234 N. Star Rd. #567
Richardson, Texas 75082
mmmfadden@protypeltd.com

(972) 555-1234

SUMMARY

Published writer with B.A. in journalism, emphasis in public relations. Six Sigma certified. Writing experiences encompass cover and feature stories, Web content, business communications, press releases, tip sheets, and newsletters. Trained in *Associated Press* Stylebook. PR experience comprises areas of healthcare, construction, and technology. Personable interviewer and confident presenter. Persuasive communicator and creative idea generator. Other key strengths include:

Accountability	*Strategic Planning*	*Coordination*	*Vision*
Assertiveness	*Integrity*	*Organization*	*Motivation*
Relationship Building	*Negotiation*	*Prioritization*	*Delegation*
Facilitation	*Perception*	*Dedication*	*Follow-through*

EDUCATION

B.A. in Journalism with emphasis in Public Relations, GPA: 3.74, University of North Texas, Denton, Texas   **May 2004**
Internships:
MAX WHITMAN & CO. PUBLIC RELATIONS, Addison, Texas, Fall 2001 and Spring 2002
Wrote news releases, tip sheets, and newsletters for healthcare and construction clients. Attended agency-client strategy meetings and observed client management. Researched speaking opportunities and RFPs. Manually compiled media list.

FAIRFIELD TECHNOLOGIES, INC., Richardson, Texas, Spring 2001
Coordinated targeted communication tactics for high-tech clients. Compiled editorial calendars; participated in creative strategy planning; pitched story ideas; and garnered placement in *New Jersey Business News*.

KBUX RADIO STATION, Dallas, Texas, Fall 2000
Designed mass mailing lists and filed ad traffic reports for top account executive. Exposed to daily routine of an account executive.

RELEVANT EXPERIENCE

Communications Specialist, INDUSTRIAL RESEARCH, INC., Dallas, Texas   **2004 – present**
Coordinate communication strategy and implementation of enterprise-wide software change involving 78,000 employees. Wrote content for system Web site; served as system spokesperson and trainer for employee population, coordinated placement and distribution of collateral materials with seven international business units. Manage complaints and interface with ad agency and corporate communications. Present a professional image.
- Integral member of the Raytheon team.

OTHER WORK EXPERIENCE

Loan Officer, MARIMAX HOME EQUITY, Lewisville, Texas   **2001 – 2004**
Qualified, designed, and sold mortgage loans in the fast-paced environment of a Fortune 500 company.
- Averaged quarterly sales of $1+ million.

PUBLICATIONS

- Cover feature story for international *Medhunter's Magazine*
- Covered science/technology for *The North Texas Daily*
- Feature stories for *The Lexington Leader*
- Feature story for *Inside Collin County Business*

PROFESSIONAL ASSOCIATIONS

- Member, Public Relations Society of America, 2000 – present
- Past member and president, Public Relations Student Society of America

COMPUTER SKILLS

- Computer literate with proficiency in MS Office Suite, QuarkXPress, Photoshop, Illustrator, PA Powerbase, Internet.

5 Address Positions

People must be able to locate you, but your address and phone number are some of the least important marketing details on a résumé. Some managers spend only a few seconds perusing a résumé and might get through the first third of it, if you are lucky. The reader's eyes should be drawn immediately to the things that will motivate him or her to read all the way to the bottom.

However, you don't want to make the reader work too hard when it comes time to make that critical call for an interview! You should make the address section part of the overall design of the résumé so it doesn't detract from the text, much as you did with your name, but keep it in an easy-to-find location. That can be done by placing the address(es) either at the top or the bottom of the résumé. If your résumé is more than one page, you should place your contact information on the first page, but you can also repeat it on the second page (pages 84 and 85).

Two addresses, a current and permanent, are often needed when a person is still in school or will be moving in a few months. Presenting them at the top sometimes creates design problems and requires a bit of imagination (pages 70 and 78). Placing two addresses at the bottom is often easier.

An address at the top of the résumé should be made part of the design so that the reader's eyes easily skip over it to begin reading the text. Graphic lines are particularly useful in this case (pages 72, 74, 76, 81, 82, 86, and 90), and so is creative placement (pages 73, 80, and 88).

Matching lines at the bottom of a résumé sometimes help to create a sense of balance so the résumé is not top heavy (pages 91 and 94).

The address can be centered under or between the line(s) (pages 72, 82, 86, and 91), made to follow the same format as the text of the résumé (page 88), or right flushed (pages 81, 82, 90, and 94).

If you have an e-mail address, always include it on your résumé. The same goes for your Web page address if you have a portfolio online.

PRESENT ADDRESS:
P.O. Box 789
Wadsworth, OH 44282
330-555-1234

gbender@protypeltd.com

CLUB ADDRESS:
4321 Wales Ave. NW
Massillon, OH 44646
330-555-5678

GREGORY D. BENDER

MANAGER ◆ SUPERINTENDENT ◆ SUPERVISOR

PROFILE

◆ Managed numerous projects totaling over $2.5 million.

◆ Skilled at planning, managing, and supervising projects from start to finish.

◆ Exceptional ability to recognize problems and provide resolutions.

◆ Consistent record of achievements to improve quality while staying within budget.

◆ Proven ability to train, motivate, and supervise staff.

◆ Educational speaker at 1997 GCSAA National Conference and Show, Las Vegas.

PROFESSIONAL EXPERIENCE

GREEN GABLE COUNTRY CLUB, Massillon, OH   12/97 – 12/05
Superintendent

Challenge: Inherited irrigation and drainage problems that caused degradation of greens and poor drainage that led to loss of customer base, especially during periods of frequent rains. Charged with managing the project to improve overall appearance of clubhouse and course.

Action: Successfully supervised projects as follows: new well drilling, which tied into 40-year-old irrigation system; several irrigation upgrades, including green perimeter heads; and extensive drainage work that solved 40 years of problems. Completed greenside bunker renovation; major dredging of creek, including new bridges, boulder work, and new pond and dams; new cart paths; major electrical upgrades; significant tree work; and complete regrassing of fairways.

Result: Maximized efficiency of irrigation system which restored dead greens and improved drainage 100 percent with no playing days lost even in a year of record rainfall. Improved overall appearance of the course and grounds. Membership increased as a result.

PINE HARBOR COUNTRY CLUB, Phoenix, MD   12/89 – 9/97
Superintendent

Challenge: Install much-needed computerized irrigation system and new drainage system. Re-landscape new clubhouse and improve traffic flow of carts on course.

Action: Coordinated and supervised an intricate new drainage system (Cambridge Drainage System). Regrassed putting surface. Designed and supervised reconstruction of practice facility, involving construction of new tees, four target-green complexes, regrassing entire area, installation of permanent, artificial mats and new landscaping. Completed re-landscaping of the new clubhouse. Planned, coordinated, and supervised installation of new cart paths and re-routing of existing paths.

Result: Produced a more aesthetically pleasing course and solved course cart-traffic problems.

SCENIC VIEW COUNTRY CLUB, Baltimore, MD   6/85 – 12/89
Assistant Superintendent

Challenge: Recover East and West courses (Baltimore Country Club) with disease problems and prepare for U.S. Women's Open.

Action: Monitored disease activity; pesticide, irrigation and fertilizer requirements and applications on East and West courses. Directly involved in preparation and recovery of course for 1988 U.S. Women's Open. Accomplished complete reconstruction of West course including grow-in period.

Result: Significantly improved general appearance of greens and course in general.

PRIOR RELEVANT EXPERIENCE

MAPLE RIDGE COUNTRY CLUB, Baltimore, MD   9/87 – 1/88
Interim Superintendent
Consulted on general improvement of turfgrass conditions

HOLLY HILLS COUNTRY CLUB, Baltimore, MD   8/86 – 11/86
Interim Superintendent
Conferred with management and assisted with completely regrassing three bent grass greens

GREEN TURF COUNTRY CLUB, Akron, OH   Summers 1982 – 1984
Golf course maintenance crew
Performed daily maintenance procedures
Involved in bookkeeping and inventory

MOON HOLLOW COUNTRY CLUB, Akron, OH   1/79 – 10/79
Golf course maintenance crew
Performed general maintenance procedures

PROFESSIONAL ORGANIZATIONS

Golf Course Superintendents Association of America
Ohio Turfgrass Council
United States Golf Association
Northern Ohio Golf Course Superintendents Association board member – (four years)

EDUCATION

THE OHIO STATE UNIVERSITY, Agricultural Technical Institute, Wooster OH
Associate of Applied Science, Turfgrass Management (June 1986)

THE UNIVERSITY OF AKRON, Akron, OH
Bachelor of Arts, Food and Nutrition (May 1984)

Briseyda E. Darling

711 Terry Brook Drive, New York, NY 10025, Tel: 555-123-4567, Cell: 407-929-7428, bedarling@protypeltd.com

"Nurses have come a long way in a few short decades. In the past, our attention focused on physical, mental, and emotional healing. Now we talk of healing your life, healing the environment, and healing the planet."
~Lynn Keegan, 1994

PROFILE

Caring and competent entry-level nurse with a passion to meet patients' needs. Offering to contribute holistic and empathetic nursing practices. Bilingual (Spanish and English) with experience in clinical settings and a successful background in office administration. Windows XP, MS Word, Internet.

- Interpersonal Communications
- Head-to-Toe Assessment
- Droplet Precautions
- Therapeutic Communication
- Contact Isolation
- Compassionate Care
- Critical Thinking
- Office Administration
- Patient Education

EDUCATION & ASSOCIATIONS

LaGuardia Community College: **Associate in Nursing**
Expected gradation date: June 2005, NCLEX: Summer 2005

Key Nursing Courses Taken:

Fundamentals of Nursing
Perspectives on Nursing

Medical Surgical Nursing I
Medical Dosage

Psychiatric Nursing
OB-GYN and Pediatrics

Associations:
Student Nurse Association
Laguardia Nursing Club

NURSING / CLINICAL EXPERIENCE

Honed nursing skills by adapting classroom knowledge into clinicals and internship. Demonstrated active listening skills and assessed patients' comfort needs. Administered injections, provided wound care, dispensed medications, and took accurate vital signs. Consoled patients and clarified care plans with sensitivity and patience. Improved patient emotional health by advocating self-care. Aided doctors by translating treatments and prognosis in Spanish, successfully abating panic.

Jamaica Hospital, Jamaica, Queens
OB-GYN and Pediatrics

September 2004 to present

Elmhurst Hospital, New York, NY
Oncology and Renal (Summer Intern)

July to August 2004

Elmhurst Hospital, New York, NY
Medical Surgical Floor

March to June 2004

NorthShore Hospital, New York, NY
Medical Surgical Floor

September to January 2003

TRACEY LITHGLOW

- ♦ Well-organized and detail-orientated accounting professional with 10+ years of experience in the credit card industry.
- ♦ Known affectionately as the "Credit Card Queen" due to ability to process customer accounts quickly and accurately.
- ♦ Proven track record of implementing change that significantly improves productivity, customer relations, and the bottom-line.
- ♦ Proficient using MS Word, MS Excel, and proprietary software.
- ♦ Recognized for integrity, dedication, and going the extra mile.

lithglow@protypeltd.com ♦ (507) 555-1234 ♦ Rochester, MN 55902 ♦ 1234 45th Ave NW

SUMMARY

EXPERIENCE

"I know I can count on Tracey to get things done and get them done right!"
– Mobil Service Station Customer

"Tracey is a highly motivated and talented individual. Prior to her start date, the credit card department was disorganized and highly inefficient, customers couldn't get their questions answered, and equipment was disappearing. Within three months, Tracey had completely turned around the department and customers were calling not to complain but to praise Tracey for the great job she was doing."
– Jon Vanheld, Supervisor

"Tracey's understanding of accounts receivable data, coupled with her enthusiasm and dedication for the task at hand, was impressive."
– Charles Chin, Owner

EDUCATION

Credit Card/Accounting Clerk
Dunway Fuel Products, Rochester, MN, 1994 – present

Manage all aspects of credit card department serving 500 gas stations and airports in eight states. Complete invoices for accounts receivable. Cut checks and enter data for accounts payable. Program POS equipment and maintain inventory.

Selected Accomplishments

- ♦ Improved customer relations and efficient handling of credit card transactions by developing a procedures book specific to each customer's needs and learning the terminology unique to each customer's brand.
- ♦ Promoted to a salaried position as a result of proven ability to develop processes that lead to increased productivity.
- ♦ Increased the dollar amount of credit card transactions completed per year from 3M to 11M while successfully maintaining accuracy and efficiency in all other areas of responsibility.
- ♦ Developed procedures guide for the credit card department resulting in a more efficiently run office.
- ♦ Saved the company $22,000 per year by researching and resolving the problem of lost equipment.

Inventory/Promotions Clerk
Leslie's Bridal Wear, Rochester, MN, 1993 – 1994
- ♦ Managed inventory, ensuring availability of items for customers.
- ♦ Supervised special projects and created promotional materials.

Accounts Receivable Clerk
Chin Restaurant Equipment & Supply, Rochester, MN, 1990 – 1992
- ♦ Implemented network accounting system and effectively trained employees on POS equipment.
- ♦ Assisted with accounts receivable, accounts payable, and payroll.

Minnesota Riverland Technical College, Rochester, MN
Bookkeeping Clerk, 1994

Austin Community College, Austin, MN
Microcomputer Applications, 1992

Georgeanne M. Dacapo

27223 N.E. 61ˢᵗ Lane • Portland, Oregon 55555

geemd@protypeltd.com

555-123-4567

geemd@protypeltd.com

Office Management • Administrative Support

Professional Profile

Multi-disciplined, proactive *Administrative Assistant* with a strong background in *Office Management* and a commitment to professionalism. Well-developed office techniques, strong liaison abilities, and effective in managing a wide variety of projects independently or as a team member. Outstanding communications and interpersonal skills. History of attention to detail and thoroughness beyond expectations. Creative, innovative, and tenacious with the ability to envision and create successful strategies and strong follow-through on all details. Loyal, dependable worker who is committed to a job well done.

"I can state with pleasure that her technical and organizational skills are at the highest level."
– *Kelly G. McJohn, PE, PLS, McJohn Engineering*

Expertise Includes

- Accounting
- Accounts Payable
- Accounts Receivables
- Bank Reconciliation
- Collections

- Customer Service
- Database Management
- Human Resources
- Mailings
- Marketing

- Operations
- Payroll
- Proposals
- Purchasing
- Reception

- Research
- Secret Clearance
- State and Federal Taxes
- Teleprospecting
- Training

Software Includes

- MS Word (70+ wpm)
- Excel

- Outlook
- QuickBooks Pro

- Goldmine
- Onyx

"Georgeanne's mature and calm manner has been an asset when dealing with difficult situations."
– *Nathan Greggs, VP Sales & Marketing, CAChe Group-Fujitsu America, Inc.*

Outstanding Accomplishments and Achievements

- ✓ Created 40-page marketing plan for selling plasma displays to Egyptian government.
- ✓ Relentlessly pursued supervisor's "lemon law" claim resulting in an award of a new vehicle.
- ✓ Voluntarily delivered an electronics shipment to LAX the evening before Thanksgiving to meet an international deadline.
- ✓ Consistently implemented proactive measures to upgrade quality and improve the efficiency of office systems.
- ✓ Achieved and maintained top-secret clearance status.

History of Employment

Office Administration/Reception • CAChe Software-Fujitsu America, Inc. • Beaverton, Oregon • *2002*

CAChe office liaison with parent company (Fujitsu America, Inc.) in California. Created new procedures, increasing the level of cooperation between the two offices. Processed orders, manufacturing, distribution, product releases, reception, payables, office operations, sales support, and marketing communications. Researched and corrected ECCN designation for exporting software products.

continued ...

74

Telemarketer • Timberline Software Corporation • Beaverton, Oregon • *2001 – 2002*
Teleprospecting, Internet research, and database management.

Office Manager • *1997 – 2001*
Big Bear Magazine and Foothill Builders Home Improvement Co. • Big Bear Lake, California
Total Administrative Office Management for two separate businesses.
Magazine publishing: Managed mailing list, invoicing, A/P and A/R, statements, fiscal reports, collections, small claims court appearances, proofreading, phones, faxing, emailing, layout, and planning. Communicated with outside vendors and advertisers. Worked closely with the sales, editorial, and graphics staff. Trained new advertising account executives.
Home remodeling: Prepared bid and proposal, change orders, and contracts. Assisted with physical home inspections, client reports, job costing, invoicing, A/P and A/R, bank reconciliation, tax and unemployment department filings. Served as liaison with city and county building departments. Prepared payroll data and employee forms. Answered phones, prepared correspondence, ordered supply, and maintained office equipment.

Administrative Assistant • McJohn Engineering and Consulting, Big Bear Lake, California • *1992 – 1996*
Civil Engineering and Land Surveying. Researched and prepared lot surveys. Supplied extensive proposal work. Worked closely with city and county building inspectors, planning departments, and FEMA.

Administrator, International Business Development Operations (AA) • *1984 – 1988*
Interstate Electronics Corporation, Anaheim, California
Obtained Top-Secret Clearance for this position.
Provided complex administrative support to the Director of International Marketing, including initiating applications for demo electronic equipment and CARNET licenses. Served as liaison with the contracts department for applicable U.S. Department of State or Commerce licensing of plasma displays and GPS receiver equipment to end-users or IEC's distributor/representative. Initiated sales and delivery orders. Tracked progress of license applications. Coordinated timely shipments with manufacturing, QA department, and air freight forwarding company. Company courier for overseas documents. Advised customers of purchase order changes of status. Provided re-export documentation for repair orders.

Affiliations

Beaverton Arts Council Board of Directors • **Portland Center for the Performing Arts** • **Portland Art Museum** • **Oregon Convention Center** • **OMSI**

Certifications and Recognitions

Certificate in International Business • University of Southern California, College of Continuing Education
Export Control of Technology • Federal Publications, Inc., Washington, D.C.
Certificate of Completion, Harmonized Base Schedule B • International Marketing Association of Orange County, California
NESRA • National Employee Services and Recreation Association Award for Membership
Certificate of Achievement, Action Team Leader, Quality Circles • Interstate Electronics Corporation, California
Program Director Award • Dawnbusters Rotary Club, California

STEPHEN P. SMITH

555 5th Ave. smith@email.net (Home) 555-123-4567
Shoretown, NJ 11111 (Cell) 555-765-4321

SUMMARY

Retail Store Manager with extensive experience in a variety of industries, including music, food, entertainment, and hospitality. Effective interpersonal and communication skills are utilized to develop and maintain customer relationships. Known for product knowledge and superior customer service. Strong organization and prioritizing skills are used to successfully manage large diverse inventories. Highly respected and valued by peers and employees for positive and practical management style, integrity, hard work, and business expertise.

PROFESSIONAL EXPERIENCE

CD Superstore, Northfield, New Jersey Nov. 1997 – present
Manager

Managed the financial and physical operations of an independent, high-volume retail store selling compact discs and related items. Supervised staff and personally provided sales and service to customers. Maintained accurate inventory, and ordered and received products and supplies. Selected and installed software, and performed computer maintenance.

- Led staff in attaining 125 percent sales growth in four years.
- Guided employees in achieving company standards by controlling problems, identifying trends, solving personnel issues, and rewarding accomplishments.
- Increased repeat customers by providing superior service, demonstrating product knowledge, and personally addressing questions and concerns.
- Maintained accurate records for over $1 million worth of inventory. Compiled detailed sales and purchase reports, reconciled cash registers, and delivered bank deposits.

Boardwalk Casino Hotel, Atlantic City, New Jersey Feb. 1995 – Nov. 1997
Administration Services / Reservations Clerk

Performed administrative duties for record retention department, including processing requests, researching confidential records, distributing interoffice correspondence, and compiling information for various departments within high-profile casino and hotel. As reservations clerk, interacted effectively with patrons to coordinate and confirm reservations.

- Avoided fines and penalties by adhering to all Casino Control Commission regulations.
- Consistently processed requests quickly and accurately in a fast-paced environment utilizing strong organization and prioritizing skills.
- Met or exceeded company and departmental guidelines for responding to calls and coordinating reservations while demonstrating quality customer service.

ShoreAirlines, Egg Harbor Township, New Jersey   Sept. 1993 – Feb. 1995
Flight Representative, Line Service

Performed a variety of activities personally and by telephone to provide customer service and support to the airline and its passengers, including gate services and reservations.

- Maintained radio communications with flight crews directly after takeoff and before landing to relay pertinent information regarding aircraft and airport status, ensuring proper procedures, security, and passenger safety.
- Requested and performed additional duties on the flightline in order to facilitate the daily operations of the airline.

World Casino Hotel, Atlantic City, New Jersey   April 1993 – Sept. 1993
Diamond Club Ambassador

Promoted the casino's Diamond Club program to patrons and photographed jackpot winners.

- Consistently exceeded daily goals for enlisting new members by effectively presenting membership benefits to patrons.

Bruno's Finer Foods, Atlanta, Georgia   Jan. 1990 – Feb. 1993
Assistant Front End Manager (1992 – 1993)

Supported the financial and physical operations of a high-volume, full-service grocery store, supervising up to 10 cashiers per shift and maintaining the cash offices.

- Ensured accurate transactions and financial records while leading employees to exceed company standards for customer service.

Maintenance Activity Clerk (1991 – 1992)

Received large volumes of products, maintained inventory, and ensured accurate pricing for every store item, utilizing an electronic inventory system.

Cashier (1990 – 1991)

Completed customer transactions promptly and accurately. Promoted to Maintenance Activity Clerk in recognition of product knowledge and professional initiative.

EDUCATION

The Art Institute of Atlanta, Atlanta, GA   March 1990
Associate Degree, Music Entertainment Management

PROFESSIONAL DEVELOPMENT

Cash Office Management   *Successful Customer Relationships*

JAMES A. DAXTON

Permanent Address:
1234 West 15th Avenue
Emporia, KS 66801
Home: (620) 555-1234

Email: jadax@protype.com
Cellular: (719) 555-1234

Present Address:
300 East 79th Street
New York, NY 10016
Home: (212) 555-5678

PROFILE

- Confident leader with the proven ability to develop new revenue sources and accomplish both long- and short-term corporate objectives.
- Dedicated professional with vast experience in managing corporate operations, outsourcing agreements, and IT development for large international corporations.
- Especially adept at increasing profitability without negatively impacting customer satisfaction.
- Successful at managing multi-million-dollar programs in fast-paced environments.
- Effective team player who works well with others and strives to create win-win relationships.
- Able to motivate management and operating personnel to achieve maximum results.

EXPERIENCE

SENIOR CLIENT EXECUTIVE (2004 – present)
Hewlett-Packard, New York, New York

- Manage all end user computing worldwide (30,000 seats) for Credit Suisse First Boston, whose parent company is Credit Suisse Group Zurich, one of the world's largest investment firms with offices in all major financial markets and trading floors in London and New York City.
- Transferred 300+ client employees and contractors under HP's umbrella June 1, 2004, and assumed full P&L responsibility for a five-year service-level agreement valued at $185 million.
- Maintain executive client relationships and assure total client satisfaction with help desk, engineering, planning, desk-side support, and break-fix services.
- Currently migrating the New York City and London service desk to HP facilities in Toronto and Dublin, which will result in better performance for the client and cost savings for HP.
- Will migrate certain engineering activities to Bangalore, India, from London and New York City during 2005, resulting in significant reduction in HP expenses and improved customer service.

VICE PRESIDENT, IT GOVERNANCE (2001 – 2003)
MCI Worldcom, Colorado Springs, Colorado

- Served as lead negotiator and managed a $7 billion EDS outsourcing service agreement.
- Renegotiated terms and conditions of the EDS contract, saving $83 million per year and gaining approval for the final agreement from the bankruptcy court.
- Scope of the contract covered IT operations and the support group that performed all data center services and billing document production across multiple computing platforms.
- Developed and managed a $400+ million operating budget and several million dollars in capital assets.

VICE PRESIDENT, UUNET (2000 – 2001)
MCI Worldcom, Colorado Springs, Colorado

- Accepted the additional responsibility of overseeing managed hosting services, which provided IT services to external clients throughout the world.
- Directed the operations of seven data centers in the U.S. staffed by 400 employees.
- Succeeded in generating significant revenue from global clients.

VICE PRESIDENT, IT OPERATIONS (1997 – 2000)
MCI Worldcom, Colorado Springs, Colorado

- Led all of MCI's American-based data operations supporting all corporate systems and network services capabilities.
- Responsible for more than 1,000 employees in 15 corporate data centers and four mega-data centers.
- Successfully developed and managed a $400 million operating budget.
- Reduced operating costs of the department by 25–35% over two years through aggressive employee realignments and contract renegotiations.
- Hold patent #6,317,746 B1 for software date and time conversion services.

EXPERIENCE
(continued)

DIRECTOR, CORPORATE APPLICATION DEVELOPMENT (1996 – 1997)
MCI Telecommunications, Colorado Springs, Colorado
- Selected to turn around the Commercial Order Processing Group that was producing a series of costly code errors in very large, complex applications, resulting in low morale and frequent turnover.
- Responsible for 400 application developers and support personnel who process service orders and develop customer-facing business unit applications.
- Accepted the challenge of improving serviceability and introducing new products on time and under budget.
- Instituted measurements and metrics to track errors and created a cross-functional skills training program to improve employee confidence.
- Formed cooperative teams to allow a single group to follow production from the requirements phase all the way through testing, which improved accountability.
- Led the unit to become the number one producer of top quality code with the highest team morale.

DIRECTOR, IT OPERATIONS (1992 – 1995)
MCI Telecommunications, Colorado Springs, Colorado
- Managed all IT operations, fourth-level service support, and service-level creation.
- Created the operating vision for the future through automation, strategic data center design and construction, and a centralized organizational structure.
- Succeeded in transforming this divisional IT organization into a centralized, highly automated, and cost-efficient group.
- The organization won the Gartner Group Award for Best in Class Data Center Operations in the telecom sector.
- When this organization was outsourced to EDS in 2000, EDS recognized the quality of operations and used it as a benchmark for its own processes throughout the company.

DIRECTOR, CORPORATE PROGRAM MANAGEMENT (1990 – 1991)
MCI Telecommunications, Dallas, Texas
- Translated internal customer requirements into complex national IT programs by managing the product development life cycle (requirements analysis, time lines, budgets, portfolios, capital funding proposals, development, launch, and testing).
- Served as an interface between product marketing, engineering, and application developers.
- Accountable to the senior vice president for delivering such products as *Friends and Family, Network-Based Automatic Call Distribution (ACD), Directory Assistance,* and *Toll Services for the Hearing Impaired.*

DIRECTOR, IT OPERATIONS (1986 – 1990)
MCI Telecommunications, Washington, DC
- Recruited by a former AT&T senior vice president to fix the massive problems in billing and computerized traffic systems.
- Developed a new system for delivery of tapes from switch directors that increased the efficiency of billing from 45% to 98.6% in only four months and 99+% in six months.

REGIONAL VICE PRESIDENT (1985 – 1986)
Sycom Systems, Orlando, Florida
- Stepped out of a traditionally large-company role into the contracting world.
- Placed application contractors at AT&T, Coca-Cola, Martin Marietta, and other large companies.

COMMUNITY
SERVICE
- Advisor, Colorado Governor's Technology Board (1999 – 2000)
- MCI Liaison, University of Colorado, Colorado Springs (UCCS), Advanced Degree and Curriculum Advisory Board (1998 – 1999)
- Member, Board of Directors, Colorado Springs Greater Chamber of Commerce (1998)

INTERESTS
Private Pilot, AOPA • Golf

Mike Moore

119 S. Second St.
Rossford, OH 45872
718-541-5993
moore@protypeltd.com

CLIENTS

Chili Z Creative
Cherub Films
Frozen Man Films
Casting Creative
Comedy Central
Rupp Productions
MTV
William Street Films
Taxi Films
NBA Entertainment
Viacom
Dragon Films
Girabaldi Productions
Big Blue Advertising

EDUCATION

Ohio State University
1982 – 1986

Operations / Production Management

Associate Producer   Assistant Director   Line Producer

Summary

Innovative entertainment industry professional with 12 years of experience in commercial film production. **Possess exceptional planning skills**, able to handle multiple projects and work well under tight deadlines. Demonstrated strong interpersonal skills in working with staff, vendors, and talent.

Work Experience

Operations Manager—Outlined staff responsibilities, created rate cards, tracked and actualized budgets, and assisted in licensing images.
- Chili Z Creative, 2004

Associate Producer—Facilitated casting and monitored budget goals.
- Chili Z Creative, Fannie May Foundation, 2004
- Blue Worldwide, 2003

Production Manager—Purchased grip, electrical, and camera equipment. Managed account information and time frame for delivery for all vendors. Drafted and created pre-production booklet. Booked all key personnel.
- William Street Films, *Yellow Fever*, 2003
- Taxi Films, *Taxi Driver Specials*, 2003
- Frozen Man Films, *Racing Stripes*, 2002
- Girabaldi Productions, *Subzero*, 2002
- Dragon Films, *Medicare*, 2000
- Dragon Films, *Verizon*, 2000

Assistant Director—Logistically set up locations. Managed and led shoots. Planned shooting schedule. Determined call times for crew, talent, and equipment.
- NBA Entertainment, *Cable Guy*, 2003
- NBA Entertainment, *Dreammaker*, 2003
- Viacom, Nick at Nite, *Road House*, 2003
- Comedy Central, *Nicky*, 2000
- Rupp Productions, *Divorce Court*, 2000
- MTV Promos, *Reality Weddings* 2000
- Dragon Films, *Connecticare*, 2000
- Dragon Films, *AT&T*, 2000

Line Producer —Prepared and actualized shooting budgets. Coordinated post- production schedules and advance locations for shoots.
- Casting Creative, *Ted Kennedy for Senate*, 2000
- Casting Creative, *Christie Whitman for Senate*, 2000
- Casting Creative, *Joe Lieberman for Senate*, 2000

Agency/Post Producer—Managed post production operations.
- Big Blue Advertising Agency, *National Association of Broadcasters*, 2001
- Cherub Films, 2001

"Mr. Jones . . . providing mortgage brokers with an exceptional level of service and responsiveness."   *Press Release 6/21/2004*

ALBERT A. JONES

12345 E. Adobe Dr. ■ Scottsdale, AZ 85255
Phone: 602-555-1234 ■ Email: jones@protypeltd.com

PROFILE   Effective Regional Manager with four years experience in the wholesale and correspondent lending industry
- Exceptional management and sales record
- Valuable hiring manager with strong training and mentoring skills
- Adept at presenting to large groups
- Strong communication skills in sales and team building
- Compelling analytical and forecasting skills for decision-making
- Proficient in using computer applications
- Masters in Business Administration

EXPERIENCE

DOWNEY SAVINGS & LOAN ASSOCIATION, F.A., Scottsdale, AZ   **2002 – present**
Southwest Regional Manager
- Transformed the struggling regional office from funding $12 to $60 million per month in one year
- Personally selected, trained, and mentored 20 employees
- Created an eight-member call center to call on brokers
- Manage 12 field reps for the western US, excluding California
- Present to groups up to 100 people on market trends and bank products
- Analyze, forecast, and develop revenue goals and strategic plans
- Establish and manage the budget for area of responsibility
- Conduct weekly one-on-ones with account executives to monitor pull-through and product mix
- Instrumental in office relocation to accommodate triple growth
- Travel monthly to focus areas—Seattle, Portland, Denver, and Phoenix
- Arrange and participate in trade shows
- Organize charity golf events and quarterly broker appreciation events
- Report directly to the senior vice president for wholesale lending
- Utilize Empower, Internet, MS Word, Excel, PowerPoint, and Outlook

HOME CAPITAL FUNDING, San Diego, CA   **2000 – 2002**
Sales Manager
- Sold through correspondent channels—instrumental in growth of business
- Achieved salesman of the month two times—a top producer
- Prepared and presented projections and pull-through reports to senior management
- Directed and managed junior loan officers and processors

EDUCATION

Masters in Business Administration   **2004**
University of Phoenix, AZ

Bachelor of Science in Business, Emphasis in Management   **2001**
University of Phoenix, AZ

PROFESSIONAL ORGANIZATIONS

- National Association of Mortgage Brokers (NAMB)
- Arizona Association of Mortgage Brokers (AAMB)
- Washington Association of Mortgage Brokers (WAMB)
- Oregon Association of Mortgage Brokers (OAMB)
- Colorado Association of Mortgage Brokers (CAMB)
- Colorado Mortgage Lenders Association (CMLA)
- Arizona Mortgage Lenders Association (AMLA)

Sara A. Swett

Home: (719) 555-1234
Cellular: (719) 555-5678

123 Mosca Pass Court, Colorado Springs, Colorado 80917   Email: sara.swett@protypeltd.com

PROFILE
- Well-organized Administrative Assistant with a strong desire to excel.
- Quick learner who enjoys working in a challenging, multi-tasking environment.
- Upbeat, courteous team player with strong communication and interpersonal skills.
- Self-motivated worker committed to working hard to get the job done on time.

EDUCATION

BACHELOR OF ARTS, PSYCHOLOGY (Spring 2005)
University of Colorado, Colorado Springs, Colorado
- **Psychology Course Work:** Psychology Research and Measurement, Psychology of Diversity, Philosophy, Social Psychology, Psychology and the Law, Psychology of Personality, Psychology and Health, Biopsychology, Human Sexuality, Developmental Psychology, Sociology, Abnormal Psychology, General Psychology
- **Communications Course Work:** Rhetoric and Writing, Public Speaking, Composition, Interpersonal Communication
- **Business Course Work:** Microeconomics, Introduction to Business, Ethics

EXPERIENCE

MEMORIAL HOSPITAL, Colorado Springs, Colorado (2001 – present)
Administrative Support III, Sleep Disorder Center (April 2003 – present)
- Provide administrative support to doctors and allied health professionals in the Sleep Disorders Clinic.
- Schedule patients for appointments, greet them upon arrival in the clinic and register them in the hospital computer system, and provide instruction for testing.
- Responsible for preauthorization processes, report preparation, and filing.
- Serve as the core trainer for computer software systems in the department.
- Answer telephones, return messages, and confirm appointments for the next work day.
- Process sleep study reports by accessing transcribed dictation, printing reports, matching information with the raw sleep study data, and distributing reports to physicians and medical records. Enter and track study data in the sleep database. Complete and audit patient charges.
- Ensure compliance with Medicare, JCAHO, American Academy of Sleep Medicine, and HIPAA regulations.
- Prepare patient charts for testing and ensure that the medical director performs all reviews prior to the beginning of the sleep study.
- Type and proofread policies, procedures, staff meeting agendas, memos, and meeting minutes.
- Maintain the physician professional fees spreadsheet, perform end-of-the month calculations, and send a receiving report to Finance to pay professional fees.
- Review and edit employee time cards and train staff in badge swiping and calendaring.
- Maintain and order the inventory of office and technician supplies, and keep the department's budget book and spreadsheet.

Key Accomplishments:
- Developed new forms and systems to make the department more efficient, including an administrative assistant handbook, patient reference book, performance improvement guides, and a new logo for the Sleep Center.
- Created the AVATAR Stars program, which extracted information from the patient satisfaction rating form, and formalized employee appreciation and review of negative comments.

EXPERIENCE

MEMORIAL HOSPITAL
Administrative Support III (continued)
- Received multiple Memorial Appreciation (MAP) Awards after being nominated by patients, family members, physicians, supervisors, and co-workers.
- Achieved 100% accuracy on patient charges.
- Reduced report turnaround for sleep studies from nine to seven days.
- Helped to develop a unique memo system for night shift communications.

Unit Clerk, Rehab Patient Care Unit (July 2001 – April 2003)
- Assisted the clinical manager and nursing staff in maintaining an organized, highly efficient nursing unit.
- Performed clerical and receptionist duties and ensured that bed utilization was maximized.
- Collaborated with other departments in delivering quality patient care.
- Answered the telephone courteously and promptly, and accurately transferred messages.
- Compiled new charts and maintained current ones, ensuring patient confidentiality.
- Maintained department records, TPR reports, census sheets, and other forms.
- Performed order entry for labs, dietary, radiology, respiratory, cardiopulmonary, and other requests.
- Entered unit-specific and patient charges; transcribed and transmitted doctor's orders.
- Requisitioned maintenance and service repairs, and maintained department supplies and equipment.

COLORADO SPRINGS STAR VIDEO, Colorado Springs, Colorado (1998 – 2001)
Manager, Sales Associate
- Helped to manage a private video store for its owners.
- Rented videos and accepted cash, checks, and credit cards.
- Provided exceptional customer service.

QUIZNO'S CLASSIC SUBS, Colorado Springs, Colorado (1997 – 1998)
Supervisor
- Assisted the manager with opening and closing the store, supervising a staff of four, and balancing the cash registers at the end of the day.
- Took customer orders, made sandwiches, cleaned the work space, and accepted money from customers.

CONTINUING EDUCATION

Memorial Hospital Training:
- Franklin Covey's Time Management (2004)
- Medical Terminology (2001)
- Unit Clerk Basics (2001)
- Healthcare Provider Basic Life Support (2001)
- Various computer applications training

COMPUTERS
- General Applications: MS Word, Excel, PowerPoint, Access, Lotus Notes
- Healthcare Applications: Patient Access Management System (PAMS), Pathway Healthcare Scheduling (PHS), Clinician View, Boise Internet Ordering, Hospital Information Services (HIS), Electronic Time Card (ETC), M-Net (Memorial's Intranet)

SARA ANNE STEELE

(719) 555.1234

ACADEMIC DEGREES

1997   **Master of Fine Art, Jewelry / Metalsmithing,** *UNIVERSITY OF WASHINGTON*, Seattle, WA
1994   **Bachelor of Fine Art, Metals / Jewelry,** *TEXAS TECH UNIVERSITY*, Lubbock, TX

TEACHING EXPERIENCE

Assistant Department Chair, *PUEBLO COMMUNITY COLLEGE, Pueblo, CO*   *Fall 2003*
Assisted in maintaining the art department, formulated class schedules, reviewed instructors, tabulated statistical information on individual programs.

Instructor, *PUEBLO COMMUNITY COLLEGE, Pueblo, CO*   *2000–2005*
Taught a wide variety of jewelry and metalsmithing classes emphasizing imagination, originality, and craftsmanship. Taught painting, 2-D and 3-D design, helping students to expand basic skills and broaden creativity. Formulated assignments based on approved curriculum, made grading decisions, offered input and encouragement, and facilitated group critiques. Instructed AVEP student. Taught and lectured in two sections of Art Appreciation, developed assignments, raised current art issues, and assigned team presentations on several art topics. Gave individual attention to each student.

- Spring 2004 / Jewelry Shop I and II, Jewelry Design I and II, Beginning and Advanced Stone Setting, Advanced Wax and Moldmaking
- Fall 2003 / Art Jewelry, Jewelry Shop I and II, Jewelry Design I and II, Beginning and Advanced Stone Setting, Advanced Wax and Moldmaking
- Summer 2003 / Jewelry Internship
- Spring 2003 / Jewelry Shop I and II, Jewelry Design I, Beginning Stone Setting, Advanced Wax and Moldmaking, Gemology
- Fall 2002 / Jewelry Shop I and II, Jewelry Design I, Beginning and Advanced Stone Setting, Advanced Wax and Moldmaking
- Summer 2002 / Gemology
- Spring 2002 / Jewelry Shop I and II, Jewelry Design I, Beginning and Advanced Stone Setting, 3-D Design
- Fall 2001 / Jewelry Shop I, Jewelry Design I and II, Advanced Wax and Moldmaking, Beginning Stone Setting
- Spring 2001 / Painting I and II, Watercolor I, Drawing I, Art Appreciation
- Fall 2000 / Painting I and II, 2-D and 3-D Design, Art Appreciation and Art Appreciation ACE

Teaching Assistant, *UNIVERSITY OF WASHINGTON, Seattle, WA*   *1996*
Taught basic skills in drawing and 3-D design, formulated assignments, made grading decisions, initiated group critiques and met individually for detailed input.

- Spring 1996 / Drawing II, Sections 122B, 122C
- Winter 1996 / 3-D Fundamentals, Sections 124B, 124C

OTHER RELEVANT EMPLOYMENT

Self-Employed, Sara Anne Steele, Artist   *2001–current*
Jewelry Sales and Repair, *SUTTON HOO, Colorado Springs, CO*   *2000*

8080 Alturas Dr. **Colorado Springs, CO 80911** ⬤ *sasteele@protypeltd.com*

EXHIBITIONS

2004   **Steel City.** Sangre De Cristo Arts Center, Pueblo, CO. June – August 2004. Group Show.

2002   **Better Than Nude.** Business of Art Center, Colorado Springs, CO. December 1 – 30, 2002. Group Show.

2000   **Pikes Peak Community College Faculty Art Show.** Downtown Studio Campus Gallery, Colorado Springs, CO. September 8 – October 13, 2000. Group Show.

1999   **Carapace.** Project 416, Seattle, WA. May 6 – 31, 1999. Group Show.

1998   **Encasements, Out of Body Experiences, and Affordable Comforts.** UMC Art Gallery, Boulder, CO. April 6 – May 15, 1998. Group Show.

       Kink: A Woman's Perspective. Leather Archives and Museum, Chicago, IL. August 9 – September 30, 1998. Group Show.

       SOIL. SOIL Art Gallery, Seattle, WA. July 2 – August 14, 1998. Group Show.

1997   **New Works by New Members.** *SOIL Art Gallery*, Seattle, WA. November 6 – 30, 1997. Group Show.

       Ephemeral Trappings. *Metropolis Contemporary Art Gallery*, Seattle, WA. July 3 – 25, 1997. Group Show.

       4th Annual Erotic Art Show. *Metropolis Contemporary Art Gallery*, Seattle, WA. June 5 – 27, 1997. *Invitational*.

       Killing Shame. *Henry Art Gallery*, University of Washington, Seattle, WA. May 24 – June 15, 1997. Graduate Show.

AWARDS AND HONORS

- March Scholarship, 1996, $500
- Gonzales Scholarship, 1995, $1000
- Teaching Assistantship, University of Washington, 1995, $18,000
- Acceptance into Contemporaries Competition, 1994
- Honorable Mention, Student Sterling Competition, 1994, $260

PROFESSIONAL AFFILIATIONS

- Club Sponsor, Jewelers Edge, 2003
- Member, Society of North American Goldsmiths, 2002–present
- Member, Colorado Metalsmithing Association, 2002–present
- Member, SOIL Artist's Cooperative, 1997–1998

LECTURES

1997   **Fetishism and Sadomasochism in Art.** University of Washington, Winter Quarter

SALLY SIMMONS TAFT

26 Benmore Terrace
Bayonne, NJ 07002

(201) 123-4567
sstaft@protypeltd.com

Strategic HR Business Partner
Start Ups ▪ High Growth ▪ Union/Non-Union Environments ▪ Profit and NonProfit
MA, Industrial/Organizational Psychology ▪ SPHR

- *11+ years of experience managing human capital initiatives that support company strategic plans/vision.*
- *Organizational development specialist with expertise in change management, team building, performance planning, individual coaching, and counseling.*
- *Innovative generalist with success building HR infrastructures and introducing company-wide total rewards, recruiting, and employee relations programs.*
- *Adjunct professor and mentor for the SHRM PHR and SPHR certification programs.*

CORE COMPETENCIES

Recruitment/Retention
Employee Referrals
Job-Posting
Campus Recruiting
Background Checks
Employee Recognition Service
Awards

Compensation
Competitive Benchmarking
Pay for Performance Job
Descriptions
Spot Rewards

Benefits
Vendor Selection
Open Enrollment
Plan Administration
Plan Descriptions
401K Implementation
Transit Check

Development
Performance Reviews
Career Pathing
Tuition Reimbursement
Interview Training
New Hire Orientation

PROFESSIONAL EXPERIENCE

NATIONAL INSTITUTE ON DRUG ABUSE (NIDA), New York, NY   2000 – 2004
Director of Human Resources—*Launched HR function within this growing $14 million agency. Member of senior management team reporting directly to EVP. Supported client group of 200 in six locations, directed staff of four, and managed a $2.5 million budget.*

Cost Savings
- Trimmed recruiting expenses by $80,000+ over a one-year period by cutting advertising budget and implementing an employee referral and job-posting program.
- Virtually eliminated workers' compensation claims by introducing a workplace safety program.

Productivity Gains
- Revamped the performance appraisal process and transitioned to a merit-based compensation strategy, realizing a 30 percent shift in productivity.
- Restructured workflow by dividing employees into nine teams with a dedicated supervisor, allowing agency to service 81 more clients per day.

Process Improvement
- Slashed turnover in a 200-person agency by 28 percent by realigning recruiting and compensation strategies.
- Spearheaded a career progression program that complemented the annual appraisal and contributed to an increase in internal promotions and retention statistics.
- Successfully averted an attempt to unionize by conducting 200 one-on-one employee interviews to address employee relations issues.
- Boosted department funding by 15 percent by offering team incentives for successfully retaining clients in treatment and placing them in competitive employment.

NEW YORK INSTITUTE OF TECHNOLOGY, New York, NY   2002 – present
Adjunct Professor, Society for Human Resource Management (SHRM) Certification Program—*Provide HR professionals and line managers with an overview of human resources management. Prepare students seeking accreditation as a Professional in Human Resources (PHR) or Senior Professional in Human Resources (SPHR).*

CORE COMPETENCIES

Labor Relations
Union Environments
Collective Bargaining
Agreements, (CBA)
Grievance Procedures
Civil Service Hearings

Policy Writing, Training, and Compliance
Affirmative Action, Anti/Sexual Harassment, EEOC, ADA, FMLA, OSHA, ERISA, HIPPA Safe Harbor Act, Workforce Safety and Ergonomics, Drug Testing, Workers' Compensation

Employee Relations
Employee Handbook
Corrective Action
Adverse Impact
Outplacement
Exit Interviews

PROFESSIONAL AFFILIATIONS

Board Member, HRO Today, 2003 – present

Chair, HRO Today Newsletter Committee, 2003 – present

Editor, Inside HRO Today, 2003 – present

Co-Chair, HRO Today Public Relations Committee, 2003 – 2004

Member, Society for Human Resource Management (SHRM)

Member, American Society of Training and Development (ASTD)

Member, Association for Not-for-Profits

- Teach two fundamental human resources management courses and two national certification exam courses to 115 students each year.

McMILLIAN MEDICAL HOME, Hoboken, NJ   1997
Consultant *for this three-month assignment to develop position descriptions, evaluations, and compensation programs to attract, retain, and reward medical home personnel.*

- Challenged previous union-dominated grievance procedures and replaced with proactive corrective action plans that detailed employee accountability and empowered the supervisory team.
- Significantly reduced tardiness and absenteeism and increased productivity among certified nurse's aides by offering a competitive nursing scholarship and subsequent placement within the organization to the top two performers.

SOMERSET COUNTY PERSONNEL DEPARTMENT, Franklin, NJ   1993 – 1996
HR Representative *for this government agency. Tasked with recruiting for all open positions in 3,500-employee union and non-union environment. Supervised staff of two.*

- Liaised with 12 unions and their attorneys and shop stewards. Participated in 15 civil service hearings. Represented agency in eight negotiations for CBA renewal.
- Debuted first supervisory training program in the agency's history.

LEHMAN BROTHERS, INC., New York, NY   1986 – 1993
Employment Representative *charged with coaching employees and team of 30 managers in the technology division on employee relations and policy issues. Hired, trained and supervised staff of two.*

- Recruited for 500 exempt /non-exempt positions during period of explosive growth. Pioneered division's job-posting program, reducing agency fees by 20 percent. Renegotiated agency contracts, resulting in a $75,000 annual savings.
- Counseled 90 employees on outplacement and severance packages during corporate restructuring; prepared adverse impact analysis.

EDUCATION / CERTIFICATIONS

Certificate, Senior Professional Human Resource Management, SHRM	**2002**
MA, Industrial/Organizational Psychology, New York University, New York, NY	**2000**
BA, Psychology, Rutgers University, Camden NJ, Summa Cum Laude	**1998**

COMPUTER SKILLS

Microsoft Word, Excel, PowerPoint, Peoplesoft

José J. "Jimmy" Martinez

CONTACT

Address: 1234 Riverview Lane, Colorado Springs, Colorado 80916
Phone: (719) 555-1234 • **Email:** martinez705@protype.com

SUMMARY

- Experienced manager with a proven track record in:
  - Administration
  - Human resource management
  - Training and development
  - Motivation
  - Policy and procedures development
  - International relations
- Solid reputation of high core values, integrity, and strong work ethic.
- Effective team player with excellent communication and interpersonal skills.
- Proven track record of leading in culturally diverse settings. Fluent in English and Spanish. Knowledge of German.

EDUCATION

MASTER OF SCIENCE, INTERNATIONAL RELATIONS (1993)
Troy State University, European Division, Troy, Alabama

BACHELOR OF SCIENCE, MANAGEMENT (1988)
University of Maryland, European Division, College Park, Maryland

ASSOCIATE OF SCIENCE, AEROSPACE CONTROL AND WARNING SYSTEMS (1986)
Community College of the Air Force, Maxwell AFB, Alabama

EXPERIENCE

MANAGEMENT/ADMINISTRATION

- As one of four Air Warning Center Crew Chiefs, aggressively coordinated and evaluated high volumes of time-critical information during the highest defense condition the North America Air Defense Command had experienced in more than 30 years following the September 11th attacks. Prevented further destruction of national infrastructure and loss of life.
- Mentored and managed more than 25 binational personnel in support of the NORAD mission. Responsible for personnel administration, morale, welfare, and professional development.
- Selected to manage the day-to-day security of the Sensitive Compartmented Information Facility. Responsible for ensuring controlled access to Top Secret/SCI information.
- Compiled data for briefing senior management to accurately reflect the disposition of organization assets.
- Served as an expert resource for issues relating to equal employment opportunity and affirmative action programs.
- Completed college course work in speech/communications, advertising, business management, motivation and performance organization, managerial leadership, labor relations, consumer fraud, marketing, promotion management, organizational behavior, women in advertising, accounting, cost accounting, taxes, business finance, business law, organizational theory, and retail management.

INTERNATIONAL

- Recognized by the National Image, Inc., with the 1997 Meritorious Service Award for contributions to the increase in opportunities for Hispanics in the military and the community in the areas of civil rights, education, and employment.
- Completed a graduate degree in international relations, including course work in political geography, survey of international relations, geostrategic studies, international organization, international economics, international political analysis, theories of international relations, government and politics of the Third World, Latin America in world affairs, international business management, international marketing, research methods in international relations, and international terrorism.

EXPERIENCE

INTERNATIONAL (continued)

- Escorted 11 American cadets to the International Air Cadet Exchange in Canada in 2001 and 14 cadets to Germany in 1996.
- Served as a liaison between the Venezuelan Air Force and U.S. military forces. Hand-picked to lay the groundwork for future operations in Venezuela by setting up transportation, billeting, and refueling operations for U.S. Customs Service aircraft and personnel.
- Supported counter-narcotics detection/monitoring missions and sensitive reconnaissance operations in the Caribbean Regional Operations Center for four years. Served as a Spanish linguist/translator and overcame the language barrier by effectively coordinating letters of agreement with the Puerto Rican Air National Guard.
- Hosted Peruvian mission representatives and coordinated operations briefings. Provided expert advice to Peru's endeavor to enhance military operational procedures.
- Coordinated battle information for the Seventh Air Force in Osan, Republic of Korea.
- Commended for services rendered to the American Red Cross during the Cuban refugee crisis in 1995, including translation and delivery of messages to and from families and refugees.
- Served as a radio and telecommunications operations watch officer in Bogota, Colombia.
- Served as a Master Tracker and Master Tracker Technician in Saudi Arabia. Responsible for managing surveillance data received from the message processing center during periods of high threat.

TRAINING/INSTRUCTION

- Managed academic training, proficiency training, and exercise programs for the Cheyenne Mountain Operations Air Warning Center personnel. Created and distributed monthly recurring training lesson plans and packages. Directed course and curriculum development.
- Supervised all simulated battle management exercises and ensured the proficiency of all weapons simulation technicians conducting training exercises for international officers.
- Assisted the flight commander in leading 14 personnel in the execution of two international weapons controller training courses.
- Selected to train newly assigned personnel because of a history of quality training and the highest quality proficiency standards.
- Administered the Air Defense Notification Center's qualifications and continuation training programs for five years at the International Airport in Frankfurt, Germany. Developed, updated, and administered monthly academic examinations. Administered monthly academic examinations. Evaluated trend analysis data for training program improvements.

TECHNICAL

- Supervised the detection and identification of aircraft. Operated the air defense warning network for short-range air defense and ground defense forces. Monitored and operated the air defense integrator system and message networks for critical operations information.
- Managed the maintenance of a precise radar surveillance picture, integrating nine fixed ground-based radars, five Aerostat radars, two over-the-horizon backscatter radars, and participating airborne and shipborne radars covering more than 2.6 million miles of Caribbean airspace.

HISTORY

UNITED STATES AIR FORCE, MASTER SERGEANT (1980 – present)
Manager, Air Warning Center Training, Cheyenne Mountain AB, Colorado
Air Warning Center Crew Chief/Crew Superintendent, Cheyenne Mountain AB, Colorado
Flight Superintendent, International Training Course, Tyndall AFB, Florida
Battle Director Technician, Osan, Korea
Mission Crew Commander Technician, Tyndall AFB, Florida
Joint Surveillance Supervisor/Operator, Key West, Florida
Unit Training Officer, Rhein Main, Germany
Air Defense Notification Center Technician, Rhein Main, Germany
Identification Officer Clerk, Neubrucke AIN, Germany
Unit Surveillance Scope Operator, Eglin AFB, Florida

Todd Williams

123 Scott Boulevard #103 ▪ Castle Rock, Colorado 80104
Home Phone: (303) 555-1234 ▪ Cellular: (719) 555-5678

E-mail: toddw@protypeltd.com

SUMMARY

- Goal-oriented worker with a proven track record of exceeding goals.
- Self-motivated and assertive top performer who sets objectives and achieves them.
- Effective team leader with strong communication and interpersonal skills.
- Proficient in Windows, MS Word, Excel, Outlook, e-mail, and Netscape.

EXPERIENCE

SELF-EMPLOYED MORTGAGE NOTARY, Denver, Colorado, 2003 – present
- Provide mobile signing services for various national notary companies as an independent contractor.
- Facilitate loan closings by reviewing documents with borrowers, ensuring they are signed and returned to the title company in a timely manner.
- Sustained continued business growth by establishing a strong network of clients through direct solicitation.

THE MOVING WORLD, Denver, Colorado
Sales Ambassador, 2002
- Called on prospective customers and generated quotes for moves through Allied and other major van lines.
- Responded to warm leads from online inquiries, estimated moving costs, and closed the sale.
- Built rapport with clients, identified needs, and educated them on available services.
- Led sales staff in booked revenue for the month of September with more than $30,000.

WELLS FARGO HOME EQUITY (Formerly Norwest Direct), Colorado Springs, Colorado
Mortgage Consultant II, 2000 – 2001; **Mortgage Consultant I**, 1999 – 2000
- Sold home equity loans and lines of credit via outbound sales calls.
- Assisted customers in determining financial needs and recommended appropriate credit solutions.
- Analyzed customer financial information, made quality credit decisions, processed loans, and advised customers of approval or denial.
- Selected for the 2000 Leader's Club Award for achieving 150% of goal; received an all-expenses paid trip to the Miami sales conference.
- Led the channel in total sales and funding for seventeen months.
- Set a record as the first outbound sales representative to fund $4.37 million in one month (423% of quota).
- First outbound sales representative to fund more than 100 loans/lines in a single month.

COMMNET CELLULAR, Englewood, Colorado
Supervisor of Customer Loyalty (Retention), 1998
Supervisor of Credit and Collections, 1997 – 1998
- Served as primary point of contact for field personnel on complex customer issues.
- Responded to escalated customer calls; made counteroffers to retain business in a highly competitive market.
- Identified areas of process improvement to enhance the overall quality of customer service.
- Hired, trained, and supervised 51 personnel; provided employee performance evaluation and feedback.
- Managed the computer-based Mosaix predictive autodialer system.

Inside Sales Representative, 1997
- Led staff in revenue-generating sales campaigns through aggressive solicitation of existing customers.

Collection Analyst, 1995 – 1997
- Identified, researched, and resolved customer billing issues to minimize churn.
- Ensured timely follow-up with customers to maximize total dollars collected and to reduce write-offs.
- Suspended/disconnected service and made recommendations to management for account write-offs when payment resolution efforts failed.

EDUCATION

BACHELOR OF ARTS, PSYCHOLOGY (*cum laude*)
University of Colorado, Colorado Springs (1993)

Lisa I. Calisto

PROFILE

- Self-motivated sales professional with more than fifteen years of proven experience.
- Top performer with a strong background in building new territories and using creative marketing approaches.
- Respected for the ability to get to the decision maker and close the sale.
- Demonstrated ability to create client loyalty beyond the sales relationship.
- Entrepreneurial thinker who works well independently or as part of a team.

EXPERIENCE

SALES REPRESENTATIVE, Waxie Sanitary Supply, Denver, Colorado (2000 – present)
- Sell paper products, chemicals, equipment, and cleaning supplies to large corporate clients, including The Pepsi Center, Coors Field, Invesco, Coors Brewery, casinos, hospital, and various other market segments.
- Formulated a two-year strategic sales plan for territory growth and built the territory from zero to $1.2 million.
- Create and conduct onsite training programs for end users focusing on the safe use of chemicals and equipment.
- Make sales presentations to upper-level management based on comprehensive needs analyses.

SALES REPRESENTATIVE, Unisource, Denver, Colorado (1992 – 2000)
- Sold paper products, chemicals, and cleaning supplies to large corporate and government clients, including hospitals, hotels, casinos, City of Denver, and Coors.
- Formulated a strategic plan for the territory and grew the account base by 350% through effective cold calling and account development.
- Created and conducted sales presentations to upper-level management, assessed their needs, and developed unique customer applications.
- Successfully regained former customers through effective marketing and follow-up.
- Designed and executed training programs for key clients.
- Achieved the President's Club through exceptional sales performance; ranked the number one salesperson in the Denver metropolitan territory.

SALES REPRESENTATIVE, Moore Business Forms, Denver, Colorado (1988 – 1990)
- Sold customized business forms to companies in the Denver territory.
- Increased sales to existing customers and developed the territory by 178%.
- Designed special forms to fit proprietary computer systems.
- Created a forms management program for the Poudre Valley Hospital.

SALES REPRESENTATIVE, Pitney Bowes, Denver, Colorado (1985 – 1988)
- Developed markets for Pitney Bowes copiers throughout 20 zip codes in the Denver metropolitan area.
- Consistently exceeded production quotas by as much as 250%, producing nearly half a million dollars a year in sales.
- Honored as one of the top five Pitney Bowes salespeople in the state of Colorado.

EDUCATION

BACHELOR OF ARTS IN BUSINESS MARKETING
Colorado State University, Fort Collins, Colorado

CONTINUING EDUCATION
- Ongoing sales and motivation training, Dale Carnegie course
- Hazardous materials, OSHA, material safety data, and SARA regulatory training

1234 Grand Cypress Lane • Lone Tree, Colorado 80124
Phone: (303) 555-1234 • Cellular: (303) 555-5678 • E-mail: lisor@protypeltd.com

Kathie R. Dodd

1234 East Shady Lane • Highlands Ranch, Colorado 80126

Home: (303) 555-1234 • Cell: (303) 555-5678

PROFILE
- Experienced manager with the ability to motivate others to excel.
- Well-organized worker who is adept at managing multiple tasks simultaneously.
- Proven public speaker with experience in providing on-the-job and classroom training.
- Effective team player with strong interpersonal and communication skills.

EDUCATION

MASTER OF BUSINESS ADMINISTRATION (December 2004)
University of Colorado, Denver, Colorado

BACHELOR OF ARTS IN HUMAN RESOURCE MANAGEMENT (2002)
Colorado Christian University, Colorado Springs, Colorado

EXPERIENCE

QWEST COMMUNICATIONS (2000 – present)
Data Services Planner and Engineer, Denver, Colorado
- Supervise field engineers in the design of DSL networks, expedite procurement of materials, and ensure that projects are completed on time and within budget.
- Manage the installation and testing of DSL networks, overseeing five technicians per project and supervise quality auditors to ensure that projects met OSHA guidelines.
- Coordinate subtending systems to permit proper communication of installed systems.
- Engineer and order materials for new technology projects. Constantly study new technologies to ensure that products meet customer needs and are properly installed.
- Collaborate with the Vice President and Director to plan for the retirement of equipment to protect tax credits.
- Work with marketing to forecast network usage to meet customer needs.
- Collaborate with data services, outside plant, real estate, and city planning departments.

Achievements:
- Succeeded in preventing power embargoes by constantly monitoring DC plant loads in the power inventory database and communicating with power technicians.
- Minimized rework and escalations by accurately defining customer requirements and providing effective solutions within tight deadlines.
- Saved nearly $200,000 in 2002 by utilizing excess material inventory on 90% of all jobs.
- Selected to help develop a business plan to determine whether Rocky Mountain Propane should acquire a propane company to serve the Denver metro market or enter the market as a new competitor.
- Singled out to assist the Vice President in finding ways to improve performance and budgeting in order to prevent layoffs.
- Served as part of a three-person team responsible for performing a structural analysis of the corporation and developing solutions to present to senior management.
- Collaborated with all layers of management in the development of the 2003 business model.

Tactical Planning Engineer, Denver, Colorado
- Provided space/power planning and engineering services valued at $1.5 million for 89 central offices in Southern Colorado.
- Planned new facilities to ensure adequate capacity for future growth. Worked with planning commissions to ensure that new facilities met the needs of the community without lowering property values.
- Responsible for every installation, removal, and upgrade in each central office, including environmental notifications and disposal of hazardous materials.
- Designed and supervised the construction of 44 buildings for QWEST, working closely with vendors, architects, and maintenance workers to ensure completion deadline and contract specifications were met.
- Managed a yearly budget of $10 million for direct needs and $600 million for section needs.
- Evaluated forecasts/job orders and designed the placement of equipment, DC power plants, switches, HVAC, and AC for fiber optic, digital, and analog data/voice services.

EXPERIENCE

Technical Planning Engineer (continued)
- Identified and corrected problems with human and equipment needs during construction.
- Reviewed quotes from vendors, authorized their hire, and defended proposals to senior management for power plant upgrades and replacements.
- Represented the projects to community organizations and answered questions regarding growth, hazardous materials, and economic development, serving as the company's representative to the public and ensuring goodwill.
- Organized regular meetings between divisions and facilitated the achievement of a single goal.
- Consulted with the legal department to validate co-location charges for a 14-state region by creating a usage percentage report.

UNITED STATES AIR FORCE, ACTIVE DUTY (1995 – 1998)
Administrative Assistant to the Squadron Commander, Hurlburt Field, Florida
Inspection Team Member and Phase Coordinator, Hurlburt Field, Florida
Helicopter Crew Chief, Kirtland AFB, New Mexico
- Scheduled and conducted meetings for the purchase and sale of helicopters valued at $30 million.
- Accountable for repair and maintenance budgets of up to $5 million.
- Justified expenses and ensured adequate profit margins on each project.
- Managed project scheduling, quality control, and customer satisfaction.
- Reviewed maintenance data, evaluated trends and production effectiveness, and identified areas requiring corrective action.
- Monitored the accuracy of 900 documented discrepancy reports with an error rate 5% below goal.
- Served as the personal assistant to the squadron commander in addition to a special assignment as vice president of the Unit Advisory Council.
- Coordinated the processing of 700 squadron personnel and maintained personnel files.
- Developed a spreadsheet for tracking personnel on temporary duty.
- Notified personnel of drug tests and handled routine human resource duties.
- Made recommendations for performance evaluations.
- Managed letters of recommendation/appreciation, awards, and commendations.
Achievements:
- Consistently selected to perform noncommissioned-officer-level duties while only a senior airman.
- Discovered and corrected a deficiency in the main transmission preparation procedures, avoiding personnel injury and equipment damage and earning a suggestion award from the Air Force.
- Frequently commended for detecting damaged aircraft parts and systems, which prevented significant loss of life and critical aircraft assets.

AFFILIATIONS
- Served as a member of Qwest Women, Women's Vision, Women's Chamber of Commerce, Pinnacle Club, and Denver Telecom Professionals.
- Volunteered to conduct a market analysis for a local nonprofit organization to determine the current state of the real estate market.
- Volunteered to provide coats for a homeless shelter.

COMPUTERS   Proficient in Windows, MS Word, Excel, PowerPoint, Access, databases, LAN ordering, and research.

VANESSA L. DAVIS

PROFILE

- Self-motivated computer professional with a background in help desk support, systems analysis, technical troubleshooting, and logistics.
- Proven leader with more than fifteen years of supervisory and management experience.
- Quick learner who adapts easily to new situations and enjoys solving challenging problems.
- Loyal, responsible worker with the proven ability to thrive under pressure.
- Currently hold a DoD Secret security clearance.

TECHNOLOGY

Certifications: A+ Certification (July 2002), Network Plus Certification (July 2002), actively pursuing Microsoft Certified Systems Engineer (MCSE) certification (December 2002).

Networks: Windows NT, Windows 2000, Networking Essentials. Experienced in creating accounts, developing account policies, implementing user rights, installing and configuring network printers, providing application support, installing and configuring network protocols, managing clients, and performing Internet downloads and upgrades.

Operating Systems: Windows 95/98/ME/NT/XP/2000 installation, configuration, and navigation. Experienced in Windows customization, troubleshooting software faults using diagnostic utilities (MSD, Norton Symantec products, MMC Snap-ins, etc.), data communications, application installations and support, basic operating systems and concepts, file manager, and print manager.

Programming Languages: C++, JAVA, HTML.

Applications: MS Word, Excel, Access, PowerPoint, FrontPage, Adobe.

Hardware: Experienced in the installation, troubleshooting, upgrade, and repair of hard drives, floppy disk drives, CD-ROM drives, power supplies, CPUs, sound cards, video cards, RAM, printers, and monitors.

EDUCATION

BACHELOR OF SCIENCE, INFORMATION TECHNOLOGY (December 2003)
Colorado Technical University, Colorado Springs, Colorado
Relevant Course Work Completed: Introduction to Problem Solving C++, Fundamentals of Web Publishing, Introduction to Data Processing, Introduction to JAVA, Spreadsheet Applications, PC Maintenance, Networking Essentials Plus

COMPUTER TRAINING (1999 – 2000)
New Horizons Technical School, Colorado Springs, Colorado
Relevant Course Work Completed: A+ Certification, Microsoft Networking Essentials, TCP/IP, Introduction to Windows NT 4.0 Core

EXPERIENCE

HELP DESK SUPERVISOR (2002 – present)
Lockheed Martin (LMIT), Cheyenne Mountain AB, Colorado
- Served as the focal point for help desk support, remote and on-site fixes, and internal customer service for the LMIT contract with NORAD inside Cheyenne Mountain.
- Interviewed, made hiring recommendations, and supervised 11 help desk technicians.
- Utilized strong communication skills to get to the root of a user's difficulties and then provided timely repair, minimizing the organization's downtime and loss of productivity.
- Responsible for troubleshooting and configuring software and hardware.
- Accurately diagnosed complex technical problems and provided effective solutions.

1234 Westmeadow Drive #101 • Colorado Springs, Colorado 80906
Phone: (719) 555-1234 • Email: HawaiianS0ul@protypeltd.com

EXPERIENCE
(continued)

SYSTEM ANALYST I (2001 – 2002)
OAO Corporation, Cheyenne Mountain AB, Colorado
- Analyzed new Windows NT and 2000 computer networks within Cheyenne Mountain.
- Installed software, hardware, and peripherals.
- Set up email profiles and maintained file servers, backups, permissions, and security.
- Monitored the network for security breaches and fixed problems to minimize downtime.

AUTOMATED MANAGEMENT OFFICE SUPERVISOR (1999 – 2001)
United States Army, Fort Carson, Colorado, Bosnia
- Completed a successful career as an Army noncommissioned officer responsible for implementing logistics automated management information systems.
- Created policies and procedures for system users and supervised 7 technicians.
- Troubleshot, maintained, and repaired more than 1,200 computer systems.
- Trained personnel on the property book computer, including the conversion of the tactical computer system to desktop computers.
- Managed the automation office in Bosnia, including maintenance and repair of PCs in Tazar, Hungary, and Sarajevo as well as installation of hardware, software, and operating systems.

LOGISTICS MANAGER (1981 – 1999)
United States Army, Korea, Fort Rucker, Alabama, Germany, Fort Carson, Colorado, Fort Jackson, South Carolina
- Managed the operations of six supply rooms with 100% accountability for more than $250 million of inventory.
- Provided logistical support for daily squadron operations and special exercises.
- Conducted quarterly and semiannual inspections and monthly inventories of all squadron supply rooms.
- Wrote standard operating procedures and managed the monthly training programs.
- Requisitioned, received, and shipped supplies, ammunition, and other inventory items.
- Managed the fielding of new equipment entering the Army inventory.
- Maintained the battalion ammunition supply point for a unit deployed to the Persian Gulf, consisting of small arms, explosives, and demolition materiel. Transported food, fuel, ammunition, and mail to the units based in Iraq.
- Negotiated and managed a new laundry service contract.
- Received a Humanitarian Service Medal for rescue efforts during the 1990 Alabama flood.

MILITARY
TRAINING
- Accounting for Property, Parts I and II (1993)
- Alcohol/Drug Coordinator Course (1993)
- Logistics Management Development, Logistics Management College (1992)
- Supply Specialist Training Army Quartermaster NCO Academy (3 months, 1989 – 1990)
- Armorer Course (40 hours, 1989)
- Organizational Supply Procedures Course (6 weeks, 1985)
- Primary Leadership Course, NCO Academy (1 month, 1983)
- Financial Management Information System Course (8 hours, 1982)
- Unit Supplyman, Central Texas College (3 weeks, 1982)

DAVID F. KELLER

PROFILE
- Goal-oriented construction and marketing professional with successful experience in:
  - ‣ Sales management
  - ‣ Customer relations
  - ‣ Account management
  - ‣ Employee motivation
  - ‣ Sales training
  - ‣ Team building
  - ‣ Residential construction
  - ‣ Building design
  - ‣ Bids/estimating
- Demonstrated ability to create client loyalty above and beyond the sales relationship.
- Strong background in building territories through consultative selling.
- Bring a unique combination of experience, energy, and charisma to the job.
- Self-motivated and focused; comfortable working independently in competitive environments.
- Colorado Class C construction license; Colorado dwellings up to six flats.

EXPERIENCE

Construction
- Owned and managed a company specializing in the construction of luxury ($500,000+) homes.
- Coordinated budget, financing, building design, site selection, subcontractors, and sales.
- Supervised residential and commercial construction projects from bid through final walk-through.
- Hands-on carpentry, remodeling, and construction experience, including foundations, framing, roofing, plumbing, electrical, drywall, painting, cabinetry, and interior trim.
- Evaluated blueprints and schematics; ensured compliance with regulations and specifications.
- Consulted with clients regarding design modifications and change orders; ensured customer satisfaction throughout the project life cycle.

Management and Supervision
- Accountable for long-range planning, profit and loss, controlling costs, invoicing, recordkeeping, collecting accounts receivable, and monitoring financial performance.
- Evaluated bids from contractors, ensured the quality of their work, and resolved problems.
- Constantly evaluated margins to ensure profitability at project completion.
- Effectively managed large territories that included much of the United States at various times.
- Served as Regional Sales Manager for an international bio-technology company with regional gross sales of $16 million and a staff of 14 sales people.
- Successfully recruited, hired, trained, and motivated sales staff.
- Proven ability to develop loyalty and team cohesiveness among employees.

Training and Development
- Developed and presented high-energy, informative training sessions, including seminars on professionalism, motivation, penetrating new markets, managing sales to high security accounts, general sales techniques, and increasing sales growth by outclassing the competition.
- Mentored 32 new sales staff and prepared 13 for promotion into sales management positions.

Sales and Marketing
- Experienced in the sale of homes, chemicals, equipment, and instrumentation.
- Identified customer needs and recommended the right solutions.
- Developed and delivered effective sales presentations to prospective clients.
- Served as a liaison between technical support staff and the client to ensure satisfaction.
- Consistently exceeded sales goals and generated significant annual gross revenues.
- Grew Bio-Rad territories by 25% to 40% every year; ranked the number one sales manager in the U.S.

WORK HISTORY
Owner/Manager, Custom Classics, Inc., Berkshire Homes, Colorado Springs, CO (1991 – present)
Regional Sales Manager, Bio-Rad Laboratories, Hercules, CA (1981 – 1994)
Technical Representative, Bio-Rad Laboratories, Hercules, CA (1975 – 1981)

EDUCATION
Bachelor of Science in Education and Biological Sciences, Boston University, Boston, MA
- Honored with the Distinguished Senior Award

Continuing Education
- Tom Hopkins Boot Camp, Systems on Consultative Selling, Mercury International Selling Seminar, Anthony Robbins on Unlimited Power, and other sales, training, and marketing seminars

ADDRESS
123 Bancroft Heights, Colorado Springs, CO 80906, Home: (719) 555-1234, Cellular: (719) 555-5678

6 Headings to Define the Sections

Headings are one of the major design elements of a résumé. How you choose to divide sections determines the readability of your résumé. Graphic lines and/or white space help define groups of similar information and draw the reader's eyes down the page.

One of the keys to a readable résumé is the judicious use of white space, and consistent spacing in critical. You will notice throughout the samples in this book that more white space is used between major sections than within sections. This breaks the résumé into easily digested chunks of information. The white space between these sections should be identical throughout the résumé. Likewise, the smaller white space within sections should be the same throughout.

There are two basic positions for your headings. One is centered (pages 99, 104, 105, 107, 109, 111, and 112) with or without lines, and the other is left justified (pages 100–103, 106, 108, and 110). Which style you choose depends on what you find pleasing to your eye. There is no right or wrong way. If you like the design, then it is a good fit with your personality. Some of your options include:

- All caps (pages 99, 102, 104, 105, 109, 111, 112)
- First letter larger (pages 100, 101, 108)
- Upper/lower case (pages 103, 107, 110)
- All lower case (page 106)
- Very large fonts (pages 107, 110)
- Designer fonts (page 110)
- Graphic lines with all capital letters (pages 104 and 112)
- Reverse boxes with white lettering (page 111)

Since people read from the top to the bottom and from left to right, begin your résumé with the most important information. Then work your way down to less important information. The top half of your résumé's first page should be packed with your strongest qualifications.

So, which section goes first? Should it be education or experience? Start with the section that contains your strongest qualifications for your target job. If you have had little experience in your prospective field but have a degree that qualifies you for a starting position in the industry, then by all means list your education first. Most people eventually move their education below their experience as they get further from their school days. If you change your career and go back to school, then the education will move to the top again and begin to gravitate to the bottom as you gain relevant experience.

The same idea goes for information within each section. For instance, if you went to an Ivy League school, you can list the school before the degree. Look at the difference in emphasis between these two methods:

HARVARD, Cambridge, Massachusetts
Master of Business Administration

MASTER OF BUSINESS ADMINISTRATION
Little Known College, Backwoods, Idaho

The same principle applies to your experience. If your job title is more impressive than where you worked, then list it first.

VICE PRESIDENT OF MARKETING
Little Known Company, Boulder, Colorado

IBM CORPORATION, Boulder, Colorado
Assistant Export Coordinator

Avoid the use of underlining since it cuts into the descenders in lower case letters. For example, notice the "p" in:

Assistant Export Coordinator

It is acceptable to use underlining when the letters are all capitalized since there are no descenders, but it is a bit of overkill in most cases:

ASSISTANT EXPORT COORDINATOR

Italics, **bold**, ALL CAPITALS, First Letter Larger, or any combination of the four are all good ways to make certain information stand out within the text. However, these styles can be overdone very easily. To make them more effective, use these type treatments sparingly.

JANE A. LAMME

Home: (719) 555-1234 • Cellular: (719) 555-5678 • E-mail: JanieLamme@protypeltd.com
1809 Pejn Avenue • Colorado Springs, Colorado 80904

QUALIFICATIONS
- Results-oriented sales and marketing professional with 20 years of experience.
- Highly motivated to surpass sales quotas and attain marketing objectives.
- Proven ability to generate new leads and substantially increase sales.
- Skilled at developing long-term relationships with clients, generating loyalty above and beyond the sales relationship.
- Enthusiastic, creative team player with strong problem solving and organization skills.

EXPERIENCE

VICE PRESIDENT OF SALES

Samurai Office Supply, Inc., Colorado Springs, Colorado (2003 – present)
- Market office supplies (40,000 items) to government contractors, healthcare providers, large corporations, and small businesses in a very competitive market.
- Cold called on buyers and developed long-term relationships that resulted in repeat business.
- Effectively managed a territory that included all of Colorado as well as national accounts.
- Develop successful print advertising campaigns to reach niche markets.
- Designed sales tools and created weekly specials to send by fax to existing customers.
- Increased annual revenue 100% by bringing in an average of five new accounts per month.

ACCOUNT EXECUTIVE

The Colorado Springs Business Journal, Colorado Springs, Colorado (2001 – 2003)
- Successfully sold advertising for two weekly newspapers that were considered the authority on local business news in Colorado Springs and Pueblo.
- Developed new corporate and small business accounts through effective marketing, cold calling, networking, professional sales presentations, and follow-up.
- Created a rapport with national advertising agencies to acquire large corporate accounts.
- Assisted companies in developing and maintaining effective advertising campaigns.
- Wrote print copy and assisted in the design and layout of advertisements.
- Built relationships with local contacts that provided leads for breaking news stories.
- Highest achiever for the Book of Lists, a tabloid-sized directory containing more than 75 top lists of the area's leading industries.
- Increased the number of new advertisers and consistently exceeded sales goals, doubling sales in two years.
- Created an ACT! computerized database of more than 2,500 key contacts.
- Designed sales tools for all sales staff, including promotion sheets, commission schedules, annual advertising time lines, and sales tracking systems.

SALES & INFORMATION DIRECTOR

Direct Marketing Specialists, Colorado Springs, Colorado (1998 – 2001)
- Directed the sales of Val-Pak direct mail services in a very competitive market.
- Developed quality, long-term business relationships with an exceptionally high percentage of repeat customers and a corresponding increase in sales.
- Recognized by the national corporate office for outstanding achievement, including multiple bonuses for high sales levels and marketing performance.
- Successfully generated new leads through active networking, professional memberships, and community service activities.
- Created and implemented a customized billing service and individual quality assurance programs to ensure customer satisfaction.

EDUCATION

BACHELOR OF SCIENCE IN SOCIAL WORK, Arizona State University, Tempe, Arizona
Graduated with honors (1980)

CONTINUING EDUCATION
Dale Carnegie, Zig Ziglar, and Tony Robbins Sales Training
Extensive sales training through corporate seminars and independent study

ROBERT COSTELLO

⇨ **DRIVING EARLY- TO MID-STAGE SOFTWARE COMPANIES TO MARKET DOMINANCE**

55 Lansing Street
Philadelphia, PA 19120
267-555-1234
TopSales@protypeltd.com

SALES EXECUTIVE – SOFTWARE INDUSTRY

- ☑ SALES AND SALES MANAGEMENT
- ☑ ALLIANCE-BUILDING
- ☑ CALL CENTER IMPLEMENTATION
- ☑ NEW PRODUCT LAUNCH
- ☑ STRATEGIC PLANNING

TOP-PERFORMING SALES MANAGER AND MULTIMILLION-DOLLAR INDIVIDUAL CONTRIBUTOR with 12 years of experience selling innovative products and professional services into the enterprise software space. Fast-track career (six promotions in six years). Played a key role in a growing company from startup to $189 million in annual sales. Inspirational manager with a record of building loyal, high-performance teams. Communicate effectively up and down the organization. Passionate, competitive, and driven to succeed. MBA degree.

Regional Director MVP Award	Q3 – 2003, Q4 – 2003, Q2 – 2004, Q3 – 2004
Proclub	1999 – 2003 (all years measured)
#1 Sales Rep, #1 Sales Manager, #1 Sales Director	1998 – 2004

PROFESSIONAL EXPERIENCE

NETDOMINANT, Philadelphia, PA   1997 – present
Played key strategic sales role in growing the company from 1 customer to 825 corporate accounts and achieving number two position in emerging market of identity and access management solutions—out of 20 rivals (IBM, Sun, Novell, etc.).

Director of Sales—Northeast Region (2003 – present)
Promoted to reenergize the strategically critical Northeast territory. Direct eight sales reps and six sales engineers.

- Built and stabilized a high-powered team. Restructured existing staff and hired/mentored four sales representatives, one of whom closed the two largest deals in the company's history.
- Achieved impressive metrics for both contribution margin and overall revenue attainment.

Sales Metrics for Team	2003	2004
Sales Revenue	$21.23M	$28.77M
Quota Attainment	140%	130%
Profitability	#1 out of 7 Regions	#1 out of 7 Regions
Proclub Attainment	Highest % in North America	Highest % in North America
Forecast Accuracy	#1	#1

Director of Sales—Firewall Sales/Corporate Sales (2002 – 2003)
Tapped to lead development of inside sales/corporate sales model. Full P&L accountability for $2 million product line.

- Re-envisioned and rebuilt the call center. Developed/implemented a call center automation system. Devised creative online tools and strategies that enabled the company to sell technical products over the phone.
- Built team of eight. Established call metrics and targets. Doubled productivity per sales rep in one quarter alone.
- Grew call center business to one of company's top revenue generators at $1.4 million in Q2 2004 sales.
- Ramped up to $1.2 million per quarter within two quarters. Slashed sales cycle by 78 percent (compared to outside sales).
- Revamped firewall sales business, increasing profits by $110,000. Improved forecasting accuracy.
- Dramatically increased lead generation and sales of maintenance agreements.

100

NETDOMINANT(Continued)

Director of Alliances and Channel Sales (2001 – 2002)

Promoted to accomplish a three-fold mission: design and execute a comprehensive OEM channel strategy; develop a CRM/ERP solutions program; and eventually develop the system integrator alliances program. Managed team of five.

- Managed OEM program to a sustainable $600,000 per quarter.
- Developed a groundbreaking CRM/ERP solutions program to provide integration of access management software with ERP systems.
- Accelerated quarterly revenue achievement in the CRM/ERP solutions program from $100,000 to $1,000,000.
- Built alliances with system integrators that yielded $7+ million in indirect or influenced revenue.
- Implemented a training program, delivering over 1,000 trained system integration consultants.

Director of Sales—Strategic Global Accounts (2000 – 2001)

Challenged to develop a global accounts region across North America. Managed 30 Fortune 500 accounts. Hired and managed team of three sales reps and three sales engineers.

- Earned top ranking out of eight regions as measured by percentage of goal achieved through first half of 2001.
- Drove $11 million in 2000 revenue with 11 assigned accounts.
- Contributed 20 percent of total corporate revenue (including maintenance renewals).
- Played integral role in producing 400 percent corporate growth in 2000.

Sales Executive/Manager—Northeast Region (1997 – 2000)

Launched the major accounts program. Evangelized innovative software solutions to major corporations.

- Signed many of the company's first and largest customers—FAA, Tokai, GE, The Hartford, Liberty Mutual, Electronic Payment Services, Cigna, Akamai, CVS, State of NY, Xerox, Paychex, United Technology.
- Closed company's first $500,000 and $1 million deals.
- Delivered watershed account, valued at $2 million with follow-on revenue of $25 million.
- Exceeded quota in all 13 quarters.
- Achieved 200 percent of goal in 2000 and 30 percent in 1999.
- Leveraged partner relationships to accelerate growth into new accounts and grow size of deals.
- Established the company's most profitable territory based on resource-to-revenue ratio.

TITAN SOFTWARE, INC., Philadelphia, PA   1995 – 1997
Global provider of enterprise fax and forms solutions for AS/400 systems.

Corporate Sales Manager

Built strategic relationships with major software firms to leverage the business model.

- Ranked number one or two out of a field of eight reps for 10 straight quarters. Responsible for 30 percent of all new business.
- Generated $450,000+ in gross margin in 1996.

EDUCATION AND PROFESSIONAL DEVELOPMENT

UNIVERSITY OF PENNSYLVANIA, Philadelphia, PA

Master of Business Administration   1997

Bachelor of Science: Business Management   1993

LYN CHEN

(703) 555-1234

■ **OBJECTIVE**

Seeking to apply solid experience in e-business, e-government, and telecommunications markets for a management consulting organization in the Asian-Pacific region. Project management, market research, and cross-cultural communication skills (Western and Asian) combine with diverse business background. Bilingual in Chinese (Mandarin and Shanghai Dialect) and English.

■ **EDUCATION**

Management Consulting Projects

M.B.A. with concentration in e-Commerce Marketing, 2004
AMERICAN UNIVERSITY, SCHOOL OF BUSINESS, Washington, D.C.

- **Redman, Brotter & Williams Communications, Washington, D.C.**—Assessed business practices of this Washington, D.C.-based public relations firm. Designed a detailed e-business plan focusing on process improvement and communication strategies, and integrated order fulfillment, service delivery, and customer relationship management, resulting in a significant reduction in daily operating costs.

- **ADI Management Institute, Alexandria, VA**—Conducted an on-site analysis of the organization's management information systems requirements and designed a procurement system that integrated contracting, accounting, and receiving processes, resulting in a more responsive, user-friendly system with real-time trackable data.

- **PacSystems Inc., Arlington, VA**—Analyzed the existing business model and global expansion opportunities for a B-2-B e-marketplace serving the U.S. packaging industry. Conducted extensive research of major international packaging markets in Asia and Europe. Designed and presented to senior executives the region-specific sales/marketing for effective market positioning and entry. Commended on research depth and dynamic presentation style.

Awards

- **Case competition winner out of 10 teams** in the Managers in International Economy class on Steinway's entry strategy to the China market. Professor's comment: *"You delivered the most compelling presentation; no one else was even close."*

B.S. in Communications, graduated summa cum laude, 2002
UNIVERSITY OF NORTH CAROLINA, Chapel Hill, NC

■ **INTERNSHIPS**

MYRON INTERNATIONAL, Washington, D.C. (2003 – 2004)
ELLISON CORPORATION, Washington, D.C. (2003 – 2004)

Intern—During the MBA program, completed internships related to business outreach, e-commerce marketing, and e-business/e-government analysis.

Client Engagement Projects

Myron International—Performed market-risk analysis on telecom, Internet, and e-commerce development throughout the Greater China Region (China, Hong Kong, and Taiwan) and identified global market trends, growth areas, and investment opportunities for Aster Technologies, a client of this international investment and consulting firm. Results were published for senior decision-makers on Aster's Intranet.

Ellison Corporation—Evaluated e-business policy/leadership and e-government readiness in the China market for a global technology and policy consulting firm and its clients, including Dunston-Patterson, Jones Smythe and Hamden. Contributed research and analysis to a company publication, *"Risk E-Business: Seizing the Opportunity of Global E-Readiness."* Utilized contacts in China and acted as a liaison between the firm and Chinese Ministry of Industry Information that regulates Internet and telecommunications development.

William Rodimaker

223 W. Lakewood Circle   •   Jefferson, Oregon 97072
williamrodimaker9@protypeltd.com
208-555-1234 *home*   *cell* 208-555-5678

Mortgage Banker

Professional Profile

Top-producing, driven, and successful **Mortgage Banker** with expertise in developing and closing mortgage loans, recruiting and training bankers, and growing companies. Strong marketing and customer service abilities. Possess outstanding **management** techniques with proven branch development and expansion strengths. Committed to excellence, professionalism, and success.

Outstanding Accomplishments

- Expanded company branches, recruited, and trained new bankers.
- Top Ten Producer • Jones Financial • *2001, 2002*
- Top Producer for Jackson Mortgage • Libby, Montana • *2000, 2001, 2002*
- Rookie of the Year • Jones Financial *(20 branches)* • *2000*
- Developed, hosted, and emceed annual Missoula County Real Estate Golf Tournament • *2000–2003*
- Partnered in building Canadian Family Golf Center

Career Progression

Senior Loan Officer • Jackson Mortgage, *a division of Jones Financial* • Jefferson, Oregon • *2003–present*
Invited as 50% partner to a one-man office. *Manager-in-training.* Developed firm to eight producing officers with plans to open ten branches in the Pacific Northwest over the next few years.

Loan Officer • Jackson Mortgage, *a division of Jones Financial* • Libby, Montana • *2000–2003*
Started as rookie and quickly increased volume to nearly $17 million during 2002 as top producer in the branch and top loan officer of the company. In the first five months of 2003, closed nearly $10 million in volume. Recruited and trained three loan officers who were strong contributors to qualifying the branch as the highest producing branch in the company of 30+ branches. *Transferred to Jefferson, Oregon.*

Loan Officer • Montana Funding • Libby, Montana • *2000*
Sub-prime mortgage company.
Established loan offices in Libby and rapidly progressed from an entry-level loan officer to producing a strong volume in mortgages while recruiting two additional people. Rapidly became one of the state's highest producers for the company.

Institutional Trader • Eastwind Securities • Toronto, Canada • *1997–1999*
Assisted in opening Eastwind with a partnership option. Made markets in Canadian "Over-the-Counter" stocks and performed "Jitney" trading for Dominion Securities.

Affiliations

Committee Member • Libby County Association of Realtors • Libby, Montana • *2000–2003*
Board of Directors • Fort Brave Childcare Center • *2002–2003*
President • Business Network International • Libby, Montana • *three terms* • *2001–2002*

Education and Licenses

Licensed • Mortgage Banker • Oregon State and Montana State • *current*
Graduate • Leadership Montana • *2003*
Certificate • Canadian Securities Course
Economics • Humboldt State University • Arcata, California • *1997*

WILLIAM C. JENKINS

888 Grand Parkway • NY, NY 10451 • (347) 555-1212 • jenkins@protypeltd.com

---

EXECUTIVE SUMMARY

Highly motivated hospitality professional with sales, marketing, budgeting and forecasting experience. As part of the opening team, assumed sole responsibility for the creation and management of all sales and marketing efforts tailored to penetrate corporate, leisure, group, and meeting markets. **Ability to maximize revenues during strong and soft periods.**

KEY AREAS OF EXPERTISE

- Business Development
- Marketing Plans
- Interpersonal Skills
- Forecasting / Budgeting
- Client Relationship Building
- Employee Management
- New York City Markets
- Hands-on Leadership Skills
- GDS Marketing

PROFESSIONAL PROFILE

PROVEN METHODOLOGY / SKILLS:
- Development and maintenance of new markets through proactive sales efforts including direct mail campaigns, persuasive telemarketing, sales presentations, trade show participation and targeted advertising.
- Initiated the GDS marketing process as well as the development of all print ad creation and placement for the Le Marquis, Envoy Club, and The Avalon.
- Resolved negative issues with clients.
- Developed and managed a multitude of accounts.

DEMONSTRATED RESULTS:
- Four successful NYC/Tri-state hotel (deluxe properties) openings. Opened Loews Glenpoint Hotel in Teaneck, NJ, as Front Desk Manager.
- Increased occupancy rate from 70 percent to 90 percent over tenure for the hotel Beacon.
- Generated more than $1 million in sales in the entertainment market through relationship building for Embassy Suites, New York.
- Consistently exceeded occupancy and revenue goals over first three years for The Avalon.

WORK EXPERIENCE

Hilton Hotels, New York, NY   **2003 to present**
Regional Director of Sales
- Targeted corporate, travel agency, and group business market segments to increase global business from each of these critical areas.
- Maintain and develop relationships with key corporate and agency accounts while prospecting new corporate accounts.

Hyatt Regency Hotels, New York, NY   **2002 to 2003**
Managing Director / Sales and Leasing
- Implemented and managed all strategic sales initiatives tailored to penetrate extended stay, corporate, and leisure markets.
- Developed annual sales and marketing budget, marketing plans, and monthly projected revenue reports.

The Ritz, New York, NY   **2001 to 2002**
Director of Sales and Marketing
- Implemented and managed all strategic sales initiatives tailored to penetrate corporate and leisure markets.
- Pursued and developed new markets through proactive direct sales efforts, including sales presentations, comprehensive mail campaigns, and persuasive telemarketing.
- Directed all yield management strategies to maximize revenues in a soft post-9/11 economy.

104

Mandarin Oriental Hotel – New York, NY   **1998 to 2001**
Director of Sales and Marketing
- As part of the opening team, created and managed all sales and marketing efforts tailored to penetrate corporate, leisure, group, and meeting markets.
- Directed all yield management strategies to maximize revenues during strong and soft periods.
- Responsible for all projections, remaining apprised of corporate and leisure markets and major trade shows to accurately forecast occupancy and average room rates.
- Partnered with corporate travel managers and travel agents, coordinating client receptions and familiarization trips to maximize visibility.
- Hired, trained, supervised, and evaluated reservations, sales, and catering support staff.

Milburn, New York, NY   **1994 to 1997**
Sales Manager / Department Head
- Oversaw a multitude of account development and maintenance functions while expanding new group and transient markets.
- Developed annual marketing plans, preparing reports and projecting revenues with the general manager.

Lucerne, New York, NY   **1992 to 1993**
Director of Sales
- Directed all day-to-day sales and marketing operations for this 600-room hotel, including new market penetration, promotional projects, corporate and transient sales, staff supervision, business plan development, report generation and analysis, and other functions.

Americana Inn, New York, NY   **1990 to 1992**
Senior Corporate Sales Manager
- Responsible for the start-up and development of all sales and marketing operations for this flagship hotel, creating and attaining ambitious sales plans, evaluating competitors, and developing responsive sales and marketing strategies.

Belnord Hotel, New York, NY   **1987 to 1988**
Account Executive
- Pursued and secured high-volume corporate transient accounts for this flagship property with annual gross revenue over $1.5 million.

Loews Corporation, New York, NY   **1981 to 1987**
Various positions including Group Sales Representative
- Generated tour, convention and incentive group business for more than 300 worldwide properties through tenacious cold calling, dynamic sales presentations, extensive trade show appearances, and effective contract negotiation.

EDUCATION

Bachelor of Science Degree Candidate, Ohio State University   **1978 to 1981**

PROFESSIONAL AFFILIATIONS

New York Travel Association
National Business Travel Association
Computer Skills: Property Management Systems – Fidelia, Visual One,
Microsoft Office Products, Logistics, Homisco, Fidelio, ACT!

Cassandra Mills

2309 Craigmont Drive
San Antonio, Texas 78300

Cmills99@protypeltd.com

(210) 555-1234

(210) 555-5678 (cell)

profile

Intelligent achiever reflected in ability to complete college in only three years while working and participating in extracurricular activities ❖ Mature college senior who values continued education ❖ Dynamic team player who enjoys collaborating and brainstorming for constructive outcomes ❖ Trainable individual eager to learn and apply knowledge to make positive differences ❖ Goal- and career-oriented

education

B.B.A. in International Finance/Economics
LUBBOCK CHRISTIAN UNIVERSITY, Lubbock, Texas   2005
Major GPA: 3.6/4.0
President's List Fall 2003; Dean's List Spring 2003, 2004, 2005

Relevant Projects:

❖ Investments II: Selected a company stock and wrote a 20-page paper based on research from Internet, SMP 500, and company pro forma statements, including ROA, ROI, profit margin, and value line. Ranked in top 96 percent of class.

❖ Corporate Finance II: Selected three stocks and hypothetically invested $200,000. Tracked bi-weekly, comparing performance to industry and competitors.

experience

Wait Staff   JOSE'S   Plano/Lubbock, Texas   2002 – present
Successfully interface with customers, peers, and management, improving communication and teamwork skills. Consistently accurate with orders.

❖ Received positive customer feedback through manager.
❖ Chosen Top Server of the Week.

Manager Trainee   MODEL FINANCE   Plano, Texas   Summers 1999 – 2001
Hired and trained employees, performed inventory, and created advertising.

❖ Praised for positive attitude, diligence, and flexibility.

activities

Member, Texas Association for Superior Finance Students   2002 – present
Founding Member, Theta Theta Delta   2002 – present
    Pledge Educator   2002
    Rush Chair   2002
Member, International Finance Association   2002 – 2003

Portfolio available

Pamela Sue Denison

1234 University Village View • Colorado Springs, CO 80918 • Home: (719) 555-1234 • Cell: (719) 555-5678

Overview

Dedicated, well-organized teacher who is highly qualified in art and Spanish.
Good listener, keen observer, team player, and effective communicator.
Able to instill in children the passion to be life-long learners.
Patient, flexible instructor who enjoys working with children and believes in
setting high expectations with the belief that children will rise to them.
Knowledge of MS Word, WordPerfect, PeopleSoft, SASI, Claris Works, Internet Explorer, and E-mail.

Education

BOCES ALTERNATIVE TEACHER'S LICENSE PROGRAM (August 2004 – present)
Will earn nine Master's degree credits through the University of Colorado, Colorado Springs
Teacher in Residence Authorization through January 2007, K–12 Art

BACHELOR OF ARTS, Denison University, Granville, Ohio (May 1994)
Major in Mass Communication with a focus on International Studies
Co-chair of the Denison University Bonds of Friendship Committee; fund raising (3 years)

Career History

TEACHER, Emerson-Edison Academy, Colorado Springs, Colorado (2004 – present)
- Teach art to sixth through eighth grade students at this urban charter middle school.
- Set learning goals and develop/implement lesson plans and instructional aids/materials that meet state standards.
- Adapt teaching style to meet the unique needs of each student in various art mediums.
- Create an interactive learning environment designed to challenge students to do their best and to inspire them to be creative.
- Implement effective classroom management strategies and ensure a safe learning environment.
- Instruct students from very diverse ethnic, socio-economic, and talent levels.
- Promote the development of social skills by helping children learn to communicate their feelings and to listen to each other.
- Supervise children during activities and counseled them when social, academic, or adjustment problems arose.
- Maintain attendance records, daily notes, and student behavior reports.
- Coach girls track and volleyball as a CHSAA certified coach—coached a girl to first place in the long jump.

HUMAN RESOURCES ASSISTANT, School District 11, Colorado Springs, Colorado (2001 – 2004)
- Provided support for human resource functions related to food service, transportation, and custodial employees.
- Screened applicants to ensure they met posted qualifications and were eligible to apply.
- Called previous employers to verify information on applications, conduct background checks through BIS, fingerprint applicants, and coordinate drug testing and physicals.
- Processed hiring recommendations and prepared personnel folders, including I-9 forms, oaths, trial period statements, salary offers, and benefit information.
- Tracked tuition reimbursements, leaves of absence, and staffing by site.
- Collaborated with Risk Management Department to process workers' compensation claims and placements, ensuring compliance with federal, state, and local regulations and laws.
- Responded to HR questions, phone calls, and correspondence from the community and district employees.

Continuing Education

PIKES PEAK COMMUNITY COLLEGE, Colorado Springs, Colorado
Conversational Spanish, Art Appreciation—3 undergraduate credits each

ADAMS STATE COLLEGE, Durango, Colorado
Dreams You Can Count On (Imagination Celebration)—1 graduate credit

123 Lincoln Avenue,
Apt. 11
Eastchester, NY 10707
914-555-1234
sjones@protypeltd.com

Sheila Jones, CEC

ACCOUNT EXECUTIVE / BUSINESS DEVELOPMENT PROFESSIONAL

PROFILE

Highly motivated professional with an entrepreneurial spirit. Unique ability to successfully prospect clients and deliver sustainable revenues. Experienced in representing value-driven services and products and promoting quality relationships with an astute perception and response to client motivations. Poised at overcoming objections and forwarding action. Able to build positive relationships by providing legendary customer service, and to respond to individual needs by overcoming challenges and barriers to client satisfaction.

PERSONAL AND BUSINESS COACHING

SELF-EMPLOYED, Eastchester, NY 2003 – present
Developed a small practice providing coaching to independent consultants and professionals. Inspire clients to successfully clarify and bring into alignment their values, vision, and identity for sustainable professional and personal growth.

PRESIDENT

SHIVA DESIGN, Eastchester, NY 2000 – 2003
Provided vision and leadership for this luxury women's wear company featuring exclusive wardrobes for a high-income private clientele with individualist personalities.
- Created a unique marketing and business prospecting strategy that drew clients from New York and California.
- Successfully identified customer needs, motivation, and concerns with outstanding customer retention.
- Negotiated purchases that cut costs 30 percent and increased profit margins.

CUSTOMER RELATIONSHIP MANAGER

THE CENTER FOR NEUROPSYCHOLOGY, Katonah, NY 1996 – 2000
First line of contact at this center dedicated to meeting a full range of needs and evaluating people challenged by neuropsychological disorders.
- Managed multiple appointments in a fast-paced, complex environment that drove a steady revenue growth of 200 percent within four years.
- Successfully negotiated third-party payments on client's behalf.

GUEST RELATIONS MANAGER

SYDA FOUNDATION, South Fallsburg, NY 1991 – 1995
Responsible for the comfort and satisfaction of 5,000 guests attending 500+ programs annually at the New York regional center of this global organization. Provided inspiration and vision for a positive team environment with recruitment, training, and supervision of guest relations staff.
- Played a key role in developing the organizational mission statement that laid the foundation for a 20 percent increase in reservations over a one-year period.
- Improved staff productivity by 15 percent through design and implementation of new policies and procedures.

CERTIFIED EXECUTIVE COACH

EXECUTIVE COACHING INSTITUTE, Boston, Massachusetts

EDUCATION

UNIVERSITY OF CALIFORNIA, Berkeley, CA
Bachelor of Science

MICHAEL LOPEZ

123 Van Street ■ New York, NY 10001 ■ 646.555.1234 ■ lopez@protypeltd.com

PROFESSIONAL QUALIFICATIONS

Art and Web Design/Production Coordination/Supervision/Training/Budget Management
Seven years of progressive experience in print, film and television production and production management. Extensive experience providing creative direction and original artwork for both print and Web production. Skilled in organizing, improving, and implementing operational systems needed to execute objectives in fast-paced creative industries. Capable of reading and producing maps, grids, and traffic/pedestrian flow charts used for large-scale events or show productions. Detail-oriented with outstanding leadership, communications, and problem-solving abilities.

TECHNICAL EXPERTISE

Microsoft Office	QuarkXPress
Macromedia Flash and Freehand	Adobe Illustrator
Adobe After Effects	Adobe Premiere
Basic Final Cut Pro	Basic AutoCAD
Expert Adobe Photoshop	Windows and Macintosh

PROFESSIONAL HISTORY

Art Director/Graphic Designer
UQ Designs, Staten Island, NY, 2000—present
■ Identify and cultivate new client relationships and alliances. Design and develop corporate image, artwork, logos, marketing materials, and publications. Supervise and provide consistent and reliable creative direction to freelance staff and in-house graphic artists. Manage design projects to ensure superior creative services that are within budget and meet required deadlines. Build and retain freelance roster.
Partial Client List: Terri Woods Publishing, Triple Crown Publishing, H2O International Film Festival

Freelance Locations Manager and Assistant/Production Coordinator and Assistant
MTV Networks, New York, NY 1999—2003
■ Served as liaison between MTVN and The NYC Mayor's Office for Film and Television. Reported all permit, venue, and shooting location concerns and issues to production management department heads. Organized arrival and departure schedules of all deliveries for massive load-ins and load-outs at large venues such as Radio City Music Hall, Madison Square Garden, The Shrine Auditorium, The Hammerstein Ballroom, and The Metropolitan Opera House.
Partial Credit List: VH1 Fashion Awards 99 – 02 and Divas Live 00 – 02; MTV Video Music Awards 00 – 03; 50+ shows in four years

Extras Casting Associate
T.E.C. Casting Company, New York, NY, 1999
■ Managed a staff of 10 in the film and television casting department. Trained 15+ casting assistants and interns on booking and filing procedures.
Partial Credit List: Bamboozled (Spike Lee Films/Touchtone Films)

Principal and Extras Casting Associate/Extras Casting Assistant
Winsome Sinclair & Associates, New York, NY 1997—1999
■ Supervised film and television casting department staff. Trained more than 20 assistants and interns on booking and scheduling processes. Liaison between Casting Director and various acclaimed film and television directors and producers. Prepared and submitted casting budgets. Provided knowledgeable consultation on SAG, AFTRA, and EQUITY rules and regulations. Served as point of contact for industry union representatives. Organized open calls and auditions for principal characters and extras.
Partial Credit List: He Got Game, Summer of Sam (Spike Lee Films/Touchtone Films), New York Undercover (Fox/Universal Television), various commercials, music videos, and independent films

DETAILED CREDIT and CLIENT LIST AVAILABLE UPON REQUEST

Jessamy S. Moores
☼ *Certified Massage Therapist, NCBTMB*

1234 Cloverleaf Road • Columbia, MD 21075
(410) 555-1235 (H) • moores@protypeltd.com

☼ Profile

Dedicated to advancing holistic health and wellness through a mutually trusting and respectful therapeutic relationship.

Energized by the challenge of learning new skills and reaching higher levels of personal and professional success.

Hold high personal standards for producing quality work.

☼ Values & Strengths

- leadership – teamwork
- integrity – respect
- patience – compassion
- creativity – spirituality
- optimism – enthusiasm
- analytical problem solving
- critical thinking
- effective communication
- documentation
- adaptability

☼ Certifications

NCBTMB
  Certification #001678144
ABMP
  Insured Member #879541

☼ Education

Bachelor of Science, Physics
Millersville University of PA
Millersville, PA

☼ Professional Training

Baltimore School of Massage – Baltimore, MD   2004
Professional Massage Therapy Program
- Completed **637-hour** Professional Program, GPA 3.97
- **Core Training:** Western Massage using Swedish Strokes • Deep Tissue Massage • Myofascial Release (Barnes Method) • Human Anatomy and Physiology • Massage Theory
- **Supplemental Training:** Joint Mobilization – Dynamic Soft Tissue Manipulation • Energy Work • Reflexology • Pregnancy Massage Spa Techniques • Aromatherapy • Communications • Boundaries Ethics and Professionalism
- Certified **First Aid/CPR**
- Student of the Month, June 2004

☼ Prior Professional Experience

MedImmune – Frederick, MD   1990 – 2003
Unit Supervisor
- Supervised skilled teams refining and formulating biological vaccine and pharmaceutical injectable products in a fast-paced, highly regulated environment.
- Planned, prioritized, and executed production operations to meet departmental master schedule.
- Presented on-the-job training and promoted safety awareness.
- Maintained records and tracked all complex information.
- Employed current Good Manufacturing Practices, standard operating procedures, and corporate policies in all activities.
  – Collaborated with internal departments including QA/QC to meet constantly changing schedules and production interruptions.
  – Employed aseptic technique, universal precautions, and disinfection and sterilization procedures.
  – Recognized for excellent documentation and organizational skills.
  – Noted for maintaining high standards of compliance and quality and detail orientation.
  – Acknowledged for demonstrating effective interpersonal skills, modeling positive behavior, and encouraging mutual respect for employees and customers alike.
  – Consistently projected company core values of quality, integrity, respect for people, leadership, and collaboration.

YVETTE WILLIAMS

123 Monroe Place ♦ Staten Island, NY 10304
Home: (718) 555-1234 ♦ Mobile: (917) 555-5678
williams@protypeltd.com

PROFESSIONAL PROFILE

MERCHANDISING PROFESSIONAL
Merchandising ♦ Negotiation ♦ Training and Development ♦ Inventory Management

Eleven years progressive experience in Retail and Operations Management. Outstanding leadership and problem-solving abilities with strong relationship-building skills. Increased departmental sales 15 percent by successfully implementing creative merchandising and promotional programs. Excellent communications and technology skills with proficiency utilizing Microsoft Office and the Internet.

PROFESSIONAL EXPERIENCE

Housewares Selling Manager, Bloomingdale's, Inc., New York, NY, 9/96–present
(Promoted from Bedding Sales Manager, Tommy Hilfiger Men's Shop Manager, Towels Operational Manager, Christmas Shop Manager, Assistant Manager of Small Electronics)
Sales Associate, Enzo Angiolini, New York, NY, 7/94–9/96

MERCHANDISING
♦ Communicate merchandise needs with buyers and planners to achieve seasonal and everyday goals. Merchandise and position selling floor for promotional events. Reduced inventory 10 percent by managing merchandise shortage. Replenish department merchandise continually and consistently. Collaborate with Visual Manager to ensure team is properly trained in merchandising standards. Ensure new receipts are backstocked and logged-in properly. Organized set-up and removal of seasonal shop.

OPERATIONS
♦ Develop profitable business plans to increase department sales and customer satisfaction. Research and implement relevant market trends to promote and increase sales. Resolve customer issues by investigating problems and following-up immediately. Established strong working relationships with senior executives from designer bedding vendors including Donna Karan, Ralph Lauren, and Calvin Klein. Served as liaison between Tommy Hilfiger Company and Bloomingdale's to ensure client satisfaction and proper merchandise placement. Prepare weekly and seasonal reports of department sales for business analysis and evaluation. Developed positive work relationships with union representatives and members.

TRAINING and SUPERVISION
♦ Recruit and hire sales associates. Train and counsel over 25 sales associates on selling and customer service skills. Prepare performance appraisals to evaluate and critique sales associate work activities. Organized special team for new lease department.

EDUCATION AND TRAINING

B.S., Business Administration, State University of New York at Oswego, 1995
Federated Executive Training Program, Bloomingdale's, Inc., 1996

Kellyn Leah Scott

1234 S. Tempe Way
Centennial, CO 80015

Home: (303) 555 – 1234
scott@protypeltd.com

SUMMARY

An Advanced Math Teacher with 10 years of teaching traditional and interactive advanced mathematics to middle and high-school students, including algebra, geometry, trigonometry, statistics, and calculus at regular and advanced levels. Specialize in practical applications of math theories, continual development to enhance student understanding of math concepts, and a demonstrated concern for student understanding. Extensive experience with the Douglas and Cherry Creek School Districts' math curricula.

EDUCATION AND LICENSING

Secondary Mathematics Teaching License (current), Colorado, May 1995

Master of Liberal Studies in Mathematics Education, Regis University, Denver, CO, August 1997
- Summa Cum Laude
- Thesis Topic – "A Standards-Based Geometry Curriculum"

Bachelor of Science in Marketing, Boston College, Chestnut Hill, Massachusetts, May 1989
- Honors Program – Carroll School of Management
- Resident Advisor for University Housing
- Regional Director and Student Interviewer – University Admissions
- Co-Founder of Emerging Leaders, a freshman orientation program

Continuing Education: Advanced Placement Calculus Teacher Training

PROFESSIONAL EXPERIENCE

SELF-EMPLOYED, Centennial, CO   1999 – present
Math Tutor
Regularly tutor 10 – 12 students per week in all math subjects including trigonometry, statistics, and calculus. Students originate from Cherry Creek and Douglas County middle and high schools, home schools, and local colleges.
- Maintained current teacher's license with continuing professional educational courses.
- Refined ability to instruct to each student's individual learning styles, and implemented motivational techniques.
- Gained exposure to the diverse curricula and teaching philosophies of area schools and math departments.

CHAPPARAL HIGH SCHOOL, Parker, CO   1998 – 1999
Mathematics Teacher
Taught algebra II and geometry to high school students. Recognized for:
- Demonstrated concern for student understanding by working individually with students and collaborating with parents.
- Using innovative teaching methods to enhance student understanding.
- Communicated the relevance of mathematical concepts in real time.

PONDEROSA HIGH SCHOOL, Parker, CO   1995 – 1998
Mathematics Teacher
Taught algebra I, geometry, and honors geometry to high school students.
- Re-vamped honors geometry curriculum so that it met or exceeded Colorado-mandated mathematics standards.
- Primarily focused on student understanding and communication of the relevance of math concepts.
- Led Honors Geometry Team in the planning and evaluation of curricula.

7 Those Difficult Dates

Where should you place your dates? It all depends on how much importance you want to give them. If you have gaps in your employment history that you would rather explain in an interview, then the dates should be less obvious. You can even leave them off altogether and list totals instead (pages 123 and 132), although your reader will automatically assume you have something to hide. You need to make the decision whether leaving the dates off will harm your chances of getting an interview more than putting the dates on your résumé.

Another reason to de-emphasize dates is your age. If you would rather not give your age away, then make the reader work to figure it out. Tuck dates against the text with parentheses (pages 126-133) or bury them somewhere else in the résumé (pages 116 and 117). You can selectively choose to leave dates off your education and show them only on your experience.

So, how far back should you go when listing your experience? The answer is simple. When your past experience stops being relevant to your job search, leave it off. The usual is 10 to 15 years in the past, unless there is something in your older experience that is critical to your qualifications. This will help to deflect interest from your age.

Accuracy and *honesty* are the most important considerations when it comes to dates. Don't lie! I had a client who chose to fudge on his dates and I didn't know about it. He was invited for an interview and then lost the job when previous employers were contacted and the dates didn't match. It wasn't worth it. Honesty is always the best policy.

There are many ways to make room for the dates. One is to establish a clear column of dates to the right of a résumé, which keeps the text lines short and makes the dates easy to find. You should not use this clear column of dates on the right if you are creating a scannable résumé since this style produces three newspaper-like columns.

Putting dates on the left gives them a great deal of importance. Since people read from left to right, information on the left of the page is read first and carries greater weight. Make sure you really want your dates to be that important before placing them in the left-hand column.

You may use months with years or years only. Some people feel more comfortable with a full accounting of their time and prefer the month/year method. However, making room for all those words becomes a problem if you choose to spell out the month, as in January 2002 to February 2005. Abbreviations or numbers for months make designing your résumé a little easier:

Jan. 2002 – Feb. 2005

or

Jan 2002 – Feb 2005

or

1/02 – 2/05

It is possible to stack the dates (as on page 115) in order to make more room. For example:

Jan. 2002   or   January 2002
– Feb. 2005   to February 2005

Dot leaders .... can help draw the eye to the dates on paragraph-style résumés where it is difficult to create a clear column for the dates (pages 119 – 121, 134). However, dot leaders should not be used in a scannable résumé.

There is no single, preferred method for the positioning of dates on a résumé. The key is to create a sense of balance by placing the dates in a position that is complementary to the rest of your information, while keeping in mind how much importance you wish to give them and the scannability of your résumé.

TAMMY RICHARDS

1234 Glenda Drive, Apt. 12 • Loveland, Colorado 80537
Home Phone: (970) 555-1234

SUMMARY OF QUALIFICATIONS

- Results-oriented self-starter with strong dedication to academic excellence and advanced studies
- Experienced in balancing personal and academic priorities
- Recognized as a creative and practical problem solver
- Proven record of creativity, flexibility, and adaptability to any assignment
- Outstanding credentials and motivation
- Excellent verbal and written communication skills

EDUCATION AND LICENSES

- Graduate Pikes Peak Community College LPN Program, Colorado Springs, Colorado
- Licensed Practical Nurse, State of Colorado
- Undergraduate college-level studies, core curricula, Portland Community College, Portland, Oregon
- Graduate Certified Nursing Assistant Program, New Care Directions, Portland, Oregon
- Licensed Certified Nursing Assistant, State of Colorado
- Graduate, East West School of Massage Therapy, Oregon
- Current certifications in CPR and Basic First Aid, American Heart Association

PROFESSIONAL EXPERIENCE

LICENSED PRACTICAL NURSE February 2003
Northern Colorado Hospice and Palliative Care, Greeley, CO to present
- Provided continuous care to terminally ill patients in their homes
- Responsible for assessments, direct patient and family care, and medication administration

CERTIFIED NURSING ASSISTANT October 2000
Pikes Peak Hospice, Colorado Springs, CO to December 2002
- Maintained patient care standards and supported families, nurses, physicians, and administrators
- Reviewed patient assessments and assisted in the planning of individualized patient care
- Provided instruction to patients in daily care
- Performed typical CNA responsibilities, including taking and recording vital signs; observing, reporting, and documenting patient activities; providing physical, emotional, and social needs to patients; and implementing appropriate emergency interventions

RESEARCH INTERVIEWER September 1995
National Opinion Research Center, Colorado Springs, CO to December 2002
- Performed research interviews in Colorado Springs and Pueblo for this Illinois firm
- Located and interviewed respondents for statistical studies
- Prepared detailed reports for the principal client (Department of Labor, Washington, DC)

CLINICAL NURSE February 2000
Long-term Care Facilities, Acute Care Settings, and Hospitals, Colorado Springs, CO to November 2002
- Responsible for all phases of patient care, medication administration

INDEPENDENT LICENSED MASSAGE THERAPIST June 1992
Richardson Massage Therapy, Portland, OR to February 2000
- Provided massage therapy at various health clubs
- Completely responsible for all business development, marketing, and promotions

MEDICAL RECORDS CLERK May 1988
Good Samaritan Hospital, Portland, OR to June 1992
- Worked closely with physicians and staff nurses maintaining medical records
- Extensive computer data entry utilizing a state-of-the-art computer system

123 Amstel Drive
Colorado Springs
Colorado 80906 USA

Rita Zimmerman

Tel: (719) 555-1234
Fax: (719) 555-5678
rz@protypeltd.com

SOLO EXHIBITIONS

- Espace Meyer Zafra, Paris, "Portraits," April 2002.
- Colorado Architecture Partnership, Colorado Springs, Colorado, "The Big Paintings," April 1998.
- Colorado College, Colorado Springs, Colorado, "Portraits of Elie Wiesel," May 1997.
- Brownsboro Gallery, Louisville, Kentucky, "Heads and the Beheaded," October 1993.
- Carnegie Arts Center, Covington, Kentucky, "New Monoprints," May 1986.
- Michael Lowe Gallery, Cincinnati, Ohio, 1985.
- Greta Peterson Galerie, Cincinnati, Ohio, 1982.

MUSEUM EXHIBITIONS

- Colorado Springs Fine Arts Center, "The Pack," Colorado Springs, Colorado, June 2003.
- Colorado Springs Fine Arts Center, "Colorado 2002," Colorado Springs, Colorado, January 2002.
- Center for Contemporary Art, "Regional Expressionism," Lexington, Kentucky, 1987.
- Delaware Art Museum, "The Female Animal," Wilmington, Delaware, 1985.
- J.B. Speed Museum, "Eight States Contemporary Artists," Louisville, Kentucky, 1984.
- The Contemporary Art Center, "Figure '82," Cincinnati, Ohio, 1982.
- Center for Contemporary Art, University of Kentucky, Lexington, "Choice Painting," 1982. Juror C. Michael O'Brian, Metropolitan Museum, New York.

SELECTED GROUP EXHIBITIONS

- Bryan & Scott Gallery, Ltd., "Nine Artists," Colorado Springs, Colorado, August 2004.
- Bryan & Scott Gallery, Ltd., "Figure and Form," Colorado Springs, Colorado, August 2003.
- Espace Meyer Zafra, "Exposition Collective: Cinq artistes de la galerie," Paris, July–October 2002.
- LA BAC Fundaciòn Internacional, 19 Passage Moliere, Paris, April 2000. Curated by Nelson Castellano-Hernandez and Carmen Mistaje-Braunstein.
- Sangre de Cristo Arts Center, Pueblo, Colorado, November 2000.
- Ruth Maier Siebensterngalerie, "Kunst-melange," Vienna, Austria, 1999.
- Formfest–Business of Arts Center, Colorado Springs, Colorado, 1999.
- Hal-Barnett Gallery, New Orleans, Louisiana, 1994.
- Water Tower Annual, Louisville, Kentucky, 1988. Juror Victoria Munroe, New York.
- Robert L. Kidd Associates/Galleries, "Animals! Contemporary Visions," Birmingham, Michigan, 1986.
- Three Rivers, Pittsburgh, Pennsylvania, 1986. Juror Lynn Gumpert, 76 New Museum, New York.
- Olin Fine Arts Center, 14th Washington and Jefferson College National Painting Show, Washington, Pennsylvania, 1982.
- Goethe-Institute, Paris, 1980.

MUSEUM COLLECTIONS AND AWARDS

- Museum Purchase, University of Kentucky Art Museum, Lexington. Merit and Purchase Award. Juror C. Michael O'Brian, Metropolitan Museum, New York.
- Museum Purchase, Fine Arts Center, Colorado Springs, Colorado.
- Merit Award, Painting, Art '83, Indianapolis, Indiana.
- Juror's Special Merit Award and selection for traveling exhibition, Elizabeth, Kentucky, 1983.

REVIEWS AND CATALOGS

- Espace Meyer Zafra, 4 rue Mahler, Paris, France, 2002.
- Gil Asakawa, "Go Figure," *Colorado Springs Gazette Telegraph,* November 1994.
- Diane Heilenman, Brownsboro Gallery Exhibition, *The Courier-Journal*, Louisville, Kentucky, October 1993.
- Daniel Brown, "Sexual Stylistics," *Dialogue Arts Journal*, Ohio, July–August 1985.
- Jan Riley, "Romantic Realist," *Dialogue Arts Journal*, March–April 1985.
- Owen Findsen, "Rita Zimmerman's Animal Paintings Not the Stuff of Disney, Audubon," *The Cincinnati Enquirer*, December 16, 1984.
- Gregg Levoy, "The Young in Art: Four Profiles of Emerging Cincinnati Artists," *The Cincinnati Enquirer*, April 15, 1984.
- Ann Tower, "Louisville Display Contains In-Depth Artistic Statements," *The Lexington Herald-Leader*, November 6, 1983.
- Sarah Landsell, "Choice Painting Vibrations Lift Spirits, Raise Hopes," *The Courier-Journal*, Louisville, Kentucky, October 10, 1982.
- B.J. Foreman, "Figural Art Star of Show," *The Cincinnati Post*, May 1, 1982.
- Owen Findsen, "Springfest Opener a Figurative Fest," *The Cincinnati Enquirer*, May 2, 1982.
- Robert Stearns, "Figure '82," *Dialogue Arts Journal*, May 1982.
- Maureen Bloomfield, "Ending the Silence," *Dialogue Arts Journal*, September 1982.

FORTHCOMING EXHIBITIONS

"Die Toteninsel" (The Island of the Dead), Kunstfaktor Galerie, Berlin, Germany, May 2005
One-Person Exhibition, Espace Meyer Zafra Galerie, Paris, France, 2005
One-Person Exhibition, Galerie Stil und Bruch, Berlin, Germany, Autumn 2005

EDUCATION AND SCHOLARSHIPS

MASTER OF FINE ARTS, 1984
University of Cincinnati, Ohio
Awarded a full university scholarship

BACHELOR OF ART, 1976
University of Florida, Gainesville

SUMMER PROGRAM, 1992
Anderson Ranch Arts Center, Snowmass, Colorado
Awarded scholarship

REPRESENTED BY

Espace Meyer Zafra, 4 rue Mahler 75004, Paris, France
Ruth Maier Siebensterngalerie, Siebensterngaße 25, 1070 Vienna, Austria
Galerie Stil und Bruch, Admiralstraße 17, D-10999 Berlin, Germany
Nelson Castellano-Hernandez, 36 Bd. du Sebastopol, Paris, France
Bryan and Scott Jewelers, Ltd., 112-114 N. Tejon, Colorado Springs, Colorado 80903 USA
The Hayden-Hays Gallery, One Lake Street, Colorado Springs, Colorado 80901 USA

Tessa Schram

1234 Edmonds Way
Woodway, WA 98000

(206) 555-1234 Cell
assistu@protypeltd.com

CAPABILITIES

— Leadership / Supervision
— Budgets, Finance and General Administration
— Customer Service: Research, Troubleshooting, Problem-solving
— Fund-raising / Development
— Databases / Data Management
— Marketing, Logistics, Events
— Written / Verbal Communications: Business Letters, Bios, Scripting, Contracts, Sponsorship Proposals, Sales Presentations, Donor Relations
— Computers: MS Office (Word, Excel, Access, PowerPoint, Outlook), MS Publisher, Adobe, Raisers Edge, Docusolve, Printmaster, WordPerfect, Lotus, Visual Basic, Visio.

EDUCATION AND TRAINING

A.A. Computer Information Systems
Shoreline Community College

HIGH-LEVEL PRESENTATIONS

Edmonds Community College
Worker Retraining Program
Presenter to:

State of Washington Senate
Higher Education Senate Meeting,

State of Washington Senate
Fundraiser Dinner
Tidewater Restaurant
Higher Education Senate
Committee

Media – Interview on King 7
Re: Worker Retraining Issues

PROGRAM MANAGER ▪ SENIOR EXECUTIVE ASSISTANT

Versatile Management, Sales, and Customer Relations Professional
Proven Graphics, Database, and Project Skills. Successful record in:
Nonprofits, Financial Services, Education, Retail, and Manufacturing

ACCOMPLISHMENTS

❑ Energetic, organized administrator with proven people and computer skills.

❑ Loyal program advocate with superior written and verbal presentation skills.

❑ Consistent history of improving executive performance by improving office organization, building positive rapport with key partners, and providing customer support that yields greater opportunities.

EXPERIENCE

BOOTSTRAP WASHINGTON, Seattle, WA   2003 – present
Executive Programs Manager / Assistant to the CEO
Temp 09/03 – 03/04 ▪ Permanent 03/04 – present
— Act as "right hand" assistant to CEO and seven regional boards. Respond to board members' calls and requests. Handle all letters, meeting script, PowerPoint presentations, and meeting setup/calendering, and logistics. Coordinate travel and arrange entertainment. Support and schedule CEO's activities.
— Presentations: Prepare data and presentations for $14 million capital campaign.
— Special Events: Handle all planning and logistics for a lavish induction of Seattle VIPs, held annually at the McCaw Theater. Confirm sponsorships, including donation of site by McCaw, food from Ivar's et al.
— Meeting Minutes: Accompany CEO to critical meetings and supply notes.
— Draft high level correspondence. Compose proposals, donor bios in *Raiser's Edge*, memos for the president, scripts, and confidential communications.

BLUE SHIELD, Seattle and Redmond, WA   1991 – 2001
Business Analyst, 05/97 – 09/01
— Served as headquarter liaison supporting employees in five regions nationwide.
— Maintained all aspects of a complex laser printing workstation.
— Managed laser printing environment for residential lines insurance.
— Created and maintained ISO tables and updated rate changes.

Lead, Home Base Typing/Assembly/Distribution (TAD), Laser Group, 08/96 – 05/97
— Converted company system from dot-matrix to laser, replacing four units with two.
— Managed and trained a three-person staff.
— Managed vendor who provided maintenance for 50+ commercial lines users.
— Improved quality. Wrote user manual and procedures. Reorganized workflow.

Coordinator, Commercial Lines Systems, 04/95 – 08/96
— Provided LAN administration for six remote offices serving 3000+ staff.
— Designed and maintained Access database to track all PC equipment.
— Managed technical vendors. Provided programming support.
— Managed, serviced, and created reports to all commercial lines accounts.

Executive Secretary to Vice President of SAFESITE, 04/93 – 04/95
— Produced correspondence, regional sales reports, and presentations.
— Handled travel and calendering for 2 VPs and a system VP.
— Arranged conference calls and resolved problems.

Receptionist/Scheduler, Document Management, 05/91 – 04/93
— Designed/produced manuals for graphics, credit, and document. Processing.
— Planned and organized department social events. Typed documents.

LYNDA L. YOUNG

1234 Overlook Road, Dover, Tennessee 37058   **(931) 555-1234**

PROFILE
- Registered Medical Assistant with an Associate Degree in medical assisting.
- Experienced in recordkeeping, filing, typing (55 wpm), scheduling, phone etiquette, dictation, and most office machines.
- Knowledge of computers; experienced with WordPerfect and MEDISOFT; familiar with many other Windows and MS-DOS applications.
- Responsible and dependable professional with a strong medical ethic.
- Excellent organizer who is able to work independently and as part of a team.

MEDICAL
- Knowledge of medical terminology; trained in phlebotomy and electrocardiography.
- Hands-on experience in vital signs, patient interviews, injections, patient care, ear irrigations, and vision and hearing tests.
- Performed strep, H-Pylori, pregnancy, hemoglobin tests, urine dips, and glucose testing.
- Experience with therapeutic ultrasound equipment, BM Coumadin machine, peak flow meters, pulse oximeters, medical instruments and materials, and cleaning/sterilization procedures.
- CPR Certification, American Heart Association (Expires February 2006).

RELEVANT EXPERIENCE

REGISTERED MEDICAL ASSISTANT . . . . 2001 – 2005
Gundersen Lutheran Clinic (Family Practice), La Crosse, Wisconsin
- Performed direct patient care and telephone triage in an ambulatory setting for eight medical doctors, one nurse practitioner, and one physician's assistant.
- Interviewed patients to establish a brief history and symptoms; reviewed and updated patient medication and allergy lists; and measured and recorded vital signs.
- Administered injections, collected specimens, set up and assisted with minor surgeries, procedures, and sigmoidoscopies.
- Dispensed sample medications as directed by providers and called prescriptions to pharmacies.
- Oversaw the proper care and monthly maintenance of the department's medical equipment and instruments.
- Member of the Access collaborative department team; helped to coordinate changes that improved patient satisfaction by allowing patients immediate access to the provider of their choice at times convenient for them.

REGISTERED MEDICAL ASSISTANT . . . . 2000 – 2001
Dr. John M. Meehan, M.D. (Family Practice), Colorado Springs, Colorado
- Performed various nursing tasks for a 40-patient-a-day office, including vital signs, charting patient interviews, triage, and setting up and assisting in minor surgery.
- Oversaw inventory and ordering of medical supplies.
- Ensured laboratory protocol was in compliance with Clinical Laboratory Improvement Amendment (CLIA).
- Coordinated referrals to specialists with patients and insurance companies.
- Scheduled patients for appointments, follow-ups, and lab work.
- Prepared dictation and filed patient charts and laboratory reports.
- Answered telephones and called in prescriptions to pharmacies.

CLERK/TYPIST III . . . . 1999 – 2000
Wisconsin Physicians Service Insurance Corporation, Madison, Wisconsin
- Performed secretarial duties for 20 accountants in the Accounting Department of a large insurance company; answered telephones and arranged appointments.
- Distributed and filed interoffice correspondence; prepared final company annual statement.

EDUCATION

ASSOCIATE DEGREE IN MEDICAL ASSISTING 2000
PPI Health Career School, Colorado Springs, Colorado
- Graduated with honors, Director's List, 4.0 GPA
- Classes in Nursing (I, II, III), Anatomy, Pharmacology, Clinical Laboratory (I, II), Medical Terminology, Recordkeeping, and 3-week Externship

Betty Wilson

123 Paula Circle • Penrose, CO 80132 • Phone/Fax: (719) 555-1234 • Cell: (719) 555-4568 • bttywilson@protypeltd.com

HIGHLIGHTS OF QUALIFICATIONS

Eighteen years of professional sports management experience.
Background in event management, public relations, and marketing in the sports industry.
Experienced in all aspects of event coordination and tournament direction.
Knowledge of Windows, MS Word, Excel, and Internet Explorer computer software.

PROFESSIONAL EXPERIENCE

MANAGER . . . . *2002 – present*
Holme Roberts & Owen, *Colorado Springs, Colorado*
- *Managed the Colorado Springs office of one of the state's largest law firms offering services in sports, nonprofit, entertainment, and employment law.*
- *Recruited, screened, hired, and supervised 25 employees, including accounting, administrative support, records management, and operations personnel.*
- *Planned and coordinated special events, including seminars and client education programs.*
- *Collaborated with headquarters to develop the local marketing plan, and acquired new clients through pro-active business development in the community.*
- *Managed purchasing, capital budgets, charitable contributions, and sponsorships.*
- *Selected to participate in several firm-wide projects, including the selection of a new travel agency, replacement of phone systems and calendar management software, and review of the in-house computer contractor.*
- *Represented the firm at meetings of the Legal Marketers Association and Association of Legal Administrators.*

ASSISTANT COMMISSIONER . . . . *2001 – 2002*
Mountain West Conference, *Colorado Springs, Colorado*
- *Attended, planned, prepared, and selected site for Joint Council meetings with athletics directors, senior women administrators, faculty athletics representatives, television partners (ESPN and ABC), and bowl partners. Attended meetings as a liaison to the Ethics and Sportsmanship, Academic Initiatives and Integration, Student Athlete Well-Being, and Student Athlete Advisory Committees.*
- *Prepared research data, assisted in coordinating meetings, and made presentations to the Board of Directors.*
- *Managed championship events—selected and set up venues, managed publicity, distributed handbooks, selected officials, coordinated awards and gifts, and met with coaches to discuss eligibility, rules, regulations, and event schedules.*
- *Involved in all aspects of preparation for championships and bowl games, including public relations, media interview coordination, suite setup, ticket distribution, and meetings with athletics directors and college presidents.*
- *Built relationships with corporate sponsors and managed community outreach projects.*
- *Researched benchmarks, compiled data, and prepared a strategic plan for the Board of Directors with full assessment of the organization's first three years.*
- *Planned and coordinated special events, such as kickoff luncheons, media days, Hall of Fame events, etc.*
- *Created the outline for a crisis management plan to prepare for disasters during championship events.*
- *Developed initiatives for public outreach including the Adopt-a-Highway program, horseback riding for the disabled, and a YMCA program for underprivileged children.*
- *Served as a conference representative at the Las Vegas Bowl, Final Four competitions, and selected events in ten sports.*
- *Directed the swimming and diving championships and the indoor track and field championships in 2002.*

DIRECTOR OF OPERATIONS . . . . *1998 – 2001*
Mountain West Conference, *Colorado Springs, Colorado*
- *Coordinated with the Colorado Springs Sports Corporation to move and start up the Mountain West Conference in Colorado Springs, including facilities, furnishings, personnel relocations, computer systems, office equipment, supplies, and directories.*
- *Developed personnel processes and hired, trained, and supervised interns.*

Director of Operations (continued)
- *Set up press conferences and media interviews for the commissioner.*
- *Researched and wrote portions of rule books and handbooks for various collegiate men's and women's sports in seven states.*
- *Served as the primary communications contact for the conference and worked with the advertising agency and media to create effective advertising campaigns.*
- *Represented the conference at kickoff luncheons, media days, and events of the U.S. Olympic Committee, Halls of Fame, Colorado Springs Sports Corporation, and various football foundations.*
- *Provide administrative support to the commissioner, including travel arrangements, appointments, media interviews, etc.*

MANAGER/DIRECTOR OF TENNIS, EVENTS MANAGER . . . . *1985 – 1998*
Heatherridge Racquet Club, Cheyenne Mountain Country Club, and Woodmoor Country Club, *Denver and Colorado Springs, Colorado*
- *Hosted the Virginia Slims of Denver tournament (Kraft General Foods World Tour).*
- *Co-chair of the Player Services Committee for The Challenge (Nuveen Men's Senior Tour, Jimmy Connors, John McEnroe, Bjorn Borg, Yannick Noah), The Broadmoor, Colorado Springs, 1997.*
- *Revitalized underperforming club programs and achieved significant profitability.*
- *Recruited, hired, and supervised professional teaching staff, front desk, food/beverage, and maintenance personnel.*
- *Developed budgets and managed general pro shop operations and tennis/racquetball/fitness facilities.*
- *Responsible for vendor selection, ordering and purchasing of inventory and supplies.*
- *Developed office policies and procedures in order to ensure efficiency of operations.*
- *Experienced in marketing, advertising, and promoting special events and tennis clubs.*
- *Coordinated media appearances and press conferences for celebrities.*
- *Integral part of a team responsible for developing event promotional materials, ticket sales, and newspaper advertising.*
- *Designed and advertised programs and created promotional brochures; assisted in publication of newsletters.*

HEAD COACH AND HEAD TENNIS PRO . . . . *1985 – 1998*
Colorado College, Cheyenne Mountain Country Club, Heatherridge Racquet Club, The Broadmoor Tennis Club, Gates Tennis Center, and University of Colorado, *Denver and Colorado Springs, Colorado*
- *As a college coach, recruited and counseled athletes, selected staff, developed budgets, raised funds, made travel arrangements, scheduled competitions, and publicized events.*
- *Played in the U.S. Women's Pro Circuit; held #1 state ranking in the Colorado Tennis Association and #1 sectional ranking in the Intermountain Tennis Association; served on the Regional Ranking Committee for Division III colleges.*
- *Taught tennis to juniors, adults, and seniors; coached college men's and women's tennis teams.*
- *The Broadmoor Tennis Club program was selected by "Tennis Magazine" as one of the top five tennis teaching programs in the United States.*
- *Certified with the United States Professional Tennis Association.*
- *Sponsored by Head Sports, Fila, Reebok, and the Aspen Leaf Corporation to promote their products.*

EDUCATION

MASTER OF ARTS, University of Denver, *Denver, Colorado (1981)*
Major: Sport Science • Emphasis in Exercise Physiology and Cardiac Rehabilitation

BACHELOR OF ARTS, Western State College, *Gunnison, Colorado (1977)*
Major: Physical Education • Athletic Scholarships for Women's Varsity Tennis and Volleyball

COMMERCIAL PHOTOGRAPHY, Scottsdale Community College, *Scottsdale, Arizona (1994 – 1995)*

Randolph E. Raggen

12345 Newalla St., Oklahoma City, OK 74851, (405) 555-1234

Law Enforcement/Industrial Security

Leadership by example ◣ Excellent work ethic

Experience

UNITED STATES MARINE CORPS, Camp Lejeune, NC (Okinawa and Iraq)   5/2000 – 5/2004

Leadership/Administration:
- Supervised ten to forty soldiers engaged in field artillery fire control
- Prepared evaluations, reviewed performance, and counseled troops on job performance and personal issues
- Conducted classes on military standards
- Maintained inventory of supplies and equipment in excess of $200,000 at highest level of operations capability, cleanliness, and security

Technical:
- Prepared artillery fire position surveys, plotted data on firing charts, and computed fire direction using computer equipment systems and artillery mathematics
- Determined fire target coordinates and prepared observer reports, giving firing data and commands
- Maintained, tested, and authorized minor repairs to survey and fire control equipment
- Operated field communications equipment

Enforcement:
- Provided law enforcement, supporting commander's law enforcement and security in combat situations and peacetime
- Provided foot and motorized patrol, traffic control, crime prevention, and physical security
- Managed all forms of violation and criminal liability from misdemeanors to felonies

Education

Principles of Instruction – 12/2003
Leadership Training – 8/2003
Security Investigation – 2/2003
Martial Arts Training – 12/2002
Weapons – 9/2002
Personal Financial Management – 12/2001

Terrorism Awareness – 7/2001
Fundamentals of Marine Corps Leadership – 7/2001
Counseling – 7/2001
Field Artillery Fire Control – 3/2001
Recruit Training – 8/2000
Fundamentals of Marine Corps Leadership – 7/2000

Computer Skills – Microsoft Word, Excel, and Access

Recognition

Meritorious Mast, Combat Action Ribbon, Presidential Unit Citation, Sea Service Deployment Ribbon, National Defense Service Medal, Marine Corps Good Conduct Medal, Navy and Marine Corps Achievement Medal

Fred G. Jamisen

9999 Abernethy Road • Oregon City, Oregon 99999
555-123-4567

Professional Profile

Highly skilled, conscientious, and precise **Steamfitter** with more than six years of experience and 10,000+ hours of training in all aspects of steamfitting. Familiar with all required codes, appropriate use of equipment, steamfitting techniques, safety standards, and proper procedures to prevent injuries. Proficient in reviewing plans, blueprints, and specifications for steamfitting projects with proven ability to provide expert recommendations. Well-developed trouble-shooting skills with accurate and precise repairs. Experienced EMT willing to volunteer EMT services on the job. Excellent communication skills, personable, trustworthy, adaptable, and committed to a long-term career.

Expertise and Training Includes:

- Air Conditioning and Refrigeration Systems and Equipment
- Boilers
- Commercial and Industrial Equipment
- Conduit Flex, Duct, and Controls
- Electrical and Electronic Contracting
- HVAC: Heating, Air Conditioning, and Refrigeration
- Instrumentation
- Outdoor Installations
- Overhead Installations
- Underground Installations
- Process Systems and Equipment
- Steam and Heating Systems and Equipment
- Troubleshooting and Maintenance
- Welding Processes including Orbital Welder Arc 207
- Wire Pulling, Wiring Devices, Removal, and Finish

Licenses

Pressure Vessel and Boiler License Class V • *State of Oregon*
United Association of Steamfitters • *Local 290*

Employment History

Steamfitter • United Association of Steamfitters • Portland, Oregon • *6 years*
Assignment to various companies and projects as needed.

Paper Machine Operator • Crown Zellerbach Corp. • West Linn, Oregon • *11 years*
Previously owned by James River and Simpson Paper Company
EMT *(Emergency Medical Technician)* • Served as volunteer EMT for the paper mill.

Sales Representative • Pepsi Bottling Company • Portland, Oregon • *8 years*
Beverage sales.

Military

U.S. Army • **Specialist E-4 – Nuclear Missile Technician** • *Honorable Discharge*

Education

Associates of Applied Arts • **Humanities**
Carroll College • Helena, Montana *and* Clackamas Community College • Oregon City, Oregon

Sierra L. Carpenter

2020 Lithonia Road
Lithonia, GA 30028
(770) 555-1234
carpenter@protypeltd.com

. . .
"She instructed her teachers on fun ways to challenge my daughter, which resulted in a child who not only gained confidence in her own abilities, but also got a kick out of challenging them."

. . .
"I instantly warmed to her work ethic and her great interpersonal skills."

. . .
"I really value the contribution that you make to gifted education."

. . .
"You are making a tremendous difference for our brightest kids by supporting teachers differentiating their instruction."

. . .
"You have classroom experience, resource teacher experience, and you work well with the teachers. Above all, you have a strong knowledge of the pacing guides as well as a vast repertoire of instructional strategies."

Profile

Professional and dedicated resource teacher. Committed to excellence and creating meaningful and stimulating lessons to improve students' ability, creativity, perception, concentration, confidence, and motivation. Methodologies used include cooperative learning strategies, modeling, and outcome-based approaches designed to enhance learning. Strong knowledge of county and state curriculums. Exceptional rapport with administration, staff, parents, and students. Effective at multi-tasking, meeting deadlines, and adapting to situations as they arise. Well known for the following qualities:

- Personable
- Organized
- Focused

- Positive attitude
- Team player
- Results oriented

- Strong work ethic
- Respected by others
- Strong leadership skills

Education and Certifications

2004	Certificate of Advanced Study in Education (CASE) program, anticipated completion in 2009—University of Georgia, Athens, Georgia
2002	Certificate of Professional Development in Gifted Education, 66 hours—Center of Gifted Education at the University of Georgia, Athens, Georgia
1998	M.S., Curriculum and Instruction—Kennesaw State University, Kennesaw, Georgia
1986	B.S., Elementary Education—Kennesaw State University, Kennesaw, Georgia

Professional Development

2004	Technology and Differentiated Instruction, University of Georgia
2004	Differentiating Instruction (webcast), Carol Ann Tomlinson, University of Georgia
1998–2001	Gifted and Talented Education, Georgia State Conferences, Lanier, GA
1998	Staff Development Strategies that Impact Student Achievement, Cindy Harrison, Consultant

Teaching Experience

Gwinnett County Public Schools, Lawrenceville, Georgia   1986 – present
Gifted Education Resource Teacher (1998 – present)
Work closely with instructional leadership teams and administration at Alford and Corley elementary schools to ensure compliance with instructional standards.

- Wrote essential curriculum for the county as part of a team and remain involved in on-going revisions.
- Collect and assess formative and summative data to monitor and support school instructional programs.

. . .

"I am proud to say that my son has grasped his middle school enrichment classes with confidence and enthusiasm. We attribute his successes in part to the great instructional support we all received from Sierra Carpenter during my son's elementary years. I am sure you will agree with me that she would be an asset to any organization."

Gifted Education Resource Teacher (continued)

- Collaborate with classroom teachers to differentiate instruction to meet the needs of high-able students.
- Conduct staff development in differentiated instruction, as well as county-wide initiatives.
- Create at-home strategies, including curriculum and interventions.
- Write summer enrichment reading curriculum for the county.
- Successfully implemented gifted services model at each school for pre-K to fifth grade.
- Model best instructional practices.

Classroom Teacher (1986 – 1998)

Used creative and adaptable teaching methods to implement all aspects of the academic curriculum. Formulated appropriate performance objectives, selected and organized classroom content, designed diversified instructional strategies, and evaluated objectives.

Accomplishments

2004	Nominated for Great Books Foundation's 2003–2004 Great Books, Great Teachers celebration
2002–2003	Grant Recipient of *The Atlanta Constitution's* Educational Foundation's Grants in Education for your "Evening to R.E.A.D.–Read" project
1997–1998	Participated in John Hopkins' reading and math pilot programs, Success for All
1997	Agnes Meyer Outstanding Teacher Award Nominee
1997	Champion for Children Award, Center for Children, Gwinnett County, Georgia
1996	ARC Educator of the Year – Gwinnett County, Georgia

. . .

"… a pleasant part of our staff who demonstrates professionalism and a positive attitude at all times."

Professional Memberships

National Education Association/GSTA/EACC
National Association for Gifted Children

NORMA CARSON

12 Beacon Hill Way • Colorado Springs, Colorado 80906
Email: normacarson@protypeltd.com • Cellular: (719) 555-1234

PROFILE

- Dedicated property manager (CRM) with diverse experience in:
  - Apartments
  - Town homes
  - Corporate suites
  - Operations management
  - Budgeting and accounting
  - Sales and marketing
  - Staffing and training
  - Event coordination
  - Business development
- Proven professional with a proven track record of generating significant revenue.
- Able to maintain a personal yet professional rapport with both staff and residents.

PROPERTY MANAGEMENT EXPERIENCE

PROPERTY MANAGER (1988 – 1999, 2003 – present)
The Vineyards, Greystone Asset Management, Colorado Springs, Colorado (2003 – present)
JBT Property Management Company, Fresno and San Pablo, California (1996 – 1999)
Benart Development, Fresno, California (1991 – 1996)
HeronPointe Condominiums, Fresno, California (1988 – 1990)

- Managed large apartments, town homes, and corporate suites, including:
  - The Vineyards—300 units, 32 acres, luxury apartments, 7 employees, 70% occupancy (up from 62% in only 4 months)
  - Maroa Park—248 units, 18 acres, luxury apartments, 8 employees, 94% occupancy
  - Cypress Creek—288 units, 21 acres, luxury apartments, 10 employees, 95% occupancy
  - Shadowbrook—296 units, 18.5 acres, B-level apartments, 10 employees, 95% occupancy
  - Hilltop—324 units, 19 acres, luxury gated apartments, 13 employees, 99% occupancy
  - Villa San Marcos—246 units, 18.5 acres, luxury apartments, 7 employees, 95% occupancy
  - Four Creeks Village—144 units, 15 acres, luxury town homes, 4 employees, 95% occupancy
  - River Oaks—432 units, 33 acres, luxury condominiums, 20 employees, 98% occupancy
  - Shady Lane Village—54 units, 5 acres, apartment complex, 2.5 employees, 98% occupancy
- Developed and implemented comprehensive marketing plans utilizing radio, television, and newspaper advertising, direct marketing campaigns, and brochures.
- Managed all operations, including building/unit maintenance, club houses, fitness clubs, tennis/sports courts, swimming pools, housekeeping, ground crews, construction, and refurbishing, with the goal of achieving the highest possible resident satisfaction.
- Accountable for budgeting, accounting, accounts payable, accounts receivable, record keeping, cash handling procedures, and reporting.
- Analyzed market conditions and recommended price increases and property enhancements that significantly increased revenue.
- Planned and directed special events and grand openings. Held weekly brunches for up to 300 tenants and potential renters. Coordinated special holiday promotions to increase the perceived value of the properties.
- Hired, trained, and supervised all staff. Held weekly training sessions to ingrain a culture of exceptional customer service.
- Served as Director of Marketing for Benart Development for two years, in addition to property management responsibilities.

HOSPITALITY EXPERIENCE

CONVENTION SALES MANAGER (2002 – 2003)
Fresno Convention and Visitors Bureau, Fresno, California

- Marketed Fresno as a meeting site to state, regional, and national accounts via telemarketing, correspondence, and direct sales calls.
- Developed sales leads and traveled extensively to close sales and generate new business.
- Entertained business clients and provided tours of local hotels to potential clients.
- Created and implemented trade show participation, sales blitzes, and direct mail campaigns.
- Increased bookings and leads by 48% in only three months.

DIRECTOR OF SALES AND MARKETING (1987 – 1988)
Maxwell's Plums Restaurant, San Francisco, California

- Responsible for marketing, promotion, and sales of a five-star restaurant seating 135, in addition to three banquet rooms seating 500, and a bar/lounge holding more than 100. (This sister property to Tavern on the Green closed after the 1988 earthquake.)

(Continued)   **Maxwell's Plums Restaurant**
- Developed and implemented a comprehensive marketing program that focused on incentive programs and systematic, continuous contact with corporations that significantly increased annual sales.
- Met with concierges, secretaries, travel agents, and meeting planners to develop new business from elite clientele.
- Participated in trade shows and created special sales promotions.

DIRECTOR OF SALES AND MARKETING (1983 – 1987)
Holiday Inn, Foster and Union City, California
- Managed the sales, marketing, and catering programs of two Holiday Inn hotels, including a night club, Japanese restaurant, full-dining restaurant, and lobby bar.
- Maintained a 78% occupancy rate or better. Developed special campaigns that resulted in 100% occupancy during holidays.
- Identified potential markets and promoted maximum transient, corporate, group, tour, government, and banquet business.
- Maximized customer satisfaction and revenue goals by developing and implementing effective sales and marketing strategies for regional and national convention accounts.
- Established monthly and annual sales goals and coordinated the development of the marketing plan and budget.
- Analyzed sales trends, developed forecasts, and set rate structures to improve profitability.
- Reviewed all proposals and other written agreements to ensure an accurate understanding existed between clients and the hotel.
- Worked closely with advertising agency on ad concepts and placement for local and national advertising campaigns.
- Hired/supervised all sales staff. Trained them in customer-focused selling and quality assurance.
- Integral member of the team responsible for the construction, preopening planning, and marketing of a new property. Achieved a 76% occupancy rate for the opening through aggressive cold calling, direct mail campaigns, and sales presentations to tour directors and meeting planners. Created and promoted a grand opening gala with more than 2,000 guests, photographers, and local dignitaries.
- Successfully marketed a new night club that became the hottest spot in southern San Francisco with standing room only.

PROJECT MANAGEMENT EXPERIENCE   **IMPLEMENTATION/LEC ENGINEER** (1999 – 2002)
AT&T Local Network Services, Sacramento, California
- Provided space/power planning and engineering services for the Sacramento area.
- Analyzed traffic routing and created systems availability.
- Supervised field engineers in the design and installation of new networks, expedited procurement of materials, and ensured that projects are completed on time and within budget.
- Evaluated forecasts/job orders and designed the placement of switch equipment for fiber optic, digital, and analog data/voice services.
- Submitted and tracked access service requests to and from the incumbent local exchange carriers.
- Maintained the data in support of billing, tracking, and administrative functions.
- Certified in ALSDEN402 Prime Products and 102-OTL to LEC.

EDUCATION   **UNDERGRADUATE STUDIES IN BUSINESS ADMINISTRATION**
Alameda Junior College, Alameda, California

PROFESSIONAL DEVELOPMENT
- Institute of Real Estate Management—Completed the Certified Residential Manager (CRM) program
- Holiday Inn University—numerous seminars and workshops relating to hotel management, budgeting, marketing, sales, and advertising
- Steve Levine Seminars—Powerful Leasing and Marketing Techniques Seminar
- The Institute of Real Estate Management, National Association of Realtors—Successful Site Management Certification

SUSAN B. ALMANN

589 Brighton View
Croton, NY 10520

914.555.1234

almann@protypeltd.com

HUMAN RESOURCES EXECUTIVE

Strategic, proactive business partner to senior operating management. Guide the design and execution of performance-based, customer-centric, and market-driven organizations.

Provided vision and counsel in steering organizations through accelerated growth as well as in turning around underperforming businesses in both union and non-union environments. Diverse background includes multinational corporations in healthcare and manufacturing industries.

Core Competencies
- Long-Range Planning
- Recruitment and Staffing
- Employee Relations
- Leadership Development
- Succession Planning
- Compensation Design
- Culture Change
- M&A Integration
- HR Policies and Procedures
- Expatriate Programs

PROFESSIONAL EXPERIENCE

MARCON MANUFACTURING COMPANY, Peekskill, NY
Director, Human Resources (1996–present)

Challenge: Recruited to create an HR infrastructure to support business growth at a $30 million global manufacturing company with underachieving sales, exceedingly high turnover, and lack of cohesive management processes among business entities in the U.S. and Asia.

Actions: Partnered with the president and board of directors to reorganize the company, reduce overhead expenses, rebuild sales, and institute a solid management infrastructure.

Results:
- Established HR with staff of five, including development of policies and procedures. Renegotiated cost-effective benefit programs that saved the company $1.5 million annually.
- Reorganized operations and facilitated seamless integration of 150 employees from two new acquisitions within the parent company.
- Reduced sales force turnover to nearly nonexistent. Upgraded quality of candidates hired by implementing interview skills training and management development programs. Results led to improved sales performance.
- Recruited all management personnel, developed HR policies, procedures and plans, and fostered a team culture at the newly built Malaysian plant with 125 employees.
- Initiated a business reorganization plan, resulting in consolidation of New York and Virginia operations and $6.5 million in cost reductions.

BINGHAMTON COMPANY, New York, NY
Director, Human Resources and Administration (1993–1996)

Challenge: Lead HR and administration functions supporting 1,600 employees at $500 million manufacturer of medical equipment. Support company's turnaround efforts, business unit consolidations, and transition to consumer products focus.

Actions: Established cross-functional teams from each site and provided training in team building to coordinate product development efforts, implement new manufacturing processes, and speed products to market. Identified cost reduction opportunities. Instrumental in reorganization initiatives that included closing a union plant in Texas and building a new plant in North Carolina. Managed HR staff of 12.

Director, Human Resources and Administration continued...

Results:
- Instituted a worldwide cross-functional team culture that provided the foundation for successful new product launches and recapture of company's leading edge despite intense competition.
- Led flawless integration of two operations into a single, cohesive European business unit, resulting in profitable business turnaround.
- Restructured and positioned the HR organization in the German business unit as a customer-focused partner to support European sales and marketing units.
- Initiated major benefit cost reductions of $3 million in year one and $1 million annually while gaining employee acceptance through concerted education and communications efforts.

ARCAMED CORPORATION, New York, NY
Manager, Human Resources (1989–1993)

Challenge: Provide HR support to corporate office and field units of an $800 million organization with 150 global operations employing 4,500 people.

Actions: Promoted from Assistant Manager to lead a staff of 10 in all HR and labor relations functions. Established separate international recruitment function and designed the staffing plan to accommodate rapid business growth. Negotiated cost-effective benefits contracts for union and non-union employees.

Results:
- Oversaw successful UAW, Teamsters, and labor contract negotiations.
- Established and staffed HR function for a major contract award with a U.S. government agency.
- Introduced incentive plans for field unit managers and an expatriate program that attracted both internal and external candidates for international assignments in the Middle East.
- Managed HR issues associated with two business acquisitions while accomplishing a smooth transition and retention of all key personnel.
- Restructured the HR function with no service disruption to the business while saving $500,000 annually.

EDUCATION
M.B.A., Cornell University, New York, NY
B.A., Business Administration, Amherst College, Amherst, MA

AFFILIATIONS
Society for Human Resource Management
Human Resource Council of Albany

SUZANNE DAVIS

123 Westlake Parkway #16 ♦ Sacramento, California 95835
Home: (916) 555-1234 ♦ Cell: (916) 555-5678 ♦ E-mail: sdavis@protypeltd.com

PROFILE

♦ Experienced multimedia sales director with demonstrated success in:

– Brand definition	– New product development	– Marketing plan creation
– Market penetration	– Online advertising	– Strategic market research
– Product positioning	– Franchise building	– Sales management

♦ Innovative thinker who is willing to step outside the box and take a risk.

♦ Proven sales leader with a strong background in building new territories and using creative marketing approaches to increase revenue.

EXPERIENCE

SACRAMENTO BEE, Sacramento, California
National Advertising and New Product Development Manager (December 2003 – present)

♦ Recruited to revive the stagnant national advertising department and create new products.

♦ Significantly increased revenue by evaluating current skill levels, restructuring the sales staff, creating a new rate structure, and developing special training programs for account executives.

♦ Succeeded in improving the quality of sales presentations and other staff sales skills, which resulted in a 7% increase in monthly sales revenue over budgets.

♦ Developed and implemented new products, including an entertainment section, travel magazine, and annual magazine.

♦ Hired, supervised, and evaluated a staff of 16 account managers, art directors, and sales support representatives.

DENVER NEWSPAPER AGENCY, Denver, Colorado
Director, Retail Display Advertising (January 2003 – November 2003)

♦ Drove all of the local advertising revenue for *The Denver Post* and *Rocky Mountain News,* including new product development and online advertising sales.

♦ Supervised and evaluated 4 managers with 33 account executives.

♦ Revamped the sales team and consistently exceeded monthly sales goals.

METRO NEWSPAPERS, FREEDOM COMMUNICATIONS, Colorado Springs, Colorado
Director, Major Accounts and Motion Pictures/Entertainment (May 2002 – January 2003)

♦ Recruited by *The Orange County Register's* publisher to joint the new Metro Newspaper Division, Freedom Media Enterprises (FME). FME is an integrated information and media company designed to service marketing and advertising needs in new and exciting ways, offering one central account contact for three markets—*The Orange County Register* (Santa Ana)*, The Gazette* (Colorado Springs)*,* and *The Tribune* (Phoenix).

♦ Developed the business plan, sales plan, policies and procedures, execution, and implementation of the new organization.

♦ Developed and managed a revenue budget of more than $30 million.

♦ Grew incremental revenues to $3.1 million in the first five months of operation.

FREEDOM COMMUNICATIONS, Newspaper Division, Colorado Springs, Colorado
Vice President, Corporate Sales (June 2000 – April 2002)

♦ Recruited by *The Gazette's* parent company to develop a new business venture to generate advertising for 28 newspapers (1.1 million total circulation), 6 Internet portals, 12 Hispanic publications, and 10 military newspapers nationwide.

♦ Responsible for writing the business plan, policies and procedures, sales plan, and job descriptions.

♦ Hired, trained, and managed four account managers and an office manager.

♦ Created strategic and tactical marketing plans for the branding of Freedom Communications and generated more than $1.7 million in new revenue in the first year.

♦ Sourced contacts, developed sales presentations, made sales calls, and captured significant market share.

THE GAZETTE, Colorado Springs, Colorado
Director, Display Advertising (January 1996 – May 2000)

♦ Built a national advertising division from the ground up and managed major accounts, generating $24 million in annual advertising revenue.

♦ Recruited, hired, and managed a team of sales managers responsible for 40 account executives.

♦ Instrumental in securing advertising for the interactive division of the newspaper (coloradosprings.com).

EXPERIENCE

THE GAZETTE (continued)
- Developed the *Home in Colorado* magazine that won the 1999 Addy Award for best in-house publication with more than four colors.
- Partnered with The Broadmoor (a Mobil five-star, five-diamond resort) to deliver *The Gazette* to guests every day; created a four-color, in-room *Broadmoor Magazine* for guests that generated significant income for the paper.
- Created partnerships with cruise lines and travel agencies to give the newspaper travel section a more national feel and to offer new opportunities to readers.

LOS ANGELES TIMES, Los Angeles, California
Advertising Sales Manager, Entertainment Category (May 1994 – December 1995)
- Recruited from *The Orange County Register* because of the phenomenal success of its news entertainment section.
- Managed a team of six sales associates responsible for selling advertising space in the entertainment *Calendar* section that generated $150 million in annual revenue.
- Developed strategic plans for future growth and franchise protection.
- Created and promoted unique online advertising programs that were ahead of their time.
- Implemented performance management and team-building strategies that improved morale, reduced turnover, and increased individual sales revenue.

THE ORANGE COUNTY REGISTER, Santa Anna, California
Sales Manager, Major Accounts Division (June 1992 – May 1994)
- Recruited, hired, and supervised a staff of fourteen account executives.
- Succeeded in growing revenue to more than $50 million a year from department, grocery, electronics, and small/medium specialty stores (Target, Macy's, Homestead House, etc.).

Retail Territorial Manager (June 1990 – May 1992)
- Managed six regional sales managers responsible for generating local advertisements from retailers throughout Orange County.

Sales Manager, Entertainment Division (January 1988 – May 1990)
- Developed and launched the Show Section, an entertainment tab that competed directly with the *Los Angeles Times Calendar* section.
- Grew the insert from 80 to 124 pages through aggressive advertising sales.
- Created significant advertising revenue with innovative partnerships, promotions, and special events.

Regional Sales Manager (January 1984 – December 1987)
- Successfully managed local sales in the Huntington Beach, El Toro, and North County regions.

Account Executive, Display Advertising (January 1983 – December 1983)

Classified Account Executive (January 1982 – December 1982)

EDUCATION

SAN FRANCISCO STATE UNIVERSITY, San Francisco, California (1972 – 1976)
- Completed three years of full-time undergraduate studies

RIO HONDO COLLEGE, Whittier, California (1972 – 1974)
- Completed the Licensed Practical Nurse program

PROFESSIONAL DEVELOPMENT
- **Landmark Forum Education** (2002)
- **Community Leadership Forum**: Better Business Bureau (2001, 2002)
- **Associated Press Institute**: Publishing Your Own Newspaper (1999)
- **Center for Creative Leadership**: Leadership Development Program (1 week, 1998)
- **University of Southern California**: Management Institute (1995)
- **Aubrey Daniels**: Performance Management Training (1993)

AFFILIATIONS
- NAA Advertising Committee Board
- Better Business Bureau Board of Directors
- CASA Fund Raising Committee
- Denver Ad Federation

KENNETH T. KIRKPATRICK

SUMMARY

- Seasoned expert witness with 18 years of experience in construction-related litigation.
- Proven technical expertise in all phases of residential and light commercial construction gained through 32 years of hands-on experience in the industry.
- Able to assess inferior workmanship, construction defects, malfeasance, and catastrophic losses.
- Skilled at applying a strong knowledge of the Uniform Building Code and industry standards to reach fair conclusions.
- Effective communicator who is adept at presenting technical subjects in a way that is easy to understand.

CREDENTIALS

- Class B-1 Contractor License, El Paso County (1980 – present)
- General Residential Class C License 2555C, Teller County (1996 – present)
- Contractors License C94-257, Douglas County (1994 – 1997, 2003 – present)
- Certified Trade and Industry Instructor, Postsecondary/Adult Level, Colorado State Board for Community Colleges and Occupational Education (1980 – 1993)
- Class C Contractor License, El Paso County (1978 – 1980)

EXPERIENCE

CONSULTANT AND EXPERT WITNESS (18 years)

- Provided expert testimony in more than 130 construction cases.
- Successfully mediated cases between construction companies and their customers.
- Hired by insurance companies to estimate the cost of reconstruction in large losses.
- Consulted for El Paso County in the Bear Creek Nature Center loss. Successfully proved to the insurance company that the cost of reconstruction would be higher than their original estimate, resulting in a larger award.

GENERAL CONTRACTOR (26 years)
K.T. Kirkpatrick Construction, Colorado Springs, Colorado

- Build custom homes valued at up to $3.2 million in El Paso, Douglas, and Teller Counties.
- Manage estimating, bid preparation, drafting of plans, and project scheduling.
- Supervise all phases of construction; hire and manage employees and subcontractors.
- Consult with clients regarding design modifications and change orders; ensure customer satisfaction throughout the project life cycle.
- Source suppliers, order construction materials, and coordinate on-time delivery.
- Taught clinics for local construction supply companies in residential construction and remodeling.
- Succeeded in maintaining a perfect record with the Regional Building Department and the Better Business Bureau of the Pikes Peak Region.

COLLEGE INSTRUCTOR (14 years)
Pikes Peak Community College, Colorado Springs, Colorado

- Taught classes in blueprint interpretation, cabinetry, framing, concrete foundations, interior and exterior finishing, estimating, and construction procedures for expansive soils.
- Coordinated remodeling projects for student work-study programs.

PRESIDENT (3 years)
Carpenter's Local 515, Colorado Springs, Colorado

- Qualified journeymen carpenters and taught qualification training classes.
- Hired by the City of Colorado Springs to teach blueprint reading to local fire fighters.
- Supervised commercial construction projects.

VIETNAM VETERAN, United States Army (3 years)

ADDRESS

123 Stonegate Court • Colorado Springs, Colorado 80919
Home: (719) 555-1234 • Cellular: (719) 555-5678 • Fax: (719) 555-9876

EDUCATION

CARPENTER'S APPRENTICESHIP (4 years)
Colorado Apprenticeship Council, Denver, Colorado
United Brotherhood of Carpenters and Joiners of America, Fort Carson, Colorado

PROFESSIONAL DEVELOPMENT
- Advanced Arbitrator Training, American Arbitration Association (2003)
- Advanced Construction Law in Colorado, National Building Institute (1999)
- Construction Law Conferences, CLE International (1996, 1997, 2004)
- Construction Industry Arbitration Training, American Arbitration Association (1997)
- International Conference of Building Officials, Colorado Chapter, Educational Institute (1991)

AFFILIATIONS

- Appointed by the Colorado Springs City Council to represent the residential builders in El Paso County on the Pikes Peak Regional Building Department's Board of Review, Board of Appeals, and Advisory Board (2003 – present)
- Appointed to the American Arbitration Association (1993 – present)
- Former member of the National Association of Homebuilders (1996)

REFERENCES

In a recent case involving the defense of an architect who was sued for breach of contract and negligence in the design of an apartment complex, my firm retained Kenneth Kirkpatrick as an expert consultant. It is my belief that Mr. Kirkpatrick's assistance in this matter was a primary factor in our ability to reach a satisfactory settlement for our client. I highly recommend Mr. Kirkpatrick as an effective and experienced consultant in construction-related litigation and intend to solicit his assistance in the future. (Gail Holt, Holt & Associates, Denver, Colorado)

We have engaged Mr. Kirkpatrick's expertise to address a wide variety of issues ranging from catastrophic losses caused by flooding and expansive soils to the assessment of construction defects. In each instance, I have found Mr. Kirkpatrick's services to be professional, timely, and responsive. His opinions have been considered and well reasoned. He is a valuable resource in serving clients with construction and structurally related concerns. (James J. Schutz, Hanes & Schutz, Colorado Springs, Colorado)

Kenneth Kirkpatrick's ability to analyze an existing construction job site, identify areas of inferior workmanship and/or malfeasance are remarkable. He has total command of the Uniformed Building Code and its many nuances and has great credibility before all of our district judges here in El Paso County. His sense of fairness is acute, which gives him credibility. (Timothy G. Felt, P.C., Colorado Springs, Colorado)

Ken Kirkpatrick simplifies the complexity by breaking the problem down into manageable elements; then he communicates with me and my clients in plain English. He does not try to overwhelm his listener with technical jargon. He is plain spoken and persuasive under cross-examination. In heated adversarial situations, Ken has held his tongue and his temper. I can count on Ken Kirkpatrick's reliability. (Edward M. Murphy, P.C., Colorado Springs, Colorado)

I used Ken Kirkpatrick as an expert witness in a residential construction case. Not only was his testimony and expert opinion valuable, but Mr. Kirkpatrick provided substantial help in preparing to cross-examine the opponent's witness, including their expert witness. Mr. Kirkpatrick was able to provide ideas and information that ultimately benefitted my client's case. (Barry W. Holmes, Denver, Colorado)

Criselle Daxton, MSN RN CNNP CFNP

1234 Horn Trail • Forissant, Colorado 80816 • (719) 555-1234

Qualifications

Dedicated Family Nurse Practitioner with more than 20 years of advanced practice experience.
Background in emergency, intensive care, internal medicine, critical care, neonatal, and in-flight nursing.
Flexible quick learner who adapts easily to new situations and enjoys a challenge.
Self-motivated professional with a commitment to providing quality nursing care.
Strong organizational and communication skills.

Credentials

Registered Nurse (License #51436)
Nationally Certified Family Nurse Practitioner
Nationally Certified Neonatal Nurse Practitioner

Certifications

Basic Life Support
Pediatric Advanced Life Support
Neonatal Resuscitation Program Regional Instructor

Education

BSN, MSN, FNP, University of Colorado at Colorado Springs, May 2000
Neonatal Nurse Practitioner Certificate, Beth-El College of Nursing, Colorado Springs, Colorado, 1989
Associate Degree in Nursing, Mesa College, Grand Junction, Colorado, 1980

Professional Experience

FAMILY NURSE PRACTITIONER
Dr. John Genrich, Pediatrician, Colorado Springs, Colorado . . . . 2002 – present

NEONATAL NURSE PRACTITIONER
Memorial Hospital, Colorado Springs, Colorado . . . . 2000 – present
- Responsible for attending all deliveries and providing appropriate medical care, assessment, and case management in a level III regional medical center.
- Member of the neonatal transport team; selected as a clinical resource person for the institution.

FLIGHT NURSE/EMERGENCY ROOM NURSE
St. Mary's Medical Center, Grand Junction, Colorado . . . . 1998 – 2000
- Provided nursing care during helicopter transport of patients.

LEVEL II ICN STAFF NURSE
St. Mary's Medical Center, Grand Junction, Colorado . . . . 1997 – 1998
- Provided comprehensive nursing care to patients in a Level II ICN.

EMERGENCY DEPARTMENT STAFF NURSE
St. Anthony's Hospital, Denver, Colorado . . . . 1989 – 1997
- Served as a staff nurse in both the Emergency Room and Medical ICU.
- Hospital night supervisor.

Professional Affiliations, Research, and Publications

- Member of the American Academy of Nurse Practitioners
- Co-investigator (1992). Conventional versus high-frequency oscillatory ventilation following exosurf administration in infants with respiratory distress syndrome, Memorial Hospital
- Daxton, C., Bruce, C. E., Monaco, F. J., and Meredith, K. M. (1993). Conventional versus high-frequency oscillatory ventilation following exosurf administration in infants with respiratory distress syndrome: A preliminary retrospective review. Abstract published in *Pediatric Pulmonology*.

8 Geographic Location

With my international clients, the fact that they have worked, studied, lived, or traveled abroad strengthens their credentials for international jobs. Therefore, placing the geographic location experience or schooling in a prominent location can be to their advantage.

Other times, it is only part of the overall design of the information. However, making it prominent does give it more importance, whether that was the intention or not.

When you really want the geographic locations of your past experience—or anything else on your résumé—to stand out, the easiest way to accomplish that is to make them flush right (pages 138 and 139) or to place them in the left-hand column of the résumé. Another alternative is to tab to a fixed place on the page for each location, as in the example on pages 136 and 137.

All of the samples in this section will cause problems with a scanner, since they create multiple columns or place text in unusual places, which confuses the OCR and applicant tracking software. To avoid this, tuck the place names up against the text and use bold or italics to make them stand out instead.

Richard Philip Greene

18, rue du Fierney • F-01630 St. Genis-Pouilly, France • Home: +33 450 20 60 30 • Cellular: +33 6 88 01 94 88
E-mail: RPB2@wanadoo.fr • Website: www.Powles-Brown.com

PROFILE

- Seasoned telecom/IT professional with diverse experience in:
  - Product development
  - Project management
  - Business planning
  - Training programmes
  - HR supervision
  - Software design
  - Network architecture
  - Capacity management
  - Interactive voice response
- Effective team leader with the proven ability to motivate staff to achieve goals.
- High achiever with a passion for training others to excel in highly technical fields.

EXPERIENCE

CONSULTANT (2000 – present)
Founded a successful consulting company dedicated to resolving cutting-edge technology challenges for clients throughout Europe. Developed innovative training programmes.

Phonexion SA (7 months)   *Geneva, Switzerland*
- Sold the Digitalk platform to this rapidly growing startup company and then was hired as a consultant to integrate and maintain it.
- Facilitated the doubling of business every two months in the first six months from zero to $4 million per month.
- Created calling card and other value-added services.
- Installed and maintained new carrier interconnects and provided customer service.

Digitalk, Limited (16 months)   *France and Switzerland*
- Developed business relationships with and sold Digitalk products to telecom companies in both France and Switzerland.

Digitalk, Limited (17 months)   *Milton Keynes, UK*
- Developed the concept for and designed the complete Digitalk training programme and delivered it to engineering and sales staff, as well as customers.
- Solicited customer feedback and integrated their requirements into the software design.

DIRECTOR, TEDS SÀRL (2004 – 2005)   *Geneva, Switzerland*
- Designed and implemented new calling card and 0900, premium-rate products.
- Wrote a comprehensive business plan with pro forma financial statements.
- Sold products and services through direct marketing.
- Responsible for full profit and loss, sales, customer service, and new product development.

ENGINEERING MANAGER, Interoute SA (1997 – 2000)   *Geneva, Switzerland*
- Managed all technical and help desk aspects of the Interoute Swiss Network, including network architecture, capacity management, and operational maintenance.
- Directed operations, hired technical staff, and allocated the training budget.
- Led the installation of a $2 million, 200m^2 switch in both Geneva and Zurich, as well as its associated network operations centre, then transferred all traffic and services to it. Determined project scope, budget, location, architecture, and time lines.
- Managed network quality and proactively monitored the network.
- Developed and implemented improved processes and working practices.
- Performed an in-depth market research study of potential teleconferencing platform suppliers and their product offerings.
- Gained experience with Ericsson Diax ANS switch, Digitalk Value-Added Platform with SQL server, ECI Digital Circuit Multiplication Equipment (DCME), ATM and SDH networks, and SS7 Carrier Interconnect.

MAINTENANCE MANAGER, Certacom, Ltd. (1991 – 1997)   *Wooburn Green, UK*
- Provided pre- and post-sales support of Certacom's signaling conversion equipment; produced designs for signaling converters; and organized dealerboard installations and expansions.
- Hired, trained, and supervised four wire persons, two test technicians, one storekeeper, and two engineers.
- Designed and delivered a speech-band training course for employees and customers.
- Maintained ISO 9002 (QAG 1) license.
- Oversaw non-contract maintenance of all products supplied by the company, including echo cancellers, analogue signaling converters, voice compression equipment, dealerboards, channel banks, and high-speed data modems.

EXPERIENCE   **SENIOR ENGINEER, Extel Systems Support** (1988 – 1991)   *London, UK*
- Rapidly promoted from Engineer to Senior Engineer and then to Senior Technical Support Engineer responsible for on-site maintenance of city brokerage systems (dealerboards), videoconferencing system design, and VSAT satellite data broadcast installation and maintenance.
- Planned and developed quotes for dealerboard installation projects.
- Led a team of four engineers in the installation and maintenance of dealerboards to ISO 9002 (BS 5750/QAG 931) standards.
- Installed X.25 packet switching on the existing Extel network.
- Participated in the design of the Comms '90 show display for Extel and managed the technical side of its installation.

FIELD ENGINEER, Apricot Computers (1986 – 1988)   *Birmingham, London, UK*
- Performed field maintenance and repairs to Apricot desktop PCs, peripherals, and LANs.

EDUCATION   **OPEN UNIVERSITY**, Milton Keynes, UK
- **Technology**: Digital Telecommunications, Digital Transmission Systems, Digital Switching Systems.
- **Business**: Complexity, Management, and Change—Applying a Systems Approach, Level 3.
- **Liberal Arts**: Introduction to Psychology.
- **Special Projects**: Directed the installation of a large telecom switch (AXE 501) in Geneva, Switzerland.

BRITISH TELECOMMUNICATION, PLC, Barking, London, UK (1981 – 1986)
Telecommunications Technician Certificate, East Ham College of Technical Education
- Completed a three-year apprenticeship program that focused on data circuit and data transmission equipment provision and maintenance, as well as private data circuits and speech-band circuits.
- Served as a technician and technical officer assigned to the Data Telecommunications Unit.
- Installed and maintained a wide range of personal computers and peripherals.
- Received Best Student—Technical Studies Award.

PROFESSIONAL DEVELOPMENT
- SQL Server Administration, Moebius Business Training, 2 days (2000)
- SQL Programming—Transact, Moebius Business Training, 1 day (2000)
- Bespoke TCP/IP and Understanding ATM, The Knowledge Centre, 4 days (1999)
- Diax ANS Basic and General O&M, Ericsson Diax, 14 days (1996)
- Landmark Education Courses (1994 – 1997)
  - Self-Expression and Leadership Program
  - Communication, Access to Power
  - Communication, Performance and Power
  - Introduction to the Forum Leadership Program and subsequent coaching
- Nokia Transmission Products, Nokia, 4 days (1994)
- Apricot PC Range Training Course, Apricot Computers Limited, 5 weeks (1986)
- Provision and Maintenance of Speech-band Circuits, British Telecom, 15 days (1986)

COMPUTERS   • **Software Applications**: MS Word, Excel, PowerPoint, Outlook, Visio, Photosuite
- **Languages**: SQL, GW Basic, Assembly
- **Operating Systems**: Windows, MS-DOS
- **Networking**: LAN, WAN, TCP/IP, ATM, ISDN, networking protocols, Cisco CCNA Introduction, Ericsson DIAX ANS switching system, interactive voice transmission switching and signaling, SS7, CCITT 7

PERSONAL   • **Languages**: native English speaker, fluent in French, knowledge of German
- **International**: Lived and worked four years in Switzerland, three years in France
- **Personal**: U.K. citizen, born 8/7/65, married, three children
- **Interests**: marathon running and swimming, skiing, digital photography, building kit cars, assembling computers and servers from scratch, British MENSA

LANDON LAVIGNE

1234 SCHOOL AVENUE
MISSOULA, MONTANA 59801
HOME: 406.555.1234 * LAVIGNE@PROTYPELTD.COM * CELL: 406.555.5678

ASSOCIATE ATTORNEY

Legal career incorporating research and writing functions, client interaction and all matters pertaining to estate planning in a dynamic, community-oriented firm. Outstanding communication capabilities with unique experience in client services, business technology, and legal endeavors. Exceptional analytic, presentation, communication, and team-oriented skills embodied in a hard-working, ethical, and imaginative associate.

LEGAL COMPETENCIES

ESTATE PLANNING, PROBATE, PROPERTY, TRUSTS, and SMALL BUSINESS

- Performed estate planning—designed wills, trusts, bequests, and succession plans for asset transfers.
- Directly advised clients on legal issues, litigation strategies, and estate and trust planning.
- Developed and streamlined automated forms system, creating an efficient forms-rendering process.
- Created computerized operating modifications that increased efficiency and profitability.

BUSINESS COMPETENCIES

MANAGEMENT, MARKETING, and TECHNOLOGY INTEGRATION

- Interned in national and international for-profit and non-profit industries.
- Analyzed marketing concepts and spearheaded the strategic marketing plan for a new product launch.
- Developed a spreadsheet function for monitoring client investments.
- Helped create overarching firm strategy for a financial consulting firm.

JD/MBA, *The University of Montana, School of Law and School of Business Administration,* June 2001
BA, Political Science and English, *The University of Wyoming, Magna cum Laude,* June 1997

LEGAL PROFILE

McDOUGALL, MINNICK & SMITH LAW OFFICES, PC   June 2001 to present
Associate Attorney   *Missoula, Montana*
- Advise and counsel clients on all aspects of estate planning, including wills, revocable and irrevocable trusts, powers of attorney, advance medical directives, succession planning, and passing of assets.
- Developed and implemented an automated forms system for estate planning at increased efficiency.
- Aid managing partner in assessing workflow strategies, eliminating costs, and creating process efficiencies.
- Assist firm in the implementation and utilization of existing technology to enhance profitability.

MONTANA STATE BAR — PROBATE, TRUSTS and ESTATES DEPARTMENT   August 2000 to June 2001
Law Clerk   *Helena, Montana*
- Aided attorneys in rewriting and revising Montana probate legal forms and documents.
- Reformatted and computerized probate forms to conform to Montana Uniform District Court rules.
- Solicited and incorporated forms, not previously available to the public, into District Court Web pages.

BASTINE, MacMILLAN & SAND, PC   August 1999 to August 2000
Legal Intern   *Missoula, Montana*
- Research, review, and analyze client estate planning records for senior associate attorneys.
- Advised and counseled clients in estate planning, including wills, trusts, and powers of attorney.
- Responsible for coordinating workflow from staff attorneys to four interns, including the preparation and writing of legal pleadings, briefs, and memoranda.

FINANCIAL PROFILE

EDWARD JONES FINANCIAL SERVICES   September 1996 to June 1997
Financial Consultancy Intern   *Laramie, Wyoming*
- Performed equity and debt investment research geared toward portfolio allocation.
- Constructed allocation models for Chief Executive Officer review using Microsoft Excel.
- Schooled in gift and estate taxes, IRA distribution, insurance, and education trusts.
- Interacted with individual and business clients, financial products salespeople, and affiliates.

KELLY COMPANY   Summer 1996
Human Resources Intern   *Denver, Colorado*
- Led search and created benchmarking process for proposed company-wide performance-based bonus system linking individual and team performance to results.
- Researched and developed user-friendly, online application system for job seekers.
- Structured and executed comprehensive redesign of current compensation and benefits packages.
- Screened and segregated résumés of potential employees for senior recruiters, assisting with recruitment of over 200 professional staff.

AMERICAN HEART ASSOCIATION   Summer 1995
Intern and Instructor   *Boulder, Colorado*
- Taught First Aid, CPR, babysitting, and crisis management courses in the community and schools.
- Organized more than 100 volunteers; managed on- and off-site presentations and fund-raisers.
- Served as safety manager to coordinate security, safety, and medical services for the Special Olympics.

PROFESSIONAL AFFILIATIONS

THE UNIVERISTY OF MONTANA – MISSOULA, SCHOOL OF LAW
    Montana Student Bar Association, Community Consultant
    Associate Students of the University of Montana, Legal Consultant

AMERICAN COLLEGE OF ESTATE LAWYERS, 2004 to present
    State Chair, 2004 – 2005

MONTANA BAR ASSOCIATION, 2002 to present
    Young Lawyers Executive Committee, 2001 – 2003
    Committee on Education, 2002 – 2003

AMERICAN BAR ASSOCIATION, 2001 to present
    Young Lawyers Division, 2001 – present
    House of Delegates, 2003 – 2005

PRESENTATIONS AND PUBLICATIONS

"Issues of Probate," *The Montana Bar Journal*, Volume XVI, No. 10, November 2004.
Tenth Annual Community Law School Seminar, Missoula, Montana, February 2003.
Streamlining and Automating Forms, Montana Bar Association Annual Meeting, Helena, Montana, 2002.

CHARITABLE ORGANIZATIONS

- Missoula Symphony, Board of Directors
- Montana Special Olympics, Fundraising
- Food Bank of Wyoming, Board of Directors
- Laramie Animal Shelter, Kennel Sponsor
- Community Legal Services of Missoula, Legal Counsel
- Habitat for Humanity, Applicant Screening Chair
- Community Dispute Resolution Center, Advisor
- American Red Cross, Fundraising Chair

CASSY SNOW

6666 99th Street, Alabaster, Texas 79000 • csnow5599@protypeltd.com

(915) 555-1234 (H) • (915) 555-5678 (C)

OBJECTIVE

Enrollment in MNA's Nurse Anesthesia School Master's Degree Program

EDUCATION

1995 – 2000	**COLLEGIATE HEALTH SCIENCES CENTER** **Bachelor of Science in Nursing, 2005** • Overall GPA 3.5 • President's List, 2001 • Dean's List, 2000, 2003, 2005	Alabaster, Texas
Relevant Study:	COLLEGIATE MEDICAL CENTER Pediatric Independent Study, 90 hours, Fall 2000	Alabaster, Texas
Relevant Projects:	• Wrote and implemented policy and procedure for urine dipstick testing for Alabaster Children's Health Clinic • Acted as case manager for local family under supervision of professor • Presented shaken baby syndrome lecture for research class • Taught senior citizens group regarding home safety • Participated in medical and nursing mission trip, Spring 2003	Alabaster, Texas Hunt, Texas Cabaso, Mexico

LICENSES AND CERTIFICATIONS

- Texas RN License – Number 999999, Expires March 2006
- ACLS Instructor and Provider, Expires March 2006
- PALS Certified, Expires July 2005
- BLS Certified, Expires August 2006
- Chemotherapy Certified, Expires May 2006
- TNNC, Expires October 2007

PROFESSIONAL EXPERIENCE

8/02 – Present	**COLLEGIATE HEALTH SCIENCES CENTER** **Faculty Associate, School of Nursing** Assist nursing students during Pediatric and PICU clinical rotations. Act as resource person assisting with procedures, medication administration, and disease assessment. Function as liaison between students and staff.	Alabaster, Texas
5/00 – Present	**CONSTANT CARE MEDICAL CENTER CHILDREN'S HOSPITAL** **Staff Nurse, RN, Pediatrics Intensive Care Unit** Provide total patient care in a 12-bed, Level II Trauma ICU including care of medical/surgical, neurology, trauma, and post-operative cardiac patients. Act as relief charge nurse, making patient assignments and ensuring all nursing and patient care standards are met. Cross-trained in pediatrics, pediatric emergency room, and NICU. Monitor vitals, administer medications, and assist with procedures. Act as patient advocate and liaison between patient, family, and physician. Assist in new employee orientation. Trained ECMO technician. • Employee of the Month, March 2003 • Member, Process Improvement Committee	Alabaster, Texas

9 Personal Information and References

There are very few times when personal information is appropriate on a résumé. Usually such facts only take up valuable white space, especially details such as age, sex, race, health, or marital status, and other information that potential employers are not allowed to ask anyway. There are exceptions to every rule in the résumé business, however! Here are some of them:

- International résumés in almost all cases require date of birth, place of birth, citizenship, marital status, sex, and a photograph.

- Students, or those who have recently graduated, often have a difficult time coming up with enough paid experience to demonstrate their qualifications. But, if they have held leadership positions in campus organizations or have supervised groups of people and organized activities on a volunteer basis, then an "Activities" section could strengthen those qualifications.

- A list of sporting interests would be helpful for a person looking for a sports marketing position.

- If you are looking for a job in sales where you would need to travel a great deal, or overseas where relocating an entire family becomes expensive, showing that you are unmarried and willing to travel could be helpful.

- Submitting a résumé to a U.S. company doing business in certain foreign countries could be another example. On such a résumé, an "Interests" section would show a prospective employer that your hobbies are compatible with the host country.

And the list goes on. It is important to use your judgment, since only you know best what qualifications are important in your field. Just remember this one rule: the information provided should be related directly to bonafide occupational qualifications for the job you are seeking.

❏ Photographs

Photographs on a résumé are required by foreign companies requesting a curriculum vita. However, in the United States, photographs are discouraged in all but a few industries. For instance, if you are trying for a job as an actor, model, newscaster, or in some other field where your appearance is, again, a bonafide occupational qualification, then a photograph is appropriate. Remember, there is an exception to every rule in the résumé business, so use your judgment.

❏ References

References are not usually presented on a résumé since most employers will not take the time to check references until after an interview. By then, they will have your completed application with a list of references. You also don't want to impose on your friends, associates, or former employers unnecessarily or too frequently. There is nothing wrong with taking a nicely printed list of personal references with you to an interview, however.

Here is one of those exceptions to the rule again. If an advertisement requests that a list of references be sent with the résumé and cover letter, then by all means supply the list. You don't want to be accused of not following directions.

Another thing: Avoid that needless line at the bottom of the résumé that says, "References available upon request." It takes up valuable white space that you need to define the sections of your résumé in order to draw the reader's eyes logically down the page.

Pretend you are an interviewer. You ask, "Will you provide references?" The interviewee replies, "Sorry, no, I can't do that." Will you even think twice about continuing to consider this candidate? I think not. It is assumed that you will provide references when requested.

It is perfectly fine to pull out some quotes from your reference letters (or performance evaluations) and use them as "decorations" on your resume (see pages 144, 145, and 147).

Kelly A. Messerly

1234 Summernight Terrace • Colorado Springs, Colorado 80909
Home: (719) 555-1234 • Email: kamess@protypeltd.com

SUMMARY	• Demonstrated success in television and radio announcer positions for more than 15 years. • Background in television reporting, weather forecasting, editing, production, and camera work. • Confident camera presence and broadcasting voice. • Definitive abilities in research, writing, production, and sales. • Self-motivated professional who is comfortable working independently with little supervision.
EXPERIENCE **Television**	• Completed KRDO and KKTV television internships as a weather forecaster, traffic anchor, editor, and reporter. • Presented weekend weather forecasts, including research, writing, editing, prompter setup, and on-camera performances. • As a reporter, investigated backgrounds, traveled to shoot on location, set up cameras, inter-viewed contacts, and filed stories. • Served as traffic anchor during the weekdays for Metro Networks. • Worked as a production assistant and cameraman for KOAA television. • Assisted production company in the creation of commercials by setting up cameras and lighting, writing scripts, editing videotape, and performing voiceovers. • Acted in commercials for Fountain Valley Mechanical, Sun Spot Tanning Salons, and Eagle Hardware. • Two years of college training in producing, behind-the-scenes directing, floor design, lighting, camera operations, and journalism. • Attended modeling school in 1991 to further develop camera presence.
Radio	• Sixteen years of experience as a radio announcer and on-air personality for contemporary radio stations. • Owned and operated a successful DJ service; developed markets for performances at private parties, conventions, weddings, and military gatherings. • Performed public service announcements and voiceovers. • Wrote and performed commercials for Computer Edge.
Communications	• Top trainer at Peterson Air Force Base for four years; instructed all enlisted personnel in emer-gency action procedures. • Briefed Margaret Thatcher, Dan Quayle, Ted Kennedy, visiting generals, and other distinguished visitors. • Staff reporter for the University of Southern Colorado weekly newspaper. • Member of Toastmasters International; spoken before groups as large as 800.

WORK HISTORY

Weekend Weather Anchor, KKTV Television, Colorado Springs	2003 – present
Reporter, KKTV Television, Colorado Springs	2000 – present
Radio Announcer, KKLI 106.3 and KSPZ 92.9, Colorado Springs	1998 – present
Owner, James L. Brown DJ Service, Colorado Springs	1990 – present
Radio Announcer, KKMG 98.9, Colorado Springs	1995 – 1998
Television Intern, KRDO Television, Colorado Springs	1999
Television Intern, KOAA Television, Colorado Springs	1999

EDUCATION

Meteorology Certificate, Mississippi State University, Mississippi	2003
Bachelor of Science, Mass Communications, University of Southern Colorado	1998
Associate of Applied Science, Broadcasting, Pikes Peak Community College	1996
Columbia School of Broadcasting, Hollywood, California	1992

JAMES ALLIBROW

557 110th Avenue NE ▪ Seattle, WA 98000 ▪ Home: 206.123.4567 ▪ plan@protypeltd.com

CAREER TARGET: MANAGEMENT / ADMINISTRATION

Leadership ▪ Project Management ▪ Planning / Delegation ▪ Hiring / Training

Experienced manager and administrator offering 10+ year public, private and entrepreneurial history in leading professional and represented labor in the efficient completion of projects and improved service delivery.

- Team and Project Leadership
- Data Systems and Reporting
- Budgets, A/R, A/P
- Hiring, Training, and Evaluation
- Writing: Grants, Reports, Letters
- Relationship Mgt./Project Liaison
- Compliance/Personnel Records
- Sales and Customer Service
- Computers: MS Office

"... James maintains a professional and disciplined approach to his work. He plans his activities and follows through. ... He is a well organized and disciplined officer who focuses on each job and efficiently completes it. He improves morale. ... Rated 'outstanding.'"—NOAA Evaluation

─────────────── **RELEVANT EXPERIENCE** ───────────────

City of Seahurst – Parks Department, Normandy Park, WA   2002 – 2005
ASSISTANT TO URBAN FORESTRY CREW CHIEF (01/04 – 06/04) / **TREE TRIMMER** (04/02 – 02/05)

Created office systems for field office, which markedly increased responsiveness of field crew. Managed work order system, tracking and executing assignment of orders to a seven-person crew. Processed orders for new equipment and maintenance. Completed monthly reports. Responded to questions from the public. *Achievements:*

- **Data Management and Order Backlogs**: Prioritized, dispatched, copied, and data-entered data for six months of backlogged work orders. Set up tracking system for new/existing orders, improving response time.
- **Scheduling and Prioritizing Tasks:** Tracked work requests/scheduled maintenance for 20+ parks.
- **Committees and Policies:** Established idle reduction protocol to complement the Park's air quality policy.
- **Program Development:** Created and implemented the Department's first tree replacement program.

North Face Recreational Equipment, Seattle, WA   2001 – 2002
CUSTOMER SERVICE, RENTAL WINDOW / RENTAL DEPARTMENT ASSOCIATE (12/01 – 04/02)

Staffed a busy retail counter that rented outdoor gear (i.e., skis, snowshoes, tents) to the general public. Managed rental equipment system. Scheduled reservations. Processed Visa/cash payments. *Achievements:*

- **Conflict Resolution:** Managed stress, found solutions, and calmed customers.

Shorewood Tree and Garden Care, Seattle, WA   1999 – 2001
GENERAL MANAGER – OWNER (10/99 – 11/01)

Founded a successful grounds maintenance company, handling all aspects of business development: bidding, service delivery, customer service, scheduling, budgets, A/R, A/P, and equipment purchases.

- **Sales and Customer Service:** Sold and serviced 150+ repeat residential/commercial clients.

Other: Tree Trimmer, ChemLawn Co. (10/98 – 10/99) ♦ Lead Gardener, Puget Landscaping (04/97 – 01/99)

National Oceanic & Atmospheric Administration (NOAA), Seattle/HI/NC/Global   1985 – 1995
COMMISSIONED OFFICER, NOAA CORPS (10/85 – 12/95)

Promoted five times in 10 years, achieving officer/executive team status within the NOAA organization. Handled crew hiring, training, and supervision; crew evaluation and mentoring; health and safety; tactical planning; emergency response; and budget preparation. Managed finance, administration, and daily operations for research vessels/projects in the western coastal zone.

National Oceanic & Atmospheric Administration (NOAA) – CONTINUED

PORT CAPTAIN, FIELD OPERATIONS OFFICER, Fishing Research Vessel (05/93 – 12/95)
PORT CAPTAIN / OFFICE MANAGER, Bangor, WA (02/91 – 05/93)

As Office Manager/Port Captain, managed the maintenance of a research vessel's financial and personnel records, time and attendance reports, and monthly expenditure reports. Supervised one financial administration. Prepared purchase orders, procurement requisitions, and open market purchases. Prepared travel orders and government bills of lading. Maintained radio/email fleet communications. Prepared vehicle/equipment reports. Helped compile budgets.

As Field Operations Officer. Managed the daily scientific operations of a 30-person crew. Provided administrative and logistical support to research scientists to make sure the day's research ran smoothly. Took on the role as acting executive officer aboard a scientific research vessel. Sailed during a hurricane-prone year, communicating with all on board and updating "Plan of the Day" to ensure smooth research operations and avoid bad seas. Managed staff in keeping legacy computers (VAX/SCS system) operational. *Achievements:*

- **Leadership and Administration:** Assigned second-in-command role as acting executive officer in 1995. Supervised junior officers and resolved all personnel issues.
- **NOAA Corps Field Recruiter:** Hired crew for the ship and recruited potential officer candidates.
- **Mentoring and Performance Turnarounds:** Inspired peer to take watch duty seriously, resulting in improved performance of peer and diligent completion of duties.
- **Emergency Response:** Identified shipboard fire, leading team to resolve situation quickly.
- **Computer System Upgrade Projects:** As communications liaison, took on the challenge of upgrading computer system in port office. During same period, supported six-month ship repair project.
- **Interagency Liaison:** Communications link with the University of WA, NOAA Laboratory, U.S. Coast Guard, U.S. Navy, U.S. Air Force, State of Washington, City of Seattle Harbors, and the general public.

> *"... James has been a strong supporter of diversity. He actively works with and supports the culturally diverse crew and scientific compliment aboard the ship. ..."—NOAA Evaluation*

RESEARCH SCIENTIST (01/88 – 02/91)

Coordinated scientific activities. Organized and implemented diving operations for ship safety inspection and scientific studies. *Projects:*

Project Manager – NMFS Sea Lion Distribution Study
- **Survey Design and Distribution:** Created postcard survey that received significant response and provided data on Sea Lion distribution through Alaska.
- **Consensus Building:** Secured cooperation from fishermen, who could have perceived an animal survey/protection effort as being against their interests, and gained partners in reporting lion sitings.

Divemaster – Principal Author, Research Study: Razor Clam Rehabilitation Study
- **Health and Safety Training / Procedures:** Designed dive procedures. Trained crew divers in research techniques.
- **Written Communications:** Worked with research team to compile data, write, and edit final study.

Volunteer Coordinator / Principal Author, Research Study – Plastic Marine Debris Study
- **Volunteer Recruitment and Organizing:** Worked with schools to secure and manage 20+ teenage students. Supervised plastic debris collection along the beach for characterization in study.

> *"... James did an excellent job as computer officer working with ETs to keep PCs and software operational. He installed the email system. ... His excellent performance is noteworthy, given his limited prior computer experience. He is capable and rises to the occasion."—NOAA Evaluation*

EDUCATION

B.S. Marine Science, University of Alaska / **A.S. Horticulture,** Shoreline Community College

ALLAN W. SMITH

QUALIFICATIONS
- Well-rounded, seasoned media sales professional with a diverse background in:
  - New business development – Radio   – Cold calling
  - Client relationship building   – Television   – Contract negotiations
  - Promotions/incentives   – Cable media   – Production
- True "people person" who is willing to go the extra mile to satisfy the client's need.
- Demonstrated ability to create client loyalty above and beyond the sales relationship.

SUMMARY

SALES AND MARKETING
- Successfully sold advertising in highly competitive markets for radio, television, and cable media companies.
- Cold called on corporate executives and small business owners to generate new accounts.
- Formulated and conducted effective multimedia sales presentations and established profitable business relationships with national and local advertisers.
- Created proposals, negotiated contracts, and closed sales.
- Helped clients to develop and implement promotional campaigns and strategic marketing plans for media advertising.
- Worked closely with advertising agencies to ensure the continuity of advertising messages.
- Certified Radio Marketing Consultant (CRMC) since 1989.

COMMUNICATION
- Proven ability to put the prospective customer at ease using a comfortable demeanor.
- Skilled at interpreting client needs and arranging ideas and words to create memorable impact.
- Wrote scripts for and performed in radio commercials and public service advertisements.
- Well-rounded media professional with experience as a news director and DJ for radio stations in early career. Interviewed movie/music stars and sports legends.

EXPERIENCE

SENIOR ACCOUNT EXECUTIVE
KOAA /NBC, Channel 5/30, Colorado Springs, Colorado (2004 – present)
- Sell advertising for NBC Channel 5/30, as well as for Cable Channel 9 *Weather First Now,* a local weather and news station operated by KOAA.
- Responsible for new client development, focusing on the retail sector and advertising agencies.
- Develop advertising proposals to meet each client's goals and budget.
- Create promotional ideas for *Weather First Now,* including register-to-win contests and ski resort promotions.
- Recognized as the top sales closer out of nine account executives with a 75% closing ratio.

ACCOUNT EXECUTIVE
Adelphia Media Services, Colorado Springs, Colorado (1992 – 2003)
- Sold advertising on cable television throughout Colorado's Front Range, building an account base from zero and generating more than $5 million in eleven years.
- Collaborated with advertising agencies to win national accounts from Jeep Chrysler Corporation, General Motors, and Safeway, among others.
- Negotiated annual, recurring contracts with large accounts that included Pueblo Bank and Trust, Medved AutoPlex, Cripple Creek Casino Owners Association, Gold Rush Hotel and Casino, Denver Newspaper Agency, Colorado Lottery, Peak Vision Center, Champion Windows, Clear Channel Communications, K&C RV Sales, and McDonalds.

ADDRESS

1234 Dirksland Street • Colorado Springs, Colorado 80907
Home: (719) 555-1234 • Cellular: (719) 555-5678 • Email: allansmith@protypeltd.com

146

EXPERIENCE (continued)	**ACCOUNT EXECUTIVE**

ACCOUNT EXECUTIVE
KAZY 106.7 FM, Denver, Colorado (1990 – 1992)
- Developed new accounts and maintained established corporate accounts for this classic rock radio station.
- Succeeded in generating nearly one half million dollars of annual revenue in the greater Denver metropolitan area.
- Ranked number one for new business development out of all account executives.

ACCOUNT EXECUTIVE
KKTV Channel 11, Colorado Springs, Colorado (1988 – 1990)
- Established a reputation as the top sales performer for this CBS affiliate television station.
- Developed and maintained new contract clients generating $500,000 in annual revenue.

ACCOUNT EXECUTIVE
KILO FM, Colorado Springs, Colorado (1981 – 1988)
- Transformed a small account list into one of the highest-billing radio lists in the Colorado Springs/Pueblo market for this number-one-rated radio station in Southern Colorado.
- Served as the creative force behind the development of promotional concepts.

EDUCATION

UNDERGRADUATE STUDIES
University of Dubuque, Iowa (one year of political science studies)
Brown Institute, Minneapolis, Minnesota (one year of mass communications studies)

PROFESSIONAL DEVELOPMENT
- Jim Doyle Sales Training (ongoing, completed 5 three-day workshops)
- Microsoft Office Course, School District 11 (12 weeks, 2005)
- Karen Brash Executive Sales Training (2 days, 2001)
- Certified Radio Marketing Consultant (1989)
- Jason Jennings Sales Training, Chicago (3 days, 1980)

COMPUTERS

Proficient in Windows, MS Word, PowerPoint, Outlook, Internet Explorer, and Lotus Notes.

CLIENT COMMENTS

"Allan has proven to be extremely knowledgeable and professional in executing my local Cable TV media campaigns. Having worked in cable advertising sales myself for six years, I can appreciate when a media salesperson does a great job from the initial schedule planning stage to the final invoice." Mike Slattery, Champion

"His thorough knowledge of his product and the sales process are evidence of his many years of success in media sales. I enthusiastically recommend Allen for any sales position and am confident that his competency and positive attitude would make him a valuable asset." Christin Stansbury, Academy Agency & Advisors

"As a representative for Adelphia Cable, Allan was one of the few who understands the true meaning of the word 'service.' " Robert Adams, Adams Advertising Agency

"Allan has the four traits that make him a great sales rep: friendly, responsible, efficient, and fun. If Allan is applying for a job with your company, I suggest hiring him immediately!" Brian Prescott, Hanson Marketing & Advertising

FATHY HOSNY GOZEH

Home Address • 3 Abd El Menom • Riad St. El Nadi Square • Kafr Shukr Kalubia, Egypt
Cellular: 0020 12 555 1234 • Home: 0020 2 555 5678 • E-mail: fathyg@protypeltd.com
Work Address • c/o Reception Department • Cairo Marriott Hotel & Casino • P.O. Box 123 • Zamalek, Cairo, Egypt

OBJECTIVE

A responsible position within the international hospitality, tourism, or transportation industries that would enhance professional growth and utilize strong interpersonal and linguistic skills.

PROFILE

- Dedicated professional with a strong work ethic and definitive customer service skills.
- Extensive background in the international hospitality and tourism industries.
- Experienced foreign traveler who is proficient in English, French, Arabic, and Hebrew languages.
- Effective team player with proven communication and interpersonal skills.
- Computer skills: Fidelio, Marasha, PMS, IBM HIS 36, and Windows 98/2000.

EDUCATION

BACHELOR OF ARTS (1997)
Benha University, Faculty of Arts, English Department, Benha, Egypt
- Major in English Language and Literature and American Literature

CERTIFICATE IN THE FRENCH LANGUAGE (1999)
Centre Francais de Culture et de Cooperation, Cairo, Egypt

EXPERIENCE

FRONT DESK CLERK, Marriott Hotel and Casino, Zamalek, Cairo, Egypt (1999 – present)
- Greeted, checked in, and checked out guests, made reservations, and answered the switchboard for this five-star property, the largest hotel in the Middle East with 1,250 rooms.
- Managed the cash drawer, accepted payments, and balanced daily receipts.
- Completed extensive Marriott customer service, teamwork, computer systems, and hotel procedures training programs.
- Operated the hotel's computer systems, including Marasha and PMS.

FRONT DESK CLERK, **Bed and Breakfast Hotel**, Paris, France (1999)
- Made reservations, greeted guests, assigned rooms, and accepted payments.
- Operated the switchboard, took accurate messages, and routed calls to appropriate rooms.

FRONT DESK CLERK, Hilton Resort and Casino, Taba, Egypt (1997 – 1999)
- Coordinated group check-in and check-out for this 410-room, five-star resort and conference center.
- Took reservations, operated the switchboard, received guests, and acted as cashier.
- Operated the hotel's computer systems, including Fidelio and IBM HIS 36.
- Immersed in the Hilton International Hotels procedures, philosophies, and computer systems training.

OPERATOR/RECEPTIONIST, Plaza Hotel, Alexandria, Egypt (1996)
- Operated the switchboard and greeted guests for this four-star, 160-room hotel while completing studies at the University.

WAITER, Casa Taba, Hilton, Taba, Egypt (1995)
- Provided exceptional customer service for this five-star Italian seafood restaurant.
- Prepared orders, delivered food and beverages, and served as cashier.
- Investigated and resolved food/beverage quality and service complaints, ensuring customer satisfaction.

PERSONAL

Date of Birth: 14 January 1976
Marital Status: single
Citizenship: Egypt
Military Service: exempt
Interests: Snorkeling, horseback riding, karate, foreign languages, literature, travel

148

10 Fonts and Bullets

Fonts (aka type style or type face) set the tone for the entire résumé. What is a font? It is that little bit of magic that enables humans to communicate in print. It is the alphabet set to music. It is art. Actually, a font is a set of curved, straight, or slanted shapes that your brain decodes into letters and then words, but that sounds too boring for a subject as fascinating as type style.

Every font has its own designer and its own personality. Each font projects a certain "feel." For instance, serif fonts (the kind with the little "feet" like the Utopia font used on this page) are considered more traditional. They are usually used as text fonts in books and magazines. Some samples include:

- Times New Roman
- New Century Schoolbook
- Palatino
- Bookman
- See pages 161–170 and 171 for more serif fonts.

Sans (meaning "without" in French) serif fonts, on the other hand, have no "feet" and are considered more contemporary, as in:

- Helvetica (Arial)
- Avant Garde
- CG Omega
- **Antique Olive**
- See pages 151–159 and 172 for more sans serif fonts.

Although serif fonts are commonly used as text type for the main body of published works, you don't have to restrict yourself to these types of fonts for résumés. Either style produces equally impressive résumés.

Headline fonts and wild type faces have their place in design, but only in the headlines and only for very creative professions. Remember, you want your résumé to be easy to read. You will find many samples of headline fonts on pages 173–174.

In all my many years of designing résumés, I have discovered that my clients don't have to understand the science behind fonts or the difference between serif and sans serif fonts, and neither do you. It is more important that you look at samples of good résumé fonts and then choose the one that makes your eyes "feel good." In other words, choose the one you like the best. Again, it comes down to personality.

If you are concerned about the scannability of your résumé, remember that the fonts you choose play a major role. If you haven't read Chapter 3, now is the time to read it. Pages 33 through 36 address the scannability of fonts and bullets in particular.

❏ Bullets

Bullets are special characters used at the beginning of indented short sentences to call attention to individual items on a résumé. Short, bulleted sentences are easier to read than long paragraphs of text, and they highlight the information you want the reader to see quickly. Bullets also add some variety to a résumé and make it just a touch more creative.

In both MS Word and WordPerfect, clicking on "Insert" gives you access to a myriad of special characters that are not found on your keyboard. That is how the bullets in this section were created. Your printing capabilities might not allow you to have access to all of these dingbats, wingdings, or symbols, but you can still be creative.

1234 Mohawk Trail
Cascade, Colorado 80809

Phone: (719) 555-1234
Email:engineer@protypeltd.com

PROFILE
- Experienced network administrator with broad knowledge of technical and training concepts, principles, and methods.
- Detail-oriented troubleshooter who gets to the root of the problem quickly.
- Known for the ability to create process efficiencies and getting the job done on time.
- Effective team player with proven communication and interpersonal skills.
- Hold an Interim Top Secret security clearance with access to Sensitive Compartmented Information (SCI).

TECHNICAL
Certification: Microsoft Certified Systems Engineer (MCSE)
Networks: Windows NT, Windows 2000, Windows for Workgroups, Exchange 5.5, Proxy Server 2.10, Microsoft System Management Server (SMS), Norton Ghost
Software: MS Word, Excel, PowerPoint, Outlook, Internet Explorer, Remedy, FrontPage, MS Mail, Netscape Navigator

EXPERIENCE
NETWORK ADMINISTRATOR (2001 – present)
Remtech Services, Inc., Cheyenne Mountain AB, Colorado
- Manage the daily operations of two classified networks with a total of 1,000 users, ensuring that resources are used efficiently.
- Maintain file servers, email, backups, permissions, and security.
- Continuously monitor the network and troubleshoot any problems to minimize downtime.
- Create user accounts, write procedures, and handle network vulnerability issues.
- Install, configure, and optimize software applications and resolve conflicts using standard installation techniques and Ghost images.
- Develop packages to distribute upgrades and service patches using SMS.
- Discovered a physical problem on one of the email servers, moved all users to the backup server, discovered another problem on the backup server, replaced them both, installed and configured the operating system and software, and migrated users to the new server.
- Recommended the purchase of a third-party administration tool (Hyena), which saved significant time.
- Currently helping to create an accreditation package for the network.

NETWORK ADMINISTRATOR (2000 – 2001)
Honeywell Technology Solutions, Inc., Schriever AFB, Colorado
- One of six administrators responsible for 3,000 users on an unclassified network.
- Installed, set up, and supported software products; installed service packs and hot fixes.
- Monitored network servers and responded to and resolved problems.
- Managed network/exchange accounts and share permissions.
- Provided input to generate and update project documents.
- Assist on special projects, such as network security, Windows 2000 testbed, and SMS packages.

LAN SYSTEMS ANALYST (1998 – 2000)
Honeywell Technology Solutions, Inc., Schriever AFB, Colorado
- Provided level-three help desk support for a 3,000-user, Windows NT/95 LAN via telephone, SMS, and onsite visits. Trained new users.
- Maintained a computer maintenance log documenting each user request, detailed problems description, and resolution. Analyzed information to determine potential for enterprise-wide problems/solutions.

EDUCATION
BACHELOR OF SCIENCE, INFORMATION SYSTEMS (1996)
University of Phoenix, Phoenix, Arizona

GIBRALTAR FONT

121 Pleasant Street, Colorado Springs, Colorado 80904
Phone: (719) 555-1234 • E-mail: gene701@protypeltd.com

PROFILE

- Detail-oriented manager with a strong background in television technology.
- Hard-working professional who is willing to do what it takes to get the job done.
- Effective team player with proven communication skills and a reputation for integrity.
- Software: Proficient in Windows, MS Word, Excel, PowerPoint, Outlook, Internet Explorer, Enterprise, Columbine, and MediaLine software.
- Hardware: Experienced in the operation of IBM PCs, AS400 System, and the DARE System.

EXPERIENCE

FOX KXRM TV and UPN KXTU TV, Colorado Springs, Colorado (1988 to present)
National Sales Assistant (1993 to present)

- Began this position as the assistant to the General Sales Manager, but eventually assumed the role of National Sales Manager, although the official title didn't change after the stations were sold.
- Worked closely with representative firms to market commercial advertising space.
- Maintained relationships with major national accounts, including GM, Ford, Saturn, Dodge, General Mills, Kraft, Proctor and Gamble, Budweiser, Coors, Kelloggs, 3-M, Pizza Hut, Fazoli's, Buena Vista, and Sony, among others.
- Developed a reputation as the person rep firm account executives turn to when they compete for Colorado Springs spot dollars.
- Account executive for all paid infomercials, direct response, and per-inquiry advertising.
- Formulated and conducted personal sales presentations and aggressively solicited business already under contract.
- Prepared proposals and negotiated rates, slot availability, and costs per point, ensuring profitability.
- Responsible for budgeting, sales forecasting, invoicing of all national accounts, collecting overdue accounts receivable, and traffic management for two stations.
- Analyzed and predicted the pricing behavior of the competition.
- Succeeded in growing annual advertising revenue from third place in the market to first place.
- Integral member of the team that improved the Nielsen ratings from fourth to first place.
- Input advertising schedules into the Enterprise computer system.

Chief Operator (1990 to 1993)

- Recruited, hired, trained, scheduled, and supervised six master control operators.
- Managed the upgrade of the master control from a Sony LMS to a totally digital system.
- Researched equipment options and made recommendations for the purchase of new equipment.

Master Control Operator (1988 to 1990)

- Set up, controlled, and monitored broadcasting equipment to transmit television programs and station breaks to the viewing audience.
- Observed on-air monitors to troubleshoot and then correct transmission problems.
- Set video, color, and audio levels to specifications.
- Selected as the 1989 Employee of the Year for performance excellence.

BOARDWALK USA, Colorado Springs, Colorado (1982 to 1987)
Restaurant/Arcade Manager

- Successfully managed the flagship operation of this arcade with a Godfather's Pizza restaurant.
- Responsible for food and beverage operations, as well as initial arcade setup and management.
- Diagnosed and maintained arcade machines and upgraded them to digital models.
- Accountable for cost control, budgeting, purchasing, profit and loss, payroll, and record keeping.
- Maintained expenses below budget through accurate planning, purchasing, and cost-effective operating procedures.
- Recruited, hired, supervised, scheduled, and motivated 15 staff members.
- Trained service staff to enhance customer service and increase profit margins.
- Investigated and resolved quality and service complaints, ensuring customer satisfaction.

CRADDOCK TELECOMMUNICATIONS, Colorado Springs, Colorado (1979 to 1982)
Audio Technician

- Member of the production crew for live sporting events.
- Composed music for children's television shows.

EDUCATION

UNDERGRADUATE STUDIES
University of Southern Colorado, Pueblo, Colorado

- Completed all but one year of a Bachelor's degree
- Achieved the Dean's List four consecutive semesters
- Maintained a 4.0 GPA

AVANT GARDE FONT

123 Alpine Drive ✦ Colorado Springs, Colorado 80909
Home: (719) 555-1234 ✦ Cellular: (719) 555-5678 ✦ E-mail: manager@protypeltd.com

PROFILE

✦ Dedicated manager with a strong background in community attraction operations, including:
- Administration
- Supervision
- Retail sales
- Grounds maintenance
- Safety and risk management
- Customer service
- Marketing and promotion
- Community involvement
- Construction/renovation

✦ Intuitive supervisor with strong communication and motivation skills.
✦ Proven leader who can shift gears quickly and handle multiple tasks simultaneously.
✦ Computers: knowledge of Windows, MS Word, Excel, Publisher, e-mail, and the Internet.

EXPERIENCE

GENERAL MANAGER, Seven Falls Company, A.G. Hill, Dallas, Texas (1991 – present)
✦ Direct the day-to-day operations of an outdoor scenic attraction with more than a quarter million visitors a year and $2.5 million in annual revenue.
✦ Succeeded in nearly doubling revenue and increasing visitor traffic by 40,000 in spite of a loss of advertising due to the dissolution of the Colorado Tourism Board in 1994.
✦ Interview, hire, and supervise a staff of 80 employees during peak season; succeeded in maintaining an exceptionally low turnover rate of core staff.
✦ Manage grounds maintenance, preservation of 1,400 acres of forest, and fire/flood prevention.
✦ Coordinate with local and national government agencies for safety, licensing, emergency management, fire prevention, etc.
✦ Proactively manage risk by foreseeing problems in new construction and regular maintenance.
✦ Oversee the operations of food services and three gift shops with $800,000 in inventory.
✦ Train employees to improve customer service; handle all customer complaints and problems.
✦ Responsible for marketing, promotion, and advertising; worked closely with ad agency on the creation and placement of print and billboard advertisements.
✦ Developed an Internet presence in 1992, which was forward thinking for its time.
✦ Supervised large construction and renovation projects, including the mountain elevator, tram, and waterfall stairway additions.

Special Projects:
✦ Represent the company in the annual Christmas Unlimited canyon lighting event generating $30,000 in donations a year (1971 – present).
✦ Member of the Logistics Team for the annual American Heart Association fund-raising walk, which generates $75,000 a year (1993 – present).
✦ Support the Hummingbird Festival and Water Quest events held at the Starsmore Discovery Center as the company representative (1994 – 2000).

ASSISTANT MANAGER, Seven Falls Company, Colorado Springs, Colorado (1971 – 1991)
✦ Hands-on manager responsible for general maintenance of the attraction property, including roads, grounds, buildings, outdoor lighting, forest, snow removal, and vehicle maintenance.
✦ Designed specialized structures and supervised construction.
✦ Hired and supervised a staff of up to 15 maintenance workers.
✦ Sourced suppliers and purchased all operation supplies and construction/repair inventory.

EDUCATION

UNDERGRADUATE STUDIES
University of Colorado, Colorado Springs, Colorado (1981 – 1982)
Pikes Peak Community College, Colorado Springs, Colorado (1971 – 1973)

PROFESSIONAL DEVELOPMENT
Leadership Pikes Peak: Class of 2000 (2000 – 2001)
Disney Institute: Excellence in Customer Service (1994)

AFFILIATIONS

✦ Appointed to the Rules Committee of the Colorado Passenger Tramway Safety Board; created guidelines for funicular railway rules that were adopted nationwide (1983 – 1986).
✦ Member, Board of Directors, Pikes Peak Country Attractions Association (1991 – present); Executive Board Member (1996 – 1998), Vice President (1999 – 2000), and President (2000 – 2001).
✦ Member, Trees Committee, Pikes Peak Hospice (1987 – 1999); coordinate the installation of lighting on all trees for an annual fund-raising event that generates $135,000 a year.

Lucinda Sans Font

1234 Malibu Point, Apt. 1 ♦ Colorado Springs, CO 80906 ♦ Cell: (719) 555-1234 ♦ aaroc@protypeltd.com

Qualifications

- Self-motivated production operator and failure analysis technician with a strong overall knowledge of the silicon wafer manufacturing process.
- Hard worker who enjoys the challenge of learning new things.
- Effective team player with excellent communication and interpersonal skills; able to relate well to people from diverse backgrounds and levels of authority.
- Skilled in visualizing resourceful and enterprising solutions to problems.
- Knowledge of Windows, Excel, MS Explorer, RS1, and MASS11 computer software.

Experience

Failure Analysis Technician
2000 - present

Atmel Corporation, Colorado Springs, Colorado
- Troubleshoot and analyze failures on silicon wafers using cross-sections, scanning electronic microscopes, E-DAX, curve tracers, batch top etchers, hypervision probe stations, etc.
- Responsible for maintenance and operation of Micrion 9500 focused ion beam.
- Make circuit modifications using Knights Technology CAV software.
- Used the FIB to locate and cross-section defects from downloaded Tencor and KLA defect maps.
- Supported yield enhancement and process development groups with innovative solutions to product challenges.
- Experienced in the safe use and disposal of hazardous chemicals.
- Worked from engineering drawings and change orders to ensure products matched specifications.

Buddy Trainer
1998 - 2000

Atmel Corporation, Colorado Springs, Colorado
- Trained and supervised new hires in operations and protocols.
- Cross-trained existing operators.
- Developed innovative training aides.
- Coordinated certification process with engineers and supervisors.

Production Operator
1996 - 1998

Atmel Corporation, Colorado Springs, Colorado
- Manufactured memory chip wafers in a Class 10 clean room environment.
- Performed minor troubleshooting on the line.
- In-depth experience with DNS coders, ASM steppers, batch and track developers, and IVS critical dimension measurement.
- Competent in photolithography, coding, stepping, developing, and inspecting for defects.

Education

Bachelor of Science in Electrical Engineering Studies
2004 - present

University of Colorado, Colorado Springs, Colorado

Associate of Pre-Engineering Studies
1997 - 1999

Pikes Peak Community College, Colorado Springs, Colorado
- Completed 32 credits toward a degree in electrical engineering.

Professional Development

FEI Company, Peabody, Massachusetts
2000
- Customer Maintenance, Level I Certification

ANTIQUE OLIVE ROMAN FONT

1234 Sunshine Trail • Colorado Springs, CO 80917 • Home: (719) 555-1234 • Email: jay1.5@protypeltd.com

PROFILE
- Dependable administrative assistant with a strong customer service background.
- Self-motivated and cooperative; enjoys finding creative, new ways of doing things.
- Hard working, patient team leader with strong communication and interpersonal skills.
- Possesses a high degree of integrity and dedication to exceptional customer service.
- Proficient in Windows, MS Word, Excel, QuickBooks, email, and Internet browsers.

EXPERIENCE
ADMINISTRATIVE ASSISTANT, Feature Homes, Inc., Colorado Springs, CO (2002 – present)
- Provide administrative support to the Controller of this custom residential home builder.
- Research land locations for possible purchase; communicate with land developers weekly.
- Prepare documents for new home closings, review new home contracts, and prepare related paperwork.
- Perform bookkeeping transactions—accounts payable, accounts receivable, and payroll.
- Set appointments with design companies and help determine color schemes for new homes.
- Responsible for customer service, filing, answering telephones, and preparing correspondence and spreadsheets.

BANKER/TELLER, US Bank and Pikes Peak National Bank, Colorado Springs, CO (2000 – 2001)
- Opened the bank, handled large volumes of cash, made deposits, and worked in the vault.
- Accurately handled account transactions, including merchant and personal deposits, check cashing, money transfers, cash advances, and loan payments.
- Sold cashier's checks, money orders, traveler's checks, and savings bonds.
- Balanced tax deposits, cash drawer, and ATM machine.
- Responded to customer inquiries regarding account balances, activities, and services.
- Collected money from customers who wrote checks with insufficient funds.
- Submitted forms to the IRS for high-cash-volume and suspicious transactions.
- Monitored security cameras in the main bank and ATM daily.

SALES ASSOCIATE, Dillard's Department Store, Colorado Springs, CO (1998 – 2000)
- Successfully sold women's accessories, consistently meeting or exceeding sales quotas.
- Assisted customers with buying decisions, using relationship building and suggestive selling techniques to increase store profitability.
- Developed relationships with repeat buyers and created a call list for notification of specials.
- Provided value-added service to customers by exceeding their expectations.
- Created and coordinated contests, promotional gifts, and other sales incentives.
- Merchandised inventory and created visual displays for the handbag, women's accessories, and hosiery departments.
- Received freight onto the floor and distributed merchandise to the appropriate displays.
- Marked down merchandise and performed inventory counts.

ASSISTANT MANAGER, Blockbuster Video, Colorado Springs, CO (1997 – 1998)
- Assisted in the management of this test-market store in a local grocery store.
- Opened and closed the store, balanced cash registers, made bank deposits, managed all safe transactions, and maintained inventory.
- Responsible for store planning, merchandising, signage, and product displays.
- Developed work schedules and supervised up to eight employees.
- Conducted new-hire interviews and made hiring recommendations.
- Trained new employees in store policies, processes, customer service, and computers.
- Expanded customer base through implementation of effective marketing programs and promotions.
- Maintained exceptionally high store standards for inventory presentation and service.

EDUCATION
HARCOURT LEARNING CENTERS, Certified Paralegal Course (1999 – 2001)

CG Omega (Optima) Font

1234 Horn Trail • Forissant, Colorado 80816 • (719) 555-1234

Qualifications

Dedicated Family Nurse Practitioner with more than 20 years of advanced practice experience.
Background in emergency, intensive care, internal medicine, critical care, neonatal, and in-flight nursing.
Flexible quick learner who adapts easily to new situations and enjoys a challenge.
Self-motivated professional with a commitment to providing quality nursing care.
Strong organizational and communication skills.

Credentials

Registered Nurse (License #51436)
Nationally Certified Family Nurse Practitioner
Nationally Certified Neonatal Nurse Practitioner

Certifications

Basic Life Support
Pediatric Advanced Life Support
Neonatal Resuscitation Program Regional Instructor

Education

BSN, MSN, FNP, University of Colorado at Colorado Springs, May 1998
Neonatal Nurse Practitioner Certificate, Beth-El College of Nursing, Colorado Springs, Colorado, 1986
Associate Degree in Nursing, Mesa College, Grand Junction, Colorado, 1971 – 1973

Professional Experience

FAMILY NURSE PRACTITIONER
Dr. John Genrich, Pediatrician, Colorado Springs, Colorado . . . . 1998 – present

NEONATAL NURSE PRACTITIONER
Memorial Hospital, Colorado Springs, Colorado . . . . 1986 – present
- Responsible for attending all deliveries and providing appropriate medical care, assessment, and case management in a level III regional medical center.
- Member of the neonatal transport team; selected as a clinical resource person for the hospital.

FLIGHT NURSE/EMERGENCY ROOM NURSE
St. Mary's Medical Center, Grand Junction, Colorado . . . . 1983 – 1985
- Provided nursing care during helicopter transport of patients.

LEVEL II ICN STAFF NURSE
St. Mary's Medical Center, Grand Junction, Colorado . . . . 1982 – 1983
- Provided comprehensive nursing care to patients in a Level II ICN.

Professional Affiliations, Research, and Publications

- Member of the American Academy of Nurse Practitioners
- Co-investigator. (1992). Conventional versus high-frequency oscillatory ventilation following exosurf administration in infants with respiratory distress syndrome, Memorial Hospital
- Lemmons, M. P., Bruce, C. E., Monaco, F. J., and Meredith, K. M. (1993). Conventional versus high-frequency oscillatory ventilation following exosurf administration in infants with respiratory distress syndrome: A preliminary retrospective review. Abstract published in *Pediatric Pulmonology*.

ARIAL (HELVETICA) FONT
12 Charro Drive • Colorado Springs, Colorado 80911
Home: (719) 555-1234 • Cellular: (719) 555-5678
Email: gkacolorado@protypeltd.com

QUALIFICATIONS

- Nearly seven years of commercial driving experience, four years of which have been driving concrete mixer trucks.
- Hold a current Class A Commercial Driver's License with all endorsements (Tanker, HazMat, Doubles/Triples).

EDUCATION

- United States Truck Driving School, Certificate of Completion (2004)
- Crystal River High School, Graduate (1992)

EXPERIENCE

TRUCK DRIVER / HEAVY EQUIPMENT OPERATOR
Nighthorse Enterprises, Inc., Colorado Springs, Colorado (2004 – present)
- Currently drive ready-mixed concrete trucks for a contractor with Transit Mix Concrete.
- Safely pick up and deliver ready-mixed concrete.
- Coordinate delivery with customers on the job site.
- Complete daily equipment inspections and observe safety measures.

Tarco, Inc., Colorado Springs, Colorado (2003 – 2004)
- Operated heavy equipment (from skid steers to front-end loaders) and performed various labor tasks.
- Gained experience measuring positive moisture status in the subgrade.

LaFarge, Inc., Colorado Springs, Colorado (2002 – 2003)
- Hauled concrete as an employee of LaFarge before they began opening up their driving opportunities to owner/operators.

Rocky Mountain Pre-Mix, Colorado Springs, Colorado (2001 – 2002)
- Transported ready-mixed concrete to customers.
- Met deadlines and ensured customer satisfaction.
- Responsible for equipment inspections and safety procedures.

Trans Colorado Concrete, Colorado Springs, Colorado (2000 – 2001)
- Company driver responsible for loading, transporting, and off-loading concrete mixes at customer locations.

Triple D Sanitation, Colorado Springs, Colorado (1998 – 2000)
- Drove sanitation and waste management trucks at both commercial and residential locations.

MECHANIC, BRADLEY FIGHTING VEHICLE SYSTEM (1992 – 1995)
United States Army
- Achieved the highest rank attainable for length of service—E-4 Specialist Assistant Squad Leader.
- Completed First Aid and CPR courses and mechanic training.
- Earned the Army Achievement Medal, Expert Marksmanship Qualification Badge with Grenade Bar, Driver and Mechanic Badge with Driver-M Bar, National Defense Service Medal, and Army Service Ribbon.

Tahoma Font

1234 Shadowlawn #76
Novi, Michigan 48377
Mobile: 248.555.1234

PROFESSIONAL NARRATIVES

"[Nicole] has always been willing to go the extra mile with difficult patients ... there was no question to me that she could meet the challenges given her because her clinical skills are excellent."

"Although she is a comfortable and competent nurse in an independent environment, Nicole is also a team player. She has served as both role model and preceptor to nursing personnel."

"It has been my good fortune to work with Nicole ... she has consistently demonstrated exceptional clinical knowledge and flawless professional technique in every aspect of home infusion nursing. Nicole is routinely selected to handle the most challenging home infusion patients, giving every confidence the task will be completed with precision."

SUMMARY OF QUALIFICATIONS

- Member of a select group of specialty nurses; attained highest level of intravenous therapy excellence and achievement.
- Excellent assessment skills and knowledge of medical protocols and specialized responsibilities.
- Skilled in calculating, mixing, and administering antineoplastic agents.
- Proficient with the use, care, and maintenance of infusion access devices.
- Experienced in utilizing the PYXIS/LYNX pharmacy dispensing system.
- Strong oral and written skills in conveying and discussing information; documenting thorough, concise, and reflective data.
- Consistently remain current in new methods and procedures.
- Establish priorities in multiple-demanding situations.
- Viewed as a valuable resource and preceptor.

EMPLOYMENT / EXPERIENCE

OAKPOINTE MEDICAL ASSOCIATES, Northville, Michigan
CLINIC/STAFF ONCOLOGY NURSE, 2004–2005
Proficiently assessed patients, inserted PIV and PICC, maintained vascular access devices and hepatic artery pumps. Calculated, mixed, and dosed chemotherapy, utilized PYXIS/LYNX pharmacy dispensing system, and administered care to participating Protocol patients.

FARMINGTON ONCOLOGY ASSOCIATES, Farmington, Michigan
CLINIC/STAFF ONCOLOGY NURSE, 2000–2004
Performed clinical assessments, and utilized PYXIS/LYNX pharmacy system. Calculated, mixed, and dosed antineoplastic agents via IV and hepatic artery pump.

LOGIFUSION, East Detroit, Michigan
HOME INFUSION COORDINATOR/PRECEPTOR, 1998–2000
Coordinated and performed skilled nursing visits of adult and pediatric patients requiring parental, subcutaneous, intraspinal, and enteral therapies with strong emphasis on teaching patients to become independent with therapies.

BON SECOURS HOSPITAL, Grosse Pointe, Michigan
ORIENTATION — EMERGENCY ROOM NURSING, 1998

PROVIDENCE HOSPITAL, Novi, Michigan
STAFF NURSE, MEDICAL/SURGICAL UNIT, 1994–1997
Provided all facets of nursing services, direct patient care, physician interaction, unit administration, documentation, and reporting.

ST. JOSEPH MERCY HOSPITAL, Ypsilanti, Michigan
PHLEBOTOMIST, 1992–1995
Collected blood specimens from patients using venipuncture, finger, and heel stick methods. Performed bleeding and clotting time tests.

EDUCATION / TRAINING / CERTIFICATION

OAKLAND COLLEGE; Rochester Hills, Michigan
A.A.S. DEGREE IN NURSING, 1994
Certified Registered Nurse Intravenous Therapy, 1993
Midline/PICC trained, 1992
BLS-C–American Heart Association (current)
Member of Infusion Nurses Society

Arial (Helvetica) Narrow

E-mail: sreymore@protypeltd.com

732.555.1234

177 Washington Avenue • Edison, NJ 08818

Sales/Territory Management Professional

Delivering consistent and sustainable revenue gains, profit growth, and market-share increases through strategic sales leadership of multi-site branches. Values offered:

- ✓ Driver of innovative programs that provide a competitive edge and establish company as a full-service market leader.
- ✓ Proactive, creative problem solver who develops solutions that save time, cut costs, and ensure consistent product quality.
- ✓ Empowering leader who recruits, develops, coaches, motivates, and inspires sales teams to top performance.
- ✓ Innovative in developing and implementing win-win solutions to maximize account expansion, retention, and satisfaction.

Selected Career Achievements

RANFORD COMPANY • Edison, NJ   1990 to 2004

As Branch Manager, reinvigorated the sales organization, growing company sales from $9 to $11 million, expanding account base from 450 to 680 and increasing market share 15 percent. Established new performance benchmarks and trained sales force on implementing sales-building customer inventory rationalization programs.

- **Revitalized and restored profitability of two underperforming territories** by coaching and developing territory reps.
- **Penetrated two new markets** and secured a lucrative market niche in abrasive products. Staffed, opened, and managed the two branch locations in New Jersey—one of which alone produced $3+ million over three years.
- **Initiated and advanced the skills of the sales force** to effectively promote and sell increasingly technical product lines in response to changing market demands.
- **Increased profit margins and dollar volume** through product mix diversification and expansion. Created product catalogs and marketing literature.
- Ensured that the company **maintained its competitive edge in the marketplace** by adding several cross-functional product lines.
- **Led highly profitable new product introduction with a 40 percent profit margin** that produced $100,000 annually in new business.

BERLIN COMPANY • Trenton, NJ   1985 to 1990

- **As Account Executive, rejuvenated sales performance of a stagnant territory. Turned around customer perception by cultivating exceptional relationships through solutions-based selling and delivering value-added service.** Recognized as a peak performer company-wide who consistently ranked number one in both sales and profits.
- **Positioned and established the company as a full-service supplier** to drive sales revenues by translating customer needs to product solutions.
- **More than doubled territory sales from $700,000 to $1.6 million** and grew account base from 80 to 125 through new market penetration. **Landed and managed three of the company's six largest accounts** and grew remaining three.
- **Captured a lucrative account and drove annual sales from $100,000 in the first year to $400,000 in three years**, outperforming the competition without any price cutting.
- **Mentored new and existing territory reps** on customer relationship management, solutions-selling strategies, advanced product knowledge, and customer programs.

Education

B.S. in Business Management—Rhode Island University, Providence, RI

Helvetica Condensed

12345 Clamdigger Court, Halls Creek • Swansboro, NC 28584 • (910) 555-1234 cell • (910) 555-5678 home

Account Executive

Profile

Dynamic, top performing account executive with more than 20 years of experience in media, insurance, and retail sales. Goal- and service-oriented professional who employs customer-consultant relationship strategies. High achiever with numerous awards as a top sales producer. Able to build, guide, and sustain successful sales teams. Aggressive sales representative inspired by challenge – honest and hard working.

Core Competencies

- Account Management
- Customer-focused Service
- Time Management
- Prospecting / Cold Calling

- Business Development
- Creative Thinker
- Relationship Development
- Computer—Word / Excel

- Consultative Sales Approach
- Lead Generation
- Pricing / Sales Programming
- Quality Service Focus

Relevant Experience

WCTI – TV12, New Bern, NC   1989 – present
Sr. Account Executive for the news leader in eastern North Carolina, WCTI – TV12, an ABC affiliate.

Manage sales and marketing for the Onslow County designated market area. Direct sales and support activities of five people. Established training programs for sales force—guide, direct, and motivate sales team. Develop and implement sales and marketing strategies, ideas, and programs. Develop quarterly package avails and rates for clients based on demographics.

- Received the top honor—Sledge Hammer Award

- Pacing Contest winner for highest sales in one day—$246,000

- Recognized for creating and producing commercials—wrote own scripts for 30, 60, and 90 second spots

- Executive Producer for the Cystic Fibrosis Telethon for 12 years

- Completed Perry S. Marshall marketing course (publicity and lead generation systems for technical sales (recognized by media)

- Ranked number one out of eight company sales executives

- Highest producer of "monthly to annual" clients

Education

Carteret Community College, Morehead City, NC
Intra-American University, Puerto Rico

Century Schoolbook

PROFILE
- Self-motivated account manager with more than ten years of proven experience.
- Top performer with a strong background in building territories, strengthening relationships, using creative marketing approaches, and increasing profitability.
- Respected for the ability to get to the decision maker and close the sale.
- Demonstrated ability to create client loyalty beyond the sales relationship.
- Knowledge of Windows, MS Word, Excel, PowerPoint, Lotus 1-2-3, Internet Explorer.

EXPERIENCE

ACCOUNT MANAGER/EXECUTIVE (2000 – present)
Learning Systems, LLC, Aurora, Colorado
- Quickly promoted to Account Manager within only five months; the only sales executive selected to stay with the company after it downsized the sales department.
- Built rapport with large corporate customers and training content providers nationwide, including Dell, AT&T Broadband, Oshkosh, Verizon, etc., and maintained confidence in the company despite its problems.
- Encouraged customization and upgrades to increase profitability of the company's propriety line of enterprise-wide knowledge management software solutions.
- Participated in trade shows, qualified buyers, and performed online demonstrations.

ACCOUNT REPRESENTATIVE (1999 – 2000)
John Wiley & Sons, Inc., Colorado Springs, Colorado
- Sold TheraScribe psychotherapy treatment planning software and related publications to mental health practitioners, hospitals, clinics, correctional facilities, government agencies, universities, and colleges nationwide.
- Prospected for new clients, analyzed their needs, and tailored sales presentations to achieve an unprecedented 98 percent close ratio.
- Provided after-sales service, training, and technical support.
- Created and implemented an effective contact and sales tracking system.
- Formulated a strategic plan for the territory and grew the account base through effective cold calling and market development.
- Succeeded in winning major national accounts, including the U.S. Air Force and Veteran's Administration hospitals.
- Achieved number one in sales nationwide, consistently exceeding monthly quotas by 140 percent.
- Developed a business plan for the launch of the new TheraScribe Pro software.
- Suggested a graduate school discount program that was accepted company-wide.

SENIOR NEW ACCOUNTS REPRESENTATIVE (1994 – 1997)
California Casualty, Glendale, California, and Colorado Springs, Colorado
- Developed markets for property and casualty insurance among unions, professional associations, and other groups that included police, firefighters, and educators.
- Generated more than 3,000 new accounts, producing an average of $300,000 in premiums per year.
- Earned numerous bonuses and incentive trips, and helped the sales team to achieve number one in the country.

EDUCATION

BACHELOR OF BUSINESS ADMINISTRATION (1991)
University of Colorado, Colorado Springs, Colorado
- Dual major in Marketing and Mass Communications

CENTER CITY FONT

PROFILE
- Focused retail manager with twenty years of experience.
- Background in marketing, sales, staff development, merchandising, and customer service.
- Effective team player with strong interpersonal and communication skills.
- Skilled in creating staff loyalty and empowering employees to excel.

EXPERIENCE

MANAGEMENT/ADMINISTRATION
- Directed the operations of 22 retail stores in three states with combined sales volume of $17.1 million.
- Served as a liaison between store management and home office merchandisers and senior managers.
- Approved sales goals and provided direction for floor sets (merchandising).
- Managed the daily operations of a high-volume retail clothing store; responsible for visual merchandising, floor supervision, and resolution of customer complaints and adjustments.
- Promoted from supervisor to manager of a $750,000 volume store and then to manager of a Casual Corner with more than $1 million in annual sales volume.
- Conceptualized and coordinated innovative fashion shows, breakfast clubs, and other promotions to increase sales volume and create customer loyalty.
- Developed new business through community involvement, seminars, and monthly training of sales staff to enhance customer service through the merchandise sales approach.

SUPERVISION/STAFF DEVELOPMENT
- Developed ten staff members for promotion to store manager or assistant store manager positions.
- Recruited, hired, trained, supervised, and evaluated sales associates, store supervisors, assistant managers, and store managers.
- Responsible for staff scheduling, ensuring adequate floor coverage, and overseeing payroll.

ACHIEVEMENTS
- Assumed responsibility for a failing district, closed unprofitable stores, and turned around declining units until all stores were profitable.
- Honored with membership in the Champions Club (1991–1992) for achieving #26 out of 860 stores in the country; Champions Club (1993–1994) achieving #48 out of 860 stores.
- Won numerous suit, dress, and pantyhose promotions by increasing sales over plan.
- Built sales volume through focused productivity training, visual merchandise presentation, and exceptional customer service.
- Voted President (1989–1990) and Vice President (1988) of the Towne East Square Merchants Association.
- President (1995–1996) and Vice President (1994) of Citadel Merchants Association.
- Selected as City Fashion Coordinator for Colorado Springs (1977–1978).
- Miss America Pageant Official (1977); First Runner Up, Miss Colorado Springs (1976).

WORK HISTORY

DISTRICT SALES MANAGER, Casual Corner, Denver, CO	1996 – present
MANAGER, Casual Corner, Citadel Mall, Colorado Springs, CO	1990 – 1996
MANAGER, Casual Corner, Towne East, Wichita, KS	1982–1990
MANAGER, Casual Corner, Towne West, Wichita, KS	1981–1982
SUPERVISOR, Casual Corner, Towne East, Wichita, KS	1980

TRAINING

CASUAL CORNER CORPORATE TRAINING: TRAC I-III (Personal Selling, Beyond Customer Service, Driving the Business), MOHR Management Training

BARBIZON SCHOOL OF MODELING: Graduate 1974

12 Paddleboat Court • Colorado Springs, Colorado 80906 • (719) 555-1234

Times New Roman Font

1234 5th Avenue

Rodgers@protypeltd.com   Edgewater, MD 21037   410-555-1234

Committed to reaching fair and just resolutions of legal matters

Trial attorney and mediator possessing more than 20 years of diverse experience in construction, family, personal injury, criminal, disability, and landlord/tenant law. Strive to provide clear and concise analysis and evaluation of a client's case, always considering the possibility of reaching a reasonable agreement and settlement through negotiation. Facilitate solutions by listening, observing, and communicating openly, with sound understanding of people and human nature.

MEDIATION TRAINING

Transformative Mediation, Maryland Institute for the Continuing Professional Education of Lawyers, 2003
Family/Domestic Mediation, Maryland Institute for the Continuing Professional Education of Lawyers, 1999
General Mediation, Maryland Institute for the Continuing Professional Education of Lawyers, 1999

EXPERIENCE

2002 to present
Trial Attorney   Philip Clark Jones & Associates   Annapolis, MD
Prepare and litigate construction cases in state and federal courts, arbitration hearings, and mediations.

1985 to 2001
Sole Practitioner   Private Law Practice   Edgewater, MD
Represented more than 300 individual and business clients in the general practice of law. Accepted 75+ pro bono cases in 10 years through the Homeless Persons Representation Project. Recipient of the Pro Bono Award from the Maryland State Bar Association, 1991.

ADDITIONAL EXPERIENCE

Trial Attorney   Nationwide Mutual Insurance Company   Annapolis, MD
Prepared and litigated tort defense cases, focusing on auto, homeowner, and business cases in jury and non-jury trials.

Trial Attorney   Maryland Automobile Insurance Fund   Annapolis, MD
Prepared and litigated tort defense cases. Researched issues on insurance coverage and liability. Drafted legislative and regulatory proposals.

Legal Assistant   Roman Catholic Diocese of San Diego   San Diego, CA
Researched and oversaw immigration cases for foreign religious personnel. Drafted contracts and leases. Researched land titles. Evaluated property tax exemptions.

EDUCATION

Juris Doctor, University of San Diego, California
Bachelor of Science in Foreign Service, Georgetown University, Washington, DC

ADMISSIONS

Maryland State Courts ● California State Courts
United States District Court for Maryland ● United States District Court for Southern California

163

Bookman
Light Font

123 North College
Santa Maria, CA 93454
Telephone: (805) 555-1234
E-mail: ppayne@protypeltd.com

PROFILE

- Reliable customer service professional with strong people skills.
- Able to thrive in a fast-paced environment, managing multiple tasks simultaneously.
- Versatile, quick learner who loves a challenge and adapts well to new situations.
- Skilled in working effectively as a team member or alone with minimal supervision.
- Effective team player with exceptional interpersonal and communication skills.
- Knowledge of Windows, MS Word, Excel, QuickBooks, BPI, Internet Explorer, e-mail.

EXPERIENCE

ADMINISTRATIVE ASSISTANT (1998 – present)
Foster's Body and Paint, Santa Maria, California
- Greet customers, set up job folders for repair work, and order parts for the project.
- Call insurance companies to validate coverage and obtain authorization to perform the work, ensuring that invoices will be paid when submitted and collecting past due accounts when required.
- Follow up on outstanding and overdue accounts receivable.
- Prepare monthly sales spreadsheets in Excel and weekly payroll in QuickBooks.
- Use Mitchell International proprietary management software for estimating, invoicing, and inventory management.
- Take digital photographs of damaged vehicles using ImageMate software and download them to the Webmaster for insertion in the Web site.

RECEPTIONIST (1997 – 1998)
Iversen Motor Company, Santa Maria, California
- Greeted clients, typed correspondence, and scheduled appointments for this new car dealership and body shop.
- Answered multi-line switchboard where the accurate taking of detailed messages was essential.
- Served as a liaison between management and potential customers.

ACCOUNTS RECEIVABLE CLERK (1994 – 1997)
Tri-County News, Santa Maria, California
- Compiled billing data to input into the proprietary computer software designed for magazine wholesale distributors.
- Audited delivery tickets and checked math calculations.
- Prepared invoices and statements and made bank deposits.
- Answered questions from customers regarding their bills.
- Set up the distribution of periodicals.
- Covered vacations in other departments, including returns and distribution.

EDUCATION

COMPUTER SUPPORT SERVICES, Santa Maria, California (1997)
- Completed course work in Microsoft Word, Excel, QuickBooks, and BPI software.

ASSOCIATE OF SCIENCE (1992)
Allan Hancock College, Santa Maria, California

164

Clearface Font

227 N.E. 99th Street • Vancouver, WA 77777

206-555-1234 *cell*   *home* 206-555-5678

Restaurant Management

Professional Profile

Driven, results-oriented, and energetic *professional* with 14 years of experience in *Restaurant Management* offering an exceptional teamwork spirit and a positive attitude.

Experienced in managing within budget guidelines, maintaining an effective flow of inventory, and developing a strong team attitude among employees. Proven skills in setting and achieving goals, supplying above-average training skills, and adding to the bottom dollar profit margin by improving service, reducing waste, and increasing efficiency.

Work well with all types of personalities, able to perform hiring and termination duties effectively and professionally. Conscientious, customer-service-oriented, and highly focused with strong follow-through skills and effective time management abilities. Possess strong common sense with a keen sense of humor. Committed to a job well done.

Expertise Includes

- Bookkeeping/Deposits
- Cash Handling
- Customer Service
- Event Planning
- Excellent Facilities Presentation

- HIV Awareness Training
- Inventory Management
- Operating within Budget
- POS Knowledge
- Public Relations

- Quality Assurance
- Schedule Management
- Staff Training
- Supervisor
- Team Player

History of Employment

Assistant Manager • Shari's Restaurant • Vancouver, Washington • *1995–1996; 2001–current*

Chef / Manager • Van Mall Retirement • Vancouver, Washington • *1996–2001*
 250 residents – supplied full meal services.

Kitchen / Assistant Manager • Carrows Restaurant • Vancouver, Washington • *1989–1995*

165

PALATINO FONT

1018 Highland Meadows
Sylvania, Ohio 43560
Home: **(419) 555-1234**
Mobile: **(419) 555-5678**
Email: Eliza@protypeltd.com

PROFILE

A dynamic pharmaceutical sales consultant who is a driving force in significant sales growth, territory management, and overall profitability. Expertise in strategic marketing, new product launch, market penetration, team leadership, and cultivation of lucrative, long-term client relationships.

CAREER HIGHLIGHTS

- An award-winning leader in the highly competitive pharmaceutical sales industry.
- Fastest-growing territory in three companies for seven consecutive years.
- Top 10 percent nationally of companies' sales forces throughout career.
- Number one in monthly sales of 55 representatives throughout Midwest region from 1998 to 2005.

PROFESSIONAL EXPERIENCE

SPECIALTY PRODUCTS MANAGER
Jones Jeffers Laboratories, Cleveland, Ohio   October 2002 – present

- Aggressively contributed to building company revenues from $10 million to $30 million.
- Spearheaded initiative to bolster customer relations. Administered satisfaction-oriented service strategies that prevented departure of two major accounts $5 million and $2 million.
- Designed marketing strategies and programs, increasing team sales by 45.5 percent.
- Devised and implemented a technical sales program focused on client education. Increased NRx share 3.2 percent and TRx share 1.2 percent in 10 months.

ACCOUNT MANAGER – MEDICAL CENTERS
Lowe Evans and Company, Healthcare Innovators, Detroit, Michigan   July 1999 – October 2002

- Increased account base 52 percent through positive relationship building and follow-up with target market: pharmaceutical providers, neurologists, family practitioners, and nursing homes.
- Attained 118 percent of sales goal for 2001 and 129 percent of sales goal for 2000.
- Awards: "Market Share Growth Leader," 2001 and "MVP, Phase VI," 2000

PHARMACEUTICAL SALES REPRESENTATIVE
PharmaCare Distributors, Findlay, Ohio   June 1997 – July 1999

- Built new territory from point zero to $4 million in annual sales within first year.
- Broke first-year and second-year sales records company-wide.
- Awards: "Territory Rep of the Year," 1998 and "Zone Sales Leader," 1998

EDUCATION

Professional Specialty Sales Representative   2002
CMR (Certified Medical Representative) Institute, Roanoke, Virginia

Bachelor of Science Degree, Business Administration, Marketing   1997
The University of Toledo, Toledo, Ohio
- Achievements: GPA 3.88, *Magna Cum Laude*

GAZETTE FONT

1234 Alteza Drive ♦ Colorado Springs, Colorado 80917 ♦ (719) 555-1234 ♦ atj@aol.com

PROFILE
- Experienced EMT and registered firefighter with a strong desire to help people.
- Quick thinker who enjoys a fast pace and the challenge of a job's physical demands.
- Adept at working under pressure and managing multiple tasks simultaneously.
- Effective team player with a positive attitude and strong interpersonal skills.
- Proven problem solver who enjoys getting to the root of a challenge.

CERTIFICATIONS & TRAINING
- Certified Emergency Medical Technician, Basic (Colorado #267-47-2785 through August 2008)
- Nationally Certified EMT (#B1204825 through March 2007)
- Basic Trauma Life Support (BTLS) (National #38792 through November 2007)
- Cardiopulmonary Resuscitation (CPR) (#D1523 through January 2008)
- Firefighter I, State of Colorado (June 2001)
- Basic Wildland Firefighting Course (April 2001)
- IV Certified, Swedish Medical Center (April 2000)
- Acute Care for Trauma (September 1999)

EXPERIENCE

EMT IV, AMBULANCE FIELD STAFF (August 2003 to present)
American Medical Response of Colorado, Colorado Springs, Colorado
- Provide on-scene advanced emergency medical care that includes patient assessment, advanced and basic medical procedures, introduction and maintenance of IVs, and advanced life support.
- Assess cardiac patients, perform cardiopulmonary resuscitation, and manage airways.
- Administer medications with medical direction, taking into consideration side effects, indications, contraindications, and patient medical histories.
- Transport injured and ill people, wheelchair clients, and mental health/detox patients.
- Provide a high standard of care while managing multiple priorities during emergencies.
- Able to develop a sense of trust with patients in high-stress environments.
- Responsible for vehicle deployment, maintenance, restocking, cleaning, and equipment safety.

EMT IV, EVENT SUPERVISOR, SUPPLY MANAGER (December 1999 to present)
Event Medical, Inc., Colorado Springs, Colorado
- Provide emergency and nonemergency medical care during large events throughout Southern Colorado, including PPIR races, the Renaissance Festival, Pikes Peak Hill Climb, Pikes Peak Invitational Soccer Tournament, horse shows, semi-pro football games, and concerts.
- Train and supervise new hires and ensure that proper emergency coverage is provided during events.
- Assess and restock equipment in the ambulances and track usage of supplies.

RINK OPERATOR (November 2001 to August 2003)
Mark "Pa" Sertich Ice Center, Colorado Springs, Colorado
- Zamboni pilot responsible for the maintenance and upkeep of the ice rink and facility.

FIREFIGHTER I, EMT IV (January 2000 to May 2001)
Broadmoor Fire and Rescue, Colorado Springs, Colorado
- Obtained the Forestry Red Card and provided advanced life support, basic life support, and fire suppression for the Broadmoor Fire Protection District.

EDUCATION

BACHELOR OF SCIENCE (1999 to present)
University of Colorado, Colorado Springs, Colorado
- Completing remaining 45 credits toward an undergraduate degree in geography and environmental sciences; total of 75 credits completed.

UNDERGRADUATE STUDIES (1996 to 1999)
Pikes Peak Community College, Colorado Springs, Colorado
- Completed 64 credits toward a geology degree and transferred to UCCS.

INTERESTS
Hockey, football, softball, rock climbing, Enduro motocross racing, trail riding, hiking, reading, fishing, computers, dog training, and hunting.

Felicia Font

OBJECTIVE   To build a career using strong clerical and customer service skills

SUMMARY
- Typing skills: 60 wpm
- Knowledge of Windows, Microsoft Word, Excel, Internet, and e-mail
- Experienced in operating 10-key calculators
- Background in office procedures, medical records, and accounting

EDUCATION

ASSOCIATE OF APPLIED SCIENCE, SECRETARIAL SCIENCE (1989)
Blair Junior College, Colorado Springs, Colorado

GRADUATED WITH HONORS (1987)
Stratton High School, Stratton, Colorado

SPECIAL COURSES COMPLETED: Office Technology, Business Management, Typing, Shorthand, Accounting, Vocational Business

EXPERIENCE

MEDICAL RECORDS CLERK
University Orthopaedic Associates, New Brunswick, New Jersey (1998 – Present)
- Handle the switchboard for 11 doctors in private practice.
- Prepare patient charts for appointments, make copies of medical records for attorneys and patients, and file charts and insertions.
- Pick up x-rays from hospitals and assist in the admission of patients.
- Train new records clerks and receptionists.

MEDICAL RECEPTIONIST
Rocky Mountain Cancer Center, Colorado Springs, Colorado (1998)
- Scheduled office visits for six doctors.
- Greeted and checked in patients.
- Answered telephones, prepared daily reports, and filed records.

ADMINISTRATIVE ASSISTANT
Champion Financial Services, Inc., Colorado Springs, Colorado (1996 – 1998)
Mercury Finance, Colorado Springs, Colorado (1995 – 1996)
- Assisted office managers in the day-to-day operations.
- Prepared documents for purchase of customer contracts.
- Investigated customer applications and ran credit reports.
- Requested and distributed dealer checks.
- Accepted and posted customer payments; collected past-due accounts.
- Responsible for accounts payable, filing, and telephone customer service.
- Assisted in training new employees.

ASSISTANT MANAGER
Quicksilver One-Hour Photo Lab, Colorado Springs, Colorado (1990 – 1995)
- Managed the Hi-Tech One-Hour Photo Lab owned by Quicksilver.
- Provided customer service to ensure satisfaction and repeat business.
- Opened and closed the store, including cash register accountability.
- Kept customer accounts up to date, and assisted in customer billing.
- Developed film, printed photographs, and trained new employees.

GARAMOND FONT

RE/MAX of Valencia
www.santaclaritavalleyhomes.com
sellers_a@protypeltd.com

25101 Ventura Avenue
Santa Clarita, California 91381

Home: 661 555-1234
Facsimile: 661 555-5678

REAL ESTATE PROFESSIONAL

Top-producing, accomplished, enthusiastic Realtor® with a distinguished career of 20+ years selling real estate. Goal oriented and results driven with ability to utilize cutting-edge technologies in generating new markets. Strong decision-maker with a proactive management style. Record of consistent achievement, proven P&L management skills, personal commitment, and positive corporate growth. Able to execute multiple projects simultaneously, communicate ideas to others, and bring functional groups together to achieve a common goal. Integrity is crucial to client care, and commitment to clients is to exceed their expectations.

HIGHLIGHTS OF QUALIFICATIONS

- Closed more than 1,000 transactions.
- Served three years on the SRAR South Land Association of Realtors® Education and Communication Committee.
- Served on the Board of Directors for the Santa Clarita Board of Realtors®.
- Member of the CMA (Complete Marketing Advantage) Network Group (a networking group consisting of 40 full-time agents from six companies whose purpose is to sell listed properties faster).
- Recognized for attaining top listings and developing qualified prospects.
- Skilled entrepreneurial marketing and development of competitive business strategies.
- In-depth industry knowledge; proactive approach to forestall problems.
- Adept negotiator and closer, who excels in business development and new market penetration.
- Equipped to compete in a fast-paced, aggressive sales environment.
- Persuasive and articulate communicator who functions effectively as part of a decision-making team.

PROFESSIONAL CREDENTIALS

Candidate, **Certified Property Manager (CPM)** through Institute of Real Estate Management (I.R.E.M.)
Completed Series 300, 400, 500, 700 courses
Licensed California Realtor®
Floyd Wickman Courses ▪ Member, Mike Ferry Business Planning ▪ Daniel Pendley Master Series

PROFESSIONAL EXPERIENCE

REALTOR® / SALES ASSOCIATE   1995 – present
RE/MAX of Valencia – Santa Clarita, CA
    Top-producing sales associate. Thorough knowledge of the Santa Clarita Valley. Handle the most complex transactions and all administrative functions. Continuously increase sales and maintain profitability each year.

PRESIDENT AND FOUNDER   1989 – 1995
BRYER Property Management – Frazier Park, CA
    Launched startup of this diversified real estate investment, development, and asset management company, and built its property management portfolio to 1,000+ residential units and 1,000,000+ sq.ft. of commercial property. Established relationships with property owners, builders, and developers throughout the region, and negotiated favorable, multiyear management contracts.

    Created a complete property management function, recruited experienced personnel, designed accounting and financial reporting processes, and implemented PC technologies for expanded portfolio analysis and management reporting capabilities.

    Represented private investors, banks (REOs), and limited partnerships. Consistently successful in maximizing asset value through measurable gains in occupancy, tenant satisfaction, retention, and operating cost reduction.

169

Book Antiqua Font

PROFILE
- Goal-oriented account manager with successful technical and pharmaceutical sales experience.
- Demonstrated ability to create client confidence and loyalty above and beyond the sales relationship.
- Strong background in office penetration, product presentation, and new territory development.
- Proven manager who is adept at meeting diverse challenges with creative solutions.
- Solid team orientation; able to complete projects with company peers as well as alliance partners.

EXPERIENCE

PROFESSIONAL SALES REPRESENTATIVE, LEVEL II (1998 to present)
Searle/Pharmacia, Colorado Springs, Colorado
- Sell cardiovascular, hypnotic, and NSAID pharmaceuticals to physicians in the Southern Colorado territory, including Colorado Springs, Pueblo, and Durango.
- Achieved Pro Club 1999.

ACCOUNT MANAGER, HOSPITALS/PHYSICIANS (1993 to 1998)
Boehringer Mannheim Corporation, Colorado Springs, Colorado
- Sold diagnostic equipment to hospitals, physicians, and retail outlets.
- Exceeded sales goals by more than 105%, achieving Winner's Club two of the last three years.
- Converted all military hospitals in Colorado Springs to BMC products despite the fact that an order had been placed for a competitive product.
- Converted Denver Health and Hospital Systems, Choice Care, and City Care HMOs.
- Saved hospital business along the Front Range when there was a product failure.
- Set up over twelve physician offices on proprietary computer software to switch patients to BMC glucose meters.
- Co-sponsored numerous programs and seminars with BMC alliance partner, Eli Lilly.
- Worked with distributors including Baxter and Bergen to set up distribution to BMC accounts.
- Led regional retail efforts by producing top two Kroger stores in sales; held numerous successful diabetes days in-store promotions.
- Worked with managed care entities including Qual Med and Proactive to set up meter programs.

SENIOR PHARMACEUTICAL SALES REPRESENTATIVE (1990 to 1993)
Bristol-Myers Squibb, Northern Colorado
- Sold pharmaceuticals to hospitals and doctors, including cardiovascular and antibiotic drugs.
- Won hospital approval for lead drugs at military and community hospitals.
- Achieved senior level within minimum time.
- Recognized for exceeding market share growth with new drug.
- Covered a three-state territory and trained new representatives.

SENIOR PHARMACEUTICAL SALES REPRESENTATIVE (1986 to 1990)
Upjohn Pharmaceutical Company, Fort Collins, Colorado
- Sold CNS, NSAID, and metabolic drugs to physicians and hospitals in two states.
- Obtained hospital formulary approval at several military and civilian hospitals.
- Consistently led district in percentage gains for direct business.
- Led the district Journal Club which analyzed and presented medical journal articles to the region.

EDUCATION

MASTER OF BUSINESS ADMINISTRATION
Colorado State University, Fort Collins, Colorado

MASTER OF SCIENCE, ECOLOGY
Yale University, New Haven Connecticut

BACHELOR OF SCIENCE, BIOLOGY
Rutger's University, New Brunswick, New Jersey

AFFILIATIONS
Charter Member, Rocky Mountain Professional Representatives Organization
Board Member, Southern Colorado Chapter, American Diabetes Association
Past Member, Weld County Pharmaceutical Organization

Serif Fonts

Sans Serif Fonts

Headline Fonts

11 Graphic Lines

All of the résumés in this book were typeset using common word processing software (MS Word and WordPerfect). That means you can reproduce everything you see in these pages, including the graphic lines. These lines can be either horizontal, vertical, or full page borders.

Lines at the top of the résumé can be used to set the name and address section(s) apart from the text so the reader's eyes can be drawn to the most important information first.

Horizontal lines between sections allow the reader to focus on each section separately and draw the eye from section to section, especially when there is little room for extra white space (which can serve the same purpose). The creative use of horizontal or vertical lines adds pizzazz to the design of a résumé without appearing too overdone. Résumés created with such lines can be used in all but the most conservative of industries.

It is important, however, to avoid the use of too many lines with different thicknesses on the same page. The résumé can get "busy," which makes the reader work too hard. It is a good idea to use no more than two line widths per résumé. For instance:

This line is .02 inch thick.

And this one is .005 inch thick.

You might combine the two together.

The samples that follow will give you some ideas for ways to use lines in a résumé. There are lines on almost every résumé in this book, so look at other pages for even more unique ideas.

DENISE SWIFT

1234 Whimsical Drive
Colorado Springs, CO 80917

Phone: (719) 555-1234
E-mail: dswift@protypeltd.com

PROFILE

- Innovative, shirt-sleeve manager with extensive experience in meeting organizational goals by establishing a climate that creates employee commitment and motivation.
- More than ten years of demonstrated success in:
  - Public Relations
  - Human Resource Management
  - Organizational Development
  - Strategic Planning
  - Project Management
  - Training/Development
  - Mediation
  - Conflict Resolution
  - Employee Relations
- Resourceful problem solver who enjoys the challenge of learning new things and taking on increasingly more complex responsibilities.
- Creative trainer with the ability to design and present effective training programs.

EXPERIENCE

DIRECTOR, TRANSPORTATION MANAGEMENT ASSOCIATION

DEVELOPMENT DIRECTOR

CLEAN CITIES COORDINATOR
Clean Air Campaign
Colorado Springs, Colorado
10/98 – present

Developed programs to encourage employers along the Garden of the Gods corridor to use alternative modes of transportation, including car pools, shuttles, bikes, and walking. Marketed the organization to businesses through cold calling and networking. Promoted collaboration and teamwork among local businesses encouraging them to become part of the solution.

- Re-established relationships with local businesses that were lost by the former director, including the organization's largest contributor.
- Succeeded in increasing membership by 40% within three months.
- Secured 12 television and 6 radio spots at no charge to the organization.
- Developed and implemented the marketing plan for two shuttle projects and managed their launch.
- Collaborated with elected officials to develop a partnership between the city and TMA.
- Organized a successful event to promote alternative fuel vehicles attended by 160 fleet managers.
- Researched and supervised the writing of more than 30 grants valued at over one million dollars.
- Secured funding for a corridor study that included three partners—the City of Colorado Springs, Colorado Department of Transportation, and the Garden of the Gods Road Transportation Management Association. Served as project management for the study.
- Secured more than $600,000 in funding for three years.

DIRECTOR OF OPERATIONS
University of Phoenix
Denver, Colorado
6/98 – 9/98

Directed the operations of all the Colorado campuses of the largest private university in the United States. Responsible for all student services, including five facilities, 5,000 student records, and 50 classrooms. Developed master schedules for classes and created monthly reports of current growth, forecasted growth, and retention efforts. Hired, supervised, and motivated 8 full-time employees.

- Managed the creation of an Access database for reporting, automating a previously manual process, and saving 20 hours of staff time per month.
- Brought all grade and attendance records up to date in only three months.

EXPERIENCE	**DIRECTOR OF ACADEMIC AFFAIRS** **University of Phoenix** Colorado Springs, Colorado 10/94 – 6/98	Supervised student affairs for the Colorado Springs campus and facilitated one class per quarter (Organizational Communication, Behavior, Sociology, or Introduction to University Studies). Managed the student affairs budget. Hired, supervised, and evaluated 160 contract and 5 full-time employees. Traveled to new sites to organize academic affairs departments and to ensure compliance with the accreditation body.

- Implemented a new academic governance structure that increased faculty/employee morale and significantly lowered the turnover rate.
- Enhanced community awareness of the University by conducting corporate calls, overseeing monthly information meetings, organizing an advisory board, and accepting leadership roles in various community organizations.
- Resolved disputes between students and instructors, resulting in win/win situations that improved the customer's attitude toward the organization.
- Oversaw the development of the new faculty orientation, faculty development, counselor training, and peer observation process, which increased faculty morale and performance by enhancing the training process.
- Developed marketing plans and information meetings that increased the number of faculty applicants by 40%.
- Initiated a departmental newsletter to keep faculty informed of policy and organizational changes, resulting in increased employee awareness and loyalty to the organization.
- Successfully coordinated articulation agreements with two community colleges to ensure transferability of credits.

EDUCATION	1993	**Master of Arts in Organizational Management** University of Phoenix, Colorado Springs, Colorado
	1987	**Bachelor of Arts in Psychology** University of Colorado, Colorado Springs, Colorado
	2000	**Professional Development** • Center for Creative Leadership, Community Leadership Program

COMMUNITY SERVICE	1999 – present	• Board of Directors, Care and Share—Chairman of the Board (2001 – present)
	2000 – present	• Board of Directors, Community Shares
	2000 – present	• Regional Board, Asso. of Commuter Transportation
	1999 – 2000	• Member of the YMCA Programming Committee
	1998	• Vice President of Programming for the American Society of Training and Development
	1998	• Served on the focus group for Peak Mobility 21

MARTIN JEWEL

1234 99th Street • Spirit Wind, Oklahoma 73544 • mjewel909@protypeltd.com
(580) 555-1234 (Cell)

QUALIFICATIONS SUMMARY ◆

Results-driven professional with 20 years of progressive operations management experience driving profitable growth in competitive customer service markets. Solutions-focused decision maker with strong leadership, communication, negotiation, and problem-solving skills. Talent for recruiting, training, and retaining superior staff. Entrepreneurial attitude, energy, and style. Expertise in:

Strategic Planning and Marketing	**Recruiting and Training**	**Personnel Development**
Business Development	**Finance and Budgeting**	**Enterprise Startup / Restructure**
Relationship / Team Building	**Revenue and Profit Growth**	**Customer Service**

PROFESSIONAL EXPERIENCE ◆

Owner / Partner   **2001 – 2005**
JAKE'S WEIGHT LOSS CENTERS, Haze Corner, Oklahoma and Seafarer, Texas
Bought a new Seafarer franchise and developed the market, realizing profit in only four months. Oversaw two managers and four employees. Expanded business by entering a limited partnership and opening four new stores, both in Seafarer and Haze Corner. Shared in personnel functions and developed / oversaw five store managers. Traveled extensively. Sold interest in franchise to partner.

- **Built revenue through effective business planning, just-in-time inventory control, creative area marketing and promotional events, in-house incentives, and ongoing training.**

Operations Manager   **1990 – 2001**
FLAVOR DELUXE, Spirit Wind, Oklahoma
Oversaw all aspects of the daily operations of a walk-in ice cream store including management, purchasing, inventory control, accounting/payroll, marketing, personnel, training, store maintenance, health and safety practices, and customer service functions. Used effective cash management, forecasting, and budgeting systems. Worked closely with the general manager to facilitate corporate policy and consistently exceed company standards. Personnel consisted of eight employees and one manager. Sold franchise.

- **Doubled profits within two years through improved store and product presentation, exceptional customer service, and the sale of a quality product at a fair price.**
- **Continued to increase sales by 5 to 10 percent each year.**
- **Regularly drew customers from across town.**
- **Never lost sight that people have choices as to where they spend their money.**
- **Motivated employees through goal setting, positive reinforcement, high expectations, and modeling good business practices.**
- **Consistently scored above 90 on health and safety inspections.**
- **Used outgoing, optimistic personality to enhance pleasant working environment.**
- **Maintained relatively low employee turnover of 5 percent.**

Manager   **1983 – 1989**
U-RENT-IT CORPORATION, Mountaintop, Oregon
Oversaw popular $1,000,000 a year rental facility that handled General Rental Items (GRI) as well as household moving vehicles. Responsibilities included personnel, purchasing, inventory control, building and equipment maintenance, record keeping, budgeting, billing, and customer service. Improved overall store profitability as reflected below:

- **Ranked 7th in country for GRI rentals.**
- **Ranked 29th out of 1,049 stores in overall profitability.**
- **Developed a pattern of repeat customers and client loyalty.**

EDUCATION ◆

Associate Degree in General Studies and Management (Dual Degree), Park University, Seashore, WA

SOMERSET D. SAUNDERS

123 University Drive
Bowling Green, Ohio 43402
(419) 555-1234
SSaunders@protypeltd.com

JURIS DOCTOR, ATTORNEY-AT-LAW

Attorney-at-law with 12 years of professional experience in firm management, business development and growth, consulting for high-profile clientele, implementation of judicial processes and procedures, and trial and appellate courtroom practice. Expertise in commercial, corporate, contract, insurance, and employment law, as well as transportation and railroad counsel, and civil and government litigation.

COURTS:
- Admitted to Practice before United States Supreme Court
- Admitted to Practice before United States Court of Appeals, Sixth Circuit

MEMBER, OHIO BAR ASSOCIATION, 1993 – present
- Admitted to Practice before Supreme Court of Ohio
- Admitted to Practice before United States District Court, Northern District of Ohio

PROFESSIONAL EXPERIENCE

PARTNER, *Scott, Smith and Saunders, LLP,* Perrysburg, Ohio   1997 – present
- **Law Firm Manager:** Oversee business operations and $15 million budget for three offices. Hire and supervise legal staff: assign cases; provide mentoring, technical support, and advisement.
  - Instrumental in expansion of practice from 4 to 33 attorneys.
  - Engineered 1600 percent increase in annual billings within seven years.
- **Defense Attorney:** Cultivate and maintain large base of commercial clientele in a diversity of industries, including health care, transportation, manufacturing, and insurance.

STAFF COUNSEL, *Newell A. Jones Associates,* Grand Rapids, Ohio   1995 – 1997
- **Litigation Manager** for varied trial caseload in defense of corporate and business clients, including:
  - Transline Transportation: workplace claims under Federal Employers Liability Act (FELA).
  - Big 3 Automaker: human resources issues, premises liability, and product liability cases.

ASSOCIATE, *Smith and Jones, P.C.,* Upper Sandusky, Ohio   1993 – 1995
- **Trial Attorney:** Represented companies in commercial, public, and government civil litigation.

EDUCATION

Juris Doctoral Degree, *The Ohio State University College of Law,* Columbus, Ohio   1993
Bachelor of Arts Degree with Distinction, *Business Administration,* Ohio University, Ada, Ohio   1990

Eric Trebel

Trebel@protypeltd.com

209 Heather Way • Novi, MI 48375
H: 248.555.1234 • C: 248.555.5678

SENIOR INFORMATION TECHNOLOGY PROGRAM MANAGER / PROJECT LEADER

• Network Manager • Technical Analyst • Consultant • Systems Officer • Project Manager

Hands on IT professional skilled in managing multimillion-dollar projects and delivering results that achieve efficiency, flexibility, and conformity with ultimately lower costs and greater profitability. Clearly defined proficiency in building installations from the ground up or turning around failing or substandard technologies. Experience in Fortune 500 corporations where knowledge of trouble shooting and problem solving is crucial.

- Developed and implemented long-term IT solutions that integrated the demands of complex business processes into streamlined networks that were stable, secure, and supported.

- Led critical safety measures, security implementation, and rollout.

- Recruited, hired, trained, and mentored teams for nationwide operations.

- Innovated IT solutions from concept through installation and launch and ongoing support through expertise in:

  - Systems Integration
  - Network Administration
  - Data Communication
  - Advanced Configurations
  - Multisite Locations

  - Processing Solutions
  - System Engineering
  - Network Modeling
  - Help Desk Leadership
  - ATM Networking

  - Network Migration
  - Internet Resources
  - Acquisition / Merger Integration
  - Disaster Recovery / Security Risks
  - System Design and Development

- Broad knowledge of current technologies and future trends.

CAREER EXPERIENCE

Independent Contractor • 2002 – present
Manage diverse contract IT projects for small businesses and individuals. Create efficiencies, isolate profitability factors, and integrate systems. Identify, recommend, and solve a diverse array of IT issues.

AT&T SOLUTIONS / FIFTH THIRD BANK – Alliance (1998–2002 through acquisitions and alliances)
Offering systems planning, deployment, and management services for networks

Project Manager / Team Lead / Network Manager • 2000 – 2002
Challenged to provide vision, strategy, and action plans in managing migration efforts from MichBell support to AT&T platform in 1998 alliance. Headed a team of nine on various Midwest locations for troubleshooting and implementation. Managed a staff of twelve on a 24/7/365 help desk supporting network-related issues. Provided mid-level to advanced training.

- Migrated MNB / Chicago First Bank technical center to Fifth Third's headquarters in Cleveland, Ohio from Detroit, Michigan. Helped plan and build infrastructure solutions to connect business units, people, and systems.

- Provided networking solutions and integration strategies that delivered value and tangible return on communications investment.

- Managed data and voice projects for Fifth Third, utilizing Vantive software for project tracking (assets, billables, receivables).

- Designed, established, and led methods to be followed for all Y2K compliance. Managed a team in testing, FCC compliance, and eventual certification, ensuring due diligence for all Y2K projects at all client/branch sites.

180

FIFTH THIRD BANK (prior: Chicago First Bank / MNB)

Tech Center /Helpdesk Manager • 1998 – 2000

Led a team of computer support representatives receiving requests for all network and operating system concerns, hardware problems, network connectivity issues, and problems relating to equipment. Team supported 2,500 banks throughout the Midwest.

- Integrated and transitioned people from three companies in two years; transitioning systems and networks with ever-increasing size, technology upgrades, and technical teams.

- Upgraded branch equipment controller and software to Token Ring; installed network equipment and cabling to IBM mainframe; supported the Matrix switch that connected all of MNB's network.

- Teamed on conversion project involving ATM machines; updated 2.4 circuit and dial backup modem to a 56K circuit and an ISDN modem for 6,000 ATM machines. Project finished three months before target date (NBD).

SCOTT DISCOUNT BROKERAGE CORPORATION (now: H&R Block); Detroit, MI
A full-service discount broker

Network/Helpdesk Manager • 1994 – 1998

Designed, led, and managed ongoing data network projects for the third largest discount brokerage in the U.S. (at the time). Responsible for system architecture, disaster recovery, system security system performance, capacity management and service levels, capital efficiency and budget, technology changes, integration of new service and equipment, and related operational support systems and applications for a network of 250+ branches and headquarters in 39 states, with 2,500 end users.

- Engineered the entire data center help desk from concept through all developmental phases, and then to implementation and ongoing support. Recruited/hired/trained teams for the nationwide network.

- Brought the entire network from an analog system to digital technology; developed a state-of-the-art backup system.

- Created a network with dual capacity that was utilized as a model for the industry.

- Set up internal repair depot at headquarters, canceled maintenance contract on all terminals, 3,270 controllers, and printers. Equipment was maintained with a higher quality, less down time for users, plus saved the company $100K per year.

- Deployed billing inefficiencies and recouped a half million dollars in billing discrepancies; also reduced ongoing complexities of accounting system to a more simple and streamlined process.

AS400 Operator/Maintenance Engineer • 1988 – 1994

Maintained and supported all 3270 equipment and cabling for 230 branches and headquarters. Performed system backups as well as month-end, quarterly, and year-end reporting.

- Set up a repair depot at headquarters, which saved the company $100K annually.

EDUCATION, CERTIFICATION & TRAINING

OAKLAND UNIVERSITY – **Degree in Computer Science** • 1988

AQC INSTITUTE OF MICHIGAN – Graduate • 1987

PMP Certification

MCSE Certification

3000+ hours of Project Management experience
AQC Institute of Michigan – Programmer (RPG, Structured COBOL, Assemblers, C, DOS)

TRACY SULSKI

1234 Silent Rain Drive • Colorado Springs, CO 80919

Home: (719) 555-1234
E-mail: tsulski@protypeltd.com

PROFILE

- Dedicated pharmacist with more than 15 years of experience in:
  - Pharmaceutical preparation
  - Drug utilization and evaluation
  - Drug therapy monitoring
  - Chemotherapy preparation and administration
  - Extemporaneous compounding
  - Hyperalimentations and intravenous admixtures
- Self-motivated healthcare professional with a strong work ethic and commitment to quality.
- Effective team player with proven communication and interpersonal skills.

CREDENTIALS

- Colorado Licensed Pharmacist (#13760)
- Louisiana Licensed Pharmacist (#14794)
- Pediatric Advanced Life Support (PALS) certified

EDUCATION

PHARMACY DOCTOR, University of Colorado, Denver, Colorado (2004 – 2007)
- Working toward a PharmD degree while holding down a full-time job.
- Course work completed: Evidence-Based Pharmacy Practice, Clinical Skills Foundation.

BACHELOR OF SCIENCE, PHARMACY, Northeast Louisiana University, (1990)
- Completed an undergraduate degree from an accredited school of pharmacy.

PROFESSIONAL DEVELOPMENT
- Maintained 15 continuing education units per year, including courses in AIDS/HIV, asthma, depression, hypertension, and diabetes management, among others.

EXPERIENCE SUMMARY

PHARMACEUTICALS
- Prepared and dispensed prescribed medications, drugs, and other pharmaceuticals for patient care.
- Reviewed prescriptions issued by physicians or other authorized prescribers to ensure accuracy and determine formulas and ingredients required.
- Compounded medications using standard formulas and processes.
- Assayed medications to determine their identity, purity, and strength.
- Established and followed procedures for quality assurance, security of controlled substances, and disposal of hazardous waste drugs.
- Maintained professional standards and adhered to federal and state regulations.
- Identified, resolved, and prevented drug-related problems, and ensured that desired patient outcomes were achieved through safe, timely, and cost-effective drug therapy.
- Audited and stocked crash carts for hospitals and participated in code responses to the ER, NICU, and pediatrics unit.
- Prepared inpatient medications, including sterile IVs, TPN, chemotherapy drugs, and IV antibiotics.
- Assisted with pharmacokinetic drug monitoring of aminoglycosides, Vancomycin, and Dilantin.
- Wrote procedures for and participated in clinical trials, including studies of Glutamine, surfactants, and cardiac medications.
- Developed patient care plans and participated on rounds with multi-disciplinary teams of healthcare professionals.

EXPERIENCE SUMMARY

COMMUNICATION
- Answered questions and provided information to pharmacy customers on drug interactions, side effects, dosages, and storage of pharmaceuticals.
- Prepared inpatient medications for hospital floors and provided patient education.
- Called doctors to clarify prescriptions, dosages, and refills and to ensure accurate and safe dispensing.
- Conducted in-service training for new interns and nurses on medication safety and hospital processes for ordering drugs.
- Maintained continuous communications with nursing units, physicians, and technicians.
- Developed scripts and procedures to ensure adequate counseling of patients on drug-herbal interactions. Succeeded in improving the AVATAR score from 88% to 90% (an instrument used to measure customer satisfaction with hospital services).

MANAGEMENT
- Directed pharmacy workers engaged in mixing, packaging, and labeling pharmaceuticals.
- Used the computerized pharmacy information management systems, tracked inventory, and maintained pharmacy records.
- Supervised the work of pharmacy staff to ensure the safe and legal processing, compounding, and delivery of prescriptions.

EXPERIENCE

STAFF PHARMACIST, Memorial Hospital, Colorado Springs, Colorado (1993 – present)
- Originally hired as a general staff pharmacist working in all areas of this 477-bed regional medical center providing comprehensive medical care for both adults and children. Specialties included cancer treatment, heart disease, trauma, and rehabilitation, as well as special services for women and children.
- In 1996, moved to the Children's Hospital specializing in NICU and pediatric pharmaceuticals while cross-covering the ICU, emergency room, and medical/surgical units.

PHARMACIST, PER DIEM, Semper Care Hospital, Colorado Springs, Colorado (2003 – present)
- Work one or two weekends a month for this long-term care, rehabilitation hospital.

PHARMACIST, PER DIEM, St. Anthony's Hospital, Denver, Colorado (2003 – 2004)
- Took a second job for 16 hours per week on the graveyard shift of this hospital selected as one of the 100 best in the United States by HCIA/Mercer.

STAFF PHARMACIST, LSU Medical Center, Shreveport, Louisiana (1990 – 1993)
- Gained diverse experience in all areas of pharmacy operations in this 550-bed regional medical center and teaching hospital.
- Spent one and a half years in pediatrics and the NICU and another one and a half years in the main pharmacy, supporting the SICU, oncology, med/surg units, and emergency department.

AFFILIATIONS

- Member, American Society of Hospital Pharmacists, ASHP (1990 – present)
- Member, Colorado Society of Hospital Pharmacists, CSHP (1994 – 2003)
- Member, American Pharmaceutical Association, APHA (1994 – 1997)

COMPUTERS

- Proficient in Windows, MS Word, Excel, PowerPoint, Outlook, and Internet Explorer.
- Experienced in the use of Pixis Connect, Cerner, and the HealthSystems Management System.

183

JOY DAVIS

123 Madison Avenue • Brooklyn, NY 10455 • 718.555.1234 • davis@protypeltd.com

OBJECTIVE: PRIVATE INVESTIGATOR

SUMMARY OF QUALIFICATIONS

Highly-trained Investigator with 5+ years of experience in the financial services and insurance industries seeking to transfer those skills and professional background into the private investigation field. Expertise in researching and documenting sensitive and confidential information and data, interviewing clients and handling multiple caseloads and responsibilities. Strong technology skills with the ability to work independently or in a team setting.

CERTIFICATIONS

Caliber Training Institute, New York, NY, 2003
Private Investigation • American Institute of Executive Protection
Criminal Defense Investigation

RELEVANT COURSEWORK

Private Investigation • Civil Claims • Retail, Industrial, and Institutional Security
Background Checks • Fingerprinting • Surveillance Techniques and Equipment
Law and Criminal Procedure • Interviewing Techniques • Security Hardware and Devices

PROFESSIONAL EXPERIENCE

Personal Management Assistant, MetLife Financial Services
New York, NY, 2003–present

- Assist 100+ policyholders with questions and concerns on insurance policies and general financial products and services. Provide policyholders with cash quotes and account status information. Maintain and update account and system files for account representatives. Schedule appointments and organize meetings. Prepare and distribute literature on company services to potential clients.

Long-Term Care Administration Assistant, Teachers Insurance Annuity Association
New York, NY, 2001–2003

- Reviewed various insurance options and plans available for purchase with clients. Evaluated and approved initial premium requests. Issued new policies. Collaborated with account managers on adjustments and changes made to policyholders accounts. Researched and verified client account activity with accounting and general ledger offices. Authorized journal entries to be processed by third party administrators.

Long-Term Care Service Representative, TAA-CREF
New York, NY, 1998–2001

- Collected and input new long-term care applications. Provided applicants with information on annuities and payroll deductions and cash premiums. Oversaw the transfer of cash transactions and account balances. Issued written communications to policyholders on approvals or withdrawals of cash transactions. Processed requests for policy cancellations, refund transactions, and reissues.

EDUCATION

AA, Business Administration, CUNY Borough of Manhattan Community College – 1997

12 Graphic Design Elements

The following résumés aren't extremely elaborate in their use of graphic design elements. They are still basically conservative résumés with just a little something added to make them stand out.

Keep in mind that the graphic should be directly related to your industry. You wouldn't put a world globe on a waitress's résumé or drafting tools on a paramedic's. In some more conservative professions (banking, accounting, senior management, for example) graphics on a résumé are not recommended, even if they are small and conservative.

The résumé on page 199 uses a graphic that reflects an international focus, whereas the graphics on pages 188, 192–197, 281, 283, 284, and 287 reflect the person's industry.

By becoming a little more inventive, you can incorporate scanned letters or figures that reflect your personality more than the industry (see pages 186, 187, 189–191, 198, 200 in this section and page 280 elsewhere).

The use of the graphics in this chapter is fine on a scannable résumé. The scanning software will ignore your graphics as long as they don't touch any of the words on the page. However, using a graphic image as the first initial of your name (like the résumés on pages 189, 200, and 280) will cause your name to be spelled wrong in the electronic database after scanning. Avoid such graphic images that are part of your name in a scannable résumé.

Those in more creative industries—the arts, entertainment, advertising, graphic design—have a license to be even more creative. You could definitely get away with the résumés in this chapter, but you can be as creative as the résumés in Chapter 17.

A farmer went out to sow his seed...Luke 8:5

Michael D. Williams

123 Cherrybrooke Court
Jacksonville, Florida 34688
Home: 727.555.1234
Cellular: 727.555.5678
Email: mdwilliams@protypeltd.com

PROFILE

Visionary leader and strong communicator with expertise in:
- Leading through a model of spiritual growth
- Creating dynamic and growth-oriented team cultures
- Utilizing broad experience and creativity to influence positive change
- Organizational development and advanced fund-raising strategies
- Comprehending and responding to complex problems
- Maximizing opportunities and resources
- Negotiations and deal structuring

EDUCATION

MASTER OF BUSINESS ADMINISTRATION (MBA) (1992)
Indiana Wesleyan University, Marian, Indiana
- Graduated at the top of the class; received the Outstanding Professional Award
- Focused on not-for-profit marketing and management

BACHELOR OF ARTS (1983)
Dallas Christian College, Dallas, Texas
- Received the Campus Living Award and Church Musician Award
- President, Alumni Association (1986 – 1988)

EXPERIENCE

CHAIRMAN, PRESIDENT, AND CEO (1997 – present)
The Worship Network, PraiseTV, and CNI Holdings, Clearwater, Florida
- Led this international media group through a period of dynamic growth.
- Developed and implemented a new business model maximizing Network resources.
- Instituted a vision management system ($i=rs^3$) that dramatically changed team focus and energy by linking each member to the Network vision.
- Expanded organizational spiritual capital through programs focused on intense personal growth and emotional health of team members.
- Transformed the corporate culture by focusing team on clarity of mission, vision, core values, and spirit of the enterprise.
- Assembled skilled senior leadership team focused on achieving corporate goals.
- Developed partnerships with mega-churches to broaden program appeal, increase viewership, and strengthen financial support.
- Founded a West Coast office to expand sales and production relationships.
- Lobbied Congress and the Federal Communications Commission on key issues relating to religious broadcasters. This included hundreds of personal meetings with key Congressional offices and launching a national coalition of religious broadcasters.

Key Accomplishments:
- Re-engineered the programming department to expand target audiences, enhance script development, incorporate new musical styles, and utilize higher production values while reducing production time by nearly 50%.

EXPERIENCE

Key Accomplishments (continued)

- Negotiated an innovative agreement for carriage of Worship programming on PaxTV/NBC valued at approximately $300 million over 50 years.
- Increased affiliate stations by more than 100% and expanded distribution to 75% of America.
- Grew international distribution from 25 to 50 foreign countries.
- Built net sales revenue more than 1,200% to $1.9 million in 2004. On track to achieve $2.5 million in 2005.
- Increased donation income by more than 400%.
- Coordinated acquisition, management, and sale of a TV station resulting in nearly a $3 million profit.
- Increased church income from zero to $250,000 in one year.
- Achieved this growth while reducing staff from 50 to 30 and increasing expenses by only 16%.
- Received first-time support from the White House, the FCC Chairman, and numerous Congressional members on the crucial Must-Carry regulations.

EXECUTIVE ADVISOR (1992 – 1997)

- Conducted a feasibility study and developed a comprehensive fund-raising plan for the CEO of a regional not-for-profit ministry in Michigan.
- Assisted national ministry by assessing fund-raising effectiveness and preparing plans for the future.
- Counseled entrepreneurs in Eastern European markets on business planning and capital raising.
- Provided positioning and marketing counsel to the CEO of a mid-sized consulting firm. Assisted in procuring largest client contract in the history of the firm.
- Advised CEO of a national church funding organization in planning for their largest capital campaign and launching a new division.

EXECUTIVE DIRECTOR (concurrently with Christian Network role) (1997 – 2000)
North American Christian Convention, Cincinnati, Ohio

- Recruited to revitalize this conference of independent Christian Churches during a period of leadership transition, financial crisis, and declining attendance.
- Conducted a national research project to determine attitudes and needs of the constituency.
- Hired a Managing Director to assist in assembling an effective team and efficient systems.
- Restructured an out-of-date leadership model to address future opportunities and needs.
- Maximized resources by implementing new fund-raising strategies, creating a new marketing plan and disposing of an underutilized office building.

Key Accomplishments:

- Grew attendance by 35% and income by 40%, increasing cash reserves from $200,000 to just under $1.2 million in less than three years.

OTHER SERVICE

- Numerous national, regional, and local speaking engagements.
- Member, Church Development Fund Board of Directors (2000 – present); currently serving as Chairman
- Elder, Harborside Christian Church (2000 – present)
- Member, Kentucky Christian College Board of Directors (1998 – present)
- Committee Member, North American Christian Convention (1994 – 1997)
- Board Member, Montrose Crisis Pregnancy Center (1985 – 1988)
- State Team Member, Communities for a Drug-Free Colorado (1987 – 1988)
- Substitute Teacher, Assistant Coach, and Music Teacher, Montrose Public Schools (1983 – 1988)
- Member, Christ in Youth Conference Planning Council (1986 – 1987)
- Area Youth Coordinator, Rocky Mountain Billy Graham Crusade (1987)
- Ministry Internship, Valley View Christian Church, Dallas, Texas (1982 – 1983)

Domenick Santos

123 Rich Avenue • Mount Vernon, NY 10550 • 914-555-1234

Hair Stylist experienced in serving a discerning clientele at world-renowned salons. Rapidly develop a loyal client base with a gift for appreciating each person's unique spirit. Skilled at providing a high level of customer service and artistic talent. Verbally fluent in English, Italian, Spanish, and French.

PROFESSIONAL TALENTS

✂ Razor Cuts	✂ Point Cutting	✂ Organic Vegetable Dyes
✂ Scissor Cuts	✂ Hot Towel Shave	✂ Fashion Waves / Permanents
✂ Precision Cutting	✂ Coloring Processing	✂ Iso Straightening
✂ Notching	✂ Highlights / Low-lights	✂ Shiatsu Massage

CREDENTIALS

WESTCHESTER SCHOOL OF BEAUTY CULTURE, Mount Vernon, NY   2001
1,040 Hours in Hairdressing / Cosmetology—Completed program two months ahead of schedule

PROFESSIONAL EXPERIENCE

Hair Stylist, GJOKO HAIR SALON INTERNATIONAL, Larchmont, NY   2004 — 2005
Quickly earned a reputation as a highly talented stylist known for creating trendy, European styles. Created individualized looks by fully analyzing individual features, appearance, lifestyle, and personal spirit. Specialized in edgy, messy razor cuts with chipped edges and exclusive blowout cuts.

✂ Created styles that were featured on the inside cover of "Make a Goddess" by Dweller, a Johnny Skippy Publishing (BMI) recording.

✂ Delivered a 25 percent increase in new clients as featured stylist in Fall/Winter Hair Show promotion, which subsequently aired on cable television.

Hair Stylist, DOMINIQUE SALON AT THE HOTEL PIERRE, New York, NY   2002 — 2004
Rapidly advanced from protégé to head stylist for this highly acclaimed salon distinguished by the Gold (E) Award of Excellence. Served and maintained a small, select client base ranging from affluent tourists, residents, and celebrity clients including Kathy Lee, Frank Gifford, Sean Cannon, Drew Carey, Rune Arledge, and Francesco Scavullo. Specialized in barber facials with hot towel and straight-razor shaves, hair coloring, classical and trendy hairstyles.

✂ Produced $210,000 in annual revenues by developing and implementing new marketing strategies.

✂ Increased product sales by $30,000 with introduction of new product lines.

✂ Introduced edgy, trendy styles that attracted a younger crowd seeking frequent hair maintenance.

✂ Invited to assist world-renowned stylist and salon owner, Dominique, at Fashion Week.

Assistant Colorist, JOSE EBER ALTELIER, White Plains, NY   2001 — 2002
Joined creative team as an assistant to the color director for this trend-setting salon. Administered annual budget of $78,000 for product purchasing and inventory. Played a key role in maintaining the satisfaction of a loyal client base of 100 affluent and influential clients.

✂ Developed advanced experience in European hair coloring, highlights, low-lights, Biolage Systems and hand painting. Enhanced coloring through use of vegetable dyes.

Assistant to Head Stylist, SALON SHIN, Scarsdale, NY   2001
Developed hands-on expertise in precision cutting and customer relationship management as assistant to the head stylist for this full-service salon recognized for its excellence in styling.

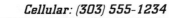

GERI WOOLERY

1234 E. Milan Court, Aurora, Colorado 80013

Cellular: (303) 555-1234

Phone: (303) 555-5678

PROFILE

- Experienced manager who understands the importance of quality service and an owner's investment.
- Proven background in operations management, negotiations, and employee motivation.
- Flexible professional who adjusts rapidly to new and challenging situations and works well under pressure to meet time-sensitive deadlines.
- Effective team leader who successfully motivates by example.

EXPERIENCE

GENERAL MANAGER, JAW PROPERTIES, INC. (1996 – present)

Regency Tower Apartments, Colorado Springs, Colorado (2000 – present)

Broadmoor Terrace Apartments, Colorado Springs, Colorado (1996 – present)

- Operate two apartment complexes with a total of 275 units valued at $15.3 million.
- Develop special events for the targeted senior community (55+) at the Regency, including monthly poolside parties, trips, and other activities.
- Maintain 99% occupancy through effective customer service and timely response to tenant concerns.
- Recruit, hire, and supervise a staff of 14, including assistant managers, maintenance personnel, leasing agents, and clerical staff.
- Developed and implemented new management policies and procedures.
- Created successful marketing campaigns that included magazine and apartment guide advertising, incentives, referral programs, and relocation specialists.
- Planned and supervised several capital improvement projects, including interiors, paint, carpeting, and parking lots.
- Developed safety programs and coordinated fire drills with the local fire department.

MANAGER (1996 – 2000)

Sundance Apartments, Colorado Springs, Colorado

- Took over the management of a rundown apartment complex with 147 units and supervised a $500,000 renovation.
- Improved security by working closely with the police department, installing security doors, and evicting problem tenants.
- Decreased vacancy rates from 40% to 2% and sold the property for a significant profit.

GENERAL MANAGER (1990 – 1996)

Pueblo Motor Inn, Pueblo, Colorado

- Upgraded guest service, amenities, and facility exteriors, which improved monthly revenue by 60%.
- Managed operations of both the hotel and restaurant, including 130 staff members and 164 rooms.
- Streamlined the operations of the restaurant, reducing food costs to 25%.
- Maintained expenses below budget through accurate planning, purchasing, and cost-effective operating procedures.

FOOD AND BEVERAGE MANAGER (1986 – 1990)

Quality Inn Hotel, Pueblo, Colorado

- Moved up the ranks from assistant manager of the restaurant/lounge to director of operations and then to general manager.
- Accountable for cost control, budgeting, profit and loss, payroll, and general accounting.
- Recruited, hired, supervised, scheduled, and motivated service staff and chefs.
- Trained service staff to enhance customer service and increase profits through suggestive selling.
- Planned menus, estimated food and beverage costs, and purchased supplies.
- Investigated and resolved food/beverage quality and service complaints, ensuring customer satisfaction.
- Developed wine lists, special events, and menus for banquets and private parties.

Douglas R. Snyder, PE

1234 Apple Lane • Penrose, Colorado 81240 • Home: (719) 555-1234 • Email: snyder@protypeltd.com

SUMMARY

- Creative thinker who wants to become part of a dynamic product development team or to work in an environment with constant challenges to make things faster, cheaper, and better.
- Able to use diverse knowledge to see problems and opportunities in a multitude of industries.
- Experienced in the design of product improvements, cost control, ergonomics, and aesthetics with a commitment to quality craftsmanship.
- Earned the Professional Engineer license (Colorado Certificate 123456).

STRENGTHS

- Adept at conceptualizing large, complex tasks and procedures while at the same time devoting requisite attention to the details.
- Can assemble and correlate ideas, theories, practical knowledge, and product information from a wide variety of fields and bring them to bear on the problem at hand.
- Able to think clearly when surrounded by distractions and when presented with conflicting information.
- Skilled at establishing rapport and facilitating a team to find unique ways to solve problems.

CREATIVITY

- Out-of-the-box thinker with the proven ability to look past assumptions to find better ways of doing things.
- Always able to see what others can't; reliable source of ideas and suggestions to solve any problem.
- Life-long avocation for automobile design—currently constructing a street rod from the ground up, including a new drive-train design and custom-built parts.
- Saw the possibilities and turned a lawnmower into a forklift.
- With a minimum of equipment, assistance, and cost, moved a large two-story hay barn from one end of the property to the other. Salvaged parts and built an elevator in the barn with a new control system.
- Solved the problem of my wife's access to a pot rack and built a motorized access system.

EXPERIENCE

COLORADO SPRINGS UTILITIES, Colorado Springs, Colorado (1991 – present)
Senior Project Engineer (1996 – present)

- Direct the construction of major utility projects. Responsible for product development, project planning, resource allocation, construction, and testing of multi-million-dollar projects.
- Currently designing a ground-up re-evaluation of control system philosophy to construct a 230kV ring-bus substation using SCADA controls without a remote terminal unit.
- Managed several large substation additions and mentoring others in project management.
- Managed the construction of a politically sensitive 115–34.5kV and 115–12.47kV substation feeding several large and important customers. Completed the project ahead of time and under budget.
- Planned, permitted, designed, and led the construction of the Woodmen 115–12.47kV substation. Effective project management skills brought the project in ahead of time and under budget. Attention to substation aesthetics permitted construction of this major substation literally in the neighborhood's backyards without a single complaint.
- Specified, evaluated, and led teams dedicated to forming strategic alliances for the purchase of switchgear, relay sheds, instrument transformers, and other major equipment.
- Led a team that completely rewrote CSU's entire transformer specification set, and implemented a strategic alliance with a transformer vendor that will enable the cost-effective purchase of up to 17 transformers.
- Wrote many transformer, switchgear, breaker, instrument transformer, disconnect switch, and other major equipment specifications.

EXPERIENCE

Key Accomplishments:
- Successfully managed the design, community integration, and public relations campaign that permitted the construction of a substation in an area that had twice rejected site development. The public participation process became an internal benchmark for the organization and resulted in magazine articles and industry presentations.
- Designed a worker-friendly unitized control shed that has since become a CSU standard. The design improved ergonomics and access and resulted in lower construction costs than the conventional layout.
- Reduced substation footprint by placing line disconnect switches on the termination towers. This saved money and improved aesthetics by reusing the existing overhead line tangent towers with added guying to handle the dead-end loads.
- Created a design to use inexpensive magnetic switches and shop-made brackets to avoid purchasing large and costly auxiliary switch assemblies for disconnects.
- Created new construction standards and updated older standards.

Engineer II (1991 – 1996)
- After successfully passing the Engineer-in-Training (EIT) examination, was transferred to the Substation and Transmission Engineering Group.
- Twice designed the relaying and control system for a large water pumping station (10 X 1500 HP) and led the team that retrofitted the new controls. Repeatedly asked by the operations of the station to consult on other matters to help guide the subsequent enlargement of the plant.
- Simplified and upgraded the WSCC-mandated under/over-frequency relaying throughout the system.

Key Accomplishments:
- Led a project to update a 1925 hydroelectric station; discovered a way to update the safety and performance of the plant while retaining its antique charm and history.

PUBLICATIONS
- Snyder, D.R. "Community Support Builds Substation," *Transmission & Distribution World*, July 2000.
- Snyder, D.R. "RFCIs Help Speed Response Times," *Transmission & Distribution World*, February 1998.

EDUCATION

UNDERGRADUATE STUDIES IN ELECTRICAL ENGINEERING
University of Colorado, Colorado Springs, Colorado
- Completed two years toward a Bachelor's Degree in Electrical Engineering
Florida Technological University, Orlando, Florida
- Completed two years of full-time study with an electrical engineering focus

CONTINUING EDUCATION
- Completed several post-graduate power engineering courses.
- Always attend every possible class, seminar, presentation, and new product demonstration, including: substation design, relay and protection, traffic engineering, video system installation, relay and control, substation equipment (motors, transmission lines, transformers, breakers, etc.).
- Recognized as an important contributor and invariably consulted on engineering matters at Colorado Springs Utilities.

PHILOSOPHY

I have long ago recognized that attractiveness and attention to aesthetics is not reserved for special occasions but is an everyday concern. Whether it be a clear and striking electrical schematic or pleasant and comforting substation landscaping, I have long advocated the view that aesthetics is not something added to a product or project but, rather, something that must be part of every design decision.

PAULA MARTIN
VETERINARY TECHNICIAN
pmartin@protypeltd.com

889 Westfield Street
Agawam, MA 06001
413.555.1234

Compassionate and competent **Veterinary Technician** with 5+ years of experience assisting veterinarians in medical and surgical procedures, ranging from routine to emergency and critical care. Recognized as efficient, skilled in multitasking and dedicated to providing prompt, courteous service. Effective communicator who enjoys working with people and animals and is able to educate owners on protecting their companion animals' health and well-being.

PROFESSIONAL EXPERIENCE

VETERINARY TECHNICIAN
HARRINGTON ANIMAL CLINIC, Agawam, MA   2000 to present
Assist five veterinarians in providing comprehensive veterinary care. Skilled in performing:

Medical & Surgical Procedures
- Assist in all types of medical treatments (and with restraints), ranging from routine office examinations to critical care, emergency situations, euthanasia, and house calls.
- Set up all equipment and prep animals for surgery: shaving, intubating, inserting IV catheters, and administrating intravenous/intramuscular drugs.
- Assist with surgeries, including spaying/neutering, exploratory, cystotomy, nasal scope, endoscopy, cruciate/luxating patella, abscess, declawing, and other procedures.
- Prepare and sterilize surgical packs in an autoclave. Monitor anesthesia and patient's vital signs. Administer subcutaneous fluids. Perform complete dentistry.
- Accurately document anesthetic drugs used during surgery. Handle post-surgical recovery—extubation, patient monitoring and calling clients to provide follow-up/status reports.
- Prepare vaccines, refill/dispense medications, administer oral medications/vaccines under supervision and provide instructions to clients. Assist with administration of chemotherapy.
- Groom and bathe animals, including fungal baths, and lion clips.
- Reverse sedation according to veterinarian's instruction.

Tests / Lab Work / Client Education
- Conduct heartworm, feline leukemia, and FIV tests. Take glucose and blood (including jugular) samples. Read results of urinalysis and fecal samples.
- Perform and develop radiographs. Assist specialists in restraining animals during ultrasounds.
- Educate clients on diseases/preventive care, home care (post-surgery, diabetic discharges, administering subcutaneous fluids and medications), grooming, diet, geriatric care, declawing alternatives, and other aspects of animal health care.

Front Office / Administration
- Cross-trained to perform front office duties, including scheduling routine health exams and surgical appointments, invoicing/cashing out, providing estimates and more.
- Greet clients and set up patients in exam rooms.
- Place orders for medications and various products per veterinarian's instructions. Sell products to clients.
- Utilize customized computer applications to process payments and enter patient records.
- Serve as a resource to new technicians by answering questions on equipment, office, and other procedures.

EDUCATION / TRAINING

A.S., Veterinary Technician; BRIARWOOD COLLEGE, Springfield, MA   2000

Additional Training:
Completed intensive, on-the-job, three-month training under guidance of licensed veterinarians at Harrington Animal Clinic.

CAMERON WOLFGANG, AIA

10747 Longview Circle
El Paso, Texas 79924
Phone: (915) 555-1234
Mobile: (915) 555-5678

Home Designed by Cameron Wolfgang

ARCHITECT
Member of the American Institute of Architects

CUSTOM RESIDENTIAL DESIGN
NEW HOMES • REMODELING • SPACE PLANNING

"Committed to Architectural Design Excellence for More Than 18 Years"

PROFESSIONAL OVERVIEW

Creative and accomplished Architect with 18+ years of experience, an excellent reputation, and a solid and *verifiable record of achievement*, gaining the trust and confidence of many of Dallas' top building contractors. Recognized for the ability to *turn a dream into a reality.* Involved in both the design stage of projects, and *hands-on* construction through final completion.

PROFILE OF STRENGTHS:

- **Unique, imaginative, and livable/comfortable floor plans** tailored to the needs of each client. Designs provide for the maximum use of space and create total environments that are functional and exciting places in which to live.
- **Strong management skills,** including strategic planning, project development and scheduling, problem solving, client relations, and quality control. Reduce building costs, improve energy efficiencies, and increase future value through good design.
- **Seasoned sales and marketing skills.** Demonstrated ability to gain trust and confidence of both builders and clients.
- **Expertise in major/minor project renovations**.
- **Solid design and construction experience in commercial projects** in addition to residential expertise.

PROFESSIONAL EXPERIENCE

Owner/ Architect
THE CJW DESIGN GROUP, Dallas, Texas

Architectural design company specializing in residential homes ranging in price from $250K to $3 million with up to 5000 sq. ft. Established a **regional reputation** for excellence and developed a loyal following with several of the top builders in North Dallas, to include:

- Monroe Custom Homes
- A. E. Homes
- Montwood Homes

EDUCATION

Bachelor of Environmental Design in Architecture
School of Architecture & Design, Dallas, Texas

ROBERT JOHN MERCER

(806) 555-1234 (h) – (806) 555-7890 (c)

9999 Hass Avenue – German Town, Texas 79000
rjmercer@protypeltd.com

SUMMARY

- Twenty years of experience piloting small corporate jets flying to domestic and international destinations.
- Seven years of overseeing operations for fixed-base and Part 135 flight services.
- Up to date with state-of-the-art flight panel and radar technology.
- In-depth understanding of aircraft systems: turboprop, turbojet, and piston propulsion.
- Consistent semi-annual flight training with Flight Safety International and Simuflite Training International, Inc., since 1990. Attended several Archie Trammel Weather Radar Schools.
- Exemplary flight record with zero accidents or violations throughout career.
- Superior knowledge of Crew Resource Management (CRM).
- Detail oriented and acutely focused on safety; skilled at recognizing unsafe weather conditions.

LICENSES

- Airline Transport Pilot—Multiple Engine Land Certification
- Flight Instructor Certification—Airplane Single and Multiengine Land Instrument Airplane

FLIGHT TIME

Total Flying Hours:	10,000+		Turbojet:	8,000
Pilot in Command:	7,000		Turboprop:	1,000
Instrument:	3,000		Simulator:	1,300

FAA TYPE RATED

Learjet 35, Citation 560XL and Citation 500

OPERATIONAL EXPERIENCE

Chief Pilot, GRAYFIELD CAPITAL CORPORATION, AAB, Germantown, Texas   1997 – 2003
Hand picked by company CEO as pilot for Albertson Alliance Bank (now GRAYFIELD CAPITAL CORPORATION). Performed operational as well as pilot duties. Typed in Learjet and Citation 560XL and Citation 500. Flew an average of three times a week throughout U.S. and Mexico averaging five to six passengers per flight.

Director of Operations, FRANKFORD AERO, Frankford, Texas   *Concurrent*   1998 – 2000
Oversaw Part 135 operation.

Pilot, AERO-MED, Grayfield, Texas   1990 – 1997
Flew Conquest I and II, Citation Type, King Air, Learjet 35 Type, and C-414 for Part 135 operation.

Self-employed, GENERAL AVIATION PILOT SERVICES & TRAINING, Grayfield, Texas   1985 – 1990

Company Pilot, WESTWARD WIND, Grayfield, Texas   1983 – 1985

EDUCATION

Bachelor of Science Degree, Technical University, Grayfield, Texas

Harry R. Moore

1200 Arroyo Chamisa % Santa Fe, NM 87505
Office: (505) 555-1234 % Mobile: (505) 555-5678

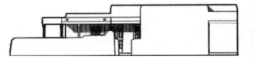

GENERAL CONTRACTOR / ARCHITECT / MASTER CRAFTSMAN
Specializing in Custom Designed/Built Adobe Homes that Capture the Spirit of Santa Fe

Award-winning, widely respected General Contractor specializing in designing and building unique, custom-made, energy-efficient *"Santa Fe Style"* adobe homes that incorporate the warmth, the spirituality, and the charm of the historical Santa Fe tradition by combining the best of both Native American and Hispanic cultures. Expert qualifications in merging modern technologies and new products with *"tried and true"* methods of building that have been around for centuries. Recognized for attention to detail and ability to create livable, high-quality homes.

Custom Aesthetic Specialties Include:

% Carved Corbels

% Plaster Ceilings with Vigas

% Latillas or Hand-Hewn Beams

% Ceramic Tile, Wood, or Flagstone Floors

% Hand-Trowelled Plaster Walls

% Arched and Curved Entryways, Doorways, and Walls

% Energy Efficient Passive Solar Designs

Home Builder's Association Awards:

Home Builder of the Year *(7-Awards)*
Winner – Best Custom Built Home
Winner – Best Custom Home Design

Professional Affiliations:

Member, National Home Builder's Association
Member, New Mexico Home Builder's Association
Member, Santa Fe Area Home Builder's Association

PROFESSIONAL BACKGROUND

Owner/General Contractor
1975–present
HARRY R. MOORE CONSTRUCTION COMPANY
Santa Fe, New Mexico

Oversee, direct, and coordinate custom-made home building projects ranging from $350K to $1.4 million. Manage all phases of project development from initial client contact, through contract negotiation and conceptual and architectural design, to the finished home. Recruit, hire, and manage 15 to 25 expert craftsmen; coordinate and direct care-fully selected subcontractors. Demonstrated commitment to quality construc-tion and ex-cep-tional client service.

EDUCATION

Bachelor of Business Administration
University of New Mexico, Albuquerque, New Mexico

YOLANDA GREENE

123 Wyckoff Street
Brooklyn, NY 11201
Phone (718) 555-1234
Yolanda@protypeltd.com

**Registered Physician
Assistant – Certified**
Gynecology / Adolescent Medicine

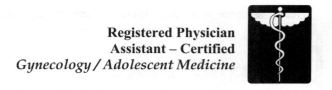

MISSION STATEMENT

To enrich the lives of all women, regardless of age, sexual orientation, race, faith, and socio-economic background by providing access to affordable, high-quality health care that successfully promotes wellness care and encourages an open, trusting dialogue between patient and practitioner.

CREDENTIALS

- ☑ U.S. D.E.A. License – National Commission on Certification of Physician Assistants
- ☑ Certified and Licensed Physician Assistant – University of the State of New York Education
- ☑ Certified in CPR and Basic Life Support
- ☑ Energetic, thorough, and compassionate practitioner.
- ☑ Gained the trust and confidence of adolescents and adults.
- ☑ Experience encompasses:
  - Colposcopic Examinations
  - Gynecological Examinations
  - Ultrasound
  - Family Planning / RU486
  - STD, HPV Screenings
  - Patient Advocacy and Counseling

EDUCATION

AMERICAN SOCIETY FOR COLPOSCOPY AND   2002
CERVICAL PATHOLOGY, Minneapolis, MN
- ☑ **Met requirements for Colposcopy Mentorship Program Examination**
- ☑ **Performed 200 colposcopic examinations**

UNIVERSITY OF MEDICINE & DENTISTRY OF NEW JERSEY, Newark, NJ   2001
- ☑ **Ultrasound Tutorial**

SUNY DOWNSTATE MEDICAL CENTER, Brooklyn, NY   2000 – 2001
- ☑ **HIV Center Seminar Series**

HIGHLAND HOSPITAL, Rochester, NY   2000
- ☑ **Accepted into family planning residency program focused on
  pelvic sonograms, MVA, and RU486**

BAYLEY SETON HOSPITAL PHYSICIAN ASSISTANT PROGRAM, Staten Island, NY   1997
- ☑ **Awarded Physician Assistant Certificate**

THE COLLEGE OF STATEN ISLAND Staten Island, NY   1997
- ☑ **Bachelor of Science: Biology**

PROFESSIONAL EXPERIENCE

AMBULATORY SURGERY CENTER OF BROOKLYN, Brooklyn, NY   1997 – 2000, 2002 – 2004
Physician Assistant
Diagnose and treat up to 40 patients daily for this privately owned clinic. Scope of diseases encompasses STDs, uterine myomas, HPV, Bartholin cysts, and PID. Obtain patient histories and perform gynecological examinations. Prescribe prescriptions and treatments; order and review sonograms and lab reports. Administrate daily activities of outpatient GYN clinic; supervise clinical team of sonographers, lab technologists, and social workers. Set the pace for receptionist to direct patients for treatment.

- ☑ Introduced and implemented RU486 (Mifepristone) treatment plan into the family planning program, with practice growth of 450 new patients annually.
- ☑ Developed colposcopy program for patients with abnormal pap smears, increasing early detection in up to 500 patients per year.
- ☑ Train and instruct nurse practitioner in routine procedures such as GYN examinations and strategies for building patient trust.

EARLY OPTIONS Affiliated with Long Island College Hospital, Brooklyn, NY   6/2001 – 12/2001
Physician Assistant
Developed experience with RU486 and manual vacuum aspiration (MVA) while providing temporary coverage at this family practice. Awarded a Buffet Foundation clinic-based research grant to study early options for patients terminating pregnancies. Accurately charted patient histories and results of physical examinations prior to medical procedures for 75 patients weekly. Dated pregnancies using sonograms.

- ☑ Identified women who were strong candidates for RU486.
- ☑ Earned a reputation for building strong rapport and provided empathetic counseling to patients.
- ☑ Provided excellent patient teaching on administration and follow-up care for medical treatments.
- ☑ Earned C.M.E. credits in sonography.

SUNY DOWNSTATE MEDICAL CENTER, Brooklyn, NY   1/2001 – 5/2001
Clinical Staff Research Associate
Conducted interviews with African-American and Caribbean female adolescents in a pilot study conducted by The Research Foundation of the State of New York and funded by Bayer Aspirin to explore the impact of unprotected sex on rising STDs/HIV rates among young women in Brooklyn, New York, the epicenter for newly diagnosed HIV cases. Established an open, honest dialogue with adolescent females.

PROFESSIONAL ASSOCIATIONS

- ☑ American Academy of Physician Assistants (AAPA)
- ☑ Association of Physician Assistants in Obstetrics & Gynecology (APAOG)
- ☑ American Society for Colposcopy and Cervical Pathology (ASCCP)

GREGORY A. POTTER

806.555.1234
6689 85th Street, #3, Lubbock, Texas 79424
gpotter@protypeltd.com

OBJECTIVE: Information Technology Specialist

EDUCATION

M.B.A. in Management and Leadership Skills, Rawls College of Business Administration (3.5)   12/04
B.B.A. in Management Information Systems, Rawls College of Business Administration (3.5)   05/03
TEXAS TECH UNIVERSITY (TTU), Lubbock, Texas

Honors:
Honors Graduate, Cum Laude › Arion Foundation Award › President's and Dean's List

Relevant Coursework:
Business Computer Programming, Systems Analysis, Advanced Applications Programming, Applications of Distributed Systems, Database Management Systems, Information Systems Project Management, Information Systems Design, Strategic Management, Conflict Negotiating, and Corporate Finance.

TECHNICAL SKILLS

Certifications:	Microsoft Office XP, MS Project 2002; Pending Microsoft Certified Professional
Operating Systems:	Microsoft PC and Mac OS
Software:	MS Office Suite, Publisher, Project, FrontPage, Oracle 8.0
Programming:	SQL+, HTML, DHTML, PHP, CGI, ASP, Perl, VB&B script, Java, and Java script
Systems Analysis and Design:	Self-taught in XML and C#; SDLC (waterfall and spiral models), UML Notation, Use-Cases/Class/Sequence/Statechart/Collaboration Diagrams, ERDs, DFDs, etc.

RELEVANT EXPERIENCE

IT Specialist, www.retedu.org (International Foundation for Retirement Education)   2003 – present
Lubbock, Texas

A nonprofit organization that provides a respected and a rigorous online educational/certification program for retirement professionals in an effort to secure the futures of today's baby boomers.

Develop and maintain two company Web sites that address online continuing education course offerings, online shopping cart, and electronic payment processing system. Report to program director. Perform data entry and update database of 1,800+ clients. Administer computer network, manage e-mail, and maintain domain registration.

Key Contributions:
- Instrumental in reengineering online ordering process to reduce confusion and increase efficiency.
- Consistently meet and exceed deadlines.

Freelance Web Designer, Lubbock, Texas
Designed Web sites for a car salesman and a piano professor promoting his book.

ORGANIZATIONS

- Member, Rawls Graduate Association, TTU   2004 – present
- Non-voting Member, Lubbock Chief Executives Roundtable Forum, TTU   2003 – present
- Member, National Society of Collegiate Scholars (NSCS), TTU   2000 – present
- Member, TTU Student Ministries   2000 – 2001
  - Leader, Freshman Family and Outreach

198

Beira d'Polizzi

123 Crocus Lane
Colorado Springs, CO 80918

Cellular: (719) 555-1234
Email: bdp@protypeltd.com

PROFILE

- Driven worker with a passion for marketing and a diverse international background.
- Bilingual in English and Spanish—fluent in both written and spoken languages.
- Effective team player with strong written and oral communication skills.
- Proven problem solver who uses logical but creative approaches to solve challenges.
- Proficient in Windows, MS Word, Excel, PowerPoint, Outlook, Internet Explorer, and Marketing Plan Pro.

EDUCATION

BACHELOR OF ARTS, INTERNATIONAL BUSINESS AND MARKETING (December 2004)
University of Colorado, Colorado Springs, Colorado
- *Marketing Course Work*: Marketing Policies/Strategies, Promotion Management, Strategy Marketing, Marketing Analysis/Planning, Contemporary Marketing, Principles of Marketing, Marketing Research.
- *International Course Work*: International Financial Management, Intercultural Communications, Spanish Grammar, International Marketing, International Economics, International Business.
- Member of the Delta Sigma Pi Professional Business Fraternity—Participated in fund raising, special events planning, community service projects, and tours of local businesses.

INTERNATIONAL EXPERIENCE

- Developed an international marketing plan for Listerine Pocket Packs in Malaysia—Analyzed the market and culture of the region, including the economic and political situation in Malaysia. Researched export issues, channel design, and distribution. Developed the pricing strategy and adaptations required for the Malaysian culture.
- Researched and created a marketing plan for Toyota N.A., including competitive analysis, pro forma financial statements, SWOT analysis, market position, and secret shopper program.
- Lived in Spain for eight years, Turkey for two years, and Italy for two years.
- Developed strong cross-cultural communication skills—able to adapt quickly to different cultures and ways of thinking.

EXPERIENCE

MARKETING INTERNSHIP (May - July 2005)
Greater Colorado Springs Chamber of Commerce, Colorado Springs, Colorado
- Completed a two-month internship in marketing, media relations, programs, and event management.
- Part of the team responsible for pre-event planning, event management (invitations, program, reservations, facilities, food, logistics, public relations), and post-event evaluation for the Small Business Expo.
- Called on sponsors to ensure customer satisfaction, and recruited celebrity models for the celebrity fashion show.
- Coordinated restaurant participation in the Taste of the Springs event—called each restaurant to schedule arrival and departure times and to confirm participation, set up banners, and decorated tables.

MARKETING INTERNSHIP (January - May 2005)
People Magazine, Colorado Springs, Colorado
- Part of a team of college students selected through EdVenture Partners to develop a marketing campaign to promote People Magazine subscriptions to a select student population.
- Formulated a marketing strategy and presented recommendations and promotional ideas to the client.
- Designed a marketing campaign targeted at college women ages 18–24.
- Prepared media kits, wrote press releases, and developed relationships with radio and television media.
- Collaborated with People Magazine's production and art departments, and met critical deadlines.

JAMES K. DOBSON

Cellular: (719) 555-1234

1234 Buttermere Drive, Colorado Springs, CO 80906

Email: jkdob@protypeltd.com

PROFILE

- Dependable manager with the proven ability to relate to clients and build trust.
- Self-motivated and focused; comfortable working independently with little supervision.
- Intuitive communicator who enjoys social interaction and speaking to groups.
- Highly proficient in Windows, MS Word, Excel, WordPerfect, QuickBooks, Dolphin Imaging, email, and the Internet.

EDUCATION

BACHELOR OF ARTS IN COMMUNICATION (2004)
University of Colorado, Boulder, Colorado
- Course work included: Rhetorical Dimensions of Communication, Empirical Research Methods, Human Communication Theory, American Sign Language I/II/III, Contemporary Mass Media, Organizational Communication, Interviewing, Communication in Society, Interpersonal Communication, Principles and Practices of Argumentation, Interaction Skills, Current Issues in Communication (Critical Thinking).

EXPERIENCE

MARKETING INTERNSHIP (2004 – present)
Greater Colorado Springs Chamber of Commerce, Colorado Springs, Colorado
- Completed a four-month internship in marketing, media relations, programs, and event management.
- Prepared and distributed promotional, public relations, and other communication materials.
- Developed and maintained a matrix to track the organization's involvement in the local media.
- Part of the team responsible for pre-event planning, event management (invitations, reservations, facilities, reception, logistics, public relations), and post-event evaluation.
- Served as an ambassador for the organization with Chamber members and the community.
- Assisted with budget review and tracking.
- Represented the organization as a speaker liaison.
- Served on the Colorado Women's Business Council advisory committee.
- Traveled with Chamber management to the annual Colorado Springs Day at the State Legislature.

OFFICE MANAGER / LAB TECHNICIAN (2001 – present)
Dr. James E. Killebrew, LLC, Colorado Springs, Colorado
- Manage the operations of a busy orthodontic practice dedicated to excellence in customer service.
- Recruit, hire, train, and supervise six staff members—an orthodontic assistant, patient coordinator, back office support, and facilities maintenance.
- Fully accountable for profit and loss of the practice, including accounts payable, accounts receivable, insurance billing, collections, payroll, quarterly tax payments, and reconciliation of bank and credit card statements.
- Forecast staffing needs, expenses, and income; prepare and manage annual budgets.
- Meet with patients to present cases and close the sale by selecting the right financing option for each patient's needs.
- Schedule appointments and referrals, prepare patients for treatments, take and develop x-rays (Ceph and Pano), and sterilize equipment.
- Design and manufacture specialty orthodontia lab retainers.

Key Accomplishments:
- Created a new scheduling system that allowed the staff to see more patients every day, which reduced the work week from 5 days to 3.5 days while at the same time increasing income by 27 percent.
- Developed Excel spreadsheets to track inventory more accurately, which significantly reduced obsolete inventory and supplies on hand.
- Reduced overhead expenses 49.4 percent by eliminating an overpriced outside janitorial service and cross-training orthodontic assistants in lab processes.

13 Paragraph Style

Good advertisements are designed in such a way that the reader's eye is immediately drawn to important pieces of information using type and graphic elements, including bold, italics, headline fonts, and so forth. Then the design must guide the reader's eye down the page from one piece of information to the next with the use of white space or graphic designs between short paragraphs.

In this science of typography, very long lines of text (longer than six or seven inches, depending on the font) and large blocks of text (more than seven typeset lines) are considered to be tiring to the reader's eye. If you look closely at textbooks, magazines, and newspapers, you will notice that the information is usually typeset in columns to reduce line lengths, and journalists intentionally write in short paragraphs because they are more reader friendly.

How does this science translate into the design of a résumé? As a general rule, you should keep your lines of text no longer than seven inches—five to six inches is even better—and your paragraphs shorter than seven lines of text each. Many people find it difficult to cram the description of a job and its accomplishments into a single paragraph while following this rule. Therefore, you will often see bulleted sentences used on résumés instead of paragraphs or following an introductory paragraph.

If you prefer the paragraph style, there are some tricks of the trade that can help you make your résumé more readable:

1. Divide your experience into related information and use several shorter paragraphs under each job description (pages 202–205 and 210).

2. List the job summary in paragraph form and then use bullets to highlight your achievements (pages 206–209).

3. Use left headings instead of centered headings (page 210) to make the line lengths shorter. This won't work, however, when the shorter line length forces your information into very long paragraphs. It is better to have longer line lengths and shorter paragraphs.

Full justification—where all the lines end at the same place on the right margin, like on this page—makes paragraph-style résumés look more formal. Ragged right margins generally give a more informal appearance (see pages 202–205, 208, and 209). Full justification creates a neater appearance any time the lines of text run all of the way to the right margin, even in bulleted résumés. However, you can choose either style and not go wrong. Again, it is just a matter of your personal preference.

AHNA D. SUTTON

1234 East North Street, Waynesboro, PA 17268
Home: 717.555.1234 ▪ Mobile: 301.555.4321 ▪ Sutton@protypeltd.com

SALES AND MARKETING EXECUTIVE
Problem Solver…Money Maker

Top-producing sales and marketing professional who is ambitious, energetic, and self-disciplined. Designer and executor of innovative marketing strategies that motivate, educate, and create demand. Mentor and coach committed to transforming novice account reps into rainmakers. Unequaled professional who embraces change and thrives on challenge.

TRACK RECORD OF SUCCESS

E-Business Development: Launched and continue to develop a unique B2B and B2C electronic shopping mall, capturing the small business market and blazing new inroads to non-traditional advertising.

Advertising Production: Conceived, designed, and published a quarterly, advertiser-funded, lifestyle and leisure magazine promoting a quad-county area of southern Pennsylvania. Circulation: 20,000/month.

Territory Development: Exploded Cellular One presence in the Chambersburg/Waynesboro, Pennsylvania, business community. Propelled the lowest producing B-mall to top producer, with sales averaging more than 300 phones per month. Orchestrated opening of two new in-line stores.

Market Penetration: Delivered an impressive first-year TV advertising sales growth from $40K to $380K by capturing the untapped auto dealership market.

Brand R & D: Forged an alliance with an auto dealership, GM/Sales, to create and launch a market brand that continues to outshine the competition. Proven skills in creating and implementing campaign budgets that work.

Leadership and Mentoring: Pioneered an in-the-trenches training ground for new sales personnel in the nuances of television advertising, motivating staff to attain third-year sales revenues approaching $190K over first-year sales.

CAREER EXPERIENCE

TELEVISION / CBS 26, Harrisburg, PA

Area's Best Shopping Sales Manager   2001 – present

> Recruited to lead a unique Internet/television advertising partnership from initial concept to full implementation. Manage a $304K annual operating budget. Hire, train, and direct sales activities of three account executives. Train and mentor 11 television sales reps.
>
> Strategically drove first-quarter profits to $8K; and project year-end to $127K. Second-year profits are expected to top $200K with $1.9 million in sales. Indirectly impacted television advertising revenues by $262K+ in less than three years.

Account Executive   1997 – 1998

> Grew Franklin County, Pennsylvania, business accounts more than 900 percent by identifying and capturing untapped business markets.

ENTREPRENEURIAL ENDEAVORS, Waynesboro, PA   1989 – present

Image Consultants Unlimited (1998 – present)

> Co-founded an advertising consulting business targeting local business with limited advertising knowledge, skills, and experience. Provide a comprehensive analysis of advertising needs and resources and big-picture management strategies to maximize ROI while trimming the fat.

202

Image Consultants Unlimited (continued)

Key Projects:

Formulated a two-year multi-faceted marketing and advertising campaign that propelled sales for a single-family home construction firm from the $140K price range to a multimillion dollar development with home sales averaging $350K.

Expanded market reach and doubled profits in one-year with a strategically designed advertising and merchandising campaign promoting an indoor/outdoor furniture retail operation.

I Do Magazine (1989 – 1991)

Conceived, designed, and published a monthly, advertiser-supported wedding planning magazine. Implemented creative marketing/distribution strategies, placing the publication into the hands of approximately 1,000 newly engaged couples each month.

CABLE ADVERTISING, Gettysburg, PA   2000 – 2001

Account Executive

Penetrated the Gettysburg, Pennsylvania, business community, which was unaccustomed to cable advertising. Drove sales from zero to $120K in only one year. Received numerous Sales Excellence Awards for consistently exceeding monthly sales goals.

WIRELESS COMMUNICATIONS/RETAIL, Chambersburg/Gettysburg, PA   1993 – 1997

Sales Manager

Within first three months of hire as Outside Sales Executive, earned corporate Giant Step Award for the greatest percentage increase in sales. This led to a promotion to Sales Manager. Tasked with oversight of mall kiosk and four sales personnel.

Grew a low-producing mall kiosk to an in-line mall store and expanded market reach by establishing a second in-line store in a neighboring community. Grew sales staff to seven. Managed a $1.2 million operating budget, inventory, promotions, and advertising for both locations.

Developed an internal communication channel, linking sales and management personnel in 25 locations across seven territories to ensure full staff coverage and networked resources for resolving operational issues and concerns.

Created a mentoring and job shadowing relationship between sales managers and top sales performers to provide them with career advancement opportunity.

PC AND WIRELESS COMMUNICATION SAVVY

PowerPoint, Excel, Word, Access, PrintShop, Publisher, FrontPage, Adobe Acrobat, Internet, E-mail, Palm Pilot, Cellular

PROFESSIONAL DEVELOPMENT

Stephen Covey, First Things First • Zig Ziglar, See You at the Top • How to Supervise People Managing for the 90s and Beyond • Influence Management Skills • Purchasing Basics for the New Buyer • Tom Peters, WOW Seminar • The Networking Seminar • Interpersonal Skills • Jim Doyle Training

CARLO PONTE

cpengineering@protypeltd.com

122 Calle Punta Arenas
Fallbrook, California 92028

Office: 760 555-1234
Cellular: 760 555-5678

GENERAL ENGINEERING CONSTRUCTION CONSULTANT

A process-oriented leader whose ability to consistently streamline operations has resulted in significant cost savings, increased productivity, and profitability.

Energetic, highly motivated, honest Consultant with extensive experience in site and infrastructure development and construction. Astute decision-maker with proactive management style; tough but fair, with outstanding interpersonal skills and strong work ethics.

- **Vision Management, Strategic Planning / Development, Cost-Efficient Project Management, and Problem Solving**. Able to perceive needs and resolve problems and conflicts during stressful situations.
- Able to build consensus across diverse political, social, cultural, and economic lines. Sensitive to staff, public, and community relations.
- Successful in negotiating public and private outsourcing agreements and partnerships, delivering strong financial results. Able to achieve cooperation, dedication, and client satisfaction.
- Well respected throughout the industry for achievement in both project construction and business management. Often requested to serve as an expert witness.

PROJECT HIGHLIGHTS

CLIENT: Heritage Partners, Ltd.

PROJECT: Rye Business Park   (1998 – present)
300-acre, $95 million commercial site and infrastructure development in Ventura, Arizona

Development and construction: rough and fine grading, storm drain and related concrete structures, sanitary sewer system, domestic water system, curb and gutter, street paving, street lights, traffic signals, dry utilities, and landscaping.

Services provided: design analysis, computerized quantity analysis, bid package and contract specifications, contractor bid analysis and award, budget and cost analysis. Manage construction activities. Coordinate subcontractor work. Verify and approve change orders as well as additional work. Develop and track multiple CPM schedules, computerized tracking of earthwork quantities for pay purposes, cash flow forecasting, and progress billing approval. Advisor to Civil Engineer.

PROJECT: L.A. Media Tech (1999 – present / concurrently)
45-acre, $70 million commercial site and infrastructure development in Los Angeles, California

Development and construction: rough and fine grading, realignment construction of existing and new construction of storm drain, sewer and water systems, street paving, and related items.

PROJECT: Henderson Business Park (2000)
Large commercial development in Temecula, California.

Site development and construction of concrete tilt-up buildings.

PROJECT: Jericho Oaks (1999)
Renovation of office building and parking lot in Thousand Oaks, California.

Tenanted improvements of office building and construction of additional parking lot.

CLIENT: The Peters Company

PROJECT: Rio Plaza (2002)
Removal and reconstruction of parking lot and new store fronts in existing shopping center.

Large aged shopping center reconstructed to upgrade and modernize up to 21st century standards. Reconstruction included removal and reconstruction of existing parking lots and truck drives, and face lift for existing buildings.

Services provided: computerized removal and paving quantities. Recommendation of several paving and subgrade options to lessen the cost dealing with subgrade material containing excessive moisture conditions accompanied by budget estimates.

CLIENT: San Bernardino New Auto Dealers Association

PROJECT: Redevelopment of San Bernardino Auto Mall (1999)
Reconstruction of infrastructure and face of San Bernardino Auto Mall and dealership store fronts.

Demolition and removals, grading, relocation of structures and utilities, curb and gutter, concrete structures, paving of streets and parking lots.

Liaison among Riverside New Auto Dealers Association, City of Riverside, and prime contractor of Riverside Construction. Services: QCQA, analysis / explanation of plans and construction to dealership owners. Attendance in weekly construction meetings.

PRESIDENT / OWNER of former SURETRUST ENGINEERING, INC.

General engineering construction company with annual contract of $12 million; 60 employees.

Locations ranged from Oceanside to Victorville, California. Project size: from $15,000 to $3 million. Clients were private, commercial, and residential developers, and public works entities, such as:

- Riverside County Transportation Department
- Riverside County Flood Control
- City of Riverside
- Los Angeles Department of Airports
- Cal-Trans
- City of Corona
- City of Hesperia
- City of Ontario
- Local Builders

CONSULTING SERVICES

- Computerized Earthwork Analysis
- Jobsite Topo Verification
- Jobsite Earthwork Tracking
- Bid Package Development
- Budget and Cost Analysis
- Plan and Cost Review
- Contracts and Specifications
- Estimating
- Project Cash Flow Forecasting
- Quality Control and Quality Assurance (QCQA)
- Jobsite / Project Management
- Computerized Critical Path Method (CPM) Scheduling
- Case Preparation for Litigation and Claims
- Expert Witness
- Storm Water Protection Prevention Plans (SWPPPs) Compliance

Hector J. Ortega

12345 Colorado Boulevard
Pasadena, California 91109

ortega@protypeltd.com

(818) 555-1234 Residence
(818) 555-5678 Cellular

PROFILE

Financial Systems Executive with more than 12 years of industry experience in managing corporate accounting systems that support the operational and financial infrastructure of large global organizations. Proactive corporate leader, successful in transitioning IT and finance areas into critical business partnerships. Accustomed to managing multiple priorities in a dynamic environment, with strong track record of leading teams responsible for interdisciplinary projects.

CAREER SKILLS AND KNOWLEDGE

Systems Expertise
- ✔ Client server/mainframe architecture
- ✔ Application specifications
- ✔ Major conversions
- ✔ Financial/management report design
- ✔ Installation/testing/debugging
- ✔ Application security implementation

Financial Systems Management
- ✔ Systems solutions consulting
- ✔ Project leadership
- ✔ Cost control/reduction
- ✔ Operations analysis/streamlining
- ✔ International liaison
- ✔ Strategic planning
- ✔ Transformation planning/management
- ✔ Productivity improvement
- ✔ Staff supervision/development (technical and nontechnical)

Client Training
- ✔ Procedural documentation
- ✔ Training manual development
- ✔ Customer support/help desk organization
- ✔ User group interface at all levels

Industry Background
- ✔ Commercial banking
- ✔ Treasury/controller operations
- ✔ Investment banking and brokerage
- ✔ Global financial services

PROFESSIONAL EXPERIENCE

UNION GLOBAL TRUST COMPANY, Pasadena, CA   1993 – present

VICE PRESIDENT, Corporate General Ledger MIS (Since 2003)

Provide full support for the infrastructure to maintain the corporate accounting systems comprised of six components integrating into a global system serving Union Global Trust offices in the United States, Europe, and Asia. Assure consistent high quality of accounting data output and ease of its accessibility for major decision-making. Advise internal financial managers bank-wide with accounting methodology and systems requirements. Determine feasibility of their requests from standpoint of criticality, development time and costs, versus expected benefits. Recommend effective alternative solutions whenever possible. Keep system downtime to a minimum.

✔ Collaborated with senior management to develop and implement an online mainframe application to control the movement of funds throughout the various business areas of the bank.
   Result: Improved accuracy of daily postings and eliminated unapplied fund transfers.

✔ Integrated two separate corporate accounting and information systems for international financial and management reporting into a structured entity.
   Result: Provided agreement between the two charts of accounts, facilitated accessibility for users, and required less staff for maintenance of the system.

✔ Directed programmers in the automation of general ledger maintenance transactions, incorporating four new applications on PC to run from Lotus spreadsheets. Completed all phasing in five months.
   Result: Drastically decreased time and labor required for monthly transaction processing and cut several days off the accounting cycle.

Continued

VICE PRESIDENT, Corporate General Ledger MIS

✓ Developed automated validation process/reports to link the data in the financial and management reporting systems and support communication between them.
   Result: Ensured the integrity of the various databases and systems tables while eliminating human errors.

✓ Selected to manage the security enforcement aspect of the Corporate Controllers' System. Set up security requirements and wrote training manuals.
   Result: Effectively supported a system having 1,000 users worldwide.

UNION GLOBAL TRUST COMPANY

ASSISTANT VICE PRESIDENT, Corporate Accounting Systems Support Unit (1998–2003)

✓ Organized and maintained a centralized support group providing help desk, multi-tiered training, and trouble-shooting assistance to users of the bank's worldwide financial and management reporting applications.
   Result: Enabled better user understanding of systems capabilities which contributed to more efficient operations.

✓ Managed a team of eight business analysts responsible for liaison between technology and system users for newly developed multi-currency accounting and reporting system. Prepared business requirements and functional specifications for system enhancements, working with technology in development and testing of system modifications prior to implementation.
   Result: Improved control of defect tracking and monitoring of system problems and enhancements for more timely resolution of system issues.

✓ Acted as a key member of management team responsible for system evaluation, quality assurance, testing, and enhancement.
   Result: Developed a disaster recovery plan and implemented a new international investment advisory accounting and reporting system that replaced an existing unstable system

✓ Coordinated installation of the division local area network and Lotus Notes for more than 100 users.
   Result: Improved system reliability and communications.

✓ Arranged the purchase and installation/upgrade of all hardware and software.
   Result: This effort replaced obsolete equipment and software to accommodate a Windows environment.

✓ Designed, developed, and implemented a Proxy Tracking database application.
   Result: Eliminated manual record-keeping for improved management reporting and better control.

SECTION MANAGER, Fiduciary Service Division (1996–1998)

✓ Managed six accountants in the Real Estate, Oil and Gas Unit. Administered the maintenance, inspection, appraisal, and sale of real estate assets held by estates and trusts. Also managed the processing and control of revenues and expenses associated with real estate and petroleum assets. Automated the preparation of oil and gas tax schedules.
   Result: Improved product quality and eliminated the need to file for IRS extensions. Also realized a 20% increase in productivity and the elimination of overtime.

✓ Created database applications to maintain property information and track revenues and expenses.
   Result: These applications eliminated paper-based file systems and reduced errors.

ASSOCIATE, Securities Processing Division (1994–1996)

UNIT LEADER, Funds Transfer Division (1993–1994)

SPECIALIST, Funds Transfer Division (1993)

EDUCATION

M.B.A., Finance — UCLA, 1993
B.A., Business Administration — UCLA, 1991

LAURA PETRY

123 Webster Avenue • New Rochelle, NY 10508
Phone (914) 555-1234 • Email laura@protypeltd.com

SENIOR MARKETING AND BUSINESS DEVELOPMENT SPECIALIST

Columbia Business School MBA / Yale University BA

Dynamic management career spanning 18 years with measurable success in marketing and business development programs. Core strengths encompass:
Market Research / Strategic Marketing Plans / Market Assessment / Risk Analysis / High Growth
Expertise in Fortune 500 Companies including Pepsi, Morgan Stanley, Pfizer, Johnson & Johnson, Start-ups, and Small Business Ventures

PROJECT HIGHLIGHTS

Market Assessment / Risk Analysis

Led an exhaustive market analysis and conducted interviews with industry experts to determine the feasibility of a full-throttle expansion into reimbursement programs for a healthcare consulting company specializing in patient information. Personally profiled market dynamics, evaluated competitive market trends and assessed risk and rewards.

Results: **Translated findings into a new product – service development tool that outlined key attributes and strategies for success as well as identified risks to be examined before aggressively pursuing expansion. Presented alternatives that offered significant opportunities for long term, sustainable growth.**

Market Strategy

Challenged to capture and disseminate extensive market intelligence into executive summary reports to define strategy for market positioning and accelerate revenue growth for one of the nation's leading healthcare / pharmaceutical companies

Results: **Played an instrumental role in contract extension with project expanding from a one-time commitment to a year-long project.**

Competitive Market Position and Business Management

Provided expertise to drive competitive market positioning and build credibility in the current news documentary marketplace and identify market opportunities consistent with the firm's strategy and brand for a small real news company. Developed market research survey and interview guide to assess strengths and vulnerabilities of management plan and brand management. Surveyed entire leadership team including internal marketing director, president, operations manager, and logistic planning team.

Results: **Influenced reversal of internal management deficiencies to favorably impact brand awareness. Identified new market development / expansion opportunities and defined strategic plans for managed growth.**

Organizational Development

Led organizational restructuring to realign customer relationship management and affiliate relationships, improve productivity, and boost morale within the internal advertising and promotion department of a private, nonprofit media. Conducted in-depth interviews with staff, customers, and affiliates to determine source and impact of internal challenges. Co-created and implemented workshops in skill building, brand development, and management.

Results: **Transitioned department to a highly functional unit that supported the organization's growth and vision.**

PROFESSIONAL HISTORY

STRATEGIC MARKETING CONSULTANT
BUSINESS DEVELOPMENT SPECIALIST   **1997 – present**

   Third-party advisor to Fortune 500 and corporate clients in the pharmaceutical, healthcare, financial services, capital markets, and media entertainment sectors. Clients include Pfizer, Morgan Stanley and Pepsi.

AT&T SOLUTIONS, New York, NY
Manager, E-Commerce   **1996 – 1997**

Played a key role in ensuring the success of the AT&T Solutions' first-ever Managed Network Solutions unit with design and development of corporate training and development program. Member of the change management team responsible for defining and communicating AT&T Solutions' unique value to external accounts. Full responsibility for account management, team deployment, management, strategic planning, time line development, deadlines, and deliverables for external projects.

ORION CONSULTANTS, New York, NY
Managing Consultant   **1991 – 1996**
Senior Associate   **1989 – 1991**
Associate   **1986 – 1988**

High-profile business development, marketing, and sales career providing expertise to the majority of Wall Street / NYC's leading investment brokerages and securities firms. Rapidly advanced through a series of increasingly responsible positions based on outstanding revenue, customer, and market growth performance. Notable achievements include:

- Architect of Orion's most successful service, the *National Fixed Income Market Study*.
- Drove 75 percent of firm's annual revenues with expansion of new business development, client relationship management, design of tactical marketing plans, and overall team leadership.
- Spearheaded development of a customized database to expand research and analysis capabilities.
- Led the development of internal policies and procedures to achieve sustainable growth.
- Analyzed, evaluated, devised, and presented marketing data and competitive analysis research results instrumental to client's performance and revenue growth.

EDUCATION

COLUMBIA BUSINESS SCHOOL, New York, NY
MBA – Marketing / Management of Organizations

YALE UNIVERSITY, New Haven, CT
BA – Sociology / Organizational Behavior

VIRGINIA A. JOHNSON

1234 Butterfield Drive
Colorado Springs, CO 80918

Home: (719) 555-1234
Cellular: (719) 555-5678

STRENGTHS

- Impeccably honest design professional with a strong customer service and sales background.
- Effective team player with a proven track record of success in consultative selling.
- Detail-oriented worker with excellent problem solving and communication skills.
- Able to build rapport and trust quickly with customers and co-workers.

EXPERIENCE

INTERIOR DESIGNER (2002 – 2005)
John William Interiors, Austin, Texas
Sell high-end furniture and completed interior design projects for prestigious clients. Use a strong sense of the esthetic—an eye for color and detail, a sense of balance and proportion, and an appreciation for beauty—to help clients create the right look for their homes and offices. Visited the client's home or office, made recommendations for the right product, closed sales (for as much as $50,000 per customer), ordered products, and monitored installation. Provided exquisite customer service that resulted in long-term relationships and return business.

INTERIOR DESIGNER (2000 – 2002)
Judy McComis Designs, Austin, Texas
Received on-the-job training in interior design that included remodels, million-dollar new homes, and commercial design projects for this full-service studio. Gained valuable experience in the building of client relationships. Researched design characteristics, including size, shape, weight, color, materials preferred, costs, ease of use, fit, and safety. Prepared sketches, diagrams, and computer models to explore design alternatives. Enhanced the function, safety, and quality of interior spaces of private homes, public buildings, and businesses, ensuring that spaces were designed to conform to federal, state and local laws and building codes. Ensured that designs for public areas met accessibility standards for the disabled and elderly. Planned the interiors of existing structures that were undergoing renovation or expansion. Researched finishes, carpet, furniture, and fixtures in catalogs and online.

DESIGN INTERN (1996 – 1998)
Design Source II, Boulder, Colorado
Worked for a year with a Denver retail lighting company selling light fixtures and learning lighting design. Spent the next two years working an average of ten hours a week with a high-end designer on residential carpet and rug projects. Researched materials and manufacturing processes, assessed project requirements, and made design recommendations. Assisted on the selection of carpets and rugs for a 15,000-square-foot custom home.

EDUCATION

BACHELOR OF ARTS, INTERIOR DESIGN (1998)
Art Institute of Colorado, Denver, Colorado
Business course work included: Ethics, Professional Practice, Psychology, Digital Presentation Techniques, Statistics, Sociology, Computer Applications, Critical Thinking.

Construction course work included: Environmental Science, Interior Architectural Detailing, Advanced Residential Design, Advanced Construction Documentation, Building and Environmental Systems, Materials and Estimates, Space Planning, History of Design and Architecture, Architectural Drafting I/II.

Design course work included: Design Development, Portfolio Presentation, Externship, Furniture Design, Hospitality Design, Corporation Programming and Design, Computer Rendering, Fundamentals of Working Drawings, Advanced Rendering, History of Design and Architecture III, Digital Design, Design Development (Residential and Commercial), Code-Barrier Free Design, Textiles/Finishes, Interior Lighting Design, Freehand Sketching for Interior Design, Computer-Aided-Design—Three-Dimensional, Interior Design Rendering, Computer-Aided Design—Two-Dimensional, Technical Perspective, Elements of Interior Design, Design Basics—Three-Dimensional, Fundamentals of Drawing, Fundamentals of Design, Color Theory.

210

14 Functional versus Chronological

There are three basic types of résumés—reverse chronological, functional, and a combination of the two.

A reverse-chronological résumé arranges your experience and education in chronological order with the most recent dates first. One of the most frequent questions I am asked as a résumé writer is, "Do I have to list all of my jobs? It makes me look so old!" My answer is always, "No, you don't have to list every single position you have ever held. The trick is to pick and choose the ones that are relevant to your objective." You can also eliminate low-level positions and positions that duplicate later experience. *Relevant* is the keyword here!

More than two-thirds of the résumés in this book are reverse-chronological, but that doesn't mean a different type of résumé might not fit your needs better. This chapter will show you what is possible with a functional résumé in case that style better fits your needs.

A functional résumé organizes your work experience by the functions you performed regardless of date. The functional résumé highlights your skills and potential instead of your work history. It allows you to play down gaps in your experience and is especially good for those people entering the job market for the first time. If you are reentering the job market, for example, after raising children, this type of résumé also allows you to list volunteer experience and community or school activities.

List your functional paragraphs in their order of importance, with the items listed first that will help you get the particular job you are targeting. Refer to Step Ten in the twelve-step résumé writing process outlined in Chapter 2 of this book for ideas on how to rearrange your résumé sentences to better capture your reader's attention.

You should know that there are very rare times when I would recommend a purely functional résumé, however. In the 1980s, true functional résumés developed a bad reputation because applicants were not listing where they gained their experience. It made recruiters suspicious that the applicant was trying to hide something. A combination functional/chronological résumé will avoid this problem. Always list a brief synopsis of your actual work experience at the bottom of your functional résumé with your title, employer, and the dates worked.

Outside of this chapter, you will find other functional résumés on pages 65, 88, 89, 96, 116, 117, 123, 143, 162, 165, 272, 273, and 283–287. On pages 53, 86, 111, 122, 128, 129, 192, 242, 243, 246–248, 268–271, and 275 you will find true chronological résumés that have added functional subdivisions under each job. You can also create a strong functional beginning to a chronological resume to highlight select skills, as on pages 74, 94, 104, 138, 146, 169, 180, 182, 183, 190, 193–195, 199, 202, 204, 205, 208, 230, 232, 234, 254, and 274.

PERRY F. ZAND

402 Maplewood Drive ▪ Colorado Springs, Colorado 80909 ▪ (719) 593-0166 ▪ pzand@protypeltd.com

A philosophy statement is the one exception where you can use personal pronouns (I, my, me). Author

TEACHING/COACHING PHILOSOPHY

Both academics and athletics demand great teaching and involve a warm, personal relationship based on trust and mutual respect between the teacher and the student. I believe this relationship is something the teacher earns through caring and dedication. Without this relationship, it is difficult to establish a connection between the subject matter and skill development. The successful teacher and coach starts by building sequential learning experiences around student needs, interests, and backgrounds to help students achieve levels of learning that they did not think was possible.

HIGHLIGHTS OF QUALIFICATIONS

Experienced coach and teacher with a background in both collegiate and secondary education settings.
Creative instructor with the ability to develop innovative learning environments that challenge students to achieve their best.
Passionate professional who cares about the students both on and off the field.
Hands-on coach who is able to build a student's skills by logically sequencing concepts based on individual needs.
Well-organized, detail-oriented problem solver who has learned from the greatest coaches in the field.

EXPERIENCE

TEACHING
- Colorado Teaching License: Physical Education K–12, Health Education K–12. Have met North Central Association requirements for junior high and middle school science.
- Taught physical education, math, and science courses to high school and middle school students.
- Taught adaptive physical education to mainstreamed and emotionally impaired students.
- Designed learning environment to meet educational development requirements, adapting teaching style to accommodate both individual and group needs
- Used teaching methods that encouraged critical thinking, problem solving, decision making, and independent learning.
- Developed curriculum materials to meet state standards and lesson objectives, incorporating experiential learning wherever possible.
- Counseled students with adjustment and academic problems and met with parents to develop proactive solutions.

COACHING
- Coached the offensive line as an Assistant Football Coach at Colorado College. Also served as PAT field goal unit coach and offensive team scout.
- Varsity offensive line coach and special teams coordinator at Coronado High School.
- Head wrestling coach at Holmes Junior High School.
- Backfield coach, assistant junior varsity football coach, head freshman coach, varsity scout, and junior varsity defensive coordinator at Doherty High School.
- Coached offensive backfield as Head Junior High Football Coach at Sacred Heart Academy.
- Volunteered as Assistant JV football coach at Doherty High School (1988) and Assistant Wrestling Coach at Coronado High School (1985).
- Analyzed the performance of players to spot weaknesses and strengths.
- Observed athletes while they performed to determine the need for individual or team improvement, and instructed them in game strategies and techniques.
- Designed and implemented activities that built team cohesiveness.
- Responsible for athlete recruitment, practice design, field implementation, game management, and team performance.
- Mentored students and assisted them with scholarships and college planning.

ACHIEVEMENTS
- Publication: "Seven Steps to Drive Blocking," *Scholastic Coach*, Vol. 24 (October 1996), pp. 23–25.
- Helped to lead the Coronado High School varsity football team to the 1991 Metro League Championship.
- Coached the Holmes Junior High wresting team to city champion twice and league champion (5 years).
- Coordinated a successful golf workshop for District 11 physical education teachers in 1997.

EDUCATION

April 2001	**Master of Arts**	**University of Phoenix**, Colorado Springs, Colorado Master's Thesis: "Steps and Movements of the Quarterback" based on research on Divisions 1 and 3 level teaching methods
June 1984	**Bachelor of Science**	**Central Michigan University**, Mount Pleasant, Michigan Major: Physical Education Minor: Health Education

---

PROFESSIONAL DEVELOPMENT

Summer 1995	The Midwest Lineman's Camp, Bloomington, Illinois (spent a week studying with Paul Alexander)
1985 – present	Attended 3 to 4 football clinics every year to hone coaching, teaching, and team management skills with some of the best coaches in the industry—Fisher Deberry, Ara Parseghian, Bill Walsh, Gene Stallings, Bo Schembechler, Lou Holtz, and Tom Osborne, among others—including the Nike Clinic, Coach of the Year Clinic, University of Colorado, Colorado State University, U.S. Air Force Academy, Notre Dame, Arizona State University, etc.

EMPLOYMENT HISTORY

1999 – present	**Physical Education Teacher**	Russell Middle School, Colorado Springs, Colorado
2002 – present	**Assistant Football Coach**	Mitchell High School, Colorado Springs, Colorado
2001	**Assistant Football Coach**	Widefield High School, Security, Colorado
1999 – 2000	**Assistant Football Coach**	Colorado College, Colorado Springs, Colorado
1993 – 1999	**Physical Education Teacher**	West Middle School, Colorado Springs, Colorado
1991 – 1998	**Assistant Football Coach**	Coronado High School, Colorado Springs, Colorado
1992 – 1993	**Science Teacher**	Holmes Junior High School, Colorado Springs, Colorado
1991 – 1993	**Physical Education Teacher**	Doherty High School, Summer Program, Colorado Springs, Colorado
1985 – 1992	**Head Wrestling Coach**	Holmes Junior High School, Colorado Springs, Colorado
1988 – 1991	**Assistant Football Coach**	Doherty High School, Colorado Springs, Colorado
1986 – 1987	**Physical Education Teacher**	North Junior High School, Colorado Springs, Colorado
1985 – 1988	**Summer Course Marshall**	Patty Jewett Golf Course, Colorado Springs, Colorado
1985	**Math-Science Teacher**	Holmes Junior High School, Colorado Springs, Colorado
1979	**Head Football Coach**	Sacred Heart Academy, Junior High, Mount Pleasant, Michigan

CAROL ANN LEWIS

PROFILE

- Experienced manager with a strong background in human resources and accounting.
- Self-motivated quick learner who enjoys new challenges.
- Effective team player with proven communication and interpersonal skills.
- Knowledge of Windows, MS Word, WordPerfect, Internet Explorer, and e-mail.

EXPERIENCE

Human Resources

- Hired, supervised, and evaluated a staff of up to 11 employees; created congenial working conditions that resulted in an average tenure of 12 years.
- Developed a benefits package for exempt and nonexempt employees, including health insurance, profit sharing, 401k programs, workers' compensation, etc.
- Established and implemented sound hiring, interviewing, and performance evaluation practices.
- Developed policies and procedures for exit interviews and ensured compliance with federal and state laws and regulations.
- Wrote employee procedure manuals and benefits handbooks.
- Shopped annually for competitive employee health insurance rates.

Management

- Owned and managed a 15-unit motel and 78-site campground; succeeded in increasing sales by 100 percent and selling the business at a profit after six years of upgrading the property's image.
- Responsible for long-range planning, budgeting, profit and loss, controlling costs, and monitoring financial performance.
- Remodeled the facilities, including a new telephone systems, furniture, and interior design.
- Served as office manager, officer of the corporation (Assistant Secretary-Treasurer), and member of the Board of Directors of a Pizza Hut franchisee with 62 stores in five states.

Accounting

- Worked closely with the corporate attorney and accountant to form an S Corporation.
- Prepared daily, weekly, monthly, and quarterly bookkeeping records and financial reports, biweekly payroll for up to 1,500 employees, and monthly profit and loss statements for 62 stores.
- Balanced the ledgers, reconciled bank accounts, made daily deposits, and prepared budgets.
- Completed all state, federal, and county tax and health reports for both service and consumer product businesses. Responsible for sales tax, payroll tax, property tax, and workers' compensation reporting in five states.
- Increased the efficiency of inputting data so profit and loss statements were available to management by the third of the month instead of the 15th or 20th, allowing problems to be detected earlier and corrective measures taken.
- Transitioned the company from double-entry bookkeeping by hand through numerous computer upgrades, including customized accounting systems that tied all 62 store cash registers to the mainframe and polled daily sales information into the office every night.

WORK HISTORY

CO-OWNER AND OPERATOR (2001 – present)
Rocky Top Motel and Campground, Green Mountain Falls, Colorado

OFFICE MANAGER (1997 – 2001)
High Plains Pizza, Inc., Liberal, Kansas

EDUCATION

UNDERGRADUATE STUDIES
Seward County Community College, Liberal, Kansas
- Completed courses in business management and computers

PROFESSIONAL DEVELOPMENT
- Training Skills for Team Leaders
- Fairness in the Workplace (Equal Employment Opportunity)
- Managing and Appraising Employee Performance
- Eliminating Violence in the Workplace (Physical and Verbal)
- Dealing with Unacceptable Employee Behavior
- How to Be a Better Trainer
- Managing for Success
- Managing Time and Tasks
- Delegation
- Improving Memory Skills

ADDRESS

1234-A Parkmoor Village Drive, Colorado Springs, Colorado 80917, Phone: (719) 555-1234

SAM M. STANCARO

QUALIFICATIONS

STRENGTHS
- Self-motivated project/field engineer with more than 18 years of experience in commercial and residential construction.
- Hard working, detail oriented professional who enjoys the challenges of the construction industry.
- Team player with strong communication and interpersonal skills.
- Experienced in Windows, MS Word, Excel, PowerPoint, Outlook, Explorer, and other software.

FIELD MANAGEMENT
- Managed large construction projects and ensured completion of permits, change orders, contract/revision logs, etc.; compiled and produced project close-out documents.
- Initiated and managed project submittals, requests for information (RFI), and project change requests (PCR).
- Analyzed costs and instituted value engineering processes, scheduled subcontractors and delivery of materials, and reviewed shop drawings.
- Served as liaison between architect, owner, and subcontractors; reviewed quality of work and compliance with specifications.
- Conducted daily meetings with project managers and weekly progress meetings with architects and owners.
- Completed more than 60 hours of OSHA safety training courses.

ENGINEERING
- Technical expert in the design and construction of concrete, steel, and wood structures.
- Extensive knowledge of site, architectural, structural, electrical, and mechanical drawings.
- Clarified drawings and provided technical assistance to field supervisors.
- Responsible for project takeoffs, estimating, and scheduling.

SURVEYING
- Experienced in field surveying, including building layout, site utilities, and curb/gutter stakeout.
- Skilled in the use of Total Station survey equipment.

PROFESSIONAL EXPERIENCE

GERALD H. PHIPPS, INC., General Contractors (1998 – 2001)
Project Engineer/Field Engineer: Remodeling of a Park County school, Fairplay, Colorado ($2.5 million)
Project Engineer/Field Engineer: Construction of a new housing development for Colorado College, Colorado Springs, Colorado ($21 million)

EMPIRE CONSTRUCTION SERVICES, General Contractors (1995 – 1998)
Project Engineer: Construction of United Airlines training facilities, Denver, Colorado ($20 million)
Field Engineer: Remodeling of Adams Mark Hotel, Denver, Colorado ($4 million)

COMMERCIAL INDUSTRIAL CONSTRUCTION, INC., General Contractors (1994 – 1995)
Project Engineer: Addition for Rose Stein Elementary School, Lakewood, Colorado ($4.5 million)

TITAN DENVER, INC., General Contractors (1993 – 1994)
Field Engineer/Assistant Superintendent: Construction of the Continental hangar at Denver International Airport ($22 million)

QUE ASSOCIATES, INC., Design-Build Architectural Engineering Firm (1989 – 1993)
Design Engineer/Project Engineer: Design and construction of residential and light commercial buildings, Washington, D.C. area

McDEVITT & STREET CONSTRUCTION COMPANY, General Contractors (1986 – 1989)
Field Engineer: Construction of three multi-story concrete/steel buildings in the Washington, D.C. area

AA BIERO COMPANY, Concrete Contractor (1984 – 1986)
Field Engineer: Construction of three multi-story concrete buildings in the Washington, D.C. area

GRANATE-BALL-GROVE, Joint Venture (Summers, 1983 – 1984)
Assistant Field Engineer and Surveyor: Construction of the largest hydroelectric power plant in the world, Sierra, California

EDUCATION

BACHELOR OF SCIENCE, CIVIL ENGINEERING, University of Maryland, College Park, Maryland (1984)

ADDRESS

1234 Broadmoor Bluffs Drive, Colorado Springs, Colorado 80906, (719) 555-1234, samstan@protypeltd.com

Dae Sung Kwan

12345 Fairway Gardens
Norcross, GA 30091

E-mail: kwan@protypeltd.com

Phone: (404) 555-1234
Cellular: (404) 555-5678

**Information Technology Management
in a client/server computing environment**

CAREER STRENGTHS

- Fifteen years of active participation in all aspects of corporate computing for industries that have included consumer products manufacturers and financial services enterprises, varying in size and complexity.
- Involved with networking technology since its inception; committed to staying abreast of new developments and adapting cutting-edge solutions to specific and rapidly changing user requirements.
- A productive, people-oriented team leader who enjoys challenges; proven ability to motivate, cross-train, and empower others to assume responsibility.
- Effective in communicating with nontechnical staff and management, simplifying advanced concepts for user-friendly comprehension.

AREAS OF EXPERTISE

- Multivendor/multiuser systems integration
- Tier III technical support and user training
- Cross-functional project management
- Migration and technical change analysis
- Systems backup and restoration of data
- Inter/Intranet Web page development

- Operations and process reengineering
- Technical planning and implementation
- Database administration
- Control/monitoring of system security
- Data warehousing
- Emerging technology research for NT servers

TECHNICAL SKILLS

Hardware
- Compaq racks, servers, and peripherals
- PCs from X86s through Pentium-based SMP
- Various Datapoint machines
- Dot matrix and laser printers

- IBM mainframes up to a 3090-600E
- Arcnet, Ethernet, and Token Ring topology
- DLT tape drives
- Scanners and MSI machines

Client Server Systems/Networks
- Sybase SQL Server systems
- Windows NT Advance server
- Microsoft SNA server
- Microsoft SQL server

- Windows NT
- Novell SFT 386 and 286
- Novell SNA Gateway
- Novell Netware

Software

Operating Platforms:	Windows NT, Windows 3.1, thru XT.
Languages:	PC/FOCUS, PC/FOCUS EIS, SPF/PC, TSO, ISPF, OS/JCL, VSAM, COBOL, FOCUS, SYNCSORT, UBASIC, Micro Focus COBOL
Utilities:	Compaq Insight Manager, Compaq Rack Builder, Seagate Backup Exec, Cheyanne Arcserve, McAfee Virus Scan, BMC Patrol, Business Objects, Norton Desktop for Windows, DBArtisan, and Transact SQL
Communications/Protocols:	Attachmate, TCP/IP, NetBIOS
Applications Programs:	MS Office (Word, Excel, PowerPoint, Access), Lotus Notes
Internet Access:	Netscape, MS Internet Explorer, HTML

(Continued)

216

PROFESSIONAL EXPERIENCE

2002 – present   PRIMARY SERVICE COMPANY—SERVER OPERATIONS GROUP, ATLANTA, GA
Team Leader, NT Field Engineering advancing from **Programmer Analyst**

- Assisted by two direct reports, currently design, purchase, configure, and install all Intel class Windows NT servers within the Atlanta corporate complex, employing more than 2,000.
- Led or served on teams providing recommendations to high-level management for buying and coordinating systems.
- Since Primary Service's transition to centralized operations, played a key role throughout the rapid growth stage of the company's computing distributing organization, which has expanded from 20 servers to 79 as of year end 2004, plus 30 network printers.
- Upgraded existing servers to optimize their performance. Integrated hardware and software into production to efficiently handle diverse data on 40 million customers and facilitate sales efforts to cross-sell Primary products.
- Created an Intranet Web page to acquaint novice users with networking features and quick fixes to common problems, thereby decreasing reliance on technical support staff.
- Contributed to team receipt of "Business Value Award" in 2003 for successful rollout of prototype on schedule.

1997 – 2002   KOREAN DIVERSIFIED INDUSTRIES, ATLANTA, GA
Application Analyst, Recording Media and Energy Product Group
Server Administrator and DBA for Windows NT and Sybase SQL Servers

- Started as FOCUS programmer to oversee the mainframe production of 50 scheduled and ad hoc reports per month.
- During restructuring of the business unit and conversion to a network environment, demonstrated aptitude for customer database design and was put in charge of a "Business Object" product that would allow users to create their own reports. Represented the business unit for all FOCUS, SQL, Business Object, and Change Management projects to Corporate MIS.
- Created and managed separate environments for user production and program development, ensuring that each ran smoothly on its own server.
- Advanced in responsibility by absorbing projects following 50 percent reduction in technical staff. Maintained a domain consisting of multiple Windows NT servers and workstations running and supporting Sybase SQL System 10 servers; migrated all systems from a SQL 4.2 Server.

1994 – 1997   COSMETCO, INC., ATLANTA, GA
Senior Programmer Analyst/LAN Administrator of a Novell Network

- Recruited as a COBOL programmer for this leading cosmetics manufacturer and worked in a team of four to convert from earlier version DOS to OS mainframe in conjunction with company's move to decentralization.
- Developed and maintained sales reporting system and databases for five business divisions, assuring functionality under different downsizing scenarios.
- Supported growth of LAN computing environment from a five-user Novell network through installation of an SNA Gateway server and more than 40 workstations with various peripherals and communication links. Performed system backups, troubleshooting, and software upgrades, as required.

1989 – 1994   EXTEL CORPORATION, MARIETTA, GA
COBOL Programmer for a Small Long-Distance Telephone Company

- Shared responsibility with another programmer for transformation and enhancement of databases for two billing system changeovers and the major development of final commission system. Utilized an early network consisting of a Datapoint mainframe linked to minicomputers.
- Learned every aspect of a very competitive business through interface with sales and accounting people, thereby adding value to the technical function.

EDUCATION AND TRAINING

- GEORGIA INSTITUTE OF TECHNOLOGY, Atlanta, GA   B.S. Computer Science (2001)
- COMPUTECH INSTITUTE, Atlanta, GA   Computer Programming Certificate (1985)
- Extensive ongoing training through hardware and software vendors including Microsoft, Sybase, and Novell.

DAVID D. DANIELSON

2269 Sample Boulevard ✦ Idaho Falls, Idaho 84444 ✦ 208-555-1234

Civil Engineer ✦ *Mechanical Engineer* ✦ *Project Engineer* ✦ *Lead Planning Engineer*
Discipline Engineer ✦ *Office Engineer* ✦ *Draftsman* ✦ *Journeyman Craftsman*

PROFESSIONAL PROFILE

Multi-disciplined *Engineer* with solid background in *Management* and *Supervisory* positions. Proven strengths in teamwork, leadership, and innovative project management, which combine to consistently contribute to corporate objectives. Outstanding communication skills and proficient negotiation abilities. Self-motivated; conscientious; well organized and detail oriented; efficient under fast pace, high stress situations; loyal; and committed to a job well done.

SIGNIFICANT ACCOMPLISHMENTS

✦ Implemented computerized document and vendor data control functions.
✦ Wrote special conditions and various contract documents.
✦ Functioned as Computer Information Analyst/Coordinator.
✦ Prepared, revised, and issued company and project procedures.
✦ Resolved internal inefficiencies in CID handling and vendor tracking.
✦ Coordinated and supervised constructability reviews and subcontract bid package preparation on contracts ranging from $1–35 million.
✦ Provided engineering support to subcontract administrator in contractual matters.
✦ Served as liaison between constructor and designer in identifying field problems prior to construction.

RELATED WORK EXPERIENCE

Morrison Knudsen Corporation   *1979–1996; 1999–present*

    Office Engineer ✦ Advanced Mixed Waste Treatment Project ✦ Idaho ✦ *1999–present*
    Lead Planning Engineer ✦ Environmental Restoration Project, Gaseous Diffusion Plant ✦ Ohio ✦ *1994–1996*
    Project Engineer ✦ Environmental Restoration Program MK-FIC, INEL ✦ Idaho ✦ *1992–1994*
    Assistant Project Engineer ✦ Fuel Processing Restoration Project MK-FIC, INEL ✦ Idaho ✦ *1991–1992*
    Engineer/Discipline ✦ Fuel Processing Restoration Project MK-FIC, INEL ✦ Idaho ✦ *1988 – 1990*
    Engineer/Civil ✦ Savannah River Site Project ✦ South Carolina ✦ *1982–1988*
    Engineer/Mechanical ✦ Washington Public Power Supply System Project MK/ES/LORD Joint Venture ✦ *1980–1982*
    Engineer/Civil ✦ Washington Public Power Supply System ✦ Washington ✦ *1980–1982*
    Draftsman ✦ Stronita Springs Dam ✦ South of Denver, Colorado, Washington Public Power Supply System ✦ *1979–1980*

CERTIFICATIONS

Hazardous Waste Operation and Emergency Response 40-hour Training ✦ 20 CFR 1910.120 (e)
    Hazardous Waste Operation and Emergency Response 8-hour Manager/Supervisor Training ✦ 20 CFR 1910.120 (e)
    Response 8-hour Manager/Supervisor Training
    Configuration Management Training ✦ Department of Energy; 1993, 1992
    Environmental Restoration Project Management Training ✦ S.M. Stroller Corp.
    Project Management Training ✦ Martin Marietta
    Radiation/Respirator Protection Training

EDUCATION

✦ **Associate of Applied Science**
✦ Boise State University ✦ Boise, Idaho

218

NICOLE JONES

123 Evelyn Court ▪ Plainfield, NJ 08821 ▪ (732) 555-1234 ▪ jones@protypeltd.com

SUPERVISING FAMILY WORKER COORDINATOR

**Case Management ▪ Investigations ▪ Employment ▪ Training ▪ Counseling
Evaluation ▪ Assessment ▪ Field Visits ▪ Reporting ▪ Community Outreach**

Eight successful years providing quality services and support to youth and adults in the social services and education fields. Outstanding leadership, problem-solving, and organizational abilities with extensive experience in employment counseling, case management, supervision, and training. Dedicated to improving the quality of life for all individuals and ensuring the proper resources and services are provided at all levels and stages in their development.

PROFESSIONAL EXPERIENCE

CASE MANAGEMENT / TRAINING / COUNSELING

- Managed a caseload of 50+ clients in child placement, stability, training, and employment.
- Referred clients to appropriate employment assignments and training programs after reviewing their history and background.
- Evaluated and monitored client's progress toward employment and placement.
- Conducted various types of investigations including: abuse, neglect, in-home supervision, residential placement, and foster care.
- Counseled clients on school issues, finances, health, and family relationships.
- Assessed the educational and training needs of clients.
- Prepared weekly progress reports and made recommendations for placement and special services.
- Conducted periodic field visits to ensure the safety of clients and children.
- Visited schools, clinics, hospitals, government agencies, and family members to gather data required to recommend court or social services actions.

PROFESSIONAL HISTORY

Family Services Specialist, DYFS, Newark, NJ	2003–2004
Employment Specialist, Essex County DOED, East Orange, NJ	2001–2003
Early Childhood Teacher, KinderCare, Piscataway, NJ	2000–2001
Elementary Teacher, KinderCare, Newark, NJ	1998–2000
Elementary Teacher, Kiddie Academy, Cranbury, NJ	1996–1998

COMMUNITY INVOLVEMENT

Plainfield YMCA Homeless Shelter
Amandela's Crossing Women and Children Shelter
Vacation Bible School Teacher

TECHNOLOGY SKILLS

Word, Excel, New Jersey State Web-based programs, Internet

EDUCATION

Bachelor of Arts in Psychology, Bloomfield College (Dean's List), May 2001

ALLEN RICHARDSON

977 East Virginia Road
Imperial, California 92251

760 555-1234
cellular: 805 555-5678
email:arich@protypeltd.com

RIG SUPERVISOR / MANAGER / CONSULTANT
DRILLING / WORKOVER / WELL SERVICE OPERATIONS
Preference: overseas rotational job in Asia, South America, and the former Soviet Union

SUMMARY OF QUALIFICATIONS

More than 26 years of broad-based knowledge and hands-on, industry-related experience encompassing a wide range of equipment and procedures used in the drilling, production, and maintenance of **oil**, **gas**, and **geothermal production and injection wells**, human resources, and field administration, including 17 years of supervision and management. A team leader, highly adaptable to varying environments across the globe (hostile environments, environmentally sensitive areas). Analytical thinker recognized for fast problem-solving actions and strong interpersonal skills. Basic conversational Spanish.

Solid experience in all phases of well operations and rig processes. Committed to leading a lean, efficient, empowered work force to achieve quality and excellence with integrity.

Proven ability to improve production efficiency, analyze and implement new processes, and achieve buy-in by production, management, and administrative staff.

- Detail-oriented, meticulous, conscientious, and results-driven; able to identify, analyze, and trouble-shoot highly complex problems.
- Quick and effective problem-solver; know when individual action is required.
- Flexible and adaptive to change; resourceful in getting the job done.
- Job completion **always** within budget and on time despite sudden setbacks and changing priorities.
- Strong planning, organizational, and estimating skills with long-term focus on the bottom line.

Technical Skills

Extremely knowledgeable in remedial and production rig work. Supervision and hands-on experience with

- Coil tubing—**large diameter units (2-3/8" – 3-1/2")**—on well cleanouts, cementing operations, plug and abandonments, stimulation and acid work, cleaning slotted liners, hydra-blasting/acid washing liner perforations, and N2 operations.
- Wireline and slickline operations—running and setting all types of production, testing, and well service tools as well as perforating and running various types of logs and surveys.
- Repair and maintenance of surface production equipment—well heads, xmas trees, flowlines, scrubbers, separators, and related production facility equipment.
- Oil and water based drilling and workover fluids—foam, aerated mud, drilling with aerated drilling fluids.

Supervision of drilling and workover operations in situations of overbalance, lost circulation, under-balance, high deviation, and extremely hazardous conditions due to extreme bottom hole temperature or pressure, lethally high concentrations of H2S, or remote location of the job site.

Key Accomplishments

- Implemented lead man position to replace traditional supervisor role. Allowed workers to develop "ownership" and provide more input into the production process—scheduling tasks, completing jobs, using their experience and intelligence to perform their jobs at a higher level.
- As key member of TQM team, instrumental in creating a quality assurance manual and training shop employees in its use.

220

Leadership Abilities

♦ Act as liaison between contractor and contractee as well as with local, state, and federal agencies; familiar with U.S. and Mexico regulations. Ensure work is carried out within specifications of company safety guidelines in a safe, environmentally responsible, and cost-effective manner.

♦ Implement safety and hazardous response programs.

♦ Manage logistical requirements and daily operations of rig area.

♦ Work in coordination with engineers and company representatives to write programs and design work flow.

♦ Supervise maintenance management program to include scheduling, equipment outage, readiness, dispatching, and inventory reporting.

♦ Complete daily job reports detailing job descriptions, number of hours worked, tools and equipment utilized, daily costs of operations, and cumulative job cost.

WORK EXPERIENCE HIGHLIGHTS

Rig Supervisor	Target Energy Services, Santa Rosa, CA	2000
Well Field Operations Supervisor	Key Enterprises, Redmond, CA	1998 – 2000
Rig Supervisor	Carlson Drilling Company, Houston, TX	1997 – 1998
Consultant (Drilling, Workover, and Well Field Operations)	Independent Consultant, Santa Fe Springs, CA	1991 – 1997

As Rig Supervisor for Carlson Drilling Company, the work required a strong hands-on approach because of the extensive use of SABA (Supplied Air Breathing Apparatus) and SCBA (Self-Contained Breathing Apparatus) and the hazards involved in moving and supplying rigs by helicopter due to extremely remote "fly-in" locations in Indonesia and South America.

EDUCATION / TRAINING / CERTIFICATIONS

Certified I.A.D.C. and M.M.S. Well Control, Supervisor's Level	Carlson Drilling Well Control School	1997
Cementing School for Service Supervisors	Dowarger Tech, Houston, TX	1987
Coiled Tubing and Nitrogen Training for Service Supervisors	Dowarger Tech, Houston, TX	1987
Personnel – Time Management	Pageant-Thompson, Anaheim CA	1985
Welex Perforating and Wireline	Training School, Ventura, CA	1984
Well Control	Ventura College, Ventura, CA	1981

PROFESSIONAL AFFILIATION

International Association of Drilling Contractors

Susan Murphy

443-555-1234 • Murphy@protypeltd.com

12345 Stonehouse Lane
Severna Park, MD 21146

RECENT COLLEGE GRADUATE WITH B.A. IN ENGLISH
Proven Leadership, Communication, and Customer Service Skills
Team Player • Self-Motivated • Flexible
Proficient in MS Word, Excel, PowerPoint

EDUCATION
B.A., Virginia Polytechnic Institute and State University, 2004, 3.4 Overall GPA

RELEVANT EXPERIENCE and SKILLS

SUPERVISORY/LEADERSHIP
- Identified Habitat for Humanity project sites and prioritized work assignments for groups of more than 100 people.
- Established contracts for work sites and identified local support agencies and resources, thus reducing project expenses and staying within a designated budget.
- Coordinated fund-raising events, transportation, lodging, and registration for service projects.
- Oversaw children's activities and assisted teachers with group projects, assuring that children were adequately supervised.

COMMUNICATION
- Conducted telephone interviews/surveys among diverse populations for medical clinical trials. Gained an understanding of medical terminology and medications, facilitating the interview process and clarifying determination for medical eligibility.
- Conducted appointment reminder calls, significantly reducing the percentage of dropped appointments.
- Prevented financial loss and scheduling confusion by notifying the supervisor of a potential problem regarding suspicious caller activity.
- Facilitated camaraderie and teamwork through group research projects and presentations, coordinating assignments, brainstorming topic interests, and developing PowerPoint presentations.

CUSTOMER SERVICE
- Eagerly assisted customers with locating merchandise and facilitating check-out in a professional, courteous, and timely manner.
- Coordinated and processed special orders and provided suggestions on specialty items, thus increasing and maintaining a loyal customer base.
- Created and arranged holiday promotional displays and rotated merchandise, enabling customers to quickly and easily locate and purchase seasonal items.
- Assisted with inventory, marked items for quick sale, and facilitated product turnover.
- Processed items for shipping and receiving, reducing surplus merchandise and saving money.

EMPLOYMENT HISTORY

Pat's Hallmark	Sales Associate	2003 to 2004
Anne Arundel Community College	Kids in College Counselor	Summer 2003
Volume II Bookstore	Sales Associate	Jan – Dec 2002
Pharmaceutical Research Plus	Telephone Interviewer	Summer 2002

COMMUNITY SERVICE: Habitat for Humanity, Woods Work Project

Ricardo Jackson

5678 S.E. Bellington Drive • Portland, Oregon 97266

ricardojackson@protypeltd.com

210-555-1234

Office Professional • Bookkeeping

Professional Profile

Highly motivated, enthusiastic **professional** with expertise in **Office Support** and **Bookkeeping.** Strong background in various office environments with strengths in accuracy, flexibility, and communication. Recent education in full-charge bookkeeping. Well-developed administrative skills. Experienced in customer service, purchasing, trouble shooting, and negotiating. Thoroughly enjoy a challenge and effective team work. Learn and adapt quickly; committed to a job well done. Honest, reliable, trustworthy, and loyal.

Skills Include:

• Computer Proficiency	• Microsoft Excel	• Purchasing	• Report Writing
• Contract Negotiation	• Multi-tasking	• Procurement	• Supervising
• Expediting	• Organization	• Project Management	• Vendor Development
• Full-Charge Bookkeeping	• Peachtree	• QuickBooks Pro	• Customer Service

Bookkeeping

Skilled in both QuickBooks Pro and Peachtree software with a thorough understanding of standard bookkeeping procedures. Practiced with accounts receivables/accounts payable, payroll, and reporting. Detail oriented with strengths in accuracy and efficiency.

Office Support

Experienced in fast-paced office environments with expertise in customer service, multi-tasking, and excellent communication skills. Strong background in research and analysis. Team oriented with computer proficiency and outstanding attendance record.

Administrative

Proven skills in project management, effective negotiation techniques, and the ability to show initiative. Background includes purchasing capital equipment, diverse manufacturing materials, and company supplies; development and review of vendor base; expedited goods and services. Personable and able to act as a liaison between customers, co-workers, and management. Flexible, well organized, and thoroughly enjoy a challenge.

History of Professional Experience

Purchasing Agent • Constar Industries • Portland, Oregon • *2000–2003*
Inside Sales • Lumber Sales Company, Inc. • Portland, Oregon • *1998–2000*
Purchasing Agent / Job Scheduler • Germantown Specialties • Portland, Oregon • *1996–1998*
Purchasing Agent • Fracker Jones & Sons • Portland, Oregon • *1990–1995*

Education

Bookkeeping, QuickBooks Pro, Peachtree, Microsoft Excel • *2003*
  Elliott Bookkeeping School • Portland, Oregon
Bachelor of Arts • **English** • State University • San Francisco, California • *1973*

ANNETTE PAGANELLI

12345 MacArthur Turnpike
Newark, New Jersey 07102

E-mail: paganelli@protypeltd.com

Home Phone: (973) 555-1234
Cell Phone: (973) 555-5678

OBJECTIVE

Pharmacy field auditor for a prescription management company.

CAREER PROFILE

Energetic and personable take-charge professional with 10 years of experience in the various operational aspects of a retail pharmacy/HBA business. Broad general knowledge of prescription medications and their generic equivalents as well as third-party billing procedures for 50+ different plans. Significant contributions to increased sales, customer relations, and efficiency in all assignments.

AREAS OF EXPERTISE

TECHNICAL OPERATIONS

- Assisted registered pharmacist with filling a large volume of prescriptions daily.
- Verified physicians' instructions for new prescriptions and refills; entered data into online computer system.
- Utilized mathematical ability to calculate conversion dosages and ensure proper strength of prescribed medications as indicated by physicians.
- Identified concurrent prescriptions, drug interactions, and cases of possible medication abuse. Brought inconsistencies to attention of pharmacist.

FINANCIAL CONTROL

- Complied with all legal requirements of different third-party plans to assure prompt payment and avoid chargebacks.
- Took responsibility for payroll and accounts payable functions.
- Administered promotional budget for best return on advertising funds. Determined items to be included in special sales circulars.
- At Third Avenue Pharmacy, implemented changes to existing check cashing service, handling more than $100,000 weekly. As a result, improved profitability of the service while freeing owner's time spent in overseeing this segment of the business.

INVENTORY CONTROL

- Carefully analyzed sales reports to identify fast-moving items in prescription medications, OTC products, and sundries.
- Compiled a Top 100 List of frequently prescribed drugs, both branded and generic, and maintained adequate stock to meet customer needs.
- Enforced security measures to reduce theft of shelf items.
- Scheduled quarterly inventory counts by an outside organization. Monitored removal of obsolete products, separation by manufacturer, and return for credit. Followed through to obtain full value for goods returned.

CUSTOMER RELATIONS

- Interacted with customers to learn their preferences and reasons for complaint.
- Ordered specific items to ensure complete satisfaction and repeat business.
- Arranged for delivery of medications for homebound patients.
- Tactfully dealt with issues of payment not covered by customer plans.

ANNETTE PAGANELLI

MERCHANDISING

- ☒ At Medi-Fair, updated merchandise, introducing new and popular items that contributed to business increase of $.5 million over previous year.
- ☒ At City Pharmacy, relocated slow-moving merchandise to new section of store to maximize its visibility and determined markdowns, which greatly increased sales.

STAFF MANAGEMENT

- ☒ Hired, supervised and evaluated performance of front end and stock personnel. Reduced high turnover by employing people who were very service-oriented, honest, and dedicated.
- ☒ Cross-trained and scheduled up to 15 full-time and part-time staff, ensuring proper coverage for busy times and special sale events.
- ☒ Encouraged a teamwork environment and open discussion of problems; acting on employees' suggestions for improvements.

EMPLOYMENT

Manager/Pharmacy Technician   2001–current
THIRD AVENUE PHARMACY, NEWARK, NEW JERSEY
Neighborhood pharmacy (5,000 sq. ft.) with 75 percent of business in prescriptions. Staff of 6.

Department Manager   1996–2001
MEDI-FAIR DRUGS & COSMETICS, NEWARK, NEW JERSEY
Large, 7,800 sq. ft. store with big HBA section. Staff of 5 stock personnel and 3 cashiers.

Pharmacy Technician/Assistant Manager   1994–1996
CITY PHARMACY, NEWARK, NEW JERSEY
Smaller, 4,500 sq. ft. store doing a large prescription and vitamin business.

EDUCATION

On-the-job training through close working relationship with store owners.

WESLEY THORPE
Tile, Marble, and Masonry Consultant

25346 Via Torino
Valley Crest, California 91327

Residence: 661 555-1234
Cellular: 661 555-5678

Well-respected, true old-world, hands-on, visionary artisan and craftsman renowned for honesty, integrity, and pride in work providing **forensic testimony**. More than 30 years of experience in ceramic and marble tile, bricks and brick pavers, cinder and glass blocks, mosaic floor, and wall mural installations/restorations. Specialize in various methods of **acid-proof flooring**. Creative layout, design, and color schemes. Outstanding cross-industry skills: advanced understanding of multiple trades, especially carpentry, drywall, tiling, masonry, and some plumbing. Passion for excellence and a contagious enthusiasm. Highly self-motivated and goal-oriented.

Innovative problem-solver, successfully restructuring inefficiencies to enhance the bottom-line. Able to foresee and forestall difficulties, thereby ensuring a smooth and safe flow of operations. Keen ability to detect construction defects before problems arise. Streamline business processes, resulting in improved safety levels and significant cost reductions. Achieved consistent, high quality control in compliance with codes and inspection standards. Ensured strict adherence to projected scheduling and costs.

Business includes a wide mix of projects: commercial, residential, institutional, and industrial, ranging from simple room additions for private residences to stores and malls. Troubleshoot homeowner complaints. Performed ADA upgrades on various local tile projects. Project highlights from completed works in The Netherlands, Germany, New Zealand (property development), and the U.S.A. including:

- 13th Century European Historic Multistory Buildings
- Los Angeles City Hall (historic east wing)
- Los Angeles Coliseum
- Los Angeles International Airport

- Anheuser Bush Plant
- High-end Housing Tracts
- Office Buildings and Hotels
- Shopping Malls

Fluent in Dutch and English.
Computer knowledgeable.

LICENSURE
C54 Contractor, State of California

STRENGTHS

Construction Defect / Malpractice
Estimating / Valuation Analysis
Destructive Testing / Nondestructive Inspection
Thorough knowledge of

- all ceramic tiles and stone (marbles, granites, slates, stone, flagstone, and sandstone)
- directional tile setting: arches, diagonal and circular flooring and walls, complex tile joints
- adjustment of irregular handmade tile and bowed walls
- different applications (plastering coat, mortar)
- wet and dry mud floor installation
- plywood underlayment
- blueprints
- foundation and form work (concrete floors, block and concrete walls)
- ADA and OSHA regulations and procedures

Experience in all areas of related home improvements and in dealing with permits and inspections.

HIGHLIGHTS OF QUALIFICATIONS

- **Ability to take control** and make sound decisions in crisis situations.
- **Interpretation of disaster-management plans** and rapid revision in response to the unique circumstances of each incident.
- **Organizational and management skills**: able to oversee multiple activities and focus on hundreds of small but essential details.
- **Leadership**: guiding, motivating, and supporting inexperienced tile setters and various trade members; directing overall program operations to ensure timely, responsible, and professional project management.

RELATED EXPERIENCE

Provide bids, estimates, and repairs currently and on an ongoing basis in addition to **consulting**, **testing**, and **expert witness engagements** as well as objective, up-to-the-minute analysis based on standard industry practices. Plan, coordinate, and supervise multiple projects and work crews. Pre-job planning, permitting, code interpretation, and daily supervision of crews, including subcontractors.

Handle projects from initial concept through design-build stages to final acceptance by client. Consultant on faulty craftsmanship, buyer / seller disputes, construction malpractice, contractual irregularities, and overexpenditure disputes. Private inspector for defect, plan, and code violations.

Inspect commercial and multi-unit residential structures to ensure all construction, alteration, and maintenance work is done in compliance with building codes and other pertinent laws and regulations. Keep detailed records, write reports and findings, justify interpretation of codes. Maintain expertise on all federal, state, and local laws, statutes, codes, and ordinances.

WORK HISTORY

FORENSIC INVESTIGATOR ▪ Forensic Investigation of Construction Defect		2000 to present
SUPERVISOR, TILE SETTER ▪ Tile Masters	Culver City, CA	1999 to 2000
TILE SETTER ▪ City of Los Angeles	Los Angeles, CA	1994 to 1997
TILE SETTER ▪ Los Angeles Airport	Los Angeles, CA	1991 to 1994
TILE SETTER ▪ Western Tile and Tile Trends, Inc.	Los Angeles, CA	Prior to 1991
CONTRACTOR / DEVELOPER ▪ Thorpe Homes	Santa Fe, NM	Prior to 1991
TILE AND BRICK MASON	The Netherlands and Germany	Prior to 1991

EDUCATION

Contractors State Licensing Board, California

Real Estate School, Santa Fe, New Mexico

Maatschappij School, Amsterdam, The Netherlands

DON EVERSON

1234 E. San Rafael Street • Colorado Springs, Colorado 80903 • (719) 555-1234

SUMMARY

- Proven construction supervisor with more than 12 years of experience, including:
  - Commercial and residential building
  - New construction and renovations
  - Estimating
  - Project scheduling
- Effective manager who is able to motivate workers to complete jobs on time.
- Proven ability to complete projects as scheduled and at or under budget.
- Skilled in analyzing tasks and breaking them down into manageable pieces.

EXPERIENCE

Project Management

- Supervised both commercial and residential construction projects.
- Developed project schedules and milestones and allocated resources.
- Sourced vendors, purchased supplies and equipment, ensured timely delivery of materials, and authorized payment of invoices.
- Evaluated blueprints and schematics to ensure compliance with codes and regulations.
- Consulted with clients regarding design modifications and change orders, ensuring customer satisfaction throughout the project life cycle.
- Scheduled and supervised 60+ skilled workers, including employees and subcontractors.
- Requested and evaluated bids from subcontractors and ensured the quality of their work.
- Implemented safety and quality control programs and regulations.
- Pulled permits, ensured that work met building and fire codes, and coordinated inspections and walk-throughs with the fire department and city inspectors. Gained experience on the fire inspection side of the business as a fire inspector for two fire districts for seven years.

Estimating

- Used hands-on experience as a trim, rough frame, and backout carpenter to perform project take-offs and estimating from blueprints and specifications.
- Completed an estimating course and prepared estimates for Crissy Fowler Lumber's truss department.

SIGNIFICANT PROJECTS

- Renovated Phil Long's old body shop and converted it to a high-end Audi service facility ($1+ million).
- Remodeled the Mitsubishi sales building to Phil Long Truck World ($750,000).
- Completed remodels of Phil Long's parts department, show room, and various small projects.
- Assistant Superintendent for Art Klein's construction of the new Ford and Saturn dealerships at Chapel Hills ($4.3 and $2.8 million).
- Served as a field supervisor for the remodel of the old Nissan facility into a Saturn dealership ($1.5 million).
- Supervised the construction of large custom homes for Art Klein.
- Worked as a trim carpenter on the Garden of the Gods Country Club remodel project.
- Supervised construction from framing to trim as a foreman with Advance Construction, a subcontractor for Watt Homes, Richmond American, Springs Ranch, and Sullivan Communities, among others.

WORK HISTORY

Construction Supervisor, Phil Long Dealerships, Colorado Springs, Colorado (2000 – 2002)
Construction Supervisor, Foreman, Trim Carpenter, Art C. Klein Construction, Colorado Springs, Colorado (1995 – 2000)
Supervisor, Foreman, Backout Carpenter, Advance Construction Company, Colorado Springs, Colorado (1990 – 1995)
Firefighter, Fire Inspector, Parker and Louvieres County Fire Districts, Colorado (1983 – 1990)
Command and Control Specialist, USAF Reserves, Peterson AFB, Colorado (1983 – 1988)
Estimator, Contract Sales, Crissy Fowler Lumber, Colorado Springs, Colorado (1981 – 1983)

EDUCATION

UNDERGRADUATE STUDIES, Northeastern Junior College, Sterling, Colorado
Completed two years of study toward a teaching degree

15 Executive Résumés

Webster defines an executive as "a person whose function is to administer or manage affairs of a corporation, division, department, group of companies, etc." This can be the president, director, chief executive officer, chief financial officer, chief information officer, controller, executive director, vice president, general manager, treasurer, principal, owner, or any other C-level manager.

Generally, a person in such a position has strategically worked his/her way to the top echelons of management over a period of at least ten years. Executives tend to have many relevant past positions, credentials, achievements, published articles, speaking engagements, community service activities, and other important qualifications.

In order to reflect this experience, an executive résumé is almost always more than one page. In fact, an executive résumé can be as long as it needs to be in order to convince the reader that the candidate has what it takes to manage an organization effectively. The first page of the résumé, however, is the most important.

Just because an executive résumé is long doesn't mean it should be wordy. The same good writing described in Chapter 2 is even more important in an executive résumé. Because the number of applicants for an executive position is generally not as large as for lower-level positions, every word of an executive's résumé will be read many times before a decision is made. Make sure every word you write serves a purpose!

As a general rule, executive résumés should be conservative in style. Senior-level management is considered a very sober position with considerable responsibility, so there is no room for frivolity or creativity. That doesn't mean, however, that the design of an executive résumé must be boring. The effective use of type style, white space, and discrete graphic lines can make your résumé stand out in the crowd.

PAUL BERNATTI

241 Vozy Lane, Planfield, IL 00000 • 857/555-1234 • Email: paul@protypeltd.com

INFORMATION TECHNOLOGY / PROJECT MANAGEMENT / STRATEGIC OPERATIONAL PLANNING

PROFILE

RESULTS-DRIVEN TECHNOLOGY EXECUTIVE with an exceptional track record of reengineering organizations to improve asset performance and operational efficiencies and to reduce expense. Proven ability to build and manage creative, highly energized, focused teams to achieve peak productivity. Possess a keen sense of bottom-line profitability.

• Accelerated profit growth from $23 million to $600 million in two years •

DEMONSTRATED COMPETENCIES:

Management

- Networking Strategy and Direction
- Budgeting and Administration
- Contract Negotiations
- Acquisition / Integration
- Training and Support Planning
- Workload Planning
- Human Resources
- Vendor Relations

Technology

- Programming Languages: COBOL, C++, Visual Basic, Progress
- Operating Systems: NT, Novell, SUN, UNIX, AIX, MVS, VM, VSE, OS/2
- Applications: MS Office, MS Project, Trend 9.0, IBM On Demand, DB2, SQL/DS, Anderson DCS, MS SQL Server, SYBase, Profit Work Bench, NXTrends Interchannel E-Commerce, ADSM, St. Paul EDI Translator
- Hardware: RS6000, Mainframes, IBM ES9000, Model 170, CISCO, Routers, NORAM RF Systems
- Certifications:
  IBM – AIX, DB2, VSE, MVS / ESA, On Demand Administration
  Novell – CNA

PROFESSIONAL EXPERIENCE

MULTIMEDIA SYSTEMS CORPORATION, Hilton, IL
Publicly traded distributor of multimedia wiring systems products for voice, data, video, and power transmission.
Executive Vice President, Information Systems, 3/96 – present
Aggressively recruited to direct and build corporate strategy, including IT systems-level management, budgetary planning, application implementation, staff recruitment / development, and acquisition implementation.

- Strategically drove company profits from $23 million to $600 million in two years.
- Acquired 14 companies and converted them to one common platform.
- Redefined staffing levels to provide enhanced customer service and reduce annual payroll expenditures.
- Reengineered systems development methodology to integrate and improve call accounting, inventory control, data warehousing, HR, Document Imaging Systems, multiple RF subsystems, and trend enterprise solutions.
- Built a self-directed staff of problem solvers through employee integration from 0 to 20 in two years.
- Designed and implemented a full disaster-recovery network, reducing maximized downtime exposure.

Continued...

JERSEY WIRING CABLE, Kansas City, MO
General Manager, 1/93 – 3/96
Promoted with full P & L responsibility for information systems and human resources of this multimillion-dollar manufacturer and distributor of cable and wiring systems. Prepared all operating budgets with full responsibility for achievement of budget goals. Supervised 12 managers and on-site staff, for a total of 250 employees. Reported directly to CEO.
- Increased revenues from $35 to $88 million.
- Led corporate-wide reorganization teams, reducing losses and improving market-share ratings.

JERSEY WIRING CABLE, Kansas City, MO
MIS Director, 4/90 – 1/93
Held full responsibility for technical application services, including five network / physical-layer programming, applications development, cost control implementation, negotiations, project management, and staff recruitment.
- Developed and implemented "Paperless Warehouses" through RF and bar code systems.
- Implemented a distribution system that resulted in increased revenues and reduced staffing requirements.
- Successfully automated human resource systems.
- Established company-wide steering committees to successfully transition departmental collaboration and prioritize organizational goals.
- Created ties between DCS and pinstripe accounting system.
- Wrote MRP cable assemblies program.

THOMASON CONSULTING, Balley, MI
Second largest consulting company nationwide
Project Manager, 1/88 – 4/90
Promoted to direct sales, marketing, customer service and contract performance for consultant and engineering projects at this firm specializing in systems applications development and project management. Supervised activities of 50 consultants.
- Generated independent cost estimates and critical analyses using Anderson's DCS system; reduced clients' annual expenses.
- Conducted distribution training / management classes.

THOMASON CONSULTING, Balley, MI
Staff Programmer, 1/88 – 4/90
- Completed programming training; promoted to project manager.

NETWORK SOLUTIONS, Balley, MI
President, 1/85 – 1/90
Founded this consulting firm specializing in the sales and installation of LAN technology, PCs, multiuser systems, and accounting software packages.
- Built sales from $0 to $3.5 million.

EDUCATION / SPECIALIZED TRAINING

Oakland University, Rochester, MI
B.S., Management Information Systems, 1988

Macomb Community College, Warren, MI
A.S., Computer Information Systems, 1984

Over 50 IBM courses with a focus on distribution operations.

SANFORD A. JEFFERSON

86 Grove Place • Rochester, NY 14604 • 585-555-1234 (Home) • 585-555-5678 (Cell)
sanford_jefferson@protypeltd.com

SOLUTIONS ENGINEER / BUSINESS ANALYST / PROJECT MANAGER
Database Management / Data Mining • Product Information Management (PIM)

Business Analyst / Solutions Engineer offering a blend of technical aptitude and business process acumen. Demonstrated success translating business needs into technical specifications and effectively communicating those specifications to developers and programmers. Successfully serve as the liaison between non-technical business process owners and technical audiences.

✓ **Successfully manage projects to develop and implement relational database applications.**

✓ **Conversant with PIM (Product Information Management) concepts and the application of those concepts to business processes; experienced with a variety of PIM applications.**

✓ **Demonstrated expertise in database management, programming, and data mapping concepts and the practical application of those concepts.**

✓ **Knowledge of data warehousing and management decision support concepts, with specific experience implementing and managing account segmentation and product categorization systems.**

✓ **Experienced with ERP product information management challenges and solutions.**

✓ **Facilitate communication among a broad array of professionals from technical, managerial, and clerical backgrounds to achieve productive collaboration on key projects.**

CAREER HIGHLIGHTS

Recruited by CrossBridge Technologies to play a key role in transitioning Product Information Management functions for Paper Now! (wholesale distributor of papers), from in-house to outsourced services. Managed the mapping and migration of data from Trigo and AS/400 applications into Content Director application provided by CrossBridge. Collaborated with IT development team to customize Content Director to successfully meet Paper Now!'s business needs. Identified areas for improvement to Content Director software package that enhanced its functionality allowing it to better serve customer business needs.

As an employee of Hart & Rogers, was integrally involved in the transition/consolidation of Product Information Management (PIM) functions following the company's acquisition by Paper Now!. Worked closely with Paper Now!'s corporate executive to develop and gain senior management approval for PIM vision that remains the firm's standard and serves as the road map for the growth and advancement of PIM operations. This vision was key to the firm's decision to outsource PIM functions to CrossBridge Technologies in order to capitalize on CrossBridge's proficiencies.

Currently working with a forest products manufacturer to develop an interface, using UCC Net to synchronize online product catalog with that of a major national retailer. Accountable for gathering requirements and developing high-level design and Statement of Work (SOW). Upon acceptance of SOW, communicated project needs to IT professionals and functioned as liaison between key client contacts and development team.

Streamlined process for implementing price changes for a wholesale distributor that reduced the new price rollout by three weeks, which was projected to deliver a $600,000 increase in profitability in a single product category for one price change event. Extrapolating over numerous product lines and multiple price changes, this approach would have potentially contributed multi-million dollar improvements to the company's bottom line.

Pioneered PIM system that led to more effective reporting to management, better tracking of day-to-day sales and marketing data, and ultimate creation of paper industry's first electronic product catalogs. Drew on knowledge of ERP applications in an AS/400 environment and collaborated with IT professionals to achieve desirable project results.

Developed a pioneering software tool for gathering specifications and preparing price quotations for printing and converting custom envelopes. Collaborated with external software consultant to create this new application. Implementation of this utility led to increased profitability and enhanced customer satisfaction by improving accuracy of quotes and orders.

PROFESSIONAL EXPERIENCE

CrossBridge Technologies (formerly ExpressData), Alpharetta, Georgia   **2000 – present**

A professional services organization offering hosted Product Information Management (PIM) software and an XML-based, real-time, business-to-business integration network (www.crossbridge.com).

Senior Solutions Engineer

- Lead or participate in PIM software implementation projects for Fortune 1000 clients. Contribute business analyses, solution design, and project management skills.
- Contribute to successful closure of several hundred thousand dollars' worth of professional service contracts by identifying customer business challenges and proposing appropriate software solutions.
- Analyze client experiences in the field and recommend product changes that contribute to the continued development of Liaison's PIM software.
- **Recruited to CrossBridge as part of transition team when Paper Now! outsourced PIM function.**

Paper Now!, Madison, Wisconsin / Rochester, New York   **1998 – 2000**

A nationwide distributor of printing papers, facility supplies, packaging materials and equipment, and graphic arts supplies. A division of International Paper. (www.PaperNow.com)

Manager, Product Information

- Led a 15-member PIM team responsible for the creation and maintenance of product and pricing information, including mainframe and AS/400 ERP systems, Internet-based content management software, and PC-based catalog publication software.
- Created the vision and secured management support for an enterprise-wide PIM roadmap.
- Managed launch of Web-based catalog management software, establishing a foundation for the PIM vision.

Hart & Rogers, Rochester, NY   **1976 – 1998**

A regional distributor of printing papers and packaging materials. Acquired by Paper Now! in 1997.

Manager, Product Information (1995 – 1998)

- Managed a six-person team responsible for ERP product and pricing information and catalog publication.
- Led successful migration of product and pricing information during ERP system conversion.
- Designed and supervised the successful development and implementation of PIM software used in support of AS/400-based ERP system; improved informational accuracy and process efficiency.
- Automated creation of catalog database utilizing ERP product information; reduced costs by eliminating redundant maintenance; and decreased time-to-market of both printed and electronic catalogs.

Manager, Upstate Envelope (1993 – 1995)

- Increased market penetration of custom envelopes.
- Designed and supervised development and implementation of envelope quotation software that enabled the capture and management of specifications, resulting in faster customer response and higher closure rate.

Various Positions (1976 – 1993)

- Provided critical support for strategic planning efforts. Identified need for and developed customer sales analysis capabilities on AS/400 ERP system, utilizing AS/400 Query, Lotus 1-2-3 / Microsoft Excel, and Microsoft Access.
- Managed corporate inventory program, making products accessible across all company locations in a timely and cost-effective manner.
- Helped develop the company's first item master file, gaining valuable experience in database management, ERP order entry and inventory management, and product information management.

TECHNICAL PROFICIENCIES

Global understanding of architecture and functionality for:

- Content Director (PIM)
- Trigo / Websphere
- PeopleSoft
- SAP / SFD
- EDI / XML
- ERP / e-commerce applications
- Visio
- Crystal Reports
- MS Office, MS Project

RACINE STEPHANS

425.123.4567 ▪ 123 Kenmore Street S.E. ▪ Bothell, WA 98000 ▪ racine@protypeltd.com

COMMUNICATIONS PROGRAM MANAGER
Strategic Corporate Communications ▪ Marketing and Promotions ▪ Recruiting Communications

Results-oriented communications project manager with 15+ year record of forging award-winning business and image growth for Fortune 500 firms. Masters graduate from Evans School of Communications with dual expertise in organizational communications, learning and design, and strategic communications. Strong project manager and program champion who can align a proposed idea with key company objectives, resulting in internal buy-in and high visibility. Effective strategist and team member.

Areas of Expertise

- Interactive Media and Message Design
- Management and Refocusing Projects
- Strategic Visioning
- Media Tours and Press Conferences

- Recruiting Communications Tools
- Internal Communications Programs
- Staff Orientation and Training
- New Program Implementation

- Promotions and Special Events
- Competitive Positioning
- Tourism and Retail Marketing
- Marketing Collateral Pieces

Value Offered

Recruiting Communications – Pioneered comprehensive $400K communication and branding program that attracted 375 high-tech candidates to Corning Incorporated in less than a year.

E-Learning – Designed, facilitated, marketed, and consulted for Ceramatec and Seattle Coffee e-learning initiatives.

Project Champion – Repeated success in energizing and aligning projects with a vision to fuel support and outcomes.

Professional History

SEATTLE COFFEE COMPANY – Contract Position via Peoplestaff – Seattle, WA   2004 – present
Communications Consultant – Strategic Communications / Partner Resources 09/04 – present

- **Seattle Coffee Global University E-Learning Program:** Hired to build a communications plan for major enterprise-wide e-learning project. Acted as a consultant to the project manager to rejuvenate and reset a stalled project in order to move to planning and launch stages. Mobilized executive management to realign team and accelerate forward momentum.

  - Benchmarked "university projects" at Ikea, Caesar's World Resorts, E-Cornell, and Samsung, applying "lessons learned" to design and re-plan the Seattle Coffee's Global University.

  - Developed integrated communications plan. Utilized design knowledge to simplify and optimize web site.

- **Partner View Survey Guide:** Worked with printing and design firms to create four-color, 20-page company survey guidebook. Managed editing process, digital print process, and color checks. Coordinated five-person team and two agencies to meet tight deadline.

Communications Consultant – Global Communications 06/04 – 08/04

Accepted temporary position to gain entry into Seattle Coffee. Wrote "Weekly Buzz" e-newsletter and "Brew Tales" product placement article. Inventoried media clips. Updated organizational announcements and Seattle Coffee web site as needed.

EVANS SCHOOL OF COMMUNICATIONS – MARIN COUNTY COLLEGE – Marin, CA   2000 – 2002
Masters Student – Communications – Paid and capstone-level projects included:

- **Women's Community Building** – Marin, CA, 2002. Developed a marketing communications plan for WCB's event facility to increase community awareness, increase operating revenue, and improve employee communications.

- **Sourdough Loan Development Corporation** – SAN FRANCISCO, CA, 2001. Redesigned communication infrastructure for the City's economic development arm. Conducted audit and delivered marketing communications intervention plan.

- **Goldwater's** – Mullholland, CA 2000. Consulting project for "Designing Systems and Branding" course. Analyzed communication processes in home decor department to identify and correct performance deficiencies.

  Performance Intervention – Identified opportunity to save $95K in lost sales and management time by improving staff meetings, teamwork, and the sales binders that outlined key sales, operations, and procedural processes.

Professional History continued...

CERAMATEC INCORPORATED – Edmonds, WA (contract and permanent status) 1991 – 2000 / 2001

Communications Intern – BETEL Park Research Facility, Integration Section (2001)

Redesigned employee orientation program. Conducted in-depth performance assessment to identify needed interventions. Designed multimedia presentations, instructional materials, and evaluation tools to improve retention and integration.

Employee Communications and Recruiting Specialist (via Peoplestaff) (2000)

- **Staffing & Training** – Hired 100+ staff in six months. Conducted interviews and team skills evaluation.

Communications Project Leader (Contract employee at Ceramatec) (1998 – 1999)

Directed PR and advertising campaigns to increase tourism in the Cascade Lakes region. Administered budget of up to $30K, managed media tours and trade shows, and held press conferences. Developed collateral, television ads, and PSAs to promote area's desirability as a tourist destination. *Key Contributions:*

- **Event Planning and Execution** – Contributed to regional branding campaign. Spearheaded "Cascade Lakes Tourism Showcase" event from concept to completion. Event became annual affair and received featured spot in Marketing News magazine as "unique promotion of place."
- **TV Advertisement Production** – Worked with award-winning film production team to create television advertisements; managed and directed talent and scene development.

Recruiting Communications Specialist (permanent Ceramatec employee) (1996 – 1998)

Orchestrated successful $300K strategic initiative that transitioned Ceramatec's public image from aerospace parts company to high-technology firm and enabled recruiting of qualified staff. Designed communication tools, facilitated cross-functional team, managed design agencies, and managed video producer in developing orientation and training collateral/multi-media materials. Worked at all levels with new recruits, HR managers, and vendors to meet goals. *Key Contributions:*

- **E-Learning Employee Orientation Programs** – Created cutting-edge online program that slashed management's time on orientation. Revamped handbook and led Employee Orientation Program, resulting in replication across divisions and recognition as world-class system by Corporate Leadership Council.
- **Multi-Media Programs** – Supported hiring of 325 staff by creating CD-ROM promoting Ceramatec. Interviewed executives, analyzed audience/relevant messages via focus groups and conceptualized video scenes.

Public Relations Coordinator – Cerametec Consumer Products Division (permanent Cerametec employee) (1991 – 1996)

Held increasing responsibility for media relations, crisis communications, promotions, special events, product placement, and core marketing/PR initiatives. Managed PR/ad agencies, contracts, video production, and budgets. *Key Contributions:*

- **Promotions** – Created successful regional promotion with Ernst. Gained exposure on two major networks.
- **Marketing Programs** – Launched national radio ad program reaching more than 2M listeners; managed product placement program, negotiating retainer fee savings of $15K over a three-year period.
- **Company Milestone Campaign** – Created PR campaign, including POP promotion that spurred 71 percent of new sales.

Education and Affiliations

M.S., Communications, 2002 – Focus: Organizational Communications, Learning & Design

MARIN COLLEGE – Evans School of Communications – Marin, CA (GPA: 3.9/4.0)

- Graduate assistantship, academic awards, and membership in *Who's Who in American Colleges & Universities*.

B.A., Sociology, 1987 – UNIVERSITY OF CALIFORNIA – Marin, CA. Graduated with Distinction.

Affiliations – American Marketing Association, 1997 – present. Membership Director/Programming Committee Member

Created and orchestrated 1st annual integrated marketing trade show event – International Association of Business Communicators, 2001 – present, Member.

Computer Skills – Intermediate-level knowledge of MS Office (PowerPoint, Word, Excel), Photoshop, and Kai's Power Show. Exposure to Director, Authorware, PageMaker, Sound Edit 16, HTML, and Dream Weaver.

12345 Silver Elm Street ❖ Smithtown, NY 11787 ❖ (718) 555-1234 ❖ vmortimer@protypeltd.com

HEALTHCARE CONTROLLER

"Jane is a consummate professional whose expertise enabled us to save more than $5 million within two years by closely examining our operations and implementing new cost controls."
Brandon Burt Smith, CEO, Braumhampton International

Agile, results-driven professional with a proven record of identifying and executing profitable solutions. More than 10 years of experience helping national and international corporations substantially improve financial operations. Expertise in healthcare supply chain management. Savvy negotiation skills combined with a keen ability to successfully network with executives, clinicians, and non-clinicians to achieve cost savings while preserving quality.

AREAS OF EXPERTISE

**Vendor Contracting ~ Business Performance Management Tools ~ Financial Reporting
Reimbursement Methodologies ~ Best Practices ~ Inventory Management**

PROFESSIONAL EXPERIENCE

BRAUMHAMPTON INTERNATIONAL, Albany, NY   1997 – 2005
Controller (2003 – 2005)

Oversaw a team of 17 direct reports and 125 support personnel. Interpreted financial and operational data to measure performance and identify organization-wide improvement opportunities for a worldwide network of healthcare facilities. Harnessed data warehouse capabilities to create operational efficiencies for purchasing and warehousing functions.

- Saved $750,000 within first three months by researching operating expenses and obtaining benchmark data resulting in utility contract renegotiations.

- Rolled out a new enterprise resource planning tool that reaped annual savings of $4.2 million and reduced the number of vendor contracts.

- Clipped supply expenses by more than $1 million within one year by analyzing high-cost healthcare categories and tightening tier commitments.

- Educated management staff in transition from material managers to supply chain directors for 15 facilities, and implemented technological enhancements in facility operations that increased productivity by 32 percent in one year.

Financial Analyst (2000 – 2003)

Prepared financial reporting, such as utilization and variance reports, for executives and board. Evaluated fiscal procedures for best practices and examined net revenue from third-party payors of network hospitals to identify cost-saving opportunities. Assisted in budget preparation and year-end closings.

- Pinpointed and resolved revenue allocation discrepancies of $1.7 million yearly from ancillary providers prior to finalization of a $1 billion joint venture.

- Achieved $12 million in network hospital savings by analyzing reimbursement schedule of major insurance carriers and identifying underpayments.

PROFESSIONAL EXPERIENCE *Continued...*

Business Analyst (1998 – 2000)

Developed, implemented, and analyzed costs for five facilities and drafted managed care contracts. Prepared monthly and quarterly business reports for resource management. Produced fiscal performance and clinical measurement reports for key personnel. Gained in-depth experience in multiple system utilization and implementation.

- Secured greater earnings in each product line by educating key department heads in three different facilities on payor and cost by product line.
- Recouped $820,000 in underpayments from insurers by reviewing high-cost claims and identifying outliers that were covered under contract rider.

Logistics Manager (1997)

Hired, trained and managed a distribution staff of 12 for a 375-bed acute care facility. Mediated disputes between department managers and buyers. Consolidated inventory levels through performance and analysis (PAR) utilization. Conducted supply chain analysis to determine areas of inefficiencies.

- Reduced internal delivery time by 20 percent and incoming complaints by 30 percent monthly. Improved fill rate by 15 percent by reorganizing logistics department. Developed accountability structure and work performance standards.

AMERICA'S HOSPITAL NETWORK, Stamford, CT   1995 – 1997
Senior Accountant/Accountant

Oversaw a $4 million budget and developed forecasting models for all business segments. Analyzed expense-to-revenue ratios for variances. Managed the general ledger for state and federal funds; provided monthly financials for board members. Participated in accounting software conversion project to upgrade financial systems for a four-facility network with six remote practices.

EDUCATION

Master of Business Administration – TEXAS UNIVERSITY – Houston, TX, 1994
Bachelor of Science in Accounting – YORK UNIVERSITY – New York, NY 1992

TECHNICAL COMPETENCIES

Expert level user of On-Line Analytical Processing (OLAP) Tools
Advanced knowledge of MS Excel, Access, and Axapta

PROFESSIONAL AFFILIATIONS AND CERTIFICATIONS

Certified Public Accountant, New York and Connecticut
Professional Association of Certified Public Accountants (PACPA)
New York Association of CPAs

Betsy Webber

1234 Thistlebrook Circle
Highlands Ranch, CO 80126

Email: betsy.webber@protypeltd.net

Home: (303) 555-1234
Cellular: (303) 555-5678

Information Technology / Business Development
Project Manager / Analyst / Programmer

Skills Summary

- Highly motivated, results-driven leader who is skilled in evaluating workflow needs and orchestrating teams to implement strategies that increase productivity, enhance quality, and improve cost effectiveness.
- Proven manager with extensive experience in technical fields, including software delivery, analysis, design, coding, change management, release packaging, and implementation.
- Astute negotiator and problem solver with excellent presentation skills; able to communicate effectively with diverse audiences of executives, software developers, and users.

Experience

Front Range Appraisal, LLC, Highlands Ranch, Colorado .... 2002 – present
Founded a residential real estate appraisal business providing professional appraisals to mortgage companies and individuals throughout the Colorado Front Range.

PRESIDENT, REAL ESTATE APPRAISER
- Prepare thorough and detailed appraisals and recertifications of single-family and multi-family properties, town-homes, and condominiums.
- Create operating income statements, rent schedules, and inspection/property/draw reports.
- Accountable for profit and loss, business planning, customer service, and new business development.

WorldCom, Highlands Ranch, Colorado .... 1997 – 2002
Simultaneously managed up to five diverse call center support teams with a staff of 30 employees and consultants. Directed the end-to-end development of large mainframe, multiple-transaction applications that focused on new technologies and improvements to existing systems. Charged with delivering on-time software releases that directly impacted sales and customer service.

MANAGER III
- Orchestrated large-scale IT engagements that incorporated structured approaches to information engineering and knowledge management (i.e., data modeling, process modeling, and event modeling).
- Responsible for business analysis, enterprise re-engineering, program/project management, application development, change management, reporting, training, and call center quality assurance. Managed a $2.0 million budget.
- Facilitated joint application development (JAD) with other customer service centers to analyze, design, and clarify requirements to support customer care when integrating MCI's architecture with the applications and processes of Worldcom.
- Also managed a team of quality assurance representatives who monitored client usage of tools and training, ensuring that they met company standards of superior customer service.
- Hired, supervised, and mentored analysts, managers, developers, and trainers, among others.
- Defined the training curriculum for new employees and tenured staff to ensure that skills were kept up to date.
- Developed performance metrics for each staff member, held monthly individual employee progress reviews, and prepared annual performance evaluations.
- Successfully balanced workloads and matrix delegation on an average of 60 concurrent IT projects.
- Ensured high-quality results by using peer reviews, audits, and project plan examinations.
- Shortened the development cycle by creatively working outside traditional interfaces to support "first to the market" product launches while at the same time ensuring that adequate time was spent on product testing and user training.

Experience

MCI Communications, Inc., Arlington, Virginia / Colorado Springs, Colorado / Denver, Colorado .... 1988 – 1997
Rapidly promoted from highly technical analyst positions to engineering and ultimately to program management.

PROGRAM MANAGER (1995 – 1997)
- Sole point of contact for the coordination of product and service implementation activities for MCI's high-revenue customers (over $900,000/year).
- Built and led a strong virtual team that provided management and technical expertise to ensure the successful activation of high-end products and services (virtual private network, Internet, toll free, and frame relay, etc.).
- Gathered project information and customer requirements and secured necessary resources through MCI, foreign alliances, and the customer.
- Notified project team members of issue status and project impact, providing first-level triage for all problems reported by the customer, subcontractors, and employer.
- Resolved capacity, diversity, and restoration issues with network planning organizations.
- Ensured customer compliance, a high level of productivity, and exceptional quality by regularly preparing project tracking reports, manpower forecasts, and analyses.

Education

Bachelor of Science, Human and Consumer Sciences (1976)
Florida State University, Tallahassee, Florida

Computer Programming Technology Certificate (1982)
Control Data Institute, Bristol, England

Colorado State Registered Appraiser (2002)
Jones Real Estate College, Denver, Colorado
License #AR 40030463
Course work included: Uniform Standards of Professional Appraisal Practice, Valuation Process,
Legal Considerations and Partial Interests, Economic Principles, Types of Value, Real Estate Markets,
Neighborhood Analysis, Site Description and Analysis, Highest and Best Use, Site Valuation,
Specific Data Collection and Preliminary Analysis, Improvement Description and Analysis, Cost Approach,
Sales Comparison Approach, Income Approach, Special Appraisal Techniques, Mathematics and Statistics

---

Technical Skills

Platforms and Operating Systems
Mainframes, midrange systems, UNIX

Programming Languages and Tools
Natural, COBOL, Visual Basic, CICS, DL/1

Databases
ADABAS, DB2, VSAM, Microsoft Access

Applications
Witness, Siebel, Proforma, Visio, MS Project, FrontPage, Crystal Reports
MS Word, Excel, PowerPoint, Outlook

HOWARD DAVIS

1111 Nantucket Bay Court • Wellington, FL 33414 • (561) 555-1234 • (561) 555-5678
hdavis@protypeltd.com

SUMMARY

More than twenty-five years of senior and executive-level management experience in Information Technology. Proven ability to direct successful teams and departments while deploying global infrastructures and company IT architecture. Highly skilled in operating departments at high service levels within approved budget parameters, while successfully communicating corporate-wide vision. Extensive Project Management, with ability to oversee all stages, from inception to launch. Background in managing technology, team, and business unit migrations. Outstanding presentation, motivation, and communication skills.

PROFESSIONAL BACKGROUND

Semi-Retired, Wellington, Florida   2000 – present
Engaged in a variety of career interests while pursuing postgraduate college credit: TV/Film Production, Professional/Licensed Yacht Captain, Professional/Certified Master Scuba Instructor and Dive Guide.

DST Systems, Inc. (Argus Health Systems, Inc.), Kansas City, Missouri   1995 – 2000
Vice President of Technology
Managed advanced technology development for a division of one of the world's largest data processing centers specializing in mutual funds, life insurance products, and health systems. Managed technical support of all Argus computing platforms: system performance/availability, capacity planning, system recovery/restart, disaster recovery, database administration, and operational preparedness.

- Designed and guided the acquisition and implementation of an IBM RS/6000 SP client/server platform, a complex of 51 parallel UNIX processors and their associated software systems.
- Directed and managed implementation of new 3-tier application architecture that became the platform for implementation of an innovative rebate tracking system.
- Operated departments within approved $15 million budget while improving employee utilization rate, reducing staff turnover, and increasing available skill sets.
- Conducted staff recruitment, development, and retention while creating incentive plans and performance reviews.
- Oversaw a staff of 35 that included consultants, system managers, as well as technical and administrative employees.
- Managed outsourcing projects for European Financial Data Services (UK) Ltd., Brentwood, England, a DST subsidiary, reporting directly to the president.
- Coordinated and led a team that built the infrastructure to migrate the core business system from mainframe to client/server with capacity to process up to 30 pharmacy transactions per second.
- Directed database administration, UNIX system programming, telecommunications systems programming, database systems operation, network management, desktop, and technical support.
- Responsible for vendor management and contract negotiations.
- Converted a disorganized, underperforming department to a high-quality service organization responsible for all vendor-supplied software/middleware.

IBM Corporation, Kansas City, MO   1987 – 1995
Senior Marketing Representative
Managed the delivery and introduction of technology services and products including ES/9000, AS/400, and RS/6000 open systems product line to Worldwide Hospital community.

- Consistently achieved high customer satisfaction ratings while exceeding $20 million per year sales quota.
- Provided consulting services and methodologies while acting as liaison for third-party vendors.
- Assisted a federally funded community health center with the successful selection and implementation of a complete replacement of infrastructure involving multiple IBM services and departments and four independent solution providers.
- Excelled in the full life-cycle sales process from needs assessment to implementation of projects, while improving the competitive advantage of IBM and its clients.
- Worked with clients to determine needs and develop specifications while monitoring project progress.
- Assured delivery of effective customer service and support, responding to and resolving any queries or issues.
- Instrumental in channel marketing efforts designed to recruit outside software/service organizations.

TECHNICAL SKILLS

Operating Systems:	Windows 95–2000/XP/NT, UNIX, AIX, MVS, VM, VSE, OS/400
Tools and Databases:	MS Project, MS Office, MS Visio, and MS FrontPage, Project Workbench, Lotus Smart Suite and Notes, IBM CICS, Encina, IMS/DB, DB2 and WebSphere, Adobe Photoshop and Premier, Avid Xpress.
Networking:	LAN/WAN, frame relay, TCP/IP, ATM, Ethernet, Sonet, fiber optics, XDSL, cable, routers, hubs, switches, Token Ring, VPN solutions, TCP wrappers, wireless.
Hardware:	IBM mainframe, midrange and minicomputers, PCs, an extensive range of peripheral equipment.
Languages:	HTML, C++, Java, Javascript, shell scripting methodologies, 390-Assembler, COBOL, Fortran, Basic.

EDUCATION AND TRAINING

BACHELOR OF SCIENCE, Mathematics, University of Missouri at Kansas City, 1977

FILM/MOTION PICTURE PRODUCTION, Palm Beach Community College, Florida
- 47 Credit Hours with a 4.0 GPA
- Member of the President's List, 2004
- Member Phi Theta Kappa (National Academic Honor Society), 2004

PROFESSIONAL DEVELOPMENT
- IBM Corporation, numerous sales and marketing training courses, both within and outside IBM

GERALD COMPTON

89 Springs Lane · Miami, FL 33101 · gc4500@protypeltd.com · (305) 555-1234(H)

Technical Project Manager
Systems engineering
Software engineering
Customer-centric management
Project turnaround
Leadership of award-winning technology projects

Delivery-driven project/program manager and technical contributor. Solid record of timely project delivery, satisfied clients, and repeat business. Effective team builder, team player, communicator, and collaborator. Possess both big-picture vision and ability to execute at the detail level. Broad systems experience:

- Scope Control
- Resource Management
- Cost/Schedule Estimation
- Budget Control
- Requirements Gathering
- Risk Analysis and Mitigation
- Execution
- Deployment
- Reporting and Closure

Qualifications:

↘ **15+ years of experience in systems engineering and software development**
↘ **Certified Program Management Professional (PMP)**
↘ **Two Master of Science Degrees (Engineering and Engineering Management)**
↘ **Won awards and achieved outside recognition for achievements on three projects**

Operating Systems: Windows (2000, NT), UNIX (including HP-UX, Solaris), Linux, VMS
Technologies: .Net, J2EE, Domino/Notes, n-tier client/server
Software/Languages: SQL Server, Oracle, MySQL, Access, SQL, VB, Perl, Java, MS Project, MS Office

PROFESSIONAL EXPERIENCE

WORLD SCIENTIFIC TECHNOLOGY CORPORATION, Miami, FL   1996 – present
Second-largest global technical services provider with $4 billion in annual revenues.

Technical Director – Southeast Division (1996 – present)
Directed six technical personnel on public and private sector projects ranging to $450,000. As technical contributor, provided systems and software engineering. Project-level P&L responsibility. Interacted with internal/external managers and technical staff. Authorized to hire/fire contractors.

Project-Management and Technology-Leadership Achievements (Selected)
- Turned around a multi-state project that had been deteriorating due to inadequate requirements definition. Led detailed specification process and achieved buy-in from stakeholders in a project to apply Web-based commercial tools to government functions. Developed an "EMall" based on Microsoft Web technology using Intelisys's electronic commerce enterprise product. Customized the solution for individual states. Enhanced customer interface functionality beyond base product capabilities.

- Brought on as program manager to save a profitable contract with the third largest U.S. bank. Rebuilt client relationships. Led marketing effort that doubled annual contract revenues to $500,000. Led software engineering team. Team-developed a niche solution to a technology integration problem, helping client retain its CRM-type business system after acquisition by second largest U.S. bank.

- On a $500,000 project for Colorado State University, managed a pioneering effort to integrate an e-commerce electronic purchasing tool into an enterprise-wide financial accounting system.

- Architected a solution for the Elections Canada project that won national recognition for excellence in government IT projects—the prestigious APEX Award. Met technical-performance challenges related to complex processing requirements. [Powerbuilder front end with Oracle (HP-UX) backend]

- Upgraded vital records to a Web-based reporting and management system for the Florida Department of Public Health. Replaced the project manager, reinvigorating client relationship and producing an additional three phases for a final total of $500,000. [Microsoft's .Net technology including C#, ASPX, and SQL Server 2000]

- Automated a Web-based campaign finance reporting system for the Florida Office of Campaign and Political Finance Systems, a $1 million project. [J2EE system with Oracle 8i backend]

NETSYNTAX, Miami, FL   1988 – 1996
Provided IT, engineering, and custom software development services.

Division Engineer/Section Manager—Enterprise Business Solutions Division
Supervised seven staff. Managed operating budgets of up to $2 million. Accountable for project management, systems architecture design, and network implementation. [Novell- and Windows NT-based networks; Lotus Notes collaboration solutions]

- Designed and engineered a voter-registration technology for Texas that was evaluated as Best-of-Breed by the Cal Tech/MIT and Carter-Ford Commission reviews. Developed a secure, Web-based WAN that enabled database replication (Oracle) and software distribution (Dephi). Supported statewide rollout of the Qualified Voter File.

- Built a prototype for the FloridaJobs Counsel, for internal/external data-sharing to be deployed at one-stop career centers. [Multi-server Lotus notes; Web-based publisher]

- Provided technical leadership on a project to build a statewide transaction database of registered voters for the Secretary of State's office in Florida. Built models to evaluate equipment options and to define parameters. Successfully implemented VRIS, which provided the largest 300 voting sites with 300 percent greater bandwidth and five times better response time with no increase in costs.

- Earned the company recognition as the "Small Business Prime Contractor of the Year" while program manager and senior technical contributor on a $550,000 feasibility study for the Defense Communications Agency. Provided validation for a concept that is under construction by Raytheon.

- Recruited to lead the company's GPS program as program manager. Managed client relationship, contributed to software development, and supervised 23 technical staff.

FLORIDA RESEARCH GROUP, Executive Vice President and CTO   1985 – 1988
Provided software and systems engineering primarily to Department of Defense clients.

EDUCATION, CERTIFICATION, LICENSURE, AND AFFILIATIONS

CORNELL UNIVERSITY, Ithaca, NY
   Master of Science, Engineering Management

UNIVERSITY OF NORTH CAROLINA, Chapel Hill, NC
   Master of Science, Electrical Engineering
   Bachelor of Electrical Engineering (Honors)

Certificate in Data Communications Technology
Program Management Professional
Professional Engineer (PE)
Data Communications Technology – Miami University 1994
Senior Member: IEEE (Institute of Electrical & Electronics Engineers)
Security Clearance: Secret

RIAZ G. KARIM

12345 Vicksburg Drive
Mesquite, Texas 75181

Home: 972.555-1234   Email: karim@protypeltd.com   Cell: 214.555.5678

SENIOR-LEVEL BANKING INDUSTRY EXECUTIVE
U.S. and Southeast Asia Operations

Dynamic leadership career combining both general and financial management responsibilities within highly competitive organizations, industries, and markets. Outstanding presentation, communication, and cross-cultural team management skills. Entrepreneurial attitude, energy, and style. MBA degree.

- Business Reengineering
- Decision-Making Authority
- Multi-Site Operations Management
- Benchmarking
- Crisis Communications
- Leadership Development
- Cross-Functional Team Leadership
- Efficiency Improvement
- P&L Management

- Continuous Process Improvement
- Proactive Leadership
- Executive Management
- Corporate Culture Change
- Team Building
- Financial Management
- Cost Reduction
- Technology Initiatives
- Turnaround Management

CORE EXPERTISE AND ACHIEVEMENTS

MUSLIM COMMERCIAL BANK LTD., KARACHI, PAKISTAN

Regional Manager, Karachi (East), Commercial Banking Group (South), 2002
Directed P&L, marketing, budgeting, planning, and branch operations functions for 28 branches of this multinational bank. Annual company revenues of $70 million dollars, 14,000 employees, five countries.

- Managed credit portfolio of $21 million, non-fund based portfolio of $43 million.
- Grew market share by 5 percent increasing liability portfolio by 8 percent and assets by 10 percent.
- Participated in initiating new market development that accelerated growth by $3.8 million.
- Supervised direct staff of 250—50 executives, 110 officers, 90 clerical.
- Collaborated with key commercial accounts to include: Phillips Electrical, Sanyo Electric, Nova Disk.
- Developed and implemented a new work-flow process that resulted in company-wide acceptance and substantial savings in time for customers and staff.
- Led an aggressive technology program to develop custom software that was accepted by management for system-wide implementation.
- Resolved staffing challenges by improving workflow, redistributing staff, and decreasing labor costs.
- Pioneered the design, development, and market launch of advanced technology for both information and telecommunications applications.

Vice President / Regional Head, Priority Banking, 2000 – 2002
Supervised regional operations with 13 branches throughout Pakistan, annual revenues of $5 million, P&L management. Disciplines: finance, marketing, personnel administration.

- Achieved 200 percent growth in revenue through phenomenal growth of incremental account base.
- Downsized annual costs 12 percent by initiating new work-flow processes, and reducing staff.
- Pioneered computerization of a product, resulting in decreasing staff and customer time by 50 percent.
- Appointed Acting Executive with full responsibility for the region in the absence of the general manager.
- Credited as first regional manager to offer corporate "Priority Culture" change for VIPs, resulting in increases of 69 percent in credit, 100 percent in deposits, 22 percent in net profits, and 200 percent in client base.
- Introduced management training program to implement "Priority Culture" changes.

244

RIAZ G. KARIM

MUSLIM COMMERCIAL BANK LTD., KARACHI, PAKISTAN

Vice President / Regional Head, Priority Banking, 2000 – 2002 (Cont'd)
- Introduced PCs to this entire Region and trained staff in use of same.
- Designed a new training program using video to demonstrate needed improvements.
- Introduced employee incentive programs (Manager of the Year, etc.) to strengthen productivity.

Assistant Vice President / Chief Manager, Clifton (Corporate) Main Branch, 1998 – 2000
Corporate branch with 42 personnel, revenues of $1 million, P&L responsibility.
- Boosted letter of credit and guaranty business by 300 percent, increased deposits by 20 percent, profits by 50 percent, and credit (advances) by 35 percent.
- Involved in landing a new account increasing share from $50,000 to $6 million.
- Slashed human resource costs 11 percent by adding key staff, improving overall workflow.
- Invited to participate in brainstorming sessions every two weeks with bank senior executives.
- Achieved branch turn-around within four months by computerization, staffing, customer service.

Assistant Vice President / Chief Manager, Saira Center Star Branch, 1995 – 1998
Supervised general banking, credit, and foreign exchange departments, 12 personnel. Finance, marketing disciplines.
- Increased revenues by 250 percent and deposit base by 200 percent through dynamic new marketing efforts.
- Managed operating and capital budgets and reduced human resources costs 20 percent.
- Handled P&L responsibilities for this entire operation.
- Introduced PC-based correspondence / reporting method resulting in acceptance by management.
- Reengineered this branch and grew to Star Branch status within two years.

Officer Grade I / Sub-Manager, Clifton Branch, 1994 – 1995
Officer Grade I / Assistant Manager Credit and Marketing, 1992 – 1993
Officer Grade I / Management Training Officer, 1992
Treasury Manager, HOUSE OF PRUDENTIAL, Karachi, Pakistan, 1991 – 1992
Financial Representative, LINCOLN SAVINGS BANK LTD., Los Angeles, California USA, 1990 – 1991

ENTREPRENEURIAL EXPERIENCE

SWIFT RENT A CAR & SALES – DALLAS, TEXAS USA, 2002 – present

Vice President / Working Partner
Start-up car sales and rental company (two years old), with annual revenues of $800,000, six employees, and two locations in Texas. Report directly to shareholders. Supervise three company officers.
- Initiated company diversification and led company through accelerated growth of 7 percent.
- Increased company sales by 20 percent in one location with start-up of new program.
- Trimmed annual budgets 30 percent by cutting labor and operations costs.
- Resolved major money problems by negotiating the initial bank credit line of $300,000.
- Spearheaded computerization of company invoicing process resulting in significant time savings.

EDUCATION

MBA – Southern New Hampshire University, Manchester, New Hampshire, 1990
(Concentration in Advanced Financial Management, Production and Operational Management, Fiscal and Monetary Policy and Marketing Strategies)

Bachelor of Science – University of Punjab-Lahore, Pakistan, 1986 (Statistics and Mathematics)

Bachelor of Commerce – Karachi University, Karachi, Pakistan, 1987 (Business Administration)

KEITH RICHARDS

12 Myrtle Drive • Charleston, South Carolina 29651 • (864) 555-1234 • keithrichards@protypeltd.com

Business Development Professional
15 years of experience

EXPERIENCE

PRESIDENT AND FOUNDER (1994 – present)
Richards & Associates, Inc., Charleston, South Carolina
Founded a multifaceted company to pursue contracts with the U.S. Government for aircraft tools and equipment. Later absorbed the export distribution business for aircraft tools from Transcon Trading Company and expanded it into 54 countries. This year, we developed an outsourcing business by reversing our supply chain and asking overseas customers to produce parts and subcomponents for clients here in the U.S.

Outsourcing

Local manufacturers are trying to improve their profit margins but are unable to raise prices due to competitive pressures. Their alternative is to lower costs, but record unemployment rates as low as 1.4% make this difficult. Richards realized that many of its overseas customers were producing quality aircraft parts for the aerospace industry, so we began approaching local companies for the purpose of outsourcing their production to low-cost countries such as Malaysia, Thailand, and Vietnam. The result has been:

- Formed a strategic alliance with Schrudder Performance Group to jointly develop a business process outsourcing proposal to Schlumberger, Ltd. The company had unsuccessfully tried to sell its gas measurement plant in Greenwood, South Carolina, twice during the past three years. Instead of selling the plant, we recommended that Schlumberger:
  - Outsource the product line to another local manufacturer (AMBAC) under contract,
  - Develop the $43 million re-manufactured market for this product line,
  - Sell the current plant and facilities for $7 million, and
  - Focus on its core competencies: brand management, marketing, and sales.
  Executed successfully, this plan would increase Schlumberger's sales from $23 million to $66 million and return $7 million in cash from the sale of the capital assets.

- Applied Six Sigma strategies to significantly reduce manufacturing costs and improve the quality of high-tech cloth seals used in industrial gas turbines produced by GE Gas Turbine in Greenville, South Carolina. Our proposal to GE simplified the manufacture of cloth seals into three distinct processes. Each process will then be outsourced to three different vendors whose core competencies best fit the application, thus saving GE $8 million in annual purchase costs and eliminating $3 million in inventory.

- Presently working with GE Gas Turbine to create a line of remanufactured turbine blades. GE currently offers only new industrial gas turbine blades (presently in short supply) and melts old blades worn by corrosion or erosion into scrap. Airfoil Services, a Richards export customer, also happens to repair gas turbine blades for GE Aircraft, Rolls-Royce, and British Aerospace. We have proposed that Airfoil rebuild the worn blades and ship them from stock in Malaysia. GE's cost of goods sold on the rebuilt blades would be barely above scrap value, and they could actually make more profit from selling the remanufactured blades than on sales of new ones. Actual sales are proprietary to GE, but they are known to exceed $100 million annually.

- Identified an offshore source for a critical-to-quality chassis component for Lemforder, AG, in Duncan, South Carolina. Lemforder's domestic production was at maximum capacity and the company had searched unsuccessfully for two years to find additional capacity outside the United States. Using a Six Sigma approach and thinking outside the box, we located a competitor plant in only six weeks (DANA in São Paulo, Brazil) that used identical high-tech eddy-current inspection methods. Even though they are competitors, we discovered that DANA had both the capacity and the desire to supply this item.

- Currently redesigning pressure vessels used in pressurized deep fryers for BKI Industries in Mauldin, South Carolina. BKI had asked us to outsource their pressure vessels from outside the U.S. in order to reduce costs. Instead of going overseas, we identified a local German manufacturer of pressure vessels (KTM) that was ASME certified and whose export business had been hurt by the currency crisis. The goal is a total redesign of the fryer and vessel to cut costs by 25 percent.

Outsourcing (continued)	• Designed and implemented a plan to outsource a new government customer sales and service center for Stanley Work's Vice President of Government Sales. Before this plan, each of Stanley's four tool divisions operated independently. Under the new process, Richards and Associates united and focused the four separate divisions into essentially one sales force. All government customer requests for quotes were funneled back to Richards, where the quotes were prepared using as many Stanley products as possible from across all divisions to meet customer expectations. Richards designed, scripted, and executed national sales programs to train hand-tool sales representatives from Proto to engage government customers in value-added sales. This business process outsourcing appeared as a seamless service to the government customer.
E-Commerce	*As a government contractor and domestic exporter, Richards receives significant discounts from its suppliers for tools and equipment. We used these discounts to create an e-commerce Web site called toolcontrol.com with 319,000 part numbers for more than 100 brands.* • Working with a local IT firm, Metaprise Consulting, we powered the site using IBM Net.Commerce, Lotus Domino Go Webserver, DB2 database, and Lotus R5. • Bowers Creative Group designed the graphics, logos, layout, flow, and text. • BruceClay.com, a meta-tag firm in California, helped us to create one custom web page for each of the 32 leading brands of tools and equipment. This allowed the various search engines to rank our Web site high according to their search string algorithms. • The Web site attracted the equity attention of Cygnus Publishing, which owns more than 50 Web sites and considered making an investment in the site. However, when Amazon.com purchased Tool Crib of the North and publicized their intention to significantly increase inventory levels and shorten delivery times, Cygnus pulled out. Amazon.com had raised customer expectations above the level at which Cygnus was prepared to invest. This appears to have been a good decision since the Amazon.com and Tool Crib partnership has not met the expectations of investors.
Government Contracting	*Developed government contracts by working with Senator Strom Thurmond's small business development office to identify government sales opportunities within the U.S. Department of Defense (DoD), including such agencies as the Army, Navy, Air Force, Marines, Coast Guard, Air National Guard, and Army National Guard.* • Successfully negotiated with Stanley Works to become an authorized Stanley Works Government Agent to the DoD. • Developed, bid, negotiated, and closed the company's first government contract with the DoD for a five-year blanket purchase agreement of more than $5 million of special military torque-related tools. • Closed several additional multi-year contracts with the DoD for military aircraft-related tools and equipment worth approximately $6 million. • Outsourced the contract manufacturing of numerous special tools and equipment that met DoD Mil-Specs, using government-approved machine shops throughout the U.S. • Richards was the only tool-related government contractor ever to be invited to the annual LRW Conference held by the Army National Guard to discuss issues and set policy nationwide for the maintenance and repair of its forces.
Export Distribution	*Upon my departure from Transcon Trading Company, many of its customers independently decided to move their accounts to Richards. We continued to expand this business to almost $1 million with distribution to 54 countries.* • Richards successfully specified, negotiated, and closed a $510,000 contract for all of the equipment for a turnkey CEPA Electric maintenance plant in Hong Kong. • CEPA built two 25MW floating power plants in the Philippines and needed an on-site maintenance shop. Richards worked with Duke Power in Oconee, South Carolina, to write the specifications. We specified, negotiated, closed, and shipped the entire project directly to Pagliabao, Philippines.

EXPERIENCE

VICE PRESIDENT (1990 – 1994)
Transcon Trading Company, Inc., Irmo, South Carolina
Recruited to this privately owned, $650,000 export management company by its founder and owner, Gerald W. Smith. Assumed profit and loss responsibility for a new division, LATCO International, which sold tools to automotive distributors in 16 countries.

- Immediately changed the company's strategic marketing and sales focus from low-value hand tools used by automotive distributors to premium, value-added production tools and equipment used by FAA-certified aircraft maintenance stations and heavy industrial companies. Managed to improve annual sales to $570,000 before being stifled by the Gulf War. Increased the global market presence from 16 to 28 countries.

- Assisted the management of our sister company, TransMedical, in developing, negotiating, and closing an outsourcing contract for $4 million of capital equipment for the Grand Cayman Island Hospital. The contract contained nine separate packages covering x-ray, laboratory, sterilization, operating room, and morgue, among other departments.

VICE PRESIDENT (1985 – 1990)
Columbia Industrial Sales Company, Inc., Columbia, South Carolina
Recruited to this privately held distributor of variable frequency drives and controls by Gary L. Traywick, the founder and owner. My specific responsibilities were to learn the business, grow it, and then buy the stock with company financing to allow the owner to retire. Mr. Traywick was a former business development manager for the Drives and Controls Division of Louis-Allis. I trained under Mr. Traywick for two years in Mexico using a variable frequency drives application program designed by Louis-Allis for motors, pumps, fans, transmissions, and controls used in the steel, paper, mining, sugar, textile, and cement industries.

- Assisted the owner in engineering and selling more than $5 million worth of drives and controls sourced from such manufacturers as GE, ABB, Siemens, Louis-Allis, and Reliance.

- Established sales offices in cities throughout Mexico (Mexico City, Monterrey, Puebla, and Guadalajara). Also opened a sales office in Guatemala City, Guatemala, that served Honduras and El Salvador.

- Led our team in closing a $3.65 million air pollution control capital equipment sale to HYLSA, a steel mill in Puebla, Mexico. At the customer's request, we searched the world to find the best-qualified manufacturer (ProceedAir of France) to fit this specific application. We created a consulting agreement at all levels of HYLSA, up through the CEO.

- Led our team in closing a $1.65 million process gas turbine capital equipment sale from Allis Chamber Compressor Corporation to Celanese de Mexico, a textile firm in Mexico.

EDUCATION

CLEMSON UNIVERSITY, Clemson, South Carolina
Bachelor of Science, Industrial Management (1983)
- Minor in Management Science
- Self-financed 100 percent of college costs

GEORGE WASHINGTON UNIVERSITY, Washington, D.C.
- Course work included: Federal Contracting Basics, Government Contract Law, Negotiation Strategies and Tactics, Procurement and the Internet, Source Selection: The Best-Value Process

SOFTWARE

Proficient in CARMA Contact Manager, IBM Net.Commerce, SAS, Lotus 1-2-3, Lotus Notes R5, Microsoft Word, PowerPoint, Excel, Access, Outlook, and Project

CLOSING THOUGHT

Nothing in the world can take the place of persistence.
Talent will not . . . nothing is more common than unsuccessful men with great talent.
Genius will not . . . unrewarded genius is almost a proverb.
Education will not . . . the world is full of educated derelicts.
Persistence, determination, these alone are omnipotent.

by Calvin Coolidge

16 Curriculum Vitae

Remember when I said that there is an exception to every rule in the résumé business? Well, here's another one. In most cases, résumés should be concise and limited to one or two pages at the most. You will carefully select your information to provide a synopsis. In the professions, however, a much longer résumé is expected, and the longer the résumé, the better your chances of getting an interview. Those industries generally include medicine, law, education, science, and media (television, film, etc.). If you are applying for a job in a foreign country, long résumés with more detail and a considerable amount of personal information are the norm (see Chapter 9).

Such a professional résumé is called a *curriculum vita* (CV) from the Latin meaning "course of one's life" (literally like running a race—and you just *thought* your life was a rat race!). For those of us who have trouble knowing how to spell the word, *vita* is singular and *vitae* is plural.

A successful CV will include not only education and experience but also publications (books, magazines, journals, and other media), certifications, licenses, grants, research, professional affiliations, awards, honors, presentations, and/or courses taught. Anything relevant to your industry is appropriate to use on a CV, and the résumé can be as long as it needs to be to present the "course of your life."

A CV—or any résumé with multiple pages for that matter—must contain a header with your name and page number on each successive page. Should the pages become separated, the reader should be able to easily put your subsequent pages in their proper order and with *your* résumé!

Victor Valentino, Ph.D.

1234 N. Richmond
Chicago, IL 60616

valentinophd@protypeltd.com

Residence: 773.555.1234
Cellular: 773.555.5678

SENIOR SCIENCE AND TECHNOLOGY MANAGER

CTO / PROJECT MANAGER / INTELLECTUAL PROPERTY / BUSINESS DEVELOPMENT

Spearheading Innovative Technology Solutions that Drive Change in a Career Spanning 14 Years

Technically sophisticated and business-savvy executive with a solid record in building new technology start-ups, state-of-the-art operations, cross-functional teams, IP assets, and organizational expansion to achieve competitive market advantages. Adept at spearheading technological innovations, global teaming, new product delivery, and commercialization. Record of success delivering simultaneous, large-scale, mission-critical projects on time and under budget. Recognized industry pioneer with 2 patents, 11 patent applications, 36 invention disclosures, and 27 periodical articles and conference papers. Bilingual: English and Spanish proficient. Ph.D. Physical Science. *Representative industries served:*

- Medical Devices
- Printing and Imaging
- Surface Mount Technology (SMT)
- Displays
- Packaging
- Nanotechnology
- RFID
- Coating
- Fuel Cells and Batteries

TECHNOLOGY / MANAGEMENT EXPERTISE

- Ground-Breaking Research Programs
- R&D Lab Management
- Full Lifecycle Project Management
- SBIR Management
- Strategic / Operational Planning
- New Product Development
- Quality, Reliability, Performance
- Competitive Benchmarking
- Technical Staffing

CAREER PROGRESSION

SUPER CAPACITOR TECHNOLOGY, INC. – Chicago, IL and Guadalajara, Mexico   1998 – present
Designer and manufacturer of the world's leading supercapacitors
Chief Technical Officer / Business Development Manager / Regional Sales Manager

Recruited to SCT in 1998 as a key member of the start-up management team to orchestrate commercialization of supercapacitor technology transfer from CSIRO. Upon building successful technology operations in Mexico, transferred to U.S. to launch the North American business enterprise. Contracted with global customers and vendors. Twelve direct reports: 1 senior scientist, 4 scientists, 3 research engineers, and 4 technicians.

HIGHLIGHTS OF ACCOMPLISHMENTS:

- **Captured the company's first multimillion-dollar sales order with the global leader in class 12 GPRS PC modems.** Research team formulated an electrolyte that exceeded the design specifications by 15 percent. SCT won 100 percent of the business. No competitors could meet specifications, driving them from this market.

- **Piloted SCT's full lifecycle, solution-focused business model in U.S.** A technology liaison—initiated business contact, generated design win, and oversaw contract manufacturer to ensure quality product delivery.

- **Chaired IP Asset Management Team that leveraged one of the industry's most viable portfolios.** Team included senior management, key scientists, and IP attorney.

- **Captured 60+ percent market share** for supercapacitors used in GPRS modems worldwide. Secured additional clientele to include the world's most recognized CPU and leading digital still camera manufacturers.

- **Reduced prototype failure rates from 85 percent to almost zero percent** via innovative performance testing and packaging technologies. **Dramatically improved product yields and lifetimes.** Patent pending.

- **Achieved 80 percent cost reduction,** designing and equipping two state-of-the-art research and coating laboratories. **Invented** novel thin-film coating formulations, techniques, and testing processes.

250

CAREER PROGRESSION, CONTINUED

ADVANCED RESEARCH INSTITUTE – Los Alamos, NM   1995 – 1997
Principal Research Investigator / Senior Scientist (Ultracapacitors), **Project Manager** (Advanced Battery)
HIGHLIGHTS OF ACCOMPLISHMENTS:

♦ **Managed** SBIR project.

♦ **Led research team** that developed advanced battery technologies for the USAF.

♦ **Achieved greater control** of process and 100 times increase in throughput by inventing a novel method of depositing capacitive material onto a substrate.

VANGUARD TECHNOLOGIES – Houston, TX   1992 – 1995
Senior Research Scientist (Lithium Ion Batteries)
HIGHLIGHTS OF ACCOMPLISHMENTS:

♦ **Developed formulations** for thin polymer electrolytes with emphasis on conductivity, coatability, and UV or E-Beam cross-linking resulting in greater uniformity of coatings and longer battery life.

♦ **Performed full IP analysis** of competitive products and manufacturing technologies. Evaluated carbon materials and methods of particle size reduction.

PATENTS AND PUBLICATIONS

Patent	9,876,543	Cathode-active material blends of Li.sub.x Mn.sub.2 O.sub.4. **Cited in 36 other patents.**
Patent	9,123,456	System and method for impregnating a moving porous substrate with active materials to produce battery electrodes.
Patents Pending	11	Supercapacitor performance and manufacturing technology.
Invention Disclosures	36	Various materials and process improvements focused on Li Polymer batteries. Some disclosures incorporated as trade secrets in preference to patenting.
Periodical Articles, Papers, Posters	27	Authored / co-authored articles published in peer reviewed journals. Delivered papers, seminars, and 15 poster presentations at professional conferences.

PROFESSIONAL PROFILE

EDUCATION

Ph.D. Physical Science
MASSACHUSETTS INSTITUTE OF TECHNOLOGY
Cambridge, MA   1989–1992

Thesis: EXAFS for Polymer Batteries. Structure conductivity in doped thin film polymer membranes. Funded by USDOE and Energy, Inc.

B.Sc. (Hons) Applied Chemistry
INSTITUTO DE TECNOLOGÍCO
Monterrey, Mexico   1986–1988

B.Tech. HD Physical Sciences
INSTITUTO DE TECNOLOGÍCO
Monterrey, Mexico   1983–1986

AFFILIATIONS

Diversity Committee
American Association for The Advancement of Science (AAAS)

Regional Chair
The Society of Mexican American Engineers and Scientists, Inc. (MAES)

Member
Society of Hispanic Professional Engineers (SHPE)

Member
Latino Alumni of MIT (LAMIT)

ADDITIONAL TECHNOLOGY SKILLS

Manufacturing Science, Supercapacitors, Materials Engineering, Electrical Engineering, Quality Control, Electrochemistry, Competitive Analysis, Reverse Engineering, Advanced Polymers, Device Testing, Batteries, Packaging Processes, Selection and Design, Anticipatory Failure Determination

COMPUTER SKILLS

Operating Systems: Windows, Mac, UNIX

Office Software: Word, Excel, Project, PowerPoint, Outlook

Programming Languages: Basic, Visual Basic, C/C++, HP Interface Basic-HPIB

Julia A. Mallard, D.O.

12345 North Queen Street, Kinston, NC 28501
(252) 555-1234 ▪ mallard@protypeltd.com

Obstetrics and Gynecology

Academic Preparation

Medical:
Doctor of Osteopathy, University of New England, College of Osteopathic Medicine, Biddeford, ME, 9/1991 – 6/1995

Undergraduate:
Bachelor of Science, Biology, State University of New York at Oneonta, Oneonta, NY, 9/1990 – 6/1991
University of New England, Biddeford, ME, 9/1988 – 6/1989
Associate Degree, Biology, Corning Community College, Corning, NY, 9/1986 – 6/1988

Medical Training

Primary Residency:
Chief Resident 7/1996 – 7/2000
William Bradford, D. O., Residency Director, Community Hospital of Lancaster, Lancaster, PA

Out Rotations:
Reproductive Endocrinology Rotation—7/1999
Samuel Thatcher, D.O., Center of Applied Reproductive Science, Johnson City, TN

Gynecologic Oncology Rotation—6/1999
Jose Misas, M.D., Harrisburg Hospital, Harrisburg, PA

Gynecologic Pathology Rotation—5/1999
Robert Kurman, M.D., Johns Hopkins Hospital, Baltimore, MD

General Surgery Rotation—10/1998
Glen Kline, D.O., Ephrata Community Hospital, Ephrata, PA, and Community of Lancaster, Lancaster, PA

Urogynecology Rotation—9/1998
Paul Sisbarro, D. O., Ephrata Community Hospital, Ephrata, PA

Maternal Fetal Medicine Rotation—6/1998
Karin Blakemore, M.D., Johns Hopkins Hospital, Baltimore, MD

Maternal Fetal Medicine Rotation—9 and 10/1997
James Hole, D.O. & Terry Tressler, D.O., Harrisburg Hospital, Harrisburg, PA

Internship:
Traditional Rotating 7/1995 – 7/1996
Jeffrey Levine, D.O., Director of Medical Education, Community Hospital of Lancaster, Lancaster, PA

Professional Licenses

North Carolina Medical Board, NC State License #200301263—2003 – present
American Samoa Health Services Regulatory Board, American Samoa License #3008-C—2002 – present
Pennsylvania State Board, PA State License #OS – 009382L—1996 – present
National Board of Osteopathic Medical Examiners – Diplomate—1996
Advanced Cardiac Life Support (Re-certification every 2 years)—1994 – present

Professional Experience

Lenoir Memorial Hospital, Kinston, NC, Staff Physician—11/2003 – present

Simply Women Healthcare, Kinston, NC, Private Practice Obstetrics and Gynecology—11/2003 – 9/2004

Lyndon Baines Johnson Tropical Medical Center, Faga'alu Village, American Samoa Socialized Medicine – Staff Physician – Obstetrics/Gynecology including Oncology, Tropical Medicine, and Dive Medicine—7/2000 – 7/2003

Professional/Academic Honors and Awards

Chief OB-Gyn Resident—1999 – 2000

Obstetrics and Gynecology Intern of the Year—1995 – 1996

National Health Service Corps Scholar, Community Hospital, Lancaster, PA

Professional Development

Advanced Fetal Monitoring—9/2004

American College of Obstetricians & Gynecologists—8/2004

OB-Gyn Coding:
Eastern Virginia Medical School, Ultrasound Workshop—11/2003

American College of Osteopathic Obstetricians and Gynecologists – Mid-Year Conference—10/2003

Lenoir Memorial Hospital – Utilization Review

Community Service

LYNDON BAINES JOHNSON TROPICAL MEDICAL CENTER
- American Samoa Project for the Primary Prevention of Diabetes Steering Committee
- Part C Infants and Toddlers Disabilities Interagency Coordinating Council
- Family Planning Coalition Teen Pregnancy Prevention
- Lyndon Baines Johnson Tropical Medical Center Library Development
- CBT Library Committee Chairman
- Medical Record Audit Committee Vice Chairman
- Tissue/Blood Bank Committee Chairman
- Pharmacy and Therapeutic Committee
- Mentoring Physicians

Affiliations

American College of Osteopathic Obstetricians and Gynecologists
American Osteopathic Association
American Medical Association

Foreign Language Abilities

Basic Communication in Spanish and Samoan

Volunteer Work

Himalayan Healthcare, Ilam, Nepal—3/2000 – present
Hospital Regional, Puerto Vallarta, Mexico—1998 – 2000

David R. Fall, LNHA

2345 Croner Avenue SW
North Canton, OH 44720
Home: 330-555-1234 ◆ Cell: 330-555-5678

DIRECTOR ◆ ADMINISTRATOR ◆ SUPERVISOR

Licensed Healthcare Professional with a B.A. in Healthcare Administration and seven years of experience. Recognized for money-saving practices, taking on additional responsibilities when needed, and skillfully overseeing construction projects. Accompanying skills include advertising/marketing, quality control, employee and resident/family member relations.

Areas of expertise and strength encompass:

▸ **Healthcare Sales and Marketing Techniques**
▸ **Epidemiology for Public Health Practice**
▸ **Legal Aspects of Healthcare Administration**
▸ **Healthcare Administration**

▸ **Human Resource Management**
▸ **Health Management Information Systems**
▸ **Health and Healthcare in the United States**
▸ **Vendor Negotiation**

CAREER HIGHLIGHTS

Demonstrated outstanding achievements as *Administrator in Training* at *Canterbury Villa* as follows:

▸ **Reduced employee turnover** from 60–70 percent to 12 percent by administering good employee relations.
▸ **Successfully increased census** from mid-60s to 84 out of 92 beds immediately following major renovation while maintaining and even increasing census during construction period.
▸ **Managed construction project**, monitoring construction groups—acting as mediator to maintain a harmonious relationship.
▸ **Saved facility money** by accepting the additional responsibility of designing company logo, brochure, and signage over and above regular job duties.

Accomplishments as *Operations Director* at *Oakhill Manor* include:

▸ **Achieved high marks** in state surveys due to proper management techniques.
▸ Assisted in implementing procedures resulting in **reduced employee injuries and resident falls** as a board member of the Safety Committee.
▸ **Ensured compliance with OSHA** and other regulatory agencies by performing daily rounds of facility.

PROFESSIONAL EXPERIENCE

CANTERBURY VILLA, Alliance, OH
(92-bed, skilled, long-term care and nursing facility)
Administrator in Training, 8/03–10/04
Completed Core of Knowledge training at Ohio State University. AIT emphasis in the business management of Medicare, Medicaid, and managed care. Reduced advertising costs by taking on added responsibility of designing logo and signage and developing radio commercials. Assisted administrator with planning, directing, and controlling general operations of facility and expanding Alzheimer's units.

PROFESSIONAL EXPERIENCE (CONT.)

Competently utilized organizational skills to manage multi-unit facility. Submitted key factor reports and conducted in-services. Aided in union management negotiations and managing union employees and team building to enhance employee relations. Collaborated in developing continuous quality improvement programs and auditing quality indicators. Assisted in the development of budgets in long term care and fiscal accountability to those budgets. Oversaw landscaping contractors and construction workers during major renovations.

OAKHILL MANOR, Louisville, OH
(114-bed, skilled, long-term care, and nursing facility),
Operations Director, 8/97–7/03
Reduced advertising costs by taking on added responsibility for designing brochures, postcards, and help wanted ads, and developing human interest articles, and radio commercials. Assisted administrator with budget and saved money by successful negotiation and comparison of vendors. Purchased office equipment and supplies. Applied working knowledge of computers, Printmaster, and word processing programs. Effectively cultivated positive employee and resident / family relations.

EDUCATION, LICENSURE, AND HONORS

Licensed Nursing Home Administrator	12/18/2004
AIT internship, Canterbury Villa, Alliance, OH	1/4–9/30/2004
Core of Knowledge – Ohio State University, Columbus, OH	8/9–8/27/2004
Bachelor of Healthcare Administration – Kennedy Western, Thousand Oaks, CA	2003
National Register's Who's Who in Executives and Professionals	2002

TRAINING SEMINARS   1998–2003
Conducting Workplace Investigations, How to Design Brochures, Legal Aspects of Human Resources, Personnel Law for Managers, Supervisor Reasonable Suspicion Training, Quality Improvement with Corporate Compliance Plans, Fire Safety, Ohio EPA, OSHA Compliance Course, Memory Enhancement Techniques, Making Supervision Super, Management Skills for the New or Prospective Manager.

PROFESSIONAL AFFILIATIONS

American College of Health Care Administrators

KERI E. ALBACH, PAC

12 Double Tree Lane • Missoula, MT 59804 • Home: (406) 555-1234 • Cell: (406) 555-5678 • kerialbach@protypeltd.com

PROFILE

- Nationally certified Physician's Assistant with diverse experience in general medicine as well as a variety of specialties.
- Passionate professional with a strong work ethic and dedication to quality patient care.
- Intellectually curious individual who welcomes new challenges.
- Self-motivated and compassionate; comfortable working independently with little supervision.
- Proficient in French; working knowledge of Spanish; cross-culturally sensitive.
- Current ACLS, CPR, and EMT certifications.

EDUCATION

BACHELOR OF SCIENCE, MEDICAL SCIENCE (May 2002)
Alderson-Broaddus College, Philippi, West Virginia

- Physician's Assistant Program
- Two years of didactic studies including: Emergency Medicine, Gerontology/Home Health Care, Surgery, Dermatology, Pediatrics, Psychiatry, OB/GYN, Clinical Practice, Applied Therapeutics, Clinical Problem Solving, Diseases of Organs and Systems, Clinical Diagnostic Procedures, History Taking and Physical Exams, Diagnostic Imaging, Pharmacology, Pathophysiology, Medical Clinical Skills/Procedures, Anatomy, Ethics, and Public Health/Community Medicine

CERTIFIED EMERGENCY MEDICAL TECHNICIAN (Spring 1996)
Loyola EMS, Chicago, Illinois

BACHELOR OF ARTS, ENGLISH LITERATURE (May 1996)
St. Lawrence University, Canton, New York

- French immersion study in Cannes, France, (Summer 1993)
- English writing and Shakespeare studies, London, England (Spring 1993)
- Completed an internship at Good Housekeeping Magazine, London, England (Spring 1993)

PROFESSIONAL EXPERIENCE

PHYSICIAN'S ASSISTANT, Colorado Joint Replacement, Denver, Colorado (2003 – 2005)

- Assisted orthopaedic physicians in primary and revision joint reconstruction.
- Provided pre-operative assessment and independent post-surgical follow-up.
- Participated in clinical research, including long- and short-term implant studies.

ORTHOPAEDIC ROTATION, Steadman-Hawkins Clinic, Vail, Colorado (2002, six weeks)

- Assisted physicians during surgery and provided pre-/post-operative care.
- Gained experience with vascular hand surgery, suturing, rehabilitation, and occupational therapy.

SURGERY ROTATION, University Health Center, Clarksburg, West Virginia (2002, six weeks)

- First and second assist in more than 200 general surgical operations.

PRIMARY CARE ROTATION, Tarboro Clinic, Tarboro, North Carolina (2002, eight weeks)

- Began as a volunteer during the Hurricane Floyd rescue mission; responsible for crisis management, setting up shelters, providing comfort care, and handling emergencies with little or no medical supplies.
- Returned for a six-week rotation and gained unique experience in primary care medicine due to the escalation of pre-existing conditions (especially among the geriatric population), communicable infections, mental health problems, and COPD caused by the crisis.

ADDITIONAL ROTATIONS (1999 – 2000)

- Pediatrics, OB/GYN, Emergency Medicine, Psychiatry, and General Internal Medicine.

RELEVANT EXPERIENCE

MEDICAL VOLUNTEER, Peace Work, Montero, Bolivia (August 2001)
- Traveled to this Third World country for the Andean Rural Health Organization.
- Provided basic medical care and immunizations; assisted in minor surgery and labor and delivery.

MEDICAL VOLUNTEER, Plains Medical Center, Limon, Colorado (1999 – 2000)
- Gained experience in small community medicine during school holidays.
- Assisted with primary care examinations, wellness counseling, and emergency procedures.

EMT, American Medical Response, Chicago, Illinois (1997 – 2000)
- Part-time position; gained hands-on experience with emergency medicine in a large city.

MEDICAL ASSISTANT, Northwestern Memorial Hospital, Chicago, Illinois (1999 – 2000)
- Assisted in providing medical/surgical and emergency medical care, including phlebotomy, EKG, and direct patient care.

MEDICAL VOLUNTEER, Loyola Orthopedic Clinic, Chicago, Illinois (1998 – 1999)
- Observed and participated in orthopedic surgery and pre-/post-operative care.

ADDITIONAL EXPERIENCE

SALES ASSOCIATE, Vegetarian Times Magazine, Chicago, Illinois (1995 – 1997)
- Sold advertising to small businesses nationwide.
- Developed marketing strategies and managed five trade shows per year.
- Wrote articles and recipes focused on nutrition and wellness.

ASSISTANT, Northwestern Memorial Hospital, Chicago, Illinois (1997 – 1998)
- Mentored by the Chief of the Immunology Laboratory; gained exposure to grant writing, diagnostic molecular biology, flow cytometry, and research.

INTERESTS

- Played college soccer for four years; selected as team captain; competed in the 1992 Nationals.
- National Scholar Athlete of the Year, 1991 (volleyball, soccer, track, and basketball).
- Enjoy skiing, hiking, waterskiing, tennis, and mountain biking.

Joyce Jacklyn Forester, RN, NHA

Phone: (719) 555-1234

1234 Valley Road, Colorado Springs, Colorado 80904

Email: jjf240@protype.ltd.com

OBJECTIVE

Progressive management role in healthcare with an emphasis on quality, cost-effective patient services and positive community relations.

PROFILE

- Experienced administrator with a progressive, holistic management approach.
- Forward-thinking manager committed to creating an environment that promotes humane, responsible care of resident populations.
- Self-motivated professional with exceptional communication and interpersonal skills.
- Colorado Licensed Nursing Home Administrator (#2097) and Registered Nurse (#57316).

EDUCATION

National Association of Boards of Examiners for Long-Term Care Administrators (2003)
- Nursing Home Administrators License

University of Colorado, Colorado Springs, CO (1999)
- Completed a Professional Advancement Certificate in Gerontology.
- Licensed to own and/or operate an assisted living facility.
- Medicaid certified.

Auburn University and Troy State University, Montgomery, AL (1990 to 1993)
- Completed credits toward a bachelor's degree in nursing.

Colorado Technical College, Colorado Springs, CO (1980 to 1982)
- Engineering studies with an emphasis on thermal energy systems.

Troy State University, Montgomery, AL (1974)
- Completed an Associate of Science in Nursing

Professional Development
- Ongoing CEUs and personal education in multiple areas of interest.

LONG-TERM CARE ADMINISTRATIVE EXPERIENCE

DIRECTOR OF NURSING
NBA Village at Skyline, Colorado Springs, CO (2002)
- Recruited to assist in opening a skilled nursing care unit to complete a continuum of care emphasizing high standards of care with a holistic approach.
- Hired 20 nursing and paraprofessional staff and successfully prepared the staff and unit for turnkey operations.
- Developed and presented in-services and nursing staff training programs.
- Customized and implemented personnel and operating policies and procedures.
- Coordinated and trained facility and outside ancillary services in the specific needs of a skilled nursing facility, including therapy, pharmacy, podiatry, dietary, security, housekeeping, human resources, and physician services.
- Supervised renovation of the existing facility to ensure that it was in compliance with state and federal regulations.
- Implemented capital expenditures and purchasing systems to obtain skilled-unit medical supplies and equipment.
- Assisted in the development and implementation of a marketing plan and toured the facility with families of prospective residents.
- Achieved state accreditation and succeeded in filling the unit within the first month.

| LONG-TERM CARE ADMINISTRATIVE EXPERIENCE (continued) | **DIRECTOR OF NURSING**
Dalraida Health Center, Montgomery, AL (1995 to 1996) |

- Managed the delivery of care to 150 geriatric patients in this long-term care facility.
- Hired to turn around this failing operation; completely overhauled the facility to comply with Medicaid, Medicare, and OSHA standards.
- Succeeded in passing inspection within three months when the facility had failed its last two inspections.
- Wrote the policy that helped resolve chronic staffing shortages.
- Provided management with better tools to evaluate staff performance and raise patient care standards.

HOSPITAL ADMINISTRATIVE EXPERIENCE

OBSTETRICS DEPARTMENT HEAD
Montgomery Regional Medical Center, Montgomery, AL (1992 to 1995)

- Hand picked to guide this hospital's new neonatal unit from the planning stage to full operation, including newborn, mother/baby (LDRP), intensive care, and transport.
- Responsible for strategic planning, capital equipment and supply purchasing, staffing, and construction supervision.
- Hired and supervised 30 RNs, LPNs, technicians, and secretaries.
- When it became difficult to hire qualified neonatal nurses, designed a complete educational and certification program that trained 15 nurses in only two months in a community-wide cooperative effort utilizing other area hospitals.
- Developed and implemented an innovative, flexible staffing program based on patient needs and cost control.
- Designed and implemented a comprehensive continuing education program for the entire staff. Once the program was successful, wrote the position description and evaluation system for a full-time nurse educator.
- Implemented all policies, procedures, and standards of care for infection control, safety, and practice.
- Designed a quality improvement plan that involved nursing staff in the development and implementation of department-specific indicators.
- Authored a security process to prevent infant abduction (Code Pink), the first policy of its kind in the city.
- Passed JCAHO survey without a single deficiency.

NURSING EXPERIENCE

STAFF AND CHARGE NURSE
St. Joseph's Convent, Colorado Springs, CO (2001 to present)
Mount St. Francis Nursing Home, Colorado Springs, CO (1998 to 2001)

- Provided compassionate nursing care to retired nuns at the St. Francis Assisted Living Facility and before that at the convent's skilled nursing facility.
- Collaborated with interdisciplinary teams to provide assessment and therapeutic management.
- Responsible for complete initial and episodic health histories and physical exams in order to identify existing and potential health problems.
- Created individualized nursing plans of care and initiated diagnostic, therapeutic, medical, and nursing actions at the request of physicians.
- Monitored and coordinated continuity of care and evaluated quality-of-life issues.
- Assessed progress, identified problems, initiated preventive measures, recognized and managed emergent problems, and initiated proper care. Documented information in residents' charts.
- Administered medication and monitored patients for side effects and adverse events.
- Provided patient and family education and support.

123 Meridian Way
Rocklin, California 95765

E-mail: klrhymes@protypeltd.com

PROFILE
- Licensed veterinarian (CA #12345, CO #6789) with an interest in internal medicine.
- Dedicated—willing to work long hours until the job is done.
- Intellectually curious professional who enjoys the challenge of learning new things.
- Self-motivated team player with strong interpersonal and communication skills.

EDUCATION

DOCTOR OF VETERINARY MEDICINE (May 1996)
Colorado State University, Fort Collins, Colorado
College of Veterinary Medicine and Biomedical Sciences
- Graduated tenth in a class of 125, *cum laude*

EQUINE SCIENCE STUDIES (1989 – 1992)
Colorado State University, Fort Collins, Colorado
College of Agricultural Sciences
- Completed 93 semester credits

EXPERIENCE

VETERINARIAN (2003 – present)
Banfield, The Pet Hospital, Sacramento, California
- Provide comprehensive medical care to companion animals with two doctors in a general veterinary practice—95% cats and dogs, 5% pocket pets.
- Perform basic surgical procedures, including routine spays/neuters, laceration repairs, and mass removals.
- Train and supervise eight veterinary technicians and office support personnel.

VETERINARIAN (2002 – 2003)
Loomis Basin Large Animal Clinic, Loomis, California
- Provided comprehensive veterinary care (approximately 80% equine, 20% food animals), alternating between routine large-animal ambulatory medicine and in-hospital management of various ICU, internal medicine, and post-operative cases.
- Assisted a board-certified equine surgeon in referral colic surgeries.
- Performed routine field surgeries and managed seasonal herd work on several local beef cattle operations.

VETERINARY MEDICAL OFFICER (2001)
USDA, Animal Plant Health Inspection Service, Richmond, Virginia
- Completed a 60-day temporary position in the United Kingdom to assist in containing and eradicating the outbreak of foot and mouth disease.
- Performed routine surveillance visits near infected areas to examine stock for clinical signs of disease.
- Collected specimens for laboratory testing and epidemiological data for analysis.
- Educated local farmers regarding appropriate biosecurity precautions and disease signs across various species.

INTERN (2000 – 2001)
LARGE ANIMAL MEDICINE AND EQUINE/FOOD ANIMAL FIELD SERVICE
Virginia/Maryland Regional College of Veterinary Medicine, Blacksburg, Virginia
- Rotated through six months of large animal internal medicine, three months of equine field service, and three months of food animal field service.
- Assisted residents and clinicians with patient diagnostics, care, and treatment.
- Performed endoscopic, bronchoscopic, and ultrasound examinations, including ultrasound guided biopsies.
- Assisted in field surgeries, including c-sections and exploratory laparotomies.
- Collected cerebrospinal fluid for analysis via atlanto-occipital and lumbosacral taps.
- Spent an elective rotation on the equine anesthesia and surgery service at the Marion duPont Scott Equine Medical Center in Leesburg, Virginia.
- Gained experience using the equine Power Float® system for routine dental floating, the placement of bit seats, and corrective dentistry methods, including hook removal, wave reduction, and incisor realignment.

EXPERIENCE **(continued)**	**VETERINARIAN** (1996 – 2000) **Captain, Veterinary Corps, United States Army,** Fort Carson, Colorado

- Provided comprehensive veterinary services in the Colorado/Wyoming region, including large and small animal care, food inspection, and zoonosis control program.
- Primary equine veterinarian for 80 horses in the cavalry battalion.
- Provided medical and surgical care for 40 military working dogs.
- Performed elective surgeries on stray facility cats and dogs, and ran clinics for privately owned pets.
- Responsible for the food inspection program at 38 military and commercial food production, storage, and delivery sites.
- Maintained liaisons with public health agencies to reduce the incidence of zoonotic diseases.
- As chief of the Fort Carson Branch Veterinary Services, trained and supervised 12 military and 7 civilian personnel.
- Wrote, published, and implemented detailed standard operating procedures for three departments.

VETERINARY ASSISTANT (1989 – 1995)
Animal Hospital Center, Englewood, Colorado (1994 – 1995)
Parker Center Animal Clinic, Parker, Colorado (Summer 1994)
Cottage Veterinary Clinic, Parker, Colorado (Summer 1993)
Squires Large Animal Practice, Parker, Colorado (Summers 1989 – 1992)

- Worked part-time and during summer breaks from college to develop skills in basic medical procedures, trauma treatment, and anesthesia.
- Assisted in emergency treatment of trauma cases, daily care and medication of hospital patients, anesthetic induction and maintenance, and animal restraint.
- Developed skills in basic medical procedures, including exposure and development of radiographs, venipuncture, intravenous catheter placement, and dental prophylaxis.
- Performed various laboratory tests, including chemistry panels and complete blood counts.
- Kept patient records; exercised and fed pets; and stocked ambulatory truck.
- Accompanied veterinarians in medical and surgical farm calls.

PROFESSIONAL **DEVELOPMENT**	**Wild West Veterinary Conference,** Reno, Nevada (2004)

California Regional Education Symposium (CARES), Pomona, California (2002)

Virginia/Maryland Regional College of Veterinary Medicine, Blacksburg, Virginia (2000 – 2001)
- **Certificate of Internship, Large Animal Internal Medicine (12 months)**

Colorado State University, Fort Collins, Colorado (1999)
- **Diagnosis and Treatment of Lameness in the Horse (3 days)**
- Equine Dentistry (3 days)

Department of Defense Military Working Dog Center (1998)
- Clinical Proficiency Course, Canine Specialist Training (1 week)

HONORS & **AWARDS**	• Member, Phi Zeta, National Veterinary Medicine Honor Society (1995) • Recipient of the Salisbury Scholarship for superior scholarship, initiative, perseverance, potential for leadership, and financial need (1995 – 1996) • Ken Lawson Award for meritorious and deserving PVM students with proven ability and probability of success with a preference for large animal practice (1993 – 1994) • Member, Alpha Zeta, Academic/Agricultural Fraternity (1991 – present) • Member, Phi Eta Sigma, Academic Honor Society (1990 – present)

COMMUNITY **SERVICE**	• Horsepower Handicapped Riding Association (1 year) • National Spinabifida Convention (1 year) • NARHA 20-Mile Benefit Rideathon for Handicapped Riding Programs (2 years) • Colorado Junior Wheelchair Sports Camp (4 years)

JASON M. LEE, MD, FACP

Contact	**Home:** 123 Roaming Road West, Monument, CO 80132
	Phone: (719) 555-1234
	Office: 1140 Amsterdam Street, Colorado Springs, CO 80907
	Phone: (719) 555-5678 ▪ **Pager:** (719) 555-4321 ▪ **Fax:** (719) 555-8765
	Email: LeeJM@protypeltd.com

Education

Bachelor of Science, Biology (1975)
Mississippi, College, Clinton, MS

Doctor of Medicine (1980)
Medical College of Wisconsin, Milwaukee, WI

Rotating Internship (1980 –1981)
William Beaumont Army Medical Center, El Paso, TX

Internal Medicine Residency (1985 –1988)
Tripler Army Medical Center, Honolulu, HI

Nuclear Medicine Fellowship (1993 –1995)
Fitzsimons Army Medical Center, Aurora, CO

Board Certifications

- American Board of Nuclear Medicine, 12345 (1995)
- American Board of Internal Medicine, 123456 (1988)
- National Board of Medical Examiners, 1-234-567-8 (1981)

Medical Licenses

- Colorado #12345
- Florida #ME 0012345

Professional Positions

Chief, Primary Care Careline (2000 – present)
Chief, Department of Nuclear Medicine (1996 – present)
Colonel, U.S. Army Medical Corps, Evans Army Community Hospital, Fort Carson, CO

0.1 FTE Administration
- Member, Risk Management Committee (1996 – present)
- Member, Radiation Control Committee (1996 – present)
- Member, Information Management Guidance Council (1998 – present)
- Member, Executive Committee of Medical Staff (1998 – present)
- Member, Credentials Committee (2000 – present)

0.7 FTE Internal Medicine Provider
- Manage a panel of patients over and under 65 years old
- Serve inpatient call, which includes such procedures as ventilator management, elective cardioversion, and central venous catheter insertion
- Perform outpatient procedures, including flexible sigmoidoscopy, treadmill and pharmacology stress tests for nuclear medicine
- Interpret PFT, EKG, Holter monitors, and sleep apnea monitors

Professional Positions (continued)	*0.2 FTE Nuclear Medicine* • Design and interpret nuclear medicine studies • Manage the Nuclear Regulatory Commission license • Diagnose and treat thyroid disorders, including outpatient and inpatient thyroid cancer and outpatient hyperthyroidism with I131 **Chief, Department of Nuclear Medicine** (1995 –1996) Fitzsimons Army Medical Center, Aurora, CO **Internal Medicine Staff** (1992) **Nuclear Surety Officer, Southern European Task Force** (1991 – 1992) **Officer in Charge, Nuclear Accident Initial Response Team** (1991 – 1992) **Chief, Department of Internal Medicine** (1990 – 1991) 45th Field Hospital, Vicenza, Italy **Chief, Department of Internal Medicine** (1988 – 1990) 196th Station Hospital, Supreme Headquarters Allied Powers Europe, Mons, Belgium **Chief Resident, Department of Internal Medicine** (1987 – 1988) Triper Army Medical Center, Honolulu, HI **Battalion Surgeon / Staff Physician** (1981 – 1985) 3/325th Airborne Infantry Combat Team / 45th Field Hospital, Vicenza, Italy

Teaching	**Evans Army Community Hospital**, Fort Carson, CO
	• Intramural Presentations Annually (1996 – present)
	  – Mortality and Morbidity Conference
	  – Grand Rounds
	• Phase II Physician Assistants (1996 – present)
	• Advanced Cardiac Life Support Instructor (1996 – present)
	• Pediatric Advanced Life Support Instructor (1998 – present)
	• Radiology Residents, University of Colorado (1999 – 2000)
	
	Fitzsimons Army Medical Center, Aurora, CO
	• Radiology Residents, Department of Nuclear Medicine (1995 – 1996)

Publications	• Lee JM., Christensen R, Lambert A, Solano RK. (1995). Assessment of dietary calcium intake, physical activity, and habits affecting skeletal health among pre-menopausal women (Abstract). • Lee JM, Christensen R, Lambert A, Solano RK. (1995). The effects of region-specific resistance exercises on bone mass in pre-menopausal military women (Abstract). • Lee JM, Kunkel MR, Friesenegger K, Solano RK, McBiles M, McNaly, PR. (1996, May 19–22). Can esophageal acid instillation precipitate myocardial ischemia in patients with known coronary artery disease (CAD): A prospective evaluation. *American Gastroenterological Association and American Association for the Study of Liver Diseases* (Abstract).

Publications (continued)	▪ Lee JM, Lambert A, Solano RK, Kim SY, Druger M, Calagan J. (1995). Simultaneous transmission/emission protocol (STEP) for attenuation correction of breast and diaphragmatic attenuation artifacts during SPECT 99mtc-Sestamibi myocardial perfusion scans in women without coronary disease (Abstract). ▪ Lee JM, Lambert A, Cote MG, Solano RK. (1995). Diuretic renogram: Past, present, and future. *Nuclear Medicine Annual*, pp. 185–216. ▪ Lee JM, Clement J, Solano K, Vanherweghem JL, van der Groen G. (1990). Hemorrhagic fever with renal syndrome in a Canadian serviceman. *CMAJ*, 143(1): 38–40.
Academic Appointments	**Instructor** (1983) Department of Military Medicine Uniformed Services University of Health Sciences, Bethesda, MD

Postgraduate Medical Education	▪ Pediatric Advanced Life Support Instructor (1998 – present)
	▪ Advanced Cardiac Life Support
	  – Instructor (1988 – present)
	  – Affiliate Faculty (1992, 1993)
	  – Course Director (1990, 1991)
	  – Provider (1981 – 1987)
	▪ Combat Casualty Management, Echelon III Course (1996)
	▪ Medical Defense Against Biological Warfare Agents Course (1996)
	▪ Medical Management of Chemical Casualties Course (1996)
	▪ Medical Officers Course in Nuclear Medicine and Radioisotope Techniques (1994)
	▪ Nuclear Hazards Training Course (1992)
	▪ Medical Effects of Nuclear Accidents Course (1991)
	▪ Advanced Trauma Life Support Provider (1987, 1991)
	▪ Combat Casualty Course (1981)

Honors	▪ U.S. Army Meritorious Service Medal (1990, 1993, 1996) ▪ U.S. Army Commendation Medal (1985) ▪ Health Professions Scholarship Program Recipient (1976)
Professional Affiliations	▪ Member, American College of Physicians ▪ Member, Society of Nuclear Medicine ▪ American College of Nuclear Physicians, Physician Outreach Program
Community	▪ Member, American Heart Association Board of Directors (1999 – 2002)
Military Qualifications	▪ Expert Field Medical Badge (1983) ▪ Airborne Parachute Jump School (1981)

DATE OF CV 04/03

PROFILE

- Certified School Psychologist with a broad range of experience in:
  - Consultation
  - Educational programming
  - Assessment
  - Behavior management
  - Individual assessment plans
  - Mentoring
  - Group therapy
  - Individual therapy
  - Play therapy
- Practical experience in assessing the cognitive, social, emotional, and adaptive needs of children with various disabilities.
- Proven ability to set high standards and motivate students to achieve success.
- Able to work with diverse age groups and populations; sensitive to each student's needs.
- Effective team player with proven listening, interpersonal, and communication skills.

EDUCATION

Ed.S. IN SCHOOL PSYCHOLOGY (2003)
University of Northern Colorado, Greeley, Colorado

MS.Ed. IN SPECIAL EDUCATION (1999)
Old Dominion University, Norfolk, Virginia
Emphasis on learning disabilities and emotional disabilities
Licensed Special Education Teacher K–12 (Colorado)

B.S. IN PSYCHOLOGY (1995)
University of Maryland, Heidelberg, Germany

PROFESSIONAL EXPERIENCE

SCHOOL PSYCHOLOGIST (2003 – present)
Harrison School District 2, Colorado Springs, Colorado

- Serve as a consultant, diagnostician, and therapist for an elementary school, middle school, alternative middle/high school, and a charter high school.
- Administer and interpret educational assessments; share findings with parents, classroom teachers, and school administrators.
- Conduct functional behavior and risk assessments and develop interventions and behavior management plans.
- Develop and conduct individual, group, and play therapy sessions.
- Consult with both regular and special education teachers to develop and implement educational strategies to facilitate learning success in the classroom.
- Create and plan educational programming for individual students.
- Developed course content and teach special education instructors how to administer and interpret special education academic testing.
- Counsel individuals with learning disabilities, physical handicaps, health impairments, behavior disorders, and those identified as gifted and talented.
- Currently mentoring a special education teacher.
- Serve as a member of the district's Strategic Planning Committee responsible for rewriting regulations to ensure compliance with the reauthorization of IDEA.
- Selected for the Positive Behavior Support Team and Student Study Support Team.

HONORARIUM INSTRUCTOR (2001 – present)
University of Colorado, Colorado Springs, Colorado

- Teach Psycho-Educational Assessment and Educational Psychology to graduate students and professional educators in the Master of Education and Master of Special Education Programs.
- Developed and implemented a unique hands-on curriculum, examinations, and multi-media presentation materials.

PROFESSIONAL EXPERIENCE

SPECIAL EDUCATION COORDINATOR (1999 – 2003)

The New Horizons Alternative School, Colorado Springs, Colorado
- Coordinated special education services for 7–12 grade students with learning and emotional disabilities.
- Developed intervention, program, and transition plans.
- Wrote Individualized Education Plans (IEPs) and psycho-educational reports.
- Facilitated multi-disciplinary team meetings.
- Developed and taught annual classes in psycho-educational assessment at the District 2 New Staff Institute.
- Supervised, trained, and evaluated special education student teachers as a cooperating teacher for the University of Colorado at Colorado Springs.
- Served as acting administrator in the absence of the principal.
- Certified ACT administrator and Accommodations Coordinator (1999 – 2003).
- Member of the interviewing and hiring team for new teachers and paraprofessionals (1999 – 2003).
- Member of the District Literacy Team responsible for developing a new literacy program, including curriculum and tests (2001 – 2002).
- Member of the District Transition Team that provided career and continuing education services to special education students between 18 and 21 years of age (1999 – 2000).

SIED TEACHER (1998 – 1999)

Southeast Cooperative Educational Program, Norfolk, Virginia
- Taught emotionally disabled students in 7–8th grade programs for the most at-risk students (expelled, violent, economically disadvantaged, and prison populations).

MENTAL HEALTH WORKER, TEACHER'S ASSISTANT (1998)

Southeast Virginia Training Center, Chesapeake, Virginia
- Worked with nonverbal adults in classroom and residential settings.
- Taught sign language to improve the communication abilities of adult autistic residents.

DISCIPLINE COORDINATOR, TEACHER'S ASSISTANT (1997 – 1998)

Chesapeake Bay Academy, Chesapeake, Virginia
- Served as an intervention specialist for this private school for learning disabled and ADHD children. Investigated incidents, determined disciplinary actions, and developed classroom interventions to prevent future problems.
- Assisted in teaching second and third grade classes for the first half of the year before being promoted to discipline coordinator for the entire K–12 population.

ACTIVE DUTY MILITARY (1990 – 1997)

United States Air Force (honorably discharged)
- Desert Storm Veteran who served four years as a paralegal and three years as a vehicle mechanic.

CONTINUING EDUCATION

- Positive Behavior Support, 12 hours (2003)
- WISC IV Training, The Psychological Corporation (2003)
- Depression: Comprehensive Assessment and Treatment of Children, Adolescents, and Adults, Medical Educational Services, 8 hours (2003)
- ADHD: Beyond the Label–Assessment, Treatment, and Educational Interventions, Medical Educational Services, 8 hours (2003)
- Crisis Response and Intervention, National Emergency Response Team, 16 hours (2002)
- Threat and Suicide Assessment, CSSP, 8 hours (2002)
- Special Education Law, Law Advisory Council, 8 hours (1999)

INTERNSHIP **SCHOOL PSYCHOLOGY INTERNSHIP** (2002 – 2003)
Harrison School District 2, Colorado Springs, Colorado
- Completed an intensive 1,200 hour internship in an elementary school, middle school, and alternative night high school program.
- Provided psycho-educational assessment, individual and play therapy, and direct/indirect consultation.

PRACTICUMS
- Cognitive Assessment, Gorman Middle School, Harrison District 2, Colorado Springs, Colorado (Fall Semester 2000)
- Personality Assessment, Colleagues and Families, Colorado Springs, Colorado (Spring Semester 2001)
- Individual Counseling, Buena Vista Elementary School, Colorado Springs District 11 (Fall Semester 2001)
- Systems Intervention, The New Horizons Alternative School, Harrison District 2, Colorado Springs, Colorado (Spring Semester 2002)

AFFILIATIONS National Association of School Psychologists

COMPUTERS Knowledge of Windows, MS Word, PowerPoint, Excel, and computerized IEP programs.

ASSESSMENT
SKILLS

WISC-IV, WISC-III	Barkley Behavior Rating Scales	R-Inventory
WPPSI	Vineland Adaptive Behavior Scales	Connors
WAIS-III	Draw a Picture, Tell a Story	PCSS
DAS	Sentence Completion	RCMAS
CAS	Madeline Thomas Stories	BASC
TONI-2	Thematic Appreciation Test	APS
GAMA	Beck Depression Inventory	PIC
Bayley	Reynolds Depression Inventories	DAP, QSS
Mullins	WJ-III	DAP, SPED
Stanford-Binet	WIAT	MAT
Unit	WRAT-III	Bender
MMPI-2	H-T-P	PPVT III

MICHAEL J. ALLAN

QUALIFICATIONS

- Passionate school superintendent with diverse experience in:
  - Organizational development
  - Strategic planning
  - Capital improvements
  - School finance/budgeting
  - Community engagement
  - Staff development
  - Consensus building
  - Partnership development
  - Technology integration
  - Appreciative inquiry model of leadership
  - Curriculum alignment
  - Assessment and accountability
  - Communication
  - Public relations
- Dedicated professional with a personal commitment to excellence in education.
- Innovative leader with the proven ability to manage a large, complex organization with integrity.
- Dynamic communicator with a talent for motivating others and building strong community networks.
- Experienced in the Malcolm Baldrige Model and Covey Principles of Leadership.

EDUCATION

MASTER OF ARTS, **University of Colorado**, Colorado Springs, Colorado (1995)
- Major in Curriculum and Instruction and Educational Leadership
- Type D Administrative Certification

BACHELOR OF ARTS, **Colorado State University**, Fort Collins, Colorado (1984)
- Major in History and Teacher Education

PROFESSIONAL EXPERIENCE

SUPERINTENDENT (June 2003 – present)
Sheridan School District, Sheridan, Colorado
Lead a metropolitan school district with more than 1,800 students, five schools, a staff of 235, and an annual budget of $29 million. Providing the leadership and change management strategies to steer an underperforming district toward academic growth. Challenged with a district where more than 80% of the elementary students are on the free or reduced lunch program, at least 40% of the student population are ELA learners, 30% of the children live outside of the district, and a high percentage are at risk. Hired staff and developed comprehensive career development programs to improve employee performance.

Accomplishments
- Created a new vision and mission statement with measurable strategic goals. Used the Appreciative Inquiry Model to assist in creating strategic direction and goals for the district.
- Turned around a district with declining enrollment and test scores (on the Accreditation Watch List), low morale, and an overall poor reputation.
- Succeeded in creating trust within the staff and community.
- Led an elementary school restructuring to better utilize staff and district resources.
- Developed a district improvement plan that aligns so well with the consolidated grant that the Colorado Department of Education uses it as a model for other districts.

Student Achievement
- Improved 2004 third grade CSAP reading scores by the highest margin in the Front Range metropolitan area.
- Led the reversal in CSAP results from a decline in 15 areas to an improvement in 13 areas out of 23 tested in 2004.
- Implemented the Colorado Reading First program in all elementary schools.
- Held an academic summit to create curriculum that is now aligned in reading, writing, and math with all content areas for PreK–12.
- Created best practices for local and state assessments and ensured that academic data reached all the way down to the student level.
- Revised the calendar to increase instructional days prior to CSAP testing.
- Developed new tools to assist in monitoring ILP and IEP students and improving grade books.

Fiscal Responsibility
- Set budget priorities and successfully administered a $16 million general fund.
- Created a budget calendar that increased stakeholder involvement at the building and community level.
- Directed the development of a capital reserve plan that strategically allocated funds to transportation and facilities improvement, dramatically increasing the quality of buses (newest was 18 years old) and the facades of buildings.
- Collaborated with a variety of partners to continue funding for the Sheridan Health Clinic, including Children's Hospital and the University of Colorado School of Nursing.

**PROFESSIONAL
EXPERIENCE •**

Fiscal Responsibility (continued)
Managed a $1.8 million Head Start budget for four districts, including Cherry Creek, Littleton, Englewood, and Sheridan.
• Directed the successful implementation of the $1+ million Colorado Reading First grant.
• Led the Board of Education in an effort to refinance bonds to save taxpayers money and to create funds for revitalizing technology.

Human Resources
• Led the district's effort to ensure that all staff met the requirements of NCLB in the area of "highly qualified."
• Directed the district team during collaboration with the teacher's union.
• Implemented an electronic timecard system to meet Department of Labor standards for classified employees.
• Developed and implemented a revised evaluation tool for teachers and classified employees.
• Created staff development plans that created two late starts per month for professional development activities.

Community Partnerships
• Led the Board of Education in developing a comprehensive community engagement plan.
• Expanded the Board of Education's community engagement model to establish sounding boards, community walks, and task forces.
• Fostered and enhanced relationships with community service organizations.

Technology
• Directed the district's efforts to create a spending plan for a $2.0 million technology refinance project.
• Created a technology integration position for the district that supports teaching staff and improves the utilization of technology resources to impact student achievement.
• Implemented Infinite Campus, a student information system that not only handles student data but also provides a parent communication tool, data management system, and a master scheduling tool.
• Brought Edison's benchmark tool to the district, which helps monitor the progress toward meeting standards.

EXECUTIVE DIRECTOR OF ASSESSMENT, RESEARCH, TECHNOLOGY SUPPORT (May 2002 – present)
Colorado Springs School District 11, Colorado Springs, Colorado
Directed all operations related to research, planning, assessment, evaluation, technology integration, and technology support for every school in the district (elementary, middle/senior high, and charter schools). Participated in the development of long-range strategic plans for the district and the department. Collaborated with the Division of Information Technology and Division of Instruction to increase school and district effectiveness. Developed assessment methodology, reporting systems, and related utilization of technology.

Served as a liaison between the Research Center of the University of Colorado at Colorado Springs and District 11's Board of Education. Developed and led the Coordination Committee responsible for bringing IT and Instruction together on a district level. Oversaw the Evaluation Unit that monitors district programs, task forces, and initiatives. Met weekly with Instructional Services to align technology integration and assessment with the needs of literacy resource teachers and instructional specialists. Prepared and presented monthly reports to the Board of Education to communicate assessment results, technology trends, and state accountability issues.

Accomplishments
• Significantly revitalized the Assessment Unit by improving communication and implementing changes based on feedback from performance measurements.
• Personally conducted teacher telephone surveys throughout the year to evaluate service delivery.
• Piloted the concept of Building Assessment Teams to promote better utilization of assessment data.
• Coordinated a Brown Bag staff development series that improved the utilization of technology tools in all schools and increased the quality of instruction.
• Improved service delivery by aligning the work of technical support, network administration, and the call center.
• Served on the District Evaluation Committee responsible for redesigning teacher evaluations so they better aligned with teaching standards and accountability.

PROFESSIONAL EXPERIENCE

PRINCIPAL, Mitchell High School, District 11, Colorado Springs, Colorado (August 1997 – May 2002)
Managed a high school with 1,500 students. Provided the leadership to improve curriculum development, instruction, administration, school climate, and academic achievement. Hired, supervised, and evaluated a staff of 125 teachers and support people. Served as a liaison between the school's administration and other principals in the district. Directed a CIVA charter school with 150 students for three years.

Accomplishments
- Selected to turn around a high school with declining enrollment, low teacher morale, a high dropout rate, deteriorating building, and poor academic reputation.
- Succeeded in revitalizing the staff and building consensus among teachers, the community, and students.
- Created a safe, productive, caring, and positive school climate through effective leadership that included modeling, rewards, communication, increased visibility, and appreciation for diversity.
- Developed and implemented innovative programs that have made Mitchell a magnet in the district.
- Implemented a variety of intervention programs to promote student achievement and retention.
- Improved attendance three percentage points by increasing the visibility of security personnel and creating an Attendance Committee that revised policies and improved parental involvement.

Student Achievement
- Designed and implemented aggressive new standards for curriculum, instruction, and assessment.
- Established an emphasis on instruction and ensured that all students were academically challenged and individually successful.
- Developed better programs and course offerings that resulted in the highest ACT improvement of any large high school on the Front Range.
- Improved writing scores on the DWA state assessments by an entire grade level.
- Achieved the highest scholarship dollar amount per graduate of any school in the district.
- Implemented the Renaissance Program to recognize academic achievement through honors, school privileges, discounts, public recognition, and incentive.

Fiscal Responsibility and Grants
- Campaigned heavily for the mill levy with school staff, parent groups, and interested community members.
- Set budgetary priorities and administered a $125,000 instruction budget and more than $100,000 in student activity accounts.
- Oversaw $90,000 in funds for the Colorado School Improvement and Incentive Program.

Technology
- Coordinated integration of technology with curriculum and instruction.
- Collaborated with Cisco to create the Cisco Networking Academy Program to prepare students for jobs in computer technology. Improved instructor technical proficiency by partnering with Pikes Peak Community College for professional development programs.
- Implemented Mastery in Motion software programs to help staff disaggregate data to assist with lesson planning and intervention.
- Implemented the Project Lead the Way program to provide hands-on career preparation and internships with local business partners in engineering fields.
- Redesigned the planetarium and added an outdoor aeroscience/space deck for advanced studies in space and aeronautical sciences.

Community Partnerships
- Recognized twice by the Chamber of Commerce for excellence in community partnerships.
- Partnered with Booz-Allen Hamilton, ARINC, WorldCom, and the Citadel Mall to adopt classes. Employees follow the students through all four years of high school, providing mentoring, career exploration, and training opportunities. Received the Colorado CAPE Award for the Booz-Allen Hamilton partnership.
- Developed a unique partnership with Peterson Air Force Base to enhance the Career Technology Center.
- Created an award-winning mentorship program with the Colorado Springs Firefighters Association that involves local firefighters mentoring at-risk students.
- Developed community partnerships to rehabilitate the physical plant using volunteer help and donated materials, which has generated a new sense of pride among Mitchell students.

Program Development
- Secured an Air Force Junior ROTC Program for the school by building support from central administration, the community, and the military. Ranked as the number one site in the entire western region.

PROFESSIONAL
EXPERIENCE

Program Development (continued)
- Created the SAIL+ Program (Student-Centered Academic Interdisciplinary Lab) for gifted ninth-grade students, leading to an Honors Endorsement Program that is individualized to each student.
- Led the development of a courtroom building that provides classroom space for pre-law courses, mock trial competitions, and simulations of actual court cases.
- Implemented a pilot mentorship program called "Choices" to teach junior and senior student leaders how to mentor freshmen classmates toward improved performance.
- Developed a partnership with the El Paso county building and construction industry to provide hands-on experience for students interested in the trade.
- Approached the El Paso County Contractors Association for grants and sponsorships for the Wheels of Learning program, which prepares students for careers in the building trades.

ADJUNCT PROFESSOR, University of Phoenix, Colorado Springs, Colorado (April 2000 – present)
- Teach graduate students and professional educators seeking advanced degrees and new certifications.
- Develop course content, examinations, and presentation materials. Certified to teach:
  - Human Relations and Organizational Behavior in Education
  - Human Resource Management in Education
  - Instruction Program Management and Evaluation
  - Critical Issues in Education
  - School Law for Educators
  - Education Finance and Budgeting
  - The Role of the Principal

HONORS &
AWARDS

- Subject of a *Rocky Mountain News* series covering the first year of a metropolitan superintendent in a challenging school district.
- Named CHSAA Activity Educator of the Month for revitalizing the Sheridan athletic program, 2004
- Finalist, District 11 Deputy Superintendent of Instruction Search, 2001
- Recipient, Chuck Gaul Award for Outstanding Principal of the Year, 2000
- International Who's Who of Administrators, 1999
- Who's Who of American Teachers, 1994, 1996, 1998, 2001
- IBM Educator of the Month, 1992, 1993
- Recipient, Doherty High School Homecoming Most Valuable Staff Member, 1993

PRESENTATIONS

- Presented "Community Engagement 101" at the 2004 Colorado Association of School Boards Conference.

DISTRICT 11 •
COMMITTEES

- Member of the District 11 Superintendent's Cabinet
- Teacher Recruitment and District Interview Teams
- District Evaluation Task Force
- Baldrige Technical Assistance Team
- Coordinating Committee
- Committee for Alternative Licensing and Student Teaching
- New Chart of Accounts Committee
- District Improvement Planning Team
- District Accountability Advisory Committee
- Safe Schools Committee
- Renaissance Committee
- Building Accountability Committee
- Conversion Committee
- Diversity in Action Committee
- Staff Development Committee
- Staff Recognition Committee
- Custodial Cuts Committee
- Community Use and Rental Committee

AFFILIATIONS

- Member of the CHSAA's Vision Development Committee responsible for promoting forward thinking on the potential delivery of CHSAA's services to the community, 2005 – present
- Vice Chair, Colorado On-Line Board, 2002 – present
- Member, DeVry University Advisory Board, 2002 – 2003
- Past President, Colorado Springs Principals Association, 2002 – 2003
- President, Colorado Springs Principals Association, 2001 – 2002

ADDRESS

1234 East Dry Creek Place • Aurora, Colorado 80016
Home: (303) 555-1234 • Cellular: (303) 555-5678 • Email: MJAllan@protypeltd.com

P.O. Box 1234
Monument, CO 80132

E-mail: kprteam@protypeltd.com

Home: (719) 555-1234
Cellular: (719) 555-5678

PROFILE

- *Innovative Registered Nurse with a reputation for astute clinical judgment and creative thinking.*
- *Compassionate caregiver who is able to quickly establish and maintain rapport with patients.*
- *Adept at working independently and in high-pressure situations that require quick thinking.*
- *Well-organized and efficient; committed to providing excellence in patient care.*

EDUCATION

BACHELOR OF SCIENCE, NURSING
University of Southern Mississippi, Hattiesburg, Mississippi

EXPERIENCE

General Nursing

- *Provided comprehensive nursing care in obstetrics, medical intensive care, and pediatric surgical units.*
- *Collaborated with interdisciplinary teams to provide assessment and therapeutic management of patients and families both in hospital and clinic settings.*
- *Responsible for complete initial and episodic health histories and physical exams in order to identify existing and potential health problems.*
- *Created individualized nursing plans of care and initiated diagnostic, therapeutic, medical, and nursing actions at the request of physicians.*
- *Monitored and coordinated continuity of care and evaluated quality-of-life issues.*
- *Assessed progress, identified problems, initiated preventive measures, recognized and managed emergent problems, and initiated proper care. Documented information in patient charts.*
- *Administered medication and blood products, monitoring patients for side effects and adverse events.*
- *Utilized basic life support skills in life-threatening crises and cardiopulmonary arrests.*
- *Provided cardiac and hemodynamic monitoring and dialysis treatments.*
- *Undergraduate degree program included public health nursing involving chronic medical, maternal-child, and occupational care.*

Specialty Nursing

- *Managed the lab operations of a busy internal medicine clinic (now under the auspices of Duke University) and served as general office nurse seeing up to 50 patients per day.*
- *Assisted with routine, Cesarean, and Lamaze deliveries as staff nurse on a hospital obstetrics unit.*
- *Performed initial baseline exams in the ER to determine obstetrical admission needs and utilized internal/external fetal monitoring devices.*
- *Assumed periodic Code Blue/Emergency Nurse responsibilities for the MICU and CCU.*
- *Served as a staff nurse with Duke University Medical Center on a 24-bed psychiatric intermediate care unit.*
- *Covered two patient populations in the psychiatric research unit—intractable pain and anorexia nervosa—and documented extensive research data.*
- *Co-facilitated psychotherapy groups and a weekly Alzheimer's family support group.*
- *Assisted patients with biofeedback and physical therapy treatments.*
- *Completed a psychiatric nursing rotation as part of undergraduate studies, involving one-on-one counseling at a local hospital, facilitating a small group at a state school for the handicapped, and directing a group at the state mental hospital. Gained intensive care experience caring for individuals with alcoholism and suicide attempts.*

Administration

- *Served as a charge nurse responsible for providing leadership in the delivery of care and utilization of resources.*
- *Made staffing assignments that considered patient needs, staff competencies, and standards of care.*
- *Assisted staff in establishing priorities for patient care and bed management.*
- *Ensured that nursing performance met all regulatory agency requirements and hospital standards.*
- *Facilitated communication with patients, families, physicians, staff members, and other healthcare professionals to achieve desired patient outcomes.*
- *Developed interview guidelines and application forms for candidates of overseas nonprofit programs.*
- *Planned and coordinated two annual mission conferences with more than 300 participants each.*
- *Part of a team responsible for revising and writing outreach policies, budgets, and financial strategies for three nonprofit organizations.*
- *Promoted and coordinated a seminar on Muslim understanding and outreach through the Billy Graham Center.*

EXPERIENCE (continued)

Teaching
- Participated in the professional development of nurses through the preceptor program and peer review process.
- Educated patients and families and provided counseling and supportive care.
- Helped to teach Red Cross orientation classes for expectant parents.
- Taught cardiopulmonary resuscitation and basic life support skills as a Certified CPR Instructor.
- Taught elementary school classes for the Colorado Springs High Country Educators and in several local nontraditional education settings.
- Organized field trips and arranged for community classes in order to encourage experiential learning.
- Home schooled two children for nine years—developed individualized curriculum for each year instead of using standardized curriculum.
- Developed and co-taught a three-month class called "Perspectives on the World Christian Movement."

HISTORY

Owner/Videographer, RetroV, Colorado Springs, CO (2001 – present)
Teacher, Home School Group, Colorado Springs, CO (1992 – 2001)
Office Nurse, Durham Medical Center, Durham, NC (1982 – 1984)
Charge Nurse, Psychiatric Unit, Duke University Medical Center, Durham, NC (1979 – 1983)
MICU Nurse, Wake County Medical Center, Raleigh, NC (1979)
Staff Nurse, Surgical-Pediatric Unit, Duke University Medical Center, Durham, NC (1978 – 1979)
Staff Nurse, Labor and Delivery, Forrest County General Hospital, Hattiesburg, MS (1978)

PRESENTATIONS

- Co-presenter, "Self-Care of the Caregiver," Duke University Medical Center, Alzheimer's Family Support Group (1982 – 1983).
- "Physician's Perceptions of the Roles and Responsibilities of the Family Nurse Practitioner in a Small Southern City," University of Southern Mississippi (USM), Final Statistical Research Paper (January 1978).
- "Health Care Delivery System in the U.S.," USM, Public Health Nursing Internship (January 1978).
- "Legal Issues in Nursing," USM, Medical/Surgical Nursing Internship (January 1977).
- "Postpartum Nutrition," USM, Obstetrical Nursing (May 1977).

CONTINUING EDUCATION

University of North Carolina, Chapel Hill and Duke University Medical Center
- RN Refresher Program: 140 hours didactic, 160 hours clinical preceptorship on a surgical oncology unit

Duke University Medical Center
- Assessment and Management of Seizures
- Biofeedback and Management of Chronic Pain
- Relaxation Techniques and Swedish Massage
- Connective Tissue Massage
- Touch as a Therapeutic Modality
- Perspectives on Psychiatric Care
- Community Mental Health
- Third-Party Reimbursement
- Ethical Dilemmas of a Psychiatric Patient's Right to Refuse Treatment
- Delivery of Mental Health Care Services to Minorities
- The Aggressive Patient: How to Prevent Explosions
- CPR Instructor Certification
- Neurology Assessment
- Brain Dysfunction
- Dementias
- Psychosomatic Patients
- Electro-Convulsive Therapy
- Assertiveness Training
- Family Assessment
- Sexual Assessment
- Implications of Ethnicity
- Implications of Aging
- The Cult Phenomenon/Life After a Cult

Wake Medical Center
- Respiratory Therapy and Arterial Blood Gas Interpretations
- Assessment of Renal Function
- Assessment and Skills for Critical Care Nursing (32 hours)
- Basic Life Support and CPR Certification (16 hours)
- Coronary Care Educational Program (72 hours)

Forrest General Hospital
- Intravenous Therapy
- Assessment and Treatment of Obstetrical Complications

PROFESSIONAL DEVELOPMENT

- "Christianity and Psychiatry: Are They Compatible?," 8-week course taught by Duke University physicians
- "Christian Psychotherapy Seminars," weekly seminars for nine months by Duke University physicians

Richard L. Henry, MA

1234 Osage Avenue, Apt. 19
Manitou Springs, Colorado 80829

Cellular: (719) 555-1234
Email: henry@protypeltd.com

PROFILE	<ul><li>Qualified instructor with a background in teaching: – sociology courses to college students – clinicians in the social services field regarding issues related to age, cultural, and gender diversity – sociology, history, social science, anthropology, and English to the at-risk youth populations</li><li>Proven ability to reach out to a diverse population regardless of ethnicity or socioeconomic status.</li><li>Effective team player with strong communication, interpersonal, and presentation skills.</li><li>Self-motivated professional who works well in groups or independently without supervision.</li><li>Proficient in Windows, MS Word, Excel, PowerPoint, Adobe Photoshop, and Internet research.</li><li>Adept at installing and maintaining computer hardware and peripherals.</li></ul>
TEACHING STRENGTHS	<ul><li>Able to teach across a broad spectrum, including sociology, anthropology, psychology, and human-services-related fields.</li><li>Strong educational background in the prime analysis and understanding of various dynamic sociological theoretical models, including structural functionalism, social conflict, and symbolic interactionism with additional theoretical strengths in gender and cultural diversity.</li><li>Proficient in the sociological aspects of Strain Theory, statistical analysis, methods of social research, criminology, deviance, and war.</li><li>Bring to the classroom a diverse perspective gained in extensive real-world experience as a psychotherapist, administrator, and program analyst/developer.</li><li>Proven ability to use innovative, cross-disciplinary resources to maximize the learning experience, including Internet resources, media, and experiential teaching.</li><li>Able to lead students and colleagues in problem solving, discussion, and logistical/tactical analysis of programmatic issues.</li></ul>
EDUCATION	**MASTER OF ARTS IN SOCIOLOGY** (1998) **University of Colorado**, Colorado Springs, Colorado <ul><li>Emphasis: Cultural/Gender Diversity and Organizational/Structural Theories</li><li>Secondary Graduate Tract: Licensing in Nonprofit Organizational Management/Human Resources</li></ul>**BACHELOR OF ARTS IN SOCIOLOGY** (1991) **University of Oklahoma**, Norman, Oklahoma <ul><li>Emphasis: Political and Cultural Theory</li><li>Minor in Social Work: Emphasis on Family Dynamics/Systems and Clinical Theory</li></ul>**PROFESSIONAL DEVELOPMENT** <ul><li>Legal and Ethical Issues in Counseling, Social Work, and Mental Health (2000)</li><li>Licensed Type III Emergency Teacher and Registered Psychotherapist, Colorado (1998 – present)</li><li>Critical Incident Stress Management (1997)</li><li>Disaster Response Protocols, Disaster Response Team (1997)</li><li>Brief Therapy Working with Adolescents, Colorado Health Networks (1996)</li></ul>
TEACHING EXPERIENCE	**PIKES PEAK COMMUNITY COLLEGE**, Colorado Springs, Colorado (2001 – present) **Adjunct Professor, Sociology Department** <ul><li>Teach classes in sociology with primary lecture material relating to social theory and the utilization of these perspectives to enhance the student's success in their chosen occupational field.</li><li>Develop curriculums, syllabuses, examinations, and appropriate lecture protocols.</li><li>Create an atmosphere of trust by encouraging open communication, positive reinforcement, and the interactive exchange of ideas.</li></ul>

MENTAL HEALTH EXPERIENCE

CEDAR SPRINGS HOSPITAL, Colorado Springs, Colorado (1998 – 1999)
Special Education Teacher, Department of Education
- Taught history, sociology, social science, anthropology, English, science, life skills, and conflict resolution to at-risk youth placed in a locked adolescent treatment center by court order. These youth exhibited marked conduct disorder personalities and were often sexual offenders.
- Maintained a safe environment conducive to learning by utilizing behavior modification techniques.
- Developed individual education plans, implemented wrap-around services with a multi-disciplinary team, and interacted with parents and caseworkers to ensure continuity of services.
- Created and maintained a computer lab for the school.
- Documented individual student progress to ensure appropriate levels of care and to meet federal and state court-ordered criteria.

LUKE-DORF, INC., Tigard, Oregon (2000 – 2001)
Sandvig Group Home Administrator
- Hired, trained, scheduled, and supervised 20 direct care staff in the delivery of care to a residential, chronically mentally ill (CMI) population.
- Documented staff interactions and assisted with crisis intervention as needed.
- Collaborated with the primary service coordinator and clinical team members to assure appropriate placement and continuity of care.
- Created in-service training to educate clinical staff in the development of treatment modalities appropriate to age, culture, gender, and ethnicity.
- Ensured compliance with appropriate state and federal regulations.

Intensive Services Coordinator (simultaneous)
- Provided intensive case management for a large, diverse group of adult CMI residents with an emphasis on continuing education and the goal of assimilation back into the general population on an appropriate functioning level.
- Evaluated residents using DSMV-IV diagnostic criteria, formulated treatment plans, and summarized progress toward treatment goals.
- Conducted mental status exams, intervened in crises, assisted with hospitalization or respite services, and followed up with discharge planning.
- Ensured continuity of care and developed positive therapeutic relationships in order to assure that the consumer's needs were met and that recidivism was minimized.
- Responsible for utilization reviews, annual reauthorizations for service, and obtaining entitlements.

Support Housing Director (simultaneous)
- Assisted CMI consumers in this transitional residential community to gain personal autonomy through enhancement of the resident's living and coping skills, educational attainment, and medication management abilities.

Administrative (on-call)
- Ensured that shifts were covered in all group homes and that appropriate after-hours crisis intervention and response was provided.
- Responsible for assuring that appropriate protocols were followed in the event of death, fire, or other critical incident.
- Collaborated with the clinical on-call professional to authorize hospitalization or respite placement.
- Followed up with hospital and clinical staff to ensure that appropriate information regarding medications, diagnoses, and treatment recommendations had been transferred appropriately.

AFFILIATIONS
- Amnesty International (1994 – present)
- University of Oklahoma Alumni Association (1994 – present)
- American Sociological Association (1994 – 1999)
- American Psychological Association (1990 – 1999)

JOYCE J ALLEN, DDS

123 Broadmoor Bluffs Drive • Colorado Springs, Colorado 80906
Home: (719) 555-1234 • Cellular: (719) 555-5678 • Email: jallen@protypeltd.com

OBJECTIVE	To enroll in a postgraduate endodontics residency program.

EDUCATION

GPR Program, Denver General Hospital, Denver, Colorado (1993 – 1994)
AEGD Program, University of Maryland, Baltimore, Maryland (1991 – 1992)
DDS Degree, University of Maryland, Baltimore, Maryland (1987 – 1991)
BS, Chemistry, George Mason University, Fairfax, Virginia (1983 – 1987)

PROFESSIONAL EXPERIENCE

Private Practice, Colorado Springs, Colorado (1997 – present)
Associate Dentist, Dr. Sally Preston, Littleton, Colorado (1997)
Associate Dentist, Drs. Bassett & Wallace, Aurora, Colorado (1994 – 1996)
Contract Dentist, Fort Carson MEDDAC, Colorado Springs, Colorado (1992 – 1993)
Associate Dentist, Dr. Marshall Fesche, Westminster, Maryland (1992)

ACADEMIC APPOINTMENT

Operative Consultant, Denver General Hospital, GPR Program (1995 – 1997)

LICENSURE

Colorado Licensed Dentist #7198 • Maryland Licensed Dentist #10868

HONORS

- Volunteer of the Year Award, Metropolitan Denver Dental Society, Colorado (1996)
- Extern for the U.S. Public Health Service, Indian Reservation, Shiprock and Crown Point, New Mexico (Summers 1990, 1991)
- Member of the Accreditation Committee for the University of Maryland Dental School (1990)
- Class Officer, University of Maryland Dental School (1987 – 1991)
- Valedictorian, Herendon High School Graduating Class of 1983—Virginia State Best and Brightest Award, luncheon with President Reagan

PROFESSIONAL DEVELOPMENT

- Various courses on esthetics, endodontics, and occlusion, Dental Convention, Denver, Colorado (1994 – present)
- Hands-on endodontic workshop with Dr. Stephen Buchanan, Santa Barbara, California (2 days each, 2002, 2004)
- Hands-on endodontic workshop with Tulsa Dental, Denver, Colorado (2 days each, 2003, 2004)
- Introduction to Dental Microscopy, Oral Facial Institute, Newport, California (2 days, 2003)
- Occlusion Course, Parts I and II, Niles Guichet Seminar, Denver, Colorado (11 days each, 1995, 1996)

VOLUNTEER

- Dentist for Kids in Need of Dentistry, Colorado Springs, Colorado (2003 – 2004)
- Dentist during educational rotations at inner city public schools, Denver Metropolitan Dental Society, Colorado (1994 – 1996)

AFFILIATIONS

- American Dental Association
- Colorado Dental Association
- American Association of Women Dentists
- Colorado Prosthodontics Society
- Rocky Mountain Dental Study Club

17 Creative Résumés

What fun to be in an industry where almost anything goes! In advertising and the arts, you have a license to be creative with your résumé. After all, creativity is one of your strongest qualifications for the job. It is the need for this creativity that determines when résumés like the ones in this chapter are appropriate. Using a creative résumé takes a very special type of person. They are not for accountants, bankers, and executives.

Needless to say, these résumés are not scannable, but the chances of a gallery, museum, graphic art firm, or ad agency scanning your résumé are almost nonexistent. Scannability in creative industries is not an issue in almost all cases. When scannability is an issue, simply create an ASCII text file résumé and send it along with your creative version (see Chapter 3).

No matter how creative you want to be, you must still keep readability in mind. If your audience can't read your résumé, what good is it?

In some career fields (artist or graphic designer, for instance), a creative résumé is the first page of a much larger portfolio, whether it is online or in a paper version that you take to an interview. The résumé doesn't replace the portfolio but summarizes it. The design must be a reflection of your "style" so it complements the entire package.

Deborah Layne

SUMMARY
- Experienced Registered Nurse with a desire to transition into pharmaceutical or medical device sales.
- Extensive knowledge of pharmacology, medical procedures, disease states, and medical terminology.
- Driven professional who thrives on challenges and works well independently.
- Highly self-motivated and responsible leader who is able to relate to physicians and healthcare providers at their professional level.
- Compassionate caregiver who quickly establishes and maintains rapport with patients, families, physicians, and colleagues.

CREDENTIALS
- Registered Nurse, Colorado
- CPR and ACLS Certified

EDUCATION

BACHELOR OF SCIENCE, NURSING (2000)
University of Southern Colorado, Pueblo, Colorado
Completed six months of additional training beyond the basic degree requirements.

CERTIFIED OPHTHALMIC ASSISTANT (1995)
REGISTERED MEDICAL ASSISTANT (1991)
CERTIFIED PHLEBOTOMIST (1991)
Denver Technical College, Colorado Springs, Colorado

PROFESSIONAL EXPERIENCE

STAFF NURSE (2004 – present)
Centura Health, St. Mary-Corwin Medical Center, Pueblo, Colorado
- Post-Anesthesia Care Unit—Provided nursing care to patients following surgery or other procedures requiring anesthesia.
- Recovered patients from general anesthesia, provided postoperative care, and prepared patients for admission or discharge.
- Administered medications, taking into consideration indications, contraindications, side effects, and patient drug history.
- Provided postoperative instructions for home care, followed up with phone calls the next day, and made recommendations for further care.

STAFF NURSE (2000 – 2004)
Memorial Hospital, Colorado Springs, Colorado
- Cardiology Step-Down Coronary Care Unit—Cared for patients following open-heart surgery, acute myocardial infarction, cardiac catheterization, pacemaker insertion, and electrophysiology studies, as well as critically ill patients with chronic heart, renal, and pulmonary disease.
- Constantly encountered medically compromised patients while at the same time juggling multiple priorities to provide only the highest quality of care.
- Developed a rapport and sense of trust with patients in high-stress environments.

PHLEBOTOMIST / NURSE'S AIDE (1998 – 2000)
Centura Health, St. Mary-Corwin Medical Center, Pueblo, Colorado
- Collaborated with nursing staff and physicians to provide quality care on the medical/surgical, geriatric, rehabilitation, oncology, and cardiac care units.
- Collected specimens of blood and body fluids for laboratory analysis.
- Ensured the proper handling of each specimen and preserved the chain of custody when performing legal draws.

1234 West Camino Pablo Drive • Fountain, Colorado 81007
Home: (719) 555-5678 • Cellular: (719) 555-1234 • Email: litnurse@protypeltd.com

278

PROFESSIONAL EXPERIENCE (continued)

NURSE'S AIDE (1995 – 1998)
Centura Health, Penrose Hospital, Colorado Springs, Colorado
- Served as a nurse's aide on the medical/surgical, geriatric, rehabilitation, oncology, and cardiac care units.
- Developed and maintained effective working relationships with doctors, nurses, and other healthcare providers.

REGISTERED MEDICAL ASSISTANT (1995 – 1998)
Alpine Internal Medicine, Colorado Springs, Colorado
- Performed direct patient care and performed triage in a medical office setting for seven doctors and three physician's assistants.
- Interviewed patients to establish medical histories and symptoms; reviewed and updated patient charts; and measured and recorded vital signs.
- Administered injections, collected specimens, and set up and assisted with medical procedures (EKGs, PFTs, and minor surgeries).
- Dispensed sample medications as directed by providers and called prescriptions to pharmacies.
- Scheduled tests and patient appointments, notified patients of test results, returned patient phone calls, and provided patient and family education services.
- Served as a patient advocate and the primary liaison between providers and patients.
- Coordinated authorization for patient care from insurance companies and managed care organizations.
- Served as the practice's OSHA and Safety Monitor Representative—Ensured compliance with OSHA regulations.

MEDICAL ASSISTANT / OPHTHALMIC ASSISTANT (1993 – 1995)
Colorado Eye Associates, Colorado Springs, Colorado
- Tested and measured eye function, including far acuity, near acuity, peripheral vision, depth perception, color perception, field of vision, and intraocular pressure, among others.
- Examined eyes for abnormalities of the cornea and anterior/posterior chambers.
- Measured axial length of the eye using ultrasound equipment.
- Conducted incoming patient interviews and preliminary examinations and maintained patient records.
- Assisted physicians in minor surgeries and RK procedures, and provided pre- and post-discharge instructions to patients.
- Participated in extensive research programs relating to glaucoma.

MEDICAL ASSISTANT (1992 – 1993)
Ronald Johnson, MD, Colorado Springs, Colorado
- Provided medical assistance and patient education in this busy dermatology practice.

MEDICAL ASSISTANT (1991 – 1992)
John Tedeschi, MD, Colorado Springs, Colorado
- Assisted an internist who specialized in geriatric medicine.

COMPUTERS

Proficient in Windows, MS Word, Email, and the Internet.

VOLUNTEER

Provided vision checks at corporate health fairs for Colorado Eye Associates.

RUSS MILLS

STRENGTHS
- Talented actor with strong stage instincts and formal training.
- Varied background that includes directing and technical work.
- Experienced in set and stage construction, lighting, and sound.
- Height: 6 feet, 0 inches – Weight: 215 lbs. – Hair: Dark Brown – Eyes: Green.

FILM

Charlie Baker's *Em@il Man*, a feature-length independent film
- Played the part of Manley, a major supporting role
- Produced by Jim Kirks and directed by Charlie Baker (summer 2002)
- Scheduled to premier at Kimball's Twin Peak Theater, Colorado Springs, Colorado (May 2003)
- Planned for release on video and DVD

O'Henry's *The Exact Science of Matrimony*, a short film
- Played the part of Jeff Tucker
- Produced and directed by Dr. Kim Walker (summer 2001)

PROFESSIONAL THEATER

Jack and the Beanstalk	The Giant	Colorado Springs Fine Arts Center, CO
Pinocchio	Candlewick	Colorado Springs Fine Arts Center, CO
Stuart Little	Leroy/Mr. Clydesdale	Colorado Springs Fine Arts Center, CO
	The Doctor/Dog 1	
H.M.S. Pinafore	Bit/Chorus	Colorado Springs Fine Arts Center, CO

UNIVERSITY THEATER

Cyrano de Bergerac	Cyrano	Colorado State University, Ft. Collins, CO
The Glass Menagerie	Tom	Colorado State University, Ft. Collins, CO
No Exit	Valet/The Devil	Colorado State University, Ft. Collins, CO
The Bald Soprano	Mr. Martin	Colorado State University, Ft. Collins, CO
Forbidden Broadway/My Fair Lady	Prof. Henry Higgins	Colorado State University, Ft. Collins, CO
Who's on First	Lou Abbott	Colorado State University, Ft. Collins, CO
The Elephant Man	Freak Handler	Colorado State University, Ft. Collins, CO
Bent	Max/SS Guard	Colorado State University, Ft. Collins, CO
Anything Goes	Ching/Chorus	Colorado State University, Ft. Collins, CO
Other People's Money	President	Colorado State University, Ft. Collins, CO

EDUCATION

University of Colorado, Colorado Springs, CO: Film production minor (2002 – present)
Colorado State University, Fort Collins, CO: Theatre major for four years (1993 – 1996)
Colorado State University, Fort Collins, CO: Tap, jazz, court, and ballroom dance (1995 – 1996)
Colorado State University, Fort Collins, CO: Stage combat (acting and directing) (1996)
Vincent Lappas Acting Seminar, Colorado Springs, CO (1999)

SPECIAL SKILLS
- Singing Voice: Contra-Tenor/Baritone
- Performance driving (civilian and military)
- Sword fighting and period fencing (stage and live)
- Experienced in rappelling
- Theater Tech Experience: fly work, set construction, light hanging, etc.

AWARDS
- Best Actor of 1990, Hamilton Southeastern, Fishers, IN
- 1995 Creative and Performing Arts Award (stipend), Colorado State University, Fort Collins, CO

ADDRESS

1234 Templeton Park Circle #12, Colorado Springs, Colorado 80917-4410
Phone: (719) 555-1234 • Email: rmills@protypeltd.com

KIMBERLY SMITH

Internship:
Corporate Interior Design Firm

EDUCATION

B.A. INTERIOR DESIGN, 5/2006, GPA 3.5
TEXAS TECH UNIVERSITY, Lubbock, TX
Minor in Marketing
Relevant Coursework:

- Computer Aided Design, (CAD)
- Construction and Building Systems
- Contract Design I
- Contract Design II
- Design I
- Design II
- History of Interior Design
- Interior Drawing
- Internship I
- Kitchen and Bath Design
- Professional Practices
- Rendering and Presentation
- Residential Design I
- Surface Materials

EXPERIENCE

RECEPTIONIST / BOOKKEEPER   **1999-2006**
SMITH & SMITH, Dallas, Texas

Worked Summers full-time for family-owned
legal practice.

- Scheduled appointments
- Greeted clients
- Routed telephone calls
- Recorded messages
- Scheduled conference room
- Performed data entry
- Balanced books
- Recorder staff meeting minutes

AWARDS & HONORS

- President's List, Fall 2004, Spring 2005
- Dean's List, Fall 2001, Spring 2004
- National Honor Society, 2005
- Who's Who, 3005
- Study Abroad, Summer 2003
- Omega Pi Honor Society, 2001
- Merit Honor Scholarship, 2000

ORGANIZATIONS

Kappa Delta Sorority, TTU, 2000-present
- Rush Chair, 2002
- President, 2004
The Marketing Association, TTU, 2004 - present
American Young Designer Association, 2005

1234 89th Streeet, #12
Lubbock, Texas 79414
Ksmith531@protypeltd.com

806.555.1234

Francine Gilroy

12345 Mountain View Drive
Clarksburg, WV 25301
(304) 555-1234
gilroy@protypeltd.com

PROFILE

- ➢ More than 10 years of experience in the guest accommodations industry, encompassing new hotel opening, renovation, and strengthening of operations.
- ➢ Proven effectiveness in maximizing profit potential through improvement of internal controls, enhancement of guest services, and implementation of innovative marketing strategies.
- ➢ Successful in recruiting quality staff members and retaining them through competitive incentives.
- ➢ Recognized for excellent team spirit and high energy level, devoting as much time and effort as necessary to accomplish company goals.

CAREER EXPERIENCE

COMFORT INNS   **1995–present**

General Manager, Clarksburg, WV (since 2001)
Currently managing operations of a 110-room facility with staff of 22, one of the largest in a chain of 78 motor lodges in the eastern United States, generating revenues of $2.9 million.

- ➢ Increased occupancy 10 percent over previous year through aggressive advertising, local business contacts, and alliances with travel agencies. Maintain 80+ percent occupancy year round despite heavy area competition.
- ➢ Developed incentive programs for staff consisting of housekeepers, maintenance workers, and front desk personnel that reduced employee turnover from more than 200 percent to less than 20 percent, and increased housekeeping productivity by 75 percent.
- ➢ Controlled labor and operating costs well below budgeted amounts due to stability and efficiency of staff.
- ➢ Virtually eliminated bad debt by instituting better control procedures with emphasis on communications between housekeeping staff and front desk regarding guest checkouts.
- ➢ In past year, staff received corporate "Hospitality Star" award for fewest complaints and most complimentary comments reported by guests.
- ➢ Appointed to Manager's Council for two consecutive years for consistently maintaining quality control levels above company standards.

General Manager, Baltimore, MD (1999–2001)
- ➢ Participated in preliminary steps involved with the opening of a new 90-room hotel at Inner Harbor. Advised selection of site based on ease of access and visibility.
- ➢ Successfully opened a new hotel, and without assistance, recruited and trained entire staff to perform to highest quality standards of guest service.
- ➢ During first year of operation, generated $1.5 million in revenue and experienced 11 consecutive "super-weeks," with occupancy at 100 percent, regarded in the trade as unusual for a newly established hotel.

General Manager, Dover, DE (1997–1999)
- ➢ Planned and organized $200,000 interior renovation project for this 94-room hotel.
- ➢ Supervised all rehabilitation work to comply with company specifications as well as time schedule and budget.

Assistant to General Manager, Rochester, NY (1996–1997)
Management Trainee, Rochester, NY (1995–1996)

SHERATON HOTEL   **1994**
Internship – Front Desk Clerk, Houston, TX

EDUCATION

UNIVERSITY OF HOUSTON   **1994**
Bachelor of Science in Hotel Management

Virginia Diane Little

12 Del Paz Drive • Colorado Springs, CO 80918 • Home Phone: (719) 555-1234

PROFILE
- Experienced painter and art educator with diverse background in:
  - Color theory
  - Presentation
  - Art therapy
  - Design
  - Drawing
  - Watercolors
  - Oil painting
  - Sculpture
  - Teaching
  - Administration
  - Marketing
  - Promotion
- Adept at encouraging creativity in students and helping them to promote themselves.

EXPERIENCE

Teaching
- Creative teacher with an interactive, hands-on teaching style; never found a student who was not teachable, regardless of ethnicity, gender, age, or life experience.
- Experienced in the instruction of student populations from diverse economic backgrounds, ages, and talent levels.
- Developed curriculum for art and art appreciation classes; committed to excellence in education.
- Taught in college and nonacademic settings, including Michael's, Hobby Lobby, retirement centers.
- Developed and conducted workshops in color theory, perspective, landscapes, seascapes, rock formations, clouds, aspens, and other types/genres of art.
- Helped students appreciate how people have used art to express ideas throughout history.
- Guided students in evaluating and critiquing 20th-century art using the Feldman Model.
- Coordinated and conducted a teaching tour of Europe for 15 art students from Tomball College.
- Recently visited the great museums of Europe, including The Louvre, The British Museum, The Vatican, and museums in Amsterdam, Germany, Florence, and Venice.
- Traveled extensively, studying the great masters in such museums as the Guggenheim (New York), the National Art Gallery (Washington, D.C.), The High Museum (Atlanta), The Art Institute of Chicago, and the Mexico Museum of Anthropology.

Art and Exhibits
- Skilled in the creative use of oils, acrylics, pen/ink, pencil, Prisma color, watercolors, and pastels.
- Two pieces of art work selected for the juried Cook Communications Art Show.
- One of 20 chosen from 400 artists for the Alternative Arts Alliance road show in Denver.
- Exhibited at the Arvada Arts Center (Denver), Cañon Arts Center (Cañon City), corporate offices, and others.
- Awarded the Lone Star Art Guild State Best of Show for an oil painting (Houston).
- Received the Artcetera Artist's Award from one of the largest Houston art leagues.
- Honored with numerous awards and ribbons from local and state art shows.
- Recipient of a full art scholarship from North Harris County College based on juried works of art, including oils, watercolors, pastels, portraits, clay sculptures, and acrylics.

Administration
- Developed marketing strategies to place art classes in innovative business settings, including Compaq Corp.
- Organized and promoted art shows, exhibits, and classes, including the first annual Tomball College Art Show.
- Efficiently managed department and classroom budgets, ensuring profitability.
- Recruited guest speakers and volunteer workers from the community and academia.
- Juried the Northwest Art League's Lone Star State Art Show with more than 500 works of art.
- Coordinated the yearbook as President of the Northwest Art League.

WORK HISTORY

Art Instructor (Art Appreciation), Pikes Peak Community College, Colorado Springs, Colorado	2001 – present
Art Instructor, Hobby Lobby, Michael's, The Bridge, Crossings, Colorado Springs, Colorado	1995 – present
Art Teacher, Compaq Computer Corporation, galleries, and stores, Houston, Texas	1984 – 1994
Art Instructor, Tomball College, Tomball, Texas	1991 – 1992
Substitute Teacher (all levels and subjects), Cypress Fairbanks School District, Houston, Texas	1980 – 1984

EDUCATION

Master of Arts, Art Education, University of Houston, Texas	1989 – 1991
Art Curriculum (29 hours), North Harris County College, Houston, Texas	1988 – 1989
Private Art Instruction under nationally known artists, including Dick Turner (portraiture), Buck Paulson (land/seascapes), and Efime Fruman (old master's techniques)	1979 – 1988

....at the center of Earth

KARL FINLEY

TEACHER AND ARTIST

123 Fair Dawn Drive
Colorado Springs
Colorado 80920

Phone: (719) 555-1234
kwfin@protypeltd.com

PROFILE

- Creative teacher with a passion for bringing the arts to life for students.
- Skilled in creating stable learning environments and inspiring others to do their best.
- Patient instructor who enjoys working with children.
- Approachable team player who is able to build rapport easily with students and parents.

EXPERIENCE

Teaching

- Developed lesson plans and instructed students in visual arts (K–12 and Gifted/Talented 7–12).
- Diverse background in teaching across the curriculum, including computers, social studies, art, math, English, industrial arts, and other subjects.
- Developed age-appropriate lessons in art history, appreciation, and production, adapting instruction to effectively target student learning styles.
- Provided students with opportunities for tangible learning through the visual arts by organizing field trips and creating thematic units that transformed classrooms into cave and moon learning extravaganzas.
- Developed an innovative Earth Day program (in collaboration with physical education, critical thinking, and music teachers) that was recognized in *TEPE Magazine* and made an annual event.
- Presented gifted and talented students with a wide variety of source material and challenges in order to promote critical thinking, problem solving, and independent learning.
- Integrated interdisciplinary units to connect art across core curriculums.
- Received the A+ Outstanding Teacher Award (1993)—one of only two teachers in the school.
- Supervised camp activities for boys 6 to 16 years old, served as a counselor, developed lesson plans, and supervised the arts budget.

Coaching

- Basketball coach for grades 7 and 8.
- Special Olympics basketball coach for grades 3 to 5.
- Coached varsity and junior high football.
- Organized and coached Tiger Cubs football team and pep club (2nd and 3rd graders).
- Sponsored and chaperoned students at high school football games.
- Supervised elementary intramural football program.

Communication

- Counseled students with adjustment and academic problems and communicated with parents.
- Rotary Club guest lecturer on community involvement in school and the arts.
- In-service lecturer and consultant on integrating arts and humanities into the curriculum.
- Presented education reform materials to administrators, teachers, and students in schools across the state of Kentucky.

Committees

- Chairman of the Equitable Schools Committee, a state program to improve individualization of education, test scores, and overall school quality.
- Chairman of the School Transformation Plan Committee; directed teachers in developing improvement plans for their classes.
- Arts Integration Consultant for regional Goals 2000 program to raise school standards.
- Appointed by the Kentucky Department of Education as Content Advisory Committee Member for Arts and Humanities for the Kentucky Education Reform Act.
- Developed assessment questions for Kentucky's KIRIS innovative testing system.
- Chairman, *Imagination Celebration* for Roosevelt-Edison Charter School.

EXPERIENCE (CONTINUED)

Entrepreneurial
- Co-owner and founder of Los Comics comic book company.
- Created an array of comic characters that have been published or are in production by Los Comics.
- Wrote and drew comic book characters and supervised the production of comic books.
- Developed the concept for a Web site and worked closely with Web development agency to implement the ideas.
- Negotiated contract with Diamond Distributors for mass distribution.
- Attended conventions and met with comic book dealers.
- Participated in San Diego Comic-Con as a comic book publisher.

EDUCATION

Completed 9 hours toward a Master of Science, Murray State University, Murray, Kentucky

Bachelor of Science in Art Education, Murray State University, Murray, Kentucky
- Student Government Association, Senator and Chairman of Student Affairs Committee.
- Recipient of Annette Schmidt Creative Arts Scholarship.
- Editorial Cartoonist for *The Murray State News*, received Kentucky Intercollegiate Press Awards.
- 3-D functional design work selected for student art shows 1989–1990.
- Attended the U.S. Space Foundation Institute Workshop 2000.

WORK HISTORY

Visual Arts Instructor (K-5), Roosevelt-Edison Charter School, Colorado Springs, Colorado	2004 – present
Owner, Los Comics, Colorado Springs, Colorado	2002 – present
Visual Arts Instructor (Elementary), High Country Christian Academy, Colorado Springs, Colorado	2004
Substitute Teacher (K-12), Widefield School District, Colorado Springs, Colorado	2004
Camp Counselor, Royal Family Kids Camp, Woodland Park, Colorado	2004
Guest Lecturer, Frontier Elementary School, District 20, Colorado Springs, Colorado	2003
Visual Arts Instructor (K-12), Fulton City Schools, Fulton, Kentucky	2002 – 2003
Visual Arts Instructor (K-6), Fulton County Schools, Hickman, Kentucky	2000 – 2002
Gifted and Talented Instructor (7-12), Fulton County Schools, Hickman, Kentucky	2000 – 2002
Coach (7-8), Fulton County Schools, Hickman, Kentucky	2000 – 2002
Camp Counselor, West Kentucky 4-H Camp	2002
Visual Arts Instructor (K-4), Robertson Elementary School, Murray, Kentucky	1997 – 1999
Daycare Director, Murray Elementary School, Murray, Kentucky	1997 – 1999
Substitute Teacher (K-8), Murray City Schools, Murray, Kentucky	1996 – 1999
Camp Counselor, Camp Canadensis, Pennsylvania	1994 – 1999

MARY PRESCOT

Advertising Major
Spanish Minor

Scheduled graduation from Texas Tech University May 2005.

Targeting reputable advertising agency needing English – Spanish bilingual advertising representative with fresh ideas.

Will relocate anywhere in the U.S.

Résumé follow-up upon request.

Role and Responsibilities

Independent worker who needs minimal instruction, also works well within team environment due to strong interpersonal, communication, and organizational skills. Held various leadership roles and self-financed 100 percent of college education.

Idea Generation

Currently utilizing advertising skills in college curriculum. Intimately involved in creating plans book and creative brief to educate the public regarding benefits the Texas Public School Systems receives from lottery funds. As a member of the creative team, contributed to all aspects of the project, including research, survey, marketing plan, plans book, and creative brief. Test market is Lubbock, Texas. If plan is successful, it will be rolled out to other cities in Texas.

Industry Marketing

Member of Tech Advertising Federation and 2001 American Advertising Federation National Student Advertising Competition team that is responsible for creating a four-year integrated marketing communications plans book and creative brief for Daimler-Chrysler. Responsible for industry analysis, public relations/sponsorship efforts, creative brief, and various other parts of the plan and ad campaign.

Cultural Insight

Received scholarship for field study in Mexico from May to June 2000. Submersed into local culture through Spanish classes at local college. Lived with family and practiced Spanish daily. Traveled around region studying and learning the Mexican culture. Dedication and accomplishments earned title of Student Ambassador, which requires presentations regarding field study in Mexico.

Proficiencies and Expertise

Most frequently used skills include, but not limited to:

- Relationship management
- Opportunity and marketing analysis
- Solid interpersonal communication
- Telemarketing experience
- Strong customer service skills
- Prioritizes assignments effectively
- Defines logical approach to problems
- Computer literate (Photoshop, Adobe Illustrator, Quark Xpress, Works, Word, PowerPoint)
- Solid office skills

Memberships and Honors

- Dean's Honors List
- Tech Advertising Federation
- 2004 American Advertising Federation Competition team
- Rho Lambda Honors Sorority
- Zeta Tau Alpha
- Red Raider Recruiter
- Mexico Field Study
- Universal Cheerleaders Assn. All-Star

"Polygonal character developed in Alias Maya from original concept design; later converted to subdivisions and rendered with Mental Ray."
–J. Medina.

Julio Medina
3138 Terry Brook Drive
Winter Park, Florida 32792
Tel: 407-555-1234 / Cell: 407-555-5678
Email: jmedina711@protypeltd.net

Character Modeler

Biddable, creative, and detailed Computer Animator skilled at replicating, from multiple references, humans, organic creatures, robotic characters, and clothing with biped and quadruped skeletal structures. Foundation in traditional art and clay sculpting that will facilitate the production pipeline from concept to manifestation. Extensive knowledge in human anatomy, kinesiology, and biomechanics.

Education

Sail Real World Education
Associate of Science Degree in Computer Animation: Graduated, Feb 2005 (Accelerated Program: 90 credits in 16 months)

Software Skills and Experience

Alias Maya
- Utilized in 14 classes for numerous graded projects: modeling, texturing, rigging, animation, dynamics, lighting, and rendering.
- Constructed organic characters, hard surface models, props, and backgrounds for independent work.
- Extensive experience modeling geometric forms with polygonal, multi-patch NURBS, and Sub-division surface topologies: Developed humans, creatures, and animals with the aforementioned modeling surfaces.
- Completed UV maps and corrective blendshapes for characters before assigning articulated rigs and texture maps.

Maxon Cinema 4D
- Created humans, humanoid creatures, props, and backgrounds for independent work.
- Extensive experience modeling with polygonal, hyper-NURBS, and splines (Freehand, Akima, Bezier, B-Spline, Linear, Cubic).

Maxon Bodypaint 3D
- Edited and completed UV maps from models imported from packages such as Cinema 4D, Maya, and Softimage XSI.
- Hand painted 3D textures for completed models with the procedurals, brush tools, and ray-brush renderer.

Adobe Photoshop
- Used during numerous courses and independent projects: texturing, painting, drawing, image manipulation, and logo design.
- Imported UV maps from models and painted color, diffuse, specular, bump, and displacement maps.

Traditional Art Background
- Completed projects and coursework in object perspective, color theory, lighting and shadows, life drawing, concept art, character development, storyboarding, and clay sculpting.
- Conceptualized art for character development, clay sculpted marquette's from observation, and built completed characters with Alias Maya.

Additional Software Skills

Adobe AfterEffects, Adobe Premiere Pro, Apple Shake, Apple Final Cut Pro HD, Corel Painter, Corel Bryce 3D, Mental Images' Mental Ray.

Relevant Coursework and Classes

Media Arts, 3D Foundations, Object Perspective, Model Creation, Shading and Lighting, Fundamentals of Logo Animation, Character Modeling, Character Rigging, Animation in 3D, Motion Study and Control, Acting for Animators, Gaming Character and Scene Design, Visual Effects, Storyboarding, Compositing and Scene Finishing, Computer Animation Final Project, Media and Society, and Demo Reel Creation.

Supporting Work History

CERTIFIED PERSONAL TRAINER, New York Health and Racquet Club, New York, NY (1996 to 2002).
- Designed detailed exercise regimes for personal clients, demonstrating fitness expertise.
- Achieved a reputation for vast knowledge of anatomy, biomechanics, and kinesiology.
- Demonstrated excellent interpersonal skills and team effort.

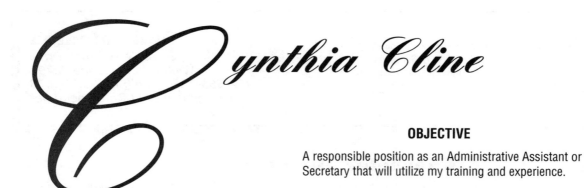
Cynthia Cline

OBJECTIVE

A responsible position as an Administrative Assistant or Secretary that will utilize my training and experience.

QUALIFICATIONS

Enthusiastic administrative assistant with an Associate Degree and experience in:
- Desktop publishing, office management, principles of accounting, research, and filing.
- Windows, MS Word, Excel, Lotus 1-2-3, WordPerfect, and other PC software.
- Typing 60 wpm, facsimile, 10-key calculators, multi-line telephones, and most office machines.

PROFILE

- Quality-conscious professional with a dedication to precision.
- Background includes customer service, public relations, and collections.
- Effective team player with strong inter-personal and communication skills.
- Comfortable taking the initiative and working independently.
- Adept at working under pressure to meet time-sensitive deadlines.

EDUCATION

ASSOCIATE OF APPLIED SCIENCE (1996)
Blair Junior College
Colorado Springs, Colorado
- Administrative Assistant major
- GPA 3.75
- Director's List for achieving 4.0 GPA
- Dean's List
- Student of the Month, August 1995

CONTACT

1234 Bluffs Island Court
Odenton, Maryland 21113
(410) 555-1234

EMPLOYMENT HISTORY

HOWARD COUNTY HEALTH DEPARTMENT, Columbia, Maryland
Office Processing Clerk II (2001 – present)
- Maintain and monitor the Substance Abuse Management Information System.
- Prepare monthly statistical reports for submission to regulatory agencies.
- Provide clerical support for the Bureau of Addictions.
- Open and close client records, and accurately enter admission/discharge information, ensuring confidentiality of medical information.
- Enter additions severity index information into the computer.
- Type general correspondence, intake/discharge summaries, and physician dictation.
- Verify daily collection of funds and determine client fees due using a sliding scale, depending on ability to pay.
- Maintain records and filing system.
- Consistently arrive early and/or stay late to ensure work is completed on time.

RIVERWOOD MENTAL HEALTH CENTER (TAD Staffing Services), Columbia, Maryland
Administrative Assistant/Receptionist (2000 – 2001)
- Greeted customers and answered five-line telephone, directing calls to their appropriate parties.
- Scheduled and cancelled appointments for the doctors.
- Updated and filed medical records.

ZURICH INSURANCE COMPANY (ADD Staff), Colorado Springs, Colorado
Administrative Assistant (1999 – 2000)
- Performed data entry using AmiPro database software.
- Sent faxes, made copies, and performed other office tasks.

NORWEST DIRECT (Western Staff Services), Colorado Springs, CO
Administrative Assistant (1997 – 1999)
- Secretary for the Adverse Actions Division of a direct marketing mortgage lending company.
- Responsible for typing and proofreading of loan denials using a Windows-based proprietary computer software.
- Interfaced closely with loan closers.
- As the first person hired in the department, trained all other administrative assistants.

18 Cover Letters, Letterheads, and Paper Colors

The first rule of cover letters: Never use a generic cover letter with only "To Whom It May Concern." With tons of work on your desk, would you be interested in such a mass mailing? You would probably consider it junk mail, right? You would be much more likely to read a letter that was directed to you personally, and so would human resources professionals.

The second rule: Every résumé sent by mail or fax needs a personalized cover letter even if the advertisement didn't request a cover letter.

The third rule: Résumés sent by e-mail don't need a true cover letter. Use only a quick paragraph with three to five sentences telling your reader where you heard about the position and why your qualifications are a perfect fit for the position's requirements. E-mail is intended to be short, sweet, and to the point. Then, cut and paste your ASCII text résumé into the e-mail message screen instead of just attaching your MS Word file (see page 46 for an example of an ASCII text file or find a copy of Barron's *e-Résumés* for detailed instructions on how to create and use an electronic résumé).

This chapter will address several cover letter types. A letter to a recruiter requires different information than a letter in answer to an advertisement. A targeted cover letter that tells a story and captures your reader's attention is ideal when possible, but such letters aren't always practical. Not everyone has the writing skills to produce an effective story, and the time involved in researching and writing the story would be impractical for mass mailings. A hard-hitting salesperson can write a dynamic cover letter, but not everyone is comfortable with that style, and a good cover letter doesn't have to be "pushy."

Before we get into specific styles, let's cover some general rules that apply to most cover letters. The letters on pages 293–301 are general cover letters following these rules.

1. Customize each cover letter with an inside address (do not use "to whom it may concern").

2. Personalize the greeting (Dear Ms. Smith). Try to get the name of a person whenever possible. A blind advertisement makes that impossible, but in other cases a quick telephone call can often result in a name and sometimes a valuable telephone conversation. When you can't get a name, use Dear Recruiter, Dear Hiring Manager, Dear Search Committee, or Dear Sir/Madam.

3. Mention where you heard about the position so your reader knows where to direct your résumé and letter. The first paragraph of your cover letter is a great place to state (or restate) your objective. Since you know the specific job being offered, you can tailor your objective to suit the position.

4. Be a name-dropper. In the first paragraph, mention the name of someone you know in the company. Hiring managers take unsolicited résumés more seriously when they assume you were referred by one of their employees or customers.

5. The second paragraph (or two) is the perfect place to mention specific experience that is targeted to the job opening. This is your "I'm super great because" information. Here is where you summarize why you are absolutely perfect for the position. Really sell yourself. Pick and choose some of your experience and/or education that is specifically related to the company's requirements, or elaborate on qualifications that are not in your résumé but apply to this particular job. If you make mention of the company and its needs, it becomes immediately obvious that your cover letter is not generic. Entice the reader to find out more about you in your résumé. Don't make this section too long or you will quickly lose the reader's interest.

6. The closing should be concise. Let the reader know what you want (an application, an interview, an opportunity to call). If you are planning to call the person on a certain day, you could close by saying, "I will contact you next Tuesday to set up a mutually convenient time to meet." Don't call on Mondays or Fridays if you can help it. If you aren't comfortable making these cold calls, then close your letter with something like: "I look forward to hearing from you soon." And remember to say, "Thank you for your consideration" or something to that effect (but don't be obsequious, please!).

❑ Story Letter

If you are planning a direct mail campaign to 50 or 100 or 400 companies, this type of letter is not for you. It just isn't practical. However, you will have to admit that the letters on pages 302–308 are great attention getters. For those dream jobs that require something special, this is the way to go. In a story cover letter, you must be able to tell a good story and write it well. If writing is not your forté, you can hire someone to write the letter, but you must still do the research and have a general outline of the story.

❑ Letters to Recruiters

There are two types of recruiters: retained and contingency. What is the difference between the two? Retained recruiters are hired by a company and are then paid by that company whether they ever find the right employee for the position or not. Contingency firms are also paid by the company but only when they find a good match and the job seeker is hired. Legitimate recruiting firms don't charge the job seeker a dime, which means they are working for their client companies and not *you*.

Because their mission is not to find the perfect job for you but to find the perfect employee for their client, they have little interest in communicating with you unless you are a prime candidate for a position they are seeking to fill *now*. Don't call recruiters; they will call you if they are interested. This affects both the beginning and ending of your cover letter. If you don't have a person's name, use Dear Recruiter. You should resign yourself to waiting for the recruiter to call you, so "I look forward to hearing from you soon" is an appropriate closing for a recruiter cover letter.

In addition to the "I'm super great because" paragraph(s), you need to add another paragraph just before the closing that tells the recruiter your ideal position title, industry, salary, and geographic preferences. Check the cover letters on pages 309–310 for examples.

❏ Dynamic Letters

Job openings that require a certain amount of dynamic spirit—like sales—deserve a more dynamic letter. This can be accomplished in the opening paragraph. The rest of the letter is written like a standard cover letter but with a little more energy than usual. The last paragraph can be a bit more aggressive—you call the hiring manager instead of waiting for him/her to call you. See pages 300, 301, and 307 for an example of a cover letter that exudes confidence and power.

❏ Thank You Letters

According to a recent survey, less than 20% of applicants write a thank you note after an interview. Of the recruiters surveyed, 94% said that a thank you letter would increase the applicant's chances of getting the job, or at least help him/her stay in the running, provided the applicant is otherwise qualified. Fifteen minutes of your time and a first class postage stamp are very inexpensive investments in your career!

Thank you letters simply thank the interviewer for his or her time and reiterate some of the important things you learned about the company in the interview. Add some key qualifications that you forgot to mention in the interview, or emphasize some of the more important things you discussed. If the interviewer shared some information that gave you an insight into the company and its culture, mention how much you appreciated it.

A thank you letter should be short—three paragraphs at the most. Don't try for the hard sell. You had your chance in the interview. The thank you letter just reinforces what you have already said. See the examples on pages 312–315.

❏ Letterheads

It is so easy to create a letterhead all your own and to make it match your résumé. Just copy into a new document the name and address you have already created for your résumé. It couldn't be simpler! It makes a very sharp impression when your cover letter and résumé match in every respect from paper color to font to letterhead.

❏ Paper Color

Color, like music, creates an atmosphere. Everyone knows that different colors evoke different feelings. Red can make a person feel warm, whereas blue does just the opposite.

Of course, you wouldn't want to use red in a résumé! . . . although an artist could get away with just about any color. As a general rule, résumé papers should be neutral or light in color. After 20 years in the résumé business, I have discovered that brilliant white linen paper is still the most popular, followed closely by a slightly off-white and then by shades of light gray.

Just make sure that the color of the paper you choose is representative of your personality and industry and that it doesn't detract from your message. For instance, a dark paper color makes your résumé hard to read.

In a scannable résumé, never use papers with a background (pictures, marble shades, or speckles). A scanner tries to interpret the patterns and dots as letters. This is a good rule to follow even for paper résumés that will never be scanned. Often companies will photocopy résumés for hiring managers, and dark colors or patterns will simply turn into dark masses that make your résumé difficult to read. If a company has multiple locations, the original résumé may even get faxed from one site to another and the same thing happens.

The type of paper (bond, linen, laid, cover stock, or coated) isn't as important, although it also projects an image. Uncoated paper (bond, linen, laid) makes a classic statement. It feels rich and makes people think of corporate stationery and important documents. Coated stock recalls memories of magazines, brochures, and annual reports. Heavy cover stock and laid paper can't be successfully folded and don't hold the ink from a laser printer or copier very well, so they must be handled gently. All of these factors play a part in your paper choice.

Regardless of the paper you choose, mail your résumé flat instead of folded. It costs a few extra cents in postage and a little more for the 9 × 12 envelope, but the impression it makes is well worth the extra cost. It also helps with the scannability of your résumé. Thank you letters and other follow-up letters can be folded in standard No. 10 business envelopes.

JOANNE A. RIDGEWAY

4321 Dexter Avenue NE ◆ Massillon, OH 44646 ◆ (330) 555-1234 ◆ ridgeway@protypeltd.com

A letter in response to an advertisement with bulleted skills that address the advertised requirements.

February 8, 2005

Attention: Christine Simmers
Alder Agency
4321 Market Avenue North, Suite 101
Canton, OH 44702

Dear Ms. Simmers:

Your advertisement in *The Repository* on Sunday, February 6, 2005, for an administrative secretary/receptionist attracted my attention. Your ad stated you are looking for candidates with strong oral and written communication skills as well as experience in Word, Excel, and Access. As my enclosed resume indicates, my qualifications closely match your requirements as follows:

- ◆ **EXPERIENCE** of more than ten years in administrative/secretarial positions with advanced computer skills in all Microsoft Office programs including Word, Excel, and Access. As technical administrative assistant at PolyOne, I streamlined production of correspondence and product specifications in Word through use of custom templates, electronic forms, macros, autotext, and modification of toolbars. I am also proficient in spreadsheet applications using Excel. At PolyOne, I was also responsible for maintaining the customer specification database and providing reports to the department manager using Access.

- ◆ **EDUCATION** at The University of Akron/Wayne College reinforced my communication and business English skills. Membership in Toastmasters International, a public speaking group, strengthened my oral communication skills.

May I come in, at your convenience, so we can discuss my qualifications more fully? I can be reached at 330-555-1234 or by email at ridgeway@protypeltd.com. If I do not hear from you by next week, I will call to see if you have any questions and to check on the status of this opportunity.

Sincerely,

Joanne A. Ridgeway

Enclosure

Regina Openhence

125 S.E. Stanley Court • Palance, Utah 99999

208-555-1234 *cell*   *home* 208-555-5678

May 16, 2005

A letter in response to an advertisement.

Attention: Lindsey Harold
Codder County Bank
P.O. Box 9229
Palance, UT 99999

Dear Ms. Harold:

In response to your recent advertisement for an experienced Commercial Loan Officer, I have enclosed a copy of my résumé for your review. As you will note, I have spent more than twenty years in the banking industry in a variety of positions. My expertise is in working in the Commercial Loan Department and one-on-one with the customers, walking them through the loan process, educating them, and making sure they are receiving the fullest benefits possible.

I have achieved numerous accomplishments and have a record for developing a strong bottom line for the bank. My personal passion as a "people person" shines through in the successes I've achieved. I am computer literate, analytical, thorough, and well experienced in the complete loan process.

I would like the opportunity to meet with you personally where we may further discuss your bank's requirements and my qualifications. It appears from your advertisement that our needs may be a very close match. Please call me at your earliest convenience to schedule a time when we may meet and review how we may mutually benefit each other. Thank you for taking the time to review my résumé, and I look forward to meeting you personally.

Sincerely,

Regina Openhence

Enclosure

Jennifer Wallace
1234 Evergreen Drive ● Baltimore, MD 21032 ● Phone: 410-555-1234 ● jwallace@protypeltd.com

October 30, 2005

A letter sent at the recommendation of a company employee.

Attn: Mary Ann Brown, Director of Sales
Marriott Corporation
3299 K Street NW, Suite 700
Washington, DC 20007

Dear Ms. Brown:

Connie Johnson, a sales director at Marriott ExecuStay in Washington, DC, suggested that I contact you regarding a marketing position with Marriott Corporation. I am familiar with Marriott's reputation as a leader in the hospitality industry as well as its variety of affiliate partners around the world. I have the knowledge, experience, and desire to uphold Marriott's world-renowned reputation for success, comfort, and quality.

As an independent consultant, I have utilized sales, marketing, and research skills to develop my business, negotiate contracts, and build positive relationships with various business leaders in my community. I am self-motivated and a great motivator of other people. I make people *want* to come to the gym, sweat, and eat right. Can you think of a better example of someone's ability to motivate others?

In addition to my entrepreneurial experience, I worked in foreign exchange and as a stock broker in a previous career. The companies I worked for placed me in managerial positions in marketing, development, and business operations. My supervisors entrusted me with significant autonomy and implemented many of my suggestions for improvements and new programs. One such "take it and run with it suggestion" I made involved setting up a foreign exchange office for the Olympics.

Ms. Brown, as you can see, I am a creative professional with great communication skills and I would be a positive asset to the Marriott Corporation. I'd like to pursue my formal introduction further with a personal interview. I'll contact you the week of February 7 unless I hear from you before then.

Thank you for your time and consideration and I look forward to speaking with you.

Sincerely,

Jennifer Wallace

Enclosure

MORGAN ALLEN

4708 Seminole Drive
Indian River, Florida 32999
914-555-1234
mallen@protypeltd.com

April 20, 2005

Mr. John Longfeld
Operations Manager
Call Center Corporation
1234 Telephone Road
Orlando, Florida 32801

> A letter for a confidential job hunt.

Dear John:

After a successful 10-year track record with Circle Technologies, I am discretely exploring new career possibilities that will capitalize on my call center operations, account management, and sales management capabilities. As part of that effort, I am contacting a few trusted colleagues to get your perspectives on the local market and seek your wisdom. Accordingly, I have enclosed for your reference a résumé that outlines my capabilities.

John, I believe that my key areas of expertise relevant to a new professional position include:

- *Managing call centers with up to 115 representatives and addressing a range of functions that have included inbound and outbound telesales, lead generation, order entry and fulfillment, customer service/customer care, and technical ("help desk") support.*

- *Assessing needs, defining project scopes, and developing contract specifications for providing services to corporate clients as an outside vendor.*

- *Managing the collection, tracking, and analyzing data related to the performance of and return on various direct marketing programs.*

- *Recruiting, hiring, training, and developing high-performing call centers and telesales teams that have delivered multi-million dollar revenues with high profit margins to my employers.*

My goal is to stay in the Greater Orlando / Central Florida region, and I am convinced that I can contribute to the success of a dynamic company. I would appreciate the opportunity to chat with you about my plans and get any insights you may be able to offer. I will call you early next week to arrange a mutually convenient time for us to have a conversation. Meanwhile, if you are aware of any opportunities that would be appropriate, please let me know whom to contact. Since no one at my current employer is aware of my plans, I trust your discretion.

Thank you for your time. I look forward to speaking with you soon.

Sincerely,

Morgan Allen

Enclosure

296

MICHAEL DOUGLASS CASSEDY

806.555.1234

9999 55th Street, Pheasant Run, Texas 79000   mdcassedy@protypeltd.com

August 1, 2005

My principal career goal is to obtain a high-impact leadership position that promotes the well being of U.S. citizens—a role that requires the ability to meet highly responsible challenges that contribute to ensuring national / international security.

Special Agent Recruiter
FBI Division of Federal Government
#1 Place Washington Avenue
Washington, DC 00999

A letter for a government position with the FBI.

RE: FBI Special Agent, Announcement # 003895703FBI

Dear Recruiter:

Officer and paratrooper training in the Special Reservists, a secret security clearance, a business degree, management experience, and a creditable background clearly translate to an FBI special agent position where structure, discipline, skill development, and applied knowledge are fundamental prerequisites. Proven trainability and promotability as a civilian and reservist also reflect noteworthy leadership skills.

Additionally, a reputation for maintaining the highest level of personal and professional reliability, dedication, bravery, and integrity also precedes me, character traits necessary to a position of this magnitude. The enclosed résumé and application package represent a sincere desire to become a member of the most elite investigative arm of the federal government, the FBI.

Augmenting my education, military training, experience, and character are skills that demonstrate leadership ability to:

Build rapport and gain trust with others, ensuring strong business relationships.

Set priorities and manage time in accordance with management goals.

Perform well under pressure, where precision and choices are critical to positive outcomes.

Make effective, timely decisions within the scope of authority.

Anticipate needs / problems, assess progress, evaluate results, and apply knowledge for an efficient operation.

Research / investigate the source of problems to create practical resolutions.

Identify objective, organize resources, and direct efforts to achieve desired results.

Analyze perspectives and assess risk factors to promote safety.

Grasp and integrate organizational mission and values to help achieve company objectives.

Share a vision, communicate goals, and delegate tasks to appropriate individuals to generate success.

Enforce compliance with policy and procedure to maintain departmental credibility.

Build a motivated work environment when tasks and procedures seem mundane.

Work supportively as a productive team player to contribute to the mission.

Remain flexible and adapt to change when transition becomes necessary.

Focus on tasks through completion, including administrative paperwork.

I am confident that you will find me to be an excellent choice for FBI special agent and look forward to a mutually beneficial personal interview to further discuss your needs and my qualifications. In the meantime, thank you for your time and consideration.

Sincerely,

Michael D. Cassedy

Enclosure: Résumé

297

JANICE MOSS, RN, BSN

12345 Cherrytree Circle
Ashland, KY 41101

(606) 555-1234   moss@protypeltd.com

□□

December 6, 2005

> The letter writer is relocating and is cold calling on possible employers.

Ms. Mary Jane Archibald, RN, MSN
Director of Nursing
Baptist Hospital
310 Healthcare Row
Durham, NC 27701

Dear Ms. Archibald:

Because of my husband's promotion, it has become necessary for us to relocate to North Carolina from Kentucky. I learned of your facility through research in the Nursing '04 Career Directory and would be interested in exploring employment opportunities as a registered nurse in a cardiac stepdown or cardiac care unit at Baptist Hospital.

As you read my enclosed résumé, you will see that, for the last seven years, I have been employed at the Highland Medical Center in Ashland, Kentucky, one of the first facilities in the state to receive the prestigious Magnet Award for outstanding nursing care. I perform both staff nurse and occasional charge nurse duties on an intermediate care cardiac medical/surgical stepdown unit. In my position, I provide primary care nursing for 4–8 patients, particularly during the critical 24-hour postoperative period following open-heart surgery.

As a nursing team participant, I routinely respond to respiratory and cardiac codes in a calm, assertive, and well-organized manner. My dedication and enthusiasm for nursing enables me to create a supportive atmosphere that is beneficial to the well-being of patients who are experiencing the extreme discomforts associated with major surgery.

My references will confirm that I maintain excellent collaborative relationships with physicians and other staff professionals in carrying out care assignments for positive patient outcomes. Many of my patients have also written me letters of appreciation. I feel confident that my broad range of skills, acquired though my professional training and clinical practice, would be of value to Baptist Hospital.

Since I plan to be in North Carolina over the holiday season and into early January, may I ask for a few minutes of your time so that I could introduce myself and learn more about your facility and nursing staff needs? I will call you to schedule a mutually convenient interview time. However, if you wish to contact me before December 22nd, please feel free to call me at the above phone number.

Sincerely,

Janice Moss

Enclosure: Résumé

JENNIE A. HALL

12345 E. Cochise Dr. ∎ Scottsdale, AZ 85259
Phone: 480-555-1234 ∎ Email: hall@protypeltd.com

March 3, 2005

A letter in response to an advertisement

Chris Jones
Director of Personnel
City of Tempe
12345 E. University
Tempe, AZ 85282

Reference: Five reasons to interview me for Call Center Manager

Dear Mr. Jones:

As a proven Customer Service and Sales Call Center Manager, I offer the skills and abilities you need for the Call Center position.

Specifically, I bring you:

> Experience in large team operations management and project management as demonstrated by receiving AT&T's highest consumer service award and completing large, complex projects.

> Proficiency in exceeding sales and customer service objectives by 120 percent.

> Expertise in training large groups, team building, and coaching one-on-one gained by managing over 200 employees and team leaders with outstanding employee opinion survey results.

> Capability to utilize and lead process improvement techniques to improve performance by working with teams of 10 to 12 people.

> Bachelor of Science in Marketing.

Based upon these highlights and those detailed in my enclosed résumé, I am certain I would be a strong match for your requirements. I would enjoy meeting with you to discuss how my qualifications can meet the needs of the City of Tempe. I look forward to hearing from you soon.

Sincerely,

Jennie A. Hall

Enclosure

JOAQUIN BETANCOURT

501 Private Beach Drive
Newport Beach, CA 92659

JBetancourt@protypeltd.com

Home/Fax: 949.000.1001
Cell: 949.000.2002

August 5, 2005

A letter requesting a senior management position in hospitality.

John E. Smith
Major Airlines
30 Rockefeller Plaza, Suite 1000
New York, NY 10112

RE: Senior Vice President of Onboard Services

Dear Mr. Smith:

Building corporate value, total quality guest environments, and workplaces that reflect a company's mission are my professional passion and expertise.

In January 2000, I was recruited by Multinational Hotels, Inc., to serve as Senior Vice President for Inter-American Operations and play a key role in the corporation's $4 billion startup. We envisioned and created an environment that thrives on the improvement process and breakthrough ideas that result from never accepting a formula just because "everyone else is doing it." Today, Multinational is the largest international hotel and leisure operations enterprise and is recognized by guests, trade publications, and the airline industry as the "World's Best Global Hotel Company."

I bring to the position of Senior Vice President of Onboard Services 20 years of proven strategic and tactical leadership in the hospitality industry. My strengths in operations management and complex negotiations are measured in multimillion-dollar revenue increases, earnings gains, reduced operating costs, and more competitive and sustainable market advantages. These core proficiencies are critical to meeting Major Airlines' financial, operating, market, superior customer service, and employee relations goals.

My team has successfully implemented innovative guest services programs that improve customer satisfaction and loyalty in collective bargaining environments. We consistently receive top approval ratings from management to front line staff. My participatory leadership style evolved from having worked through school as a doorman, busboy, server, line cook, and front desk agent. I can, and still do, walk in our employees' shoes. I do not ask any one to do anything I would not do.

As a frequent flyer, I have observed and experienced the best and the worst our industry has to offer. The same traveler who steps onto a plane also stays at our hotels. Our goals are the same—to provide an enjoyable, comfortable, safe, and hassle-free experience.

I appreciate your consideration and look forward to speaking with you regarding your search.

Sincerely,

Joaquin Betancourt

Enclosure: Résumé

John G. Warren

1st Avenue #4C – Long Island City, New York 11106 – Cell: 407-555-1234 – Home: 212-555-5678 – E-mail: jgwarren@protypeltd.com

September 12, 2005

Florida Hotel & Resort
3138 Terry Brook
Winter Park, Florida

> A letter used to gain a position in the hospitality industry without experience in that industry.

Re: General Resort Manager

Dear Employment Manager:

You need impeccable guest services, tenacious management, and a sincere desire to fulfill expectations to cement memorable experiences for customers in the hospitality industry. As an experienced General/Senior Manager with more than 10 years of experience ensuring excellent operations, propelling profits, and delivering superb service, I now offer you my assistance as your new General Resort Manager.

In order to annihilate your competition, retain your existing clientele, and win new ones, your hotel must service above the standards of your competitors and make an impression with competent and professional people. In addition, your facility must invite your existing and prospective guests with pleasing aesthetics and seductive comfort. Above all, every person in your team MUST exceed the expectations of every guest with which they interact. I offer to secure these essentials for your hotel and continue to uphold the professional image Florida Hotel & Resort exudes.

With an accomplished history under my current employer, I now seek an opportunity to contribute in the hotel industry with an upscale establishment like yours. Please review my attached résumé, and allow me to highlight the following. I have…

- ✓ Turned low-performing locations into profitable establishments that pleased directors, owners, and customers.
- ✓ Enhanced already successful establishments and produced in areas overlooked by other managers.
- ✓ Led large staffs by motivating them, infusing them with confidence, and leading them by example.
- ✓ Communicated with corporate and non-corporate personnel using language that is clear, sensible, intelligent, and persuasive.
- ✓ Developed a valuable reputation with a highly demanding clientele by delivering on promises and anticipating their comfort and service needs.
- ✓ Generated millions in annual gross by overhauling departments and decreasing expenditures.

The value I will bring to your hotel is not limited to the above. In me, you will gain a manager that can forecast financial, operational, and guest needs accurately, prioritize and manage intelligently, and own all responsibilities in your organization, which will lead to your continued success.

Thank you in advance for your time and consideration. I look forward to hearing from you.

Sincerely,

John G. Warren

MICHAEL MARTINEZ

123 London Street • Northern, IL 60099 • (847) 555-2222 • mmartinez@protypeltd.com

September 4, 2005

> A broadcasting letter for an entry-level worker.

Human Resources
Felicity, Inc.
P.O. Box 49552
Chicago, Illinois 60110

Dear Hiring Professional:

As a child my playground was most often the family restaurant. I learned early on that success depends on a strong commitment to customer satisfaction, quality, and a constant focus on the bottom line. My recent experience includes retail management roles in book, video, and game product store environments. The range of my experience spans:

Retail Store Operations Management	Merchandising / Creative Product Display
P&L Responsibility / Budgeting / AP / AR	External Marketing / Publicity
Solutions-Focused Customer Service	Special Events Coordination
Shift Supervision / Opening and Closing	Editor / Author Monthly Catalog
Primary / Peripheral Sales	Solid Communication / Teambuilding Skills
Inventory Control / Purchasing / Loss Prevention	Strong PC and Database Skills

My contributions include:

- **Editor, author, creative designer for a 20-page monthly book catalog** including writing feature articles and book / product synopses.

- **Redesigned product displays** resulting in a **50% increase in sales** in targeted merchandise sales.

- **Awarded 35 recognitions for customer service and peripheral sales**; personally exceeded all other district stores in presales of select video product.

I have approached my work with a strong sense of urgency, working well under pressure and change. I am considered a team player who has a strong commitment to the people and the organization I work for.

The sum of my experience has provided me with the qualifications to contribute to your company's long-term success. I have enclosed my résumé in anticipation that you may be interested in adding an impact player to your team. I would welcome a personal interview. Thank you for your time and consideration.

Sincerely,

Michael Martinez

Enclosure

JOSE CASTELLANOS

P.O. Box 1234 • Phoenix, Arizona 85123 • (602) 555-1234

June 26, 2005

A great example of a "story" letter.

Ms. Cindy Smith
College Relations Manager
Hallmark Cards, Inc.
P.O. Box 123456
Kansas City, Missouri 64141

Dear Ms. Smith:

It was in my hometown of Bogotá, Colombia, that as a teenager I came into contact with Hallmark for the first time. Even though I was not aware of the vision, effort, and commitment of resources that had gone into the Mother's Day card I had purchased, I was a happy customer. I never thought to wonder about the logistics of how that card had gotten to that small store or why a company more than 3,000 miles away was able to appeal to me, a kid from another country, culture, and language.

Hallmark's aggressive market penetration in more than 100 countries and its striving to provide employees with a supportive and challenging environment to best develop and apply their individual skills demonstrate to me that Hallmark is a company well worth entrusting with my career. In addition, I am impressed and attracted by Hallmark's commitment to supporting the communities in which it operates.

In light of Hallmark's international interest, you may be interested in my background. I started a small business in Colombia, which tested my energy, creativity, and initiative. The business quickly grew to be competitive as a result of innovative marketing and operation strategies. I have since learned to speak English, obtained a Bachelor of Business Administration from a U.S. university, and worked in several countries in varied positions, successfully adapting to both the people and management styles of these countries. Furthermore, in order to be better prepared for today's complex business environment, I am pursuing a Master of International Management degree, which I will complete in December.

It is my hope that my solid academic and cultural backgrounds, business experience, and interest in the international arena will convey to you that I have the qualifications to make a valuable contribution to Hallmark's efforts to remain the worldwide leader of the social expression industry.

I would like to be part of the Hallmark team that once helped me express myself through that card I gave my mother, and to take part in expanding the company to reach even more people all over the world. I would appreciate the opportunity to interview with you during your upcoming visit to Phoenix and hope that you will give the enclosed résumé favorable consideration. Thank you for your attention.

Sincerely,

Jose Castellanos

Enclosure

Gloria R. Clawson

1234 Queen Anne Way • Colorado Springs, Colorado 80917 • (719) 555-1234

A dream job with little relevant experience.

July 21, 2005

United Airlines (AFA)
Attn: F/A Employment
Box 66100
Chicago, Illinois 60666

Dear Sir/Madam:

I have dreamed of being a flight attendant since I was sixteen, but something has always prevented me from fulfilling that dream. Now that I've had a little experience with Western Pacific Airlines, I'm confident that I qualify for such a position. I would very much like to work for United Airlines, which I feel is a well-established and reputable organization.

With my twenty years of public relations experience, I would be an asset to United. I am a highly qualified individual who is ready to move forward into a more professional career. As you will see from the enclosed letters of recommendation, I am a very efficient and conscientious worker. I have a particularly strong desire to travel and work with people. With my outgoing personality and infectious smile, I know I would make a great addition to your team.

My résumé can only highlight my qualifications. A personal interview will assure you of my potential value to your company. I look forward to hearing from you so we may take the discussions of this challenging position one step further.

Sincerely,

Gloria R. Clawson

Enclosure

LORNA HURLEY

1234 Saturn Drive #123 • Colorado Springs, Colorado 80906 • (719) 555-1234

October 19, 2005

Making connections with the feelings of the reader and explaining why the job would be a good fit even though the writer is over-qualified.

Human Resources
USAA
1234 Telstar Drive
Colorado Springs, CO 80920

Ref Code: PC-COS-1234

Dear Recruiter:

I have long been a satisfied customer of USAA, as was my father before me, so when I noticed your advertisement for Customer Account Professionals in a recent edition of The Gazette, I was immediately attracted to the possibility of working for USAA again. I was a supervisor in the Communications Center in your San Antonio headquarters for two years before returning to Colorado Springs for family reasons.

Although I don't know your current hiring needs, I hope to explore the possibility of working for USAA as a customer service supervisor. I was a supervisor at Allstate insurance in the customer and agency service department, and all of my positions have involved a high level of customer service for both internal and external clients. At Allstate, I reviewed detailed policy information and relayed that information to both the insureds and their agents. I am accustomed to working in a fast-paced team environment with conflicting deadlines and have good computer skills. My college degrees and continuing professional development have prepared me for success within your customer service department.

Even though you might consider my qualifications too strong for this position, I want to assure you that I would enjoy the opportunity to learn USAA's Colorado Springs business from the ground up. I would welcome the opportunity for an interview to further discuss how my unique skills could benefit USAA. Thank you for your consideration, and I look forward to hearing from you soon.

Sincerely,

Lorna Hurley

Enclosure

GREGORY HUMPHREYS

5896 42nd Street ▪ Lubbock, Texas 79000
ghumphreys@protypeltd.com
806.555.1234 (C) ▪ **806.555.5678 (H)**

A letter requesting an informational interview at the recommendation of a mutual contact.

August 1, 2005

Mr. Gary Wintworth
Manager
ABC Company
5555 Main Street
Amarillo, Texas 78000

Dear Mr. Wintworth:

Your associate, Brady Williams, whom I met last Thursday at a Rotary Club meeting referred me to you in my quest to find out more about the telecom industry. It is with sincere interest that I request a 30-minute informational interview with you at your convenience. I am currently a manager with Intel but would like to make a transition to a related field and feel someone in a reputable company, such as yours, could enlighten me. As Brady speaks highly of you, I would very much respect any guidance you might offer.

I will call your office within the week to perhaps set up a date and time. Until then, thank you for your consideration.

Gratefully,

Gregory Humphreys

Enclosure: Business Card

Michael C. DeWitt

Permanent Address: 1234 Edgepark Road ◆ **Vienna, Virginia 22182** ◆ **Message: (703) 555-1234**
Present Address: Jan Luykenstraat 1234 ◆ **1071 CR Amsterdam** ◆ **The Netherlands**
Home: (+31) 20-555-1234 ◆ **Work: (+31) 20-555-5678** ◆ **E-mail: dewitt@protypeltd.com**

February 17, 2005

> Dynamic cover letter.

Mr. Mike Smith
Vice President, Sales
BT North America
1234 East 52nd Street
New York, NY 10022

Dear Mr. Smith:

Would you have an interest in an individual who has generated more than $50 million in global account revenues for a telecommunications leader, and who recently played a key role in the success of a new BT European joint venture? If so, I'd like to speak with you about how I can employ these skills and my knowledge of MCI/WorldCom to help BT North America achieve its revenue and business objectives in the new global marketplace.

As a successful sales and business development manager with MCI, I have a proven track record of delivering significant revenue and profit growth by building value propositions for advanced voice, data, and Internet applications. These skills have placed me within the top one percent of MCI's global sales force on three separate occasions.

In my current assignment as a member of the senior management team for Telfort in The Netherlands, I direct a group that, in just six months time, has been instrumental in contributing more than $10 million in revenue to this successful startup.

With my overseas assignment drawing to a close in April 2005, I have a strong interest in pursuing opportunities within BT North America. Should you have a current or emerging need for a proven contributor to your management team, I would appreciate your serious consideration of my qualifications outlined in the enclosed résumé.

My present travel plans call for me to be in the United States from 2/20 through 3/2. I would welcome the opportunity to meet with you in person and will contact you shortly to determine if this is convenient for you. I look forward to hearing from you soon.

Sincerely,

Michael C. DeWitt

Enclosure

KEISHA CHAMBER

1234 East Platte
Colorado Springs, CO 80903

Telephone:
(719) 555-1234

July 12, 2005

Networking letter requesting an internship or informational interview.

Stephen Smith
P.O. Box 1234
LaJunta, Colorado 81050

Dear Mr. Smith:

John Smith, Professor at UCCS, recommended that I contact you. I have just graduated from the University of Colorado at Colorado Springs with an undergraduate degree in geography and environmental sciences.

My studies, combined with my Olympic training have been particularly intense. I often devoted more than 30 hours a week to my sport and still found the time to pursue my degree and earn a 3.4 GPA. Unfortunately, this rigorous schedule didn't afford me the benefit of an internship, but it did provide me with the desire to achieve and the belief that consistent training improves performance. Now that I have graduated, I would like to spend the next year working for a company like yours and learning all there is to know about the GIS industry. I am available full time in whatever capacity you need.

The opportunity to work for your company would be a real asset to my career, and I would appreciate your serious consideration of my qualifications. If you don't see a fit with your organization at the present time, I would still like to have the opportunity to meet with you or someone in your company who could take a few minutes to provide me with some ideas for how I might break into and succeed in this industry. Thank you for your consideration, and I look forward to hearing from you soon.

Sincerely,

Keisha Chamber

Enclosure

TONY POLACEK

1234 Bridle Trail
Pueblo, Colorado 81005

Phone: (719) 555-1234
polacek@protypeltd.com

November 17, 2005

> Letter to a recruiter. Note the third paragraph that is unique in letters to recruiters.

Mr. Stefan Smith
President
Management Search, Inc.
1234 S. Cook St., Suite 12
Barrington, IL 60010

Dear Mr. Smith:

Is one of your clients looking for a Human Resources or Labor Relations Manager with a proven track record of success in both manufacturing and high-tech services industries? Then you will want to review my qualifications.

As a successful human resource generalist with extensive labor relations experience, I have become well known for my ability to improve employee morale and increase trust between unions and management. I have negotiated and administered several collective bargaining agreements and was often called in to diffuse stalled bargaining processes. My dynamic leadership style motivates change within the corporate culture and builds support from within the ranks. These skills, plus many more, would be true assets to any company whether they are unionized or not.

My target job is at the middle-management level with an innovative company that could challenge my skills in human resource management, employee relations, and compensation and benefit administration. I have no geographic preferences and would be open to relocation. My salary requirements would of course depend on the city, but I would anticipate a base salary in the area of $60,000.

Should one of your clients have a current or emerging need for a member of their human resource management team, I would appreciate your serious consideration of my qualifications as outlined in the enclosed résumé. I am free to meet with you at your convenience and look forward to hearing from you soon.

Sincerely,

Tony Polacek

Enclosure

LEE DAVID MILLER

1234 Amstel Drive • Colorado Springs, Colorado 80907 • (719) 555-1234 • E-mail: ldmiller@protypeltd.com

Letter to a recruiter.

August 13, 2005

Mr. Scott Smith
Office Manager
Korn/Ferry International
1234 S. Wacker Drive, Ste. 12
Sears Tower
Chicago, IL 60606

Dear Mr. Smith:

After a 25-year career in a number of senior management positions with high-tech computer/ communications companies in the Silicon Valley (and a short stint owning my own consulting company), I have seen many examples of great leadership and a few that were less than that. What seems to separate the truly successful senior executive from the mediocre is the degree of commitment he is able to instill in his people. I have been successful in building strong teams of productive professionals by creating comfortable, yet challenging environments that are stimulating and satisfying. Having participated in changes that have transformed the industry, I want to continue to be a part of this challenge in a senior leadership position that can take advantage of my in-depth knowledge of current technologies.

If one of your clients is looking for an experienced vice president or director who can motivate a team not only to meet but to exceed growth and financial goals, I am the person who can deliver those expectations and more. I am looking for a position that will continue to challenge me and give me the opportunity to lead a company into the 21st century. I have no geographic preferences and would expect compensation in the $130–175,000 range, exclusive of benefits.

The enclosed résumé will provide you with the details of my experience and accomplishments. I would welcome the opportunity for an interview to discuss how my skills and experience can meet your needs. Thank you for your consideration.

Sincerely,

Lee David Miller

Enclosure

DAVID F. KOVACH

Unsolicited letter to create a job.

August 16, 2005

Ms. Nancy Waite
COO, Executive Vice President
Ports of Call
3333 Quebec Street, Suite 9100
Denver, Colorado 80207-2331

Dear Ms. Waite:

Carol Ingwersen recommended that I forward a copy of my résumé for your review. I am very interested in returning to the travel industry in a sales capacity and would appreciate an opportunity to sit down with you to talk about the unique ideas I could bring to your sales process.

As you can see in my résumé, I have extensive sales and customer service experience, but what you can't see is that I have worked for travel clubs twice in my career. I succeeded in selling 450 memberships in only three months for The Diplomats in Des Moines, Iowa, and I worked as the membership director for the Texas Air Travel Club during my early career. With its own private jet and 2,500 members, the Texas Air Travel Club was very similar to Ports of Call. I developed some innovative ways of increasing memberships that would be valuable to your company.

Even though you don't have any current openings, I think you will find my ideas worthy of a trial even if you have to create a position for me. I will give you a call next week to see if there is a mutually convenience time we can get together to talk about the possibilities. Thank you for your consideration.

Sincerely,

David F. Kovach

Enclosure

SALLY RENE STEWART

5000 West 5th Street
Lubbock, Texas 79400
(806) 555-1234
srs@protypeltd.com

A thank you letter
following an interview.

August 28, 2005

Ms. Jane Young
The Design Center
Merimax Interiors, Inc.
234 Waukegan Road
Lubbock, Texas 79402

Dear Ms. Young:

Thank you for the time you extended me during our interview last Tuesday. Our discussion was enlightening and enjoyable. I am sincerely interested in a designer position with Merimax Interiors, Inc., as I was impressed with your company's culture, growth options, and mission to provide creative yet functional interior designs to clients in the medical care industry.

As you may recall, my particular strength is a positive approach to my work and a commitment to excellence in any endeavor I attempt. The honors I attained during my college career at Texas Tech University reflect my quest for distinction. The prospect of putting my color and design knowledge to work in a business environment such as yours at Merimax Interiors, Inc., is thrilling.

If you have additional questions, please feel free to contact me at (806) 555-1234. I look forward to hearing again from you in the very near future.

Again, thank you for your interest in my qualifications for your designer vacancy.

Sincerely,

Sally Rene Stewart

David M. Hudson

4321 Oakmoore Avenue NE
Massillon, OH 44646
330-555-1234

A thank you letter following an interview.

February 10, 2005

Mr. Randall Killian
Manager, Prototype Operations
Topco Industries, Inc.
4231 Seabrook Ave. NW
North Canton, OH 44720

Dear Mr. Killian:

I would like to take this opportunity to thank you for the interview Thursday afternoon at your office and to confirm my strong interest in the CNC Machinist position.

After we spoke, it became increasingly clear to me that the position we discussed would be a good fit for my skills and interest. I recognize that this is a busy department with a demanding schedule and a need for accuracy and the ability to meet deadlines. I believe my background, experience, and skills will allow me to make a positive contribution in this department. I hope you will consider me for this position.

In closing, I would like to again thank you for sharing your valuable time with me. I am excited about the possibilities of this position and remain even more convinced of the potential for a good match. I would consider it a privilege to be an employee of a company with an excellent reputation such as Topco. I look forward to a favorable outcome.

Sincerely,

David M. Hudson

1234 Ashwood Circle
Colorado Springs, CO 80906
Phone: (719) 555-1234
E-mail: lsteele@protypeltd.com

Thank you letter that drops the name of the recipient's manager.

June 7, 2005

Ms. Jeanine Smith
Director of Sales and Marketing
The Cliff House
1234 Canon Avenue
Manitou Springs, Colorado 80829

Dear Ms. Smith:

Thank you for taking the time to interview me for the Sales Manager position at The Cliff House. As we discussed, I have built two successful businesses from the ground up and am very comfortable making cold calls, networking, and building a clientele from scratch. One of those businesses was a travel agency, where I worked closely with my counterparts in the hospitality industry and made high-level presentations to corporate prospects. This experience would translate well into the hotel industry here in the Colorado Springs area.

I had the unexpected pleasure of speaking with Craig Hartman on Friday, May 28, and got a positive feeling for the management culture at The Cliff House even before meeting you. I know that I would be a good fit in the Sales Manager position. Enclosed is a copy of my reference list, as you requested. If you have any further questions, feel free to give me a call. I look forward to hearing from you soon.

Sincerely,

Liz Steele

Enclosure

314

Amy Rigby
1234 Main Street, Annapolis, MD 21401
410-555-1234 ● Rigby@protypeltd.com

July 15, 2005

A thank you letter following an interview for a nurse returning to the workforce.

Attn: Anne Johnson, Nursing Recruiter
Wayson Pavilion – Human Resources
Anne Arundel Medical Center
2001 Medical Parkway, Suite 350
Annapolis, MD 21401

Dear Ms. Johnson:

Thank you for taking time out of your busy schedule yesterday to discuss the pediatric temporary float pool clinical nursing position that is available. As we discussed, this is the perfect position where I can continue to develop my nursing skills but have the flexibility that I desire.

I am confident that I can make a positive contribution to the high quality of nursing care that is provided at AAMC. My experience working as a clinical nurse in the Pediatric Research Unit at Johns Hopkins University facilitated my ability to quickly and accurately assess patient needs and identify appropriate treatment plans. Being a team member on research protocols proved to me how important it is to clearly communicate patient needs and requirements, in writing and verbally, especially when numerous medical caregivers were involved. I learned the importance of patient advocacy and how to properly inform parents and caregivers how to monitor their children's medical needs and follow prescribed treatment plans upon hospital discharge.

These skills and more, combined with my Bachelor's Degree in Nursing from Johns Hopkins, more than qualify me for the position. I would consider it an honor and privilege to serve the staff, patients, and physicians that choose to affiliate themselves with Anne Arundel Medical Center.

Thank you for your time and consideration for this position. I look forward to speaking with you in more detail soon.

Sincerely,

Amy Rigby

MATT C. LINCOLN

8899 1st Place – Lubbock, Texas 79416
(806) 555-1234
mattlincoln89@protypeltd.com

A resignation letter, which every job seeker hopes to write eventually!

August 28, 2005

Mr. Jack Preston
Vice President
Cox & Preston Advertising
9986 Ave. G
Lubbock, Texas 79401

Dear Jack:

It is with mixed emotions that I present this letter of resignation. As you know, my parents have been ailing for the last three years. Considering their poor health, I have secured a position with Braxton and Braxton in New York City to be near them. I will relocate to that area in two months. However, it is my intention to remain in the office for at least two to four weeks to ease the transition in filling my vacancy.

I want to express to you that my ten years with you and David have been rewarding and beneficial to my growth as a layout artist. You have both been great associates and mentors. I only hope my position with Braxton and Braxton will bring me as much job satisfaction.

Please let me know if there is anything else I must do to complete the resignation process.

Sincerely,

Matt C. Lincoln

19 | Résumé Worksheets

I developed worksheets for my Barron's book *How to Write Better Résumés and Cover Letters* that have received rave reviews. Since they follow the twelve-step résumé writing process in Chapter 2 of this book, they can be useful for your résumé development. You can download free MS Word, PDF, or WordPerfect files of the questionnaires at *www.patcriscito.com* by selecting the "Pat's Books" link.

If you need more detail on how to use the worksheets than you find in Chapter 2, you might want to pick up a copy of *How to Write Better Résumés and Cover Letters* at your local library or bookstore.

You should copy as many of the College Education, Vocational/Technical Training, Professional Development, and Keyword worksheets as you need for your own experience.

COLLEGE EDUCATION

Use this form to collect information on your formal college education. Write down everything you can think of regardless of whether you use it on the final résumé. You will narrow the list later. Use a separate page for each degree. Make as many copies of this page as you need for each degree.

DEGREE _____

SCHOOL _____

CITY AND STATE _____

YEARS ATTENDED _____

YEAR GRADUATED _____ GPA _____

MAJOR _____

MINOR _____

THESIS/DISSERTATION _____

_____

_ _

SIGNIFICANT PROJECTS _____

_____

_____

_____

HONORS, AWARDS, SCHOLARSHIPS, ETC. _____

_____

_____

_____

ACTIVITIES (volunteer, leadership, sports, social groups, etc.) _____

_____

_____

_____

STUDY ABROAD (programs, school, country, special areas of study) _____

_____

_____

_____

VOCATIONAL/TECHNICAL TRAINING

Use this form to collect information on your vocational, technical, occupational, and military training. Write down everything you can think of, regardless of whether it relates to your job goal. You will narrow the list later. Make copies of this page if you need more room.

NAME OF COURSE _____

PRESENTED BY (company, school, etc.) _____

RESULT (certification, diploma, etc.) _____

DATES ATTENDED _____

YEAR GRADUATED _____

- -

NAME OF COURSE _____

PRESENTED BY (company, school, etc.) _____

RESULT (certification, diploma, etc.) _____

DATES ATTENDED _____

YEAR GRADUATED _____

- -

NAME OF COURSE _____

PRESENTED BY (company, school, etc.) _____

RESULT (certification, diploma, etc.) _____

DATES ATTENDED _____

YEAR GRADUATED _____

- -

NAME OF COURSE _____

PRESENTED BY (company, school, etc.) _____

RESULT (certification, diploma, etc.) _____

DATES ATTENDED _____

YEAR GRADUATED _____

PROFESSIONAL DEVELOPMENT

Use this form to collect information on your professional development and continuing education, including in-services, workshops, seminars, corporate training programs, conferences, conventions, etc. Write down everything you can think of, regardless of whether it relates to your job goal. You will narrow this list later. Make as many copies of this page as you need.

NAME OF COURSE _____

PRESENTED BY (company, school, etc.) _____

RESULT (certification, diploma, etc.) _____

DATES ATTENDED _____

- -

NAME OF COURSE _____

PRESENTED BY (company, school, etc.) _____

RESULT (certification, diploma, etc.) _____

DATES ATTENDED _____

- -

NAME OF COURSE _____

PRESENTED BY (company, school, etc.) _____

RESULT (certification, diploma, etc.) _____

DATES ATTENDED _____

- -

NAME OF COURSE _____

PRESENTED BY (company, school, etc.) _____

RESULT (certification, diploma, etc.) _____

DATES ATTENDED _____

- -

NAME OF COURSE _____

PRESENTED BY (company, school, etc.) _____

RESULT (certification, diploma, etc.) _____

DATES ATTENDED _____

KEYWORDS

Use this form to collect the buzz words of your industry and any synonyms. You will probably need several copies of this page to get all of the keywords on paper.

❑ Keyword: _____
   ❑ Synonym: _____
   ❑ Synonym: _____

❑ Keyword: _____
   ❑ Synonym: _____
   ❑ Synonym: _____

❑ Keyword: _____
   ❑ Synonym: _____
   ❑ Synonym: _____

❑ Keyword: _____
   ❑ Synonym: _____
   ❑ Synonym: _____

❑ Keyword: _____
   ❑ Synonym: _____
   ❑ Synonym: _____

❑ Keyword: _____
   ❑ Synonym: _____
   ❑ Synonym: _____

❑ Keyword: _____
   ❑ Synonym: _____
   ❑ Synonym: _____

❑ Keyword: _____
   ❑ Synonym: _____
   ❑ Synonym: _____

❑ Keyword: _____
   ❑ Synonym: _____
   ❑ Synonym: _____

❑ Keyword: _____
   ❑ Synonym: _____
   ❑ Synonym: _____

❑ Keyword: _____
   ❑ Synonym: _____
   ❑ Synonym: _____

❑ Keyword: _____
   ❑ Synonym: _____
   ❑ Synonym: _____

❑ Keyword: _____
   ❑ Synonym: _____
   ❑ Synonym: _____

❑ Keyword: _____
   ❑ Synonym: _____
   ❑ Synonym: _____

❑ Keyword: _____
   ❑ Synonym: _____
   ❑ Synonym: _____

❑ Keyword: _____
   ❑ Synonym: _____
   ❑ Synonym: _____

❑ Keyword: _____
   ❑ Synonym: _____
   ❑ Synonym: _____

❑ Keyword: _____
   ❑ Synonym: _____
   ❑ Synonym: _____

EXPERIENCE–JOB NO. 1

JOB TITLE _____

NAME OF EMPLOYER _____

CITY AND STATE _____

DATE STARTED _____ DATE ENDED _____

SUMMARY SENTENCE (The overall scope of your responsibility, overview of your essential role in the company, kind of products or services for which you were responsible) _____
_____
_____
_____
_____

NUMBER OF PEOPLE SUPERVISED AND THEIR TITLES OR FUNCTIONS _____
_____
_____
_____
_____

DESCRIPTION OF RESPONSIBILITIES (Don't forget budget, hiring, training, operations, strategic planning, new business development, production, customer service, sales, marketing, advertising, etc.) _____
_____
_____
_____
_____
_____
_____
_____
_____
_____
_____
_____
_____

ACCOMPLISHMENTS _____
_____
_____
_____
_____
_____
_____
_____
_____
_____
_____
_____
_____

EXPERIENCE–JOB NO. 2

JOB TITLE _____

NAME OF EMPLOYER _____

CITY AND STATE _____

DATE STARTED _____ DATE ENDED _____

SUMMARY SENTENCE (The overall scope of your responsibility, overview of your essential role in the company, kind of products or services for which you were responsible) _____

_____

_____

_____

_____

NUMBER OF PEOPLE SUPERVISED AND THEIR TITLES OR FUNCTIONS _____

_____

_____

_____

_____

DESCRIPTION OF RESPONSIBILITIES (Don't forget budget, hiring, training, operations, strategic planning, new business development, production, customer service, sales, marketing, advertising, etc.) _____

_____

_____

_____

_____

_____

_____

_____

_____

_____

_____

_____

_____

_____

ACCOMPLISHMENTS _____

_____

_____

_____

_____

_____

_____

_____

_____

_____

_____

_____

_____

EXPERIENCE–JOB NO. 3

JOB TITLE _____

NAME OF EMPLOYER _____

CITY AND STATE _____

DATE STARTED _____ DATE ENDED _____

SUMMARY SENTENCE (The overall scope of your responsibility, overview of your essential role in the company, kind of products or services for which you were responsible) _____

_____

_____

_____

_____

NUMBER OF PEOPLE SUPERVISED AND THEIR TITLES OR FUNCTIONS _____

_____

_____

_____

_____

DESCRIPTION OF RESPONSIBILITIES (Don't forget budget, hiring, training, operations, strategic planning, new business development, production, customer service, sales, marketing, advertising, etc.) _____

_____

_____

_____

_____

_____

_____

_____

_____

_____

_____

_____

_____

_____

ACCOMPLISHMENTS _____

_____

_____

_____

_____

_____

_____

_____

_____

_____

_____

_____

_____

_____

EXPERIENCE–JOB NO. 4

JOB TITLE _____

NAME OF EMPLOYER _____

CITY AND STATE _____

DATE STARTED _____ DATE ENDED _____

SUMMARY SENTENCE (The overall scope of your responsibility, overview of your essential role in the company, kind of products or services for which you were responsible) _____
_____
_____
_____
_____

NUMBER OF PEOPLE SUPERVISED AND THEIR TITLES OR FUNCTIONS _____
_____
_____
_____
_____

DESCRIPTION OF RESPONSIBILITIES (Don't forget budget, hiring, training, operations, strategic planning, new business development, production, customer service, sales, marketing, advertising, etc.) _____
_____
_____
_____
_____
_____
_____
_____
_____
_____
_____
_____
_____

ACCOMPLISHMENTS _____
_____
_____
_____
_____
_____
_____
_____
_____
_____
_____
_____

EXPERIENCE–JOB NO. 5

JOB TITLE _____

NAME OF EMPLOYER _____

CITY AND STATE _____

DATE STARTED _____ DATE ENDED _____

SUMMARY SENTENCE (The overall scope of your responsibility, overview of your essential role in the company, kind of products or services for which you were responsible) _____
_____
_____
_____
_____

NUMBER OF PEOPLE SUPERVISED AND THEIR TITLES OR FUNCTIONS _____
_____
_____
_____
_____

DESCRIPTION OF RESPONSIBILITIES (Don't forget budget, hiring, training, operations, strategic planning, new business development, production, customer service, sales, marketing, advertising, etc.) _____
_____
_____
_____
_____
_____
_____
_____
_____
_____
_____
_____
_____
_____

ACCOMPLISHMENTS _____
_____
_____
_____
_____
_____
_____
_____
_____
_____
_____
_____
_____

EXPERIENCE–JOB NO. 6

JOB TITLE _____

NAME OF EMPLOYER _____

CITY AND STATE _____

DATE STARTED _____ DATE ENDED _____

SUMMARY SENTENCE (The overall scope of your responsibility, overview of your essential role in the company, kind of products or services for which you were responsible) _____

_____

_____

_____

_____

NUMBER OF PEOPLE SUPERVISED AND THEIR TITLES OR FUNCTIONS _____

_____

_____

_____

_____

DESCRIPTION OF RESPONSIBILITIES (Don't forget budget, hiring, training, operations, strategic planning, new business development, production, customer service, sales, marketing, advertising, etc.) _____

_____

_____

_____

_____

_____

_____

_____

_____

_____

_____

_____

_____

ACCOMPLISHMENTS _____

_____

_____

_____

_____

_____

_____

_____

_____

_____

_____

_____

_____

EXPERIENCE–JOB NO. 7

JOB TITLE _____

NAME OF EMPLOYER _____

CITY AND STATE _____

DATE STARTED _____ DATE ENDED _____

SUMMARY SENTENCE (The overall scope of your responsibility, overview of your essential role in the company, kind of products or services for which you were responsible) _____
_____
_____
_____
_____

NUMBER OF PEOPLE SUPERVISED AND THEIR TITLES OR FUNCTIONS _____
_____
_____
_____
_____

DESCRIPTION OF RESPONSIBILITIES (Don't forget budget, hiring, training, operations, strategic planning, new business development, production, customer service, sales, marketing, advertising, etc.) _____
_____
_____
_____
_____
_____
_____
_____
_____
_____
_____
_____
_____

ACCOMPLISHMENTS _____
_____
_____
_____
_____
_____
_____
_____
_____
_____
_____
_____
_____
_____
_____

EXPERIENCE—JOB NO. 8

JOB TITLE _____

NAME OF EMPLOYER _____

CITY AND STATE _____

DATE STARTED _____ DATE ENDED _____

SUMMARY SENTENCE (The overall scope of your responsibility, overview of your essential role in the company, kind of products or services for which you were responsible) _____
_____
_____
_____
_____

NUMBER OF PEOPLE SUPERVISED AND THEIR TITLES OR FUNCTIONS _____
_____
_____
_____

DESCRIPTION OF RESPONSIBILITIES (Don't forget budget, hiring, training, operations, strategic planning, new business development, production, customer service, sales, marketing, advertising, etc.) _____
_____
_____
_____
_____
_____
_____
_____
_____
_____
_____
_____
_____

ACCOMPLISHMENTS _____
_____
_____
_____
_____
_____
_____
_____
_____
_____
_____

EXPERIENCE–JOB NO. 9

JOB TITLE _____

NAME OF EMPLOYER _____

CITY AND STATE _____

DATE STARTED _____ DATE ENDED _____

SUMMARY SENTENCE (The overall scope of your responsibility, overview of your essential role in the company, kind of products or services for which you were responsible) _____
_____
_____
_____
_____

NUMBER OF PEOPLE SUPERVISED AND THEIR TITLES OR FUNCTIONS _____
_____
_____
_____
_____

DESCRIPTION OF RESPONSIBILITIES (Don't forget budget, hiring, training, operations, strategic planning, new business development, production, customer service, sales, marketing, advertising, etc.) _____
_____
_____
_____
_____
_____
_____
_____
_____
_____
_____
_____
_____

ACCOMPLISHMENTS _____
_____
_____
_____
_____
_____
_____
_____
_____
_____
_____
_____
_____

EXPERIENCE—JOB NO. 10

JOB TITLE _____

NAME OF EMPLOYER _____

CITY AND STATE _____

DATE STARTED _____ DATE ENDED _____

SUMMARY SENTENCE (The overall scope of your responsibility, overview of your essential role in the company, kind of products or services for which you were responsible) _____

_____

_____

_____

_____

NUMBER OF PEOPLE SUPERVISED AND THEIR TITLES OR FUNCTIONS _____

_____

_____

_____

_____

DESCRIPTION OF RESPONSIBILITIES (Don't forget budget, hiring, training, operations, strategic planning, new business development, production, customer service, sales, marketing, advertising, etc.) _____

_____

_____

_____

_____

_____

_____

_____

_____

_____

_____

_____

_____

ACCOMPLISHMENTS _____

_____

_____

_____

_____

_____

_____

_____

_____

_____

_____

_____

RELATED QUALIFICATIONS

AFFILIATIONS (professional associations, chambers of commerce, Toastmasters, etc.) _____
_____
_____
_____
_____
_____

LANGUAGES (with levels of proficiency*) _____
_____
_____
_____

*Fluent (absolute ability, native), Highly Proficient (3 to 5 years of usage in the country), Proficient (able to understand the subtleties of the language), Working Knowledge (can conduct everyday business), Knowledge (exposure to the language, courtesy phrases)

LICENSES _____
_____
_____
_____

CERTIFICATIONS _____
_____
_____
_____

CREDENTIALS _____
_____
_____
_____

PRESENTATIONS/SPEECHES (title, meeting, sponsoring organization, city, state, date) _____
_____
_____
_____

EXHIBITS _____
_____
_____
_____

PUBLICATIONS (authors, article title, publication title, volume, issue, page numbers, date) _____
_____
_____
_____

GRANTS _____
_____
_____
_____

RELATED QUALIFICATIONS

SPECIAL PROJECTS _____
_____
_____
_____

RESEARCH _____
_____
_____
_____

UNIQUE SKILLS _____
_____
_____
_____

VOLUNTEER ACTIVITIES, CIVIC CONTRIBUTIONS _____
_____
_____
_____
_____
_____

HONORS, AWARDS, DISTINCTIONS, PROFESSIONAL RECOGNITION _____
_____
_____
_____
_____

COMPUTERS _____
_____
_____

Applications (MS Word, Excel, PowerPoint, etc.) _____
Operating Systems (Windows, Macintosh, UNIX, etc.)_____
Databases (Access, Oracle, etc.) _____
Programming Languages _____
Networking _____
Communications _____
Hardware _____

OTHER RELEVANT SKILLS _____
Actors (singing, musical instruments, martial arts, etc.)_____
Secretaries (typing speed, shorthand, etc.) _____
Welders (TIG, MIG, ARC, etc.) _____

INTERNATIONAL _____
(travel, living, cross-cultural skills, etc.) _____
_____

QUALIFICATIONS PROFILE

Keep the qualifications profile short, sweet, and to the point. I tend to limit them to five or six bullets, although there are exceptions to this rule when creating a curriculum vita or other types of professional résumés.

You can title this section with any of the following headlines: Profile, Qualifications, Highlights of Qualifications, Expertise, Strengths, Summary, Synopsis, Background, Professional Background, Executive Summary, Highlights, Overview, Professional Overview, Capsule, or Keyword Profile.

OBJECTIVE/FOCUS (this can become the first sentence of your profile or stand alone) _____
_____
_____
_____

SECOND SENTENCE (areas of expertise) _____
_____
_____
_____

STRENGTHS _____
_____
_____
_____

STRENGTHS _____
_____
_____
_____

STRENGTHS _____
_____
_____
_____

STRENGTHS _____
_____
_____
_____

STRENGTHS _____
_____
_____
_____

STRENGTHS _____
_____
_____
_____

REFERENCES

Unless an advertisement specifically requests references, don't send them with your résumé. Type a nice list of three to six references on the same letterhead as your résumé to take with you to the interview. Use this form to collect the information for your reference list. Choose people who know how you work and are not just personal friends or family members.

NAME _____
RELATIONSHIP TO YOU _____
COMPANY _____
MAILING ADDRESS _____
CITY, STATE, ZIP _____
WORK PHONE _____ CELL PHONE _____
HOME PHONE _____ E-MAIL _____

NAME _____
RELATIONSHIP TO YOU _____
COMPANY _____
MAILING ADDRESS _____
CITY, STATE, ZIP _____
WORK PHONE _____ CELL PHONE _____
HOME PHONE _____ E-MAIL _____

NAME _____
RELATIONSHIP TO YOU _____
COMPANY _____
MAILING ADDRESS _____
CITY, STATE, ZIP _____
WORK PHONE _____ CELL PHONE _____
HOME PHONE _____ E-MAIL _____

NAME _____
RELATIONSHIP TO YOU _____
COMPANY _____
MAILING ADDRESS _____
CITY, STATE, ZIP _____
WORK PHONE _____ CELL PHONE _____
HOME PHONE _____ E-MAIL _____

NAME _____
RELATIONSHIP TO YOU _____
COMPANY _____
MAILING ADDRESS _____
CITY, STATE, ZIP _____
WORK PHONE _____ CELL PHONE _____
HOME PHONE _____ E-MAIL _____

NAME _____
RELATIONSHIP TO YOU _____
COMPANY _____
MAILING ADDRESS _____
CITY, STATE, ZIP _____
WORK PHONE _____ CELL PHONE _____
HOME PHONE _____ E-MAIL _____

CONTACT INFORMATION

This final stage of information gathering will provide you with all the information you need to begin your résumé. For the contact information, you can use your full name, first and last name only, or shortened names (Pat Criscito instead of Patricia K. Criscito).

Do not use work telephone numbers or a work e-mail address on your résumé. Potential employers tend to consider that an abuse of company resources, which implies you might do the same if you are working for them. Listing a cellular telephone number on your résumé gives a hiring manager a way to reach you during working hours.

Avoid the use of "cutesy" e-mail addresses on a résumé. If you use *babycakes@aol.com* for your personal e-mail, create a second e-mail address under your account that will be more professional. If your only access to the Internet is at work, then create a free-mail account at *hotmail.com*, *juno.com*, *usa.net*, *yahoo.com*, *mail.com*, *excite.com*, *e-mail.com*, or *altavista.com*. Check *www.refdesk.com/freemail.html* for a list of even more free e-mail services.

NAME _____

MAILING ADDRESS _____

CITY, STATE, ZIP _____

COUNTRY (if applying outside the country where you live) _____

HOME PHONE _____   CELL PHONE _____

E-MAIL _____

WEB SITE _____

20 Index of Job Titles

How many times have you wished for a line or two to describe something you did in a job long ago or even just yesterday? If you are like me, it happens all the time. Unless you can get your hands on the actual job description for your position, finding the words to tell someone in a few short sentences what your duties were or what you accomplished is one of the hardest parts of writing a résumé.

That is what makes this index different from other résumé books. Instead of listing only the titles from the objectives of all the résumés in this book, it lists every job that every résumé mentions. That means you can turn to a page that has been referenced in the index and find wording somewhere in that résumé that applies to a specific job title. Sometimes it will be only one or two lines. Other times the entire résumé will be devoted to it. This should assist you in coming up with words to describe the various jobs you have performed in the past.

341

Decisions, decisions... **BARRON'S** helps you choose the right career

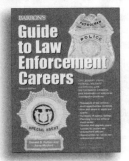
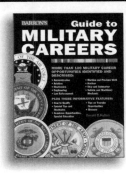

Guide to Homeland Security Careers

By Donald B. Hutton and Anna Mydlarz

From the reviews:

"A valuable guide. ... Students will come away from this book with an understanding of the variety of skills needed and the many options available in this field."
—Kathleen Ishii, *School Library Journal*, October 2003

Paperback, ISBN 0-7641-2375-0, $14.95, Can. $21.00

Guide to Law Enforcement Careers
2nd Edition

By Donald B. Hutton and Anna Mydlarz

Hundreds of jobs are listed and described in local, state, federal, military, and special law enforcement agencies. Careers cover a variety of areas including municipal police officer, deputy sheriff, corrections officer, state police officer, federal agents, criminal investigators, and many more.

Paperback, ISBN 0-7641-1551-0, $16.95, Can. $24.50

Barron's Guide to Military Careers

By Donald B. Hutton

This book describes military training and available academic and special training programs, as well as ROTC programs. Among the military career opportunities described in this book are those in administration, aviation, combat, construction, engineering, health, human services, law enforcement, machine work, public affairs, ship operations, and many more.

Paperback, ISBN 0-7641-0489-6, $18.95, Can. $27.50

100 Careers in Film and Television

By Tanja Crouch

Nearly everybody wants to get into the movies or be on television–and here's the book that shows them how! Some of the careers discussed include: Talent Agent, Apprentice Editor, Art Director, Assistant Cameraman, Assistant Director, Costume Designer, Director of Photography, Film Editor, Gaffer, Music Mixer, Production Assistant, Stage Manager, Storyboard Artist, and many more.

Paperback, ISBN 0-7641-2164-2, $14.95, Can. $21.00

100 Careers in the Music Business

By Tanja Crouch

From the reviews:

"Many teens dream of working in music, this practical overview of professions in the field will acquaint them with aspects of the industry they never knew existed."
—Paula Rohrlick, *KLIATT*, September 2001

Paperback , ISBN 0-7641-1577-4, $14.95, Can. $21.00

The Complete Job Search Guide for Latinos

Murray Mann and Rose Mary Bombella

This brand-new book instructs Latinos on ways to step up from mere jobs and into promising, high-paying careers. It offers tips on self-assessment of job skills, identifying career goals, obtaining job training, researching industries and individual companies where hiring prospects are good, building a career portfolio, writing résumés and career marketing letters, networking within a target industry, and gaining employment.

Paperback, ISBN 0-7641-2869-8, $14.99, Can. $21.99

SUCCESS WITHOUT COLLEGE SERIES
From the reviews:

"With college costs on the rise, it's become more important to have a knowledge of careers available without post-secondary education. Barron's guides fill the gap. Most helpful stories are told by industry professionals.... Important lessons on preparing a resume and job-search advice are equally useful. ... An index, appendixes with organizations and associations, bibliography and job-search tools are common to each book."
—*Today's Librarian*, September 2001

Careers in Sports, Fitness, and Recreation

By Robert F. Wilson

Paperback
ISBN 0-7641-1562-6, $10.95
Can. $15.50

Careers With Animals

By Audrey Pavia

Paperback
ISBN 0-7641-1621-5, $10.95
Can. $15.50

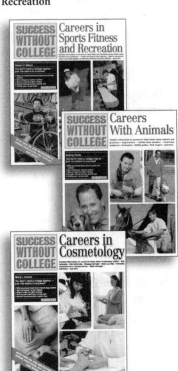

Careers in Cosmetology

By Mary L. Dennis

Paperback
ISBN 0-7641-1523-5, $10.95
Can. $18.95

All prices are in U.S. and Canadian dollars and subject to change without notice. Order from your bookstore—or directly from Barron's by adding 18% for shipping and handling (minimum charge $5.95). New York, New Jersey, Michigan, and California residents add sales tax to total after shipping and handling.

Barron's Educational Series, Inc.
250 Wireless Blvd.
Hauppauge, NY 11788
Order toll-free: 1-800-645-3476
Order by fax: 1-631-434-3217

In Canada:
Georgetown Book Warehouse
4 Armstrong Ave.
Georgetown, Ont. L7G 4R9
Canadian orders: 1-800-247-7160
Fax in Canada: 1-800-887-1594

(#128) R 9/05

More Career Advice from BARRON'S

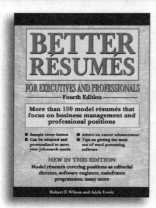

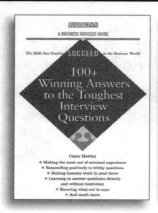

Better Résumés for Executives and Professionals, 4th Edition

Robert F. Wilson and Adele Lewis

Men and women seeking business leadership positions require a special kind of résumé. Updated, and filled with tips on getting the most out of Internet facilities and word processing software, this book presents more than 100 model résumés that apply to business management positions. Readers can use them as models for their own résumés . Model résumés include editorial director, controller, software engineer, systems engineer, mainframe programmer, and many others.

Paperback, ISBN 0-7641-1317-8, $16.95, Can$24.50

The Computer Science Résumés and Job-Finding Guide

Phil Bartlett

This brand-new book is must-read material for job-hunting computer software engineers, applications and systems programmers, database developers and administrators, systems analysts, security engineers, network engineers, test engineers, and many other specialists in the IT (information technology) profession. An opening chapter gives an overview of today's IT job market with projections through the year 2010, current top job opportunities, and a discussion of new and evolving IT employment opportunities. A following chapter discusses the job-winning process, with advice on résumé writing and distribution, getting interviews, and landing a position.

Paperback, ISBN 0-7641-2907-4, $16.95, Can$24.50

How to Write Better Résumés and Cover Letters

Pat Criscito

The stodgy, old-fashioned typewritten résumé is a thing of the past—and Barron's has a brand-new résumé manual designed to propel today's job seekers toward success! The emphasis is on organizing one's job qualifications and career experience to make the best possible presentation, but this how-to book focuses on a far broader range of job-seeking techniques than simply writing a good résumé. The author advises on taking full advantage of career planning Internet sources and college career service centers. She also points out differences between paper résumés and electronic résumés and discusses methods of preparing each. In many career fields, a well-presented paper résumé will never go out of date, and this book explains how to organize résumé material, present past accomplishments succinctly, then "sell" one's skills with dynamic sentences and power verbs. It also shows how to prepare scannable and e-mailable résumés, create dynamic cover letters, include photos and references when required, select appropriate typefaces and paper colors, and much more. The author also inspires job seekers with scores of model résumés that apply to everyone from first-time job hunters to executives seeking to advance their careers.

Paperback, 0-7641-2494-3, $14.95, Can21.95

BARRON'S BUSINESS SUCCESS SERIES

Books in Barron's popular *Business Success* series are written for career-minded men and women intent on moving up the corporate ladder or going out on their own as entrepreneurs. These titles offer advice from experienced business managers and experts on how to prosper in the corporate world and succeed at all levels of business management.

100+ Winning Answers to the Toughest Interview Questions

Casey Hawley

What do you tell a job interviewer when he asks about your background, and you know you have less experience than other job candidates? The author approaches this and other tough questions with solid advice. General tips that apply to all interview questions entail giving answers that ring true, answers that are direct and without hesitation, and answers that don't meander, but speak precisely to the questions the interviewer asks.

Paperback, ISBN 0-7641-1644-4, $7.95, Can$11.50

Interview Strategies That Lead to Job Offers

Marilyn Pincus

Helpful information about how to ace a job interview, this book gives step-by-step instructions for use as soon as a job interview is scheduled. Readers are instructed to

- Do research on prospective employer to uncover key information
- Rehearse answers to predictable questions and position yourself to succeed
- Use information interviewers reveal about their procedures to your advantage
- Know whether to follow up with e-mail, regular mail, or phone calls.

Paperback, ISBN 0-7641-0684-8, $7.95, Can$11.50

All prices are in U.S. and Canadian dollars and subject to change without notice. Order from your bookstore—or directly from Barron's by adding 18% for shipping and handling (minimum charge $5.95). New York, New Jersey, Michigan, and California residents add sales tax to total after shipping and handling.

Barron's Educational Series, Inc.
250 Wireless Blvd.
Hauppauge, NY 11788
Order toll-free: 1-800-645-3476
Order by fax: 1-631-434-3217

In Canada:
Georgetown Book Warehouse
4 Armstrong Ave.
Georgetown, Ont. L7G 4R9
Canadian orders: 1-800-247-7160
Fax in Canada: 1-800-887-1594

(#136) R 9/05